NINE SEAHORSES

A PLEA FOR SANITY IN THREE PARTS

Nine Seahorses

A Plea For Sanity In Three Parts

by

Seahorse Sam

Published by Seahorse Press Ltd 2011

Nine Seahorses: A Plea For Sanity In Three Parts

Seahorse Sam is a nom-de-plume assumed by Dr Martin Nicholas Stephen Nieland, a psychologist with significant experience of teaching both theory and research at undergraduate and postgraduate levels, implementing policy in mental health domains such as dual diagnosis and leading service development in and from the third sector.

Published in 2011 by Seahorse Press Ltd, Ilkley LS29 8HT
www.seahorsepress.co.uk

ISBN 978-0-9567142-0-6

British Library Cataloguing in Publication Data. A catalogue record for this book is available from the British Library.

Printed by Jade Press Ltd, Leeds LS9 7QL
www.jadeprint.com

Although inspired along the way by many unnamed individuals (stupendously generous instances of lovingness in particular) and, from time to time, by people in groups of various sizes and having miscellaneous purposes (whether each *raison d'être* and membership criterion had been honed finely or was barely identifiable), this book comprises merely one unaffiliated person's reflections on first hand experience of modern and contemporary psychology: in books and in journals; in academic study, research and pedagogy; in strategy and policy development including "dual diagnosis"[1]; in helping to build treatment services for drugs and alcohol problems; in mental health contexts and in psychotherapy; in visiting prisons; in religious practice and in spiritual fellowship; in social and domestic environments; moreover and superordinate, in his own experience of life and living – especially after a protracted implosion of his own making; and an unexpected, explosive awakening that was not. The author represents and speaks for no establishment, agency or organisation – nor any person living or dead but himself. There are no deliberately mischievous references to any person or organisation in his history. Hoping to provoke and entertain, but never to offend or harm, Seahorse Sam has written this volume under a *nom-de-plume* for creative reasons, but also in deference to principles embedded in his own "moral psychology". He is stoically optimistic about the book's reception; nevertheless, he hopes to spare himself any surfeit of undue credit, criticism or unsolicited scrutiny. He appreciates quietly, and without reckoning, all of the love that has come his way, and is sorry to every person he ever hurt.

---

[1] the co-occurrence of substance (any drugs) misuse (including alcohol) and mental health problems

"Walden Pond from Thoreau's Cabin"
Courtesy of the Thoreau Institute at Walden Woods, Lincoln, MA

We cracked the nut of self-deceiving

Turned away from loveless living

Dispelled pursuit of blind receiving

Found a peace in gracious giving

Contents

Part I
"It's An Inside Job"

Chapter 4   31
"Inside the machine"

Chapter 5   43
"Towards a moral psychology"

Part II
"You Can't Win A Bad Game"

Chapter 8
"Good relations"   97

Chapter 9   133
"A moral psychology"

Chapter 10   187
"A broader, pragmatic empiricism"

Intermezzo (extract from the Preface):

Part I of *Nine Seahorses* is a considered overview of the discipline of academic psychology (at least, those parts of it that speak to the "human condition" or what we might refer to as personal sanity). Part II – which is a tour of modern psychotherapy more exigent yet fecund than the outline of modern psychology afforded in Part I – opens with consideration of the "moral environment" before proceeding to a more detailed account of what is meant by a "moral psychology". Pending development of these ideas – and anticipating favourable reports of "moral psychology" in action – Part III comprises a more figurative and elucidatory (still, necessary and integral) exposition of those principles upon which living out a "moral psychology" rests.

---

[2] See also the Table "Sample falsifiable propositions …" on pp.193-204 of Chapter 10.

Part III
"The Story Of Seahorse Sam"

Chapter 14   255
"Learning to 'Let go'"

Chapter 15   267
"Say, 'Cheese!'"

Finale   278
Last thoughts on a one-faced psychology

The Rogues' Gallery with Reader's Notes   287
(or personalities in the history of psychology)

References   305
(third party works cited within *Nine Seahorses*)

Epilogue   309
~ The conclusion of the wise seahorse ~

Addendum   311
Layers of allegory in the concept of *Nine Seahorses*

List of Illustrations

List of Figures and Tables

Page(s)

Henry David Thoreau (1817–1862)
Courtesy of the Thoreau Institute at Walden Woods, Lincoln, MA

Foreword

Nine Seahorses: A Plea For Sanity In Three Parts

Having taught more generations of psychology students than I care to remember, I look back on the results with mixed feelings. Most, I feel sure (although I'm not sure I could produce the evidence to support the view), have benefited from the experience. They have learned what we psychologists have to say about human information processing (perception, memory, learning, and so on); about personality, mental illness, and social interaction; about the developmental processes that produce the adult; and about the physical basis (chiefly to be found in brain function) of psychological phenomena. Many have gone on to use what they have learned directly – as, for example, clinical, educational, or forensic psychologists, or as researchers, building on what they have learned to produce new knowledge. And those that do not use their psychology directly have an advantage in whatever they do (I like to think) that comes from a training that allows them to think scientifically about human behaviour generally.

So far so good; what gives me cause for concern, however, is that so few of these students, at the end of their formal education, seem to have views about, or interest in, the Big Questions that make psychology such a fascinating topic. How is the notion of free will to be reconciled with the mechanistic interpretation that comes from neuroscience? How should the reality of conscious experience be dealt with, given the advantages of the intellectually rigorous framework supplied by behaviourism? To what extent is our psychological make-up determined by social and environmental factors? What is the relation between the insights about human nature supplied by analytical psychology and those, seemingly very different, that emerge from an experimental, scientific approach?

The blame for this state of affairs must rest more with the teachers than with the students. Surely (although they may phrase them differently) new students come to the subject with an ache to answer questions such as these; perhaps we fail to provide a setting in which answers can be sought. For ease of presentation we divide up our topic into convenient chunks and teach them separately. We teach and examine a "module" on Conditioning and Learning (say), and this is over and done before the student moves on to Psychopathology, or Personality, or Social Psychology. No wonder that the Big Questions, which require an integration of these different areas, fail to get addressed. Students are constrained to spend their time inspecting individual trees – time spent in seeking a view of the entire wood does not lead to success in examinations.

In spite of all this, some trained psychologists (if even just a few) maintain a desire to see the bigger picture, and are brave enough to attempt the integration of the various areas of psychology that is required. The author of this book has done just that. The core of his analysis (so it seems to me) is the attempt to integrate the approach and findings of modern experimental psychology with the conclusions that derive from the analytic approach. The implications of this rapprochement are developed not only for mental illness and our attempts to treat it (the search for "sanity" in a narrow sense), but also for its general relevance for the task that all of us face in our everyday lives, trying to make sense of our place in a complex social world.

I call this enterprise "brave" with good reason. Professional and academic psychologists are usually specialists in one or another branch of the discipline, and are fully aware that they lack expertise in areas that they have not studied directly, or in which they have not practised. For the most part they are unwilling to trespass into the territory of others, if only because they are afraid that their shortcomings will be pounced on by the experts. But to make progress in constructing a comprehensive psychology, it is necessary to take the risk. The author of this book has done so, and is to be congratulated for it. Undoubtedly various experts will find fault with his treatment of their own special topic. But we may hope that it will make them think, and perhaps dare themselves to tell us how their specialism provides answers to the Big Questions that concern us all.

Geoffrey Hall
Professor of Psychology
University of York

Preface

Nine Seahorses: A Plea For Sanity In Three Parts

The present volume, combining treatise and allegorical narrative in one original argument, constitutes a modern and provocative education in psychology and psychotherapy. Its refusal to sit in those disciplines exclusively, however, renders it relevant in the domains of philosophy, religion and religious studies, spirituality and counselling; moreover, all of the social sciences including history, culture and counterculture, politics, citizenship, war and peace studies including conflict resolution, ecology and environmentalism. It anticipates 21st century thinking that is both ancient in roots yet reverberates with President Barack Obama's incumbency as President of the United States of America[3]. It roils in the groundswell of a multi-faceted "spiritual revolution" effervescing across our world. What do we mean by a "spiritual revolution" and why do we need one?

For our purposes, "spiritual" just means "unseen". Referring to that which isn't necessarily "known" to the five senses, it alludes to the "transcendent" as well as the narrowly empirical. If one is willing to contemplate that science may never explain "everything" (epistemologically, in a religious sense, or in any other manner) then "spiritual" as meant here is hardly a heretical concept, even to the atheist. Few of us would dispute the proposition that conscious, subjective experience represents our most salient and significant day-to-day reality (that much is almost too blindingly obvious), but these "inner worlds" evade consensual definition in the scientific, religious; indeed, any other vernacular. What, then, is the spiritual life? Looking at the whole of human history we live in a world that has been re-shaped fundamentally in just a half-millennium by the Scientific Revolution. Whilst modern science has benefited mankind immeasurably, it has presented us in equal measure with unscalable threats to our very existence. Science tends to polarise itself with what preceded it, i.e., religion and, arguably, it is the extremists on both sides that threaten us most. Seemingly it is neither more technology, nor more religion (certainly of the kind inspired by human rather than divine authority), that will save us from a final disgrace; rather, a civic maturity that originates in the individual.

Nine Seahorses propounds an ecumenical "moral psychology". The shape of the modern (academic) discipline is teased from its ancient beginnings through the Scientific Revolution and the Enlightenment – for it is a product of its history. Alas, these unfinished and imperfect understandings are harnessed daily for the treatment of our most psychologically imperilled – including the desperately addicted, distressed and suicidal – without the humility that might accompany an appreciation of their (in)adequacy. *Nine Seahorses* is about personal and collective sanity: it is, thereby, about mature society. It is idealistic, but it is not unrealistic, and it is possible to draw upon both strict and more pragmatic levels of empirical support to demonstrate the point. As with all things human, it matters less where we are "at" right now as where we go next; for it is direction of travel, rather than pace of progress, that assures safe homecoming whether we are destined for a personal or a professional hearthside.

---

[3] Far from condoning nationalism, and equally far from promoting Western parochialism, the significance of Barack Hussein Obama II's (1961–) incumbency as President of the United States of America – in terms of racial equality, individual dignity and the progression of human society towards maturity – surely cannot be missed or overstated.

Now, the evolutionary chain of human ideas ("memes" in fashionable philosophy) comprises innumerable links, many of which, because of a natural (or, at least, identifiably human) tendency to discriminate new ways of looking at things from the old, comprise reactions to what has gone before. This tends to polarisation of positions which, when accompanied by a certain kind of rigidity, distracts from any kind of "truth" that may lie hidden in between. This kind of process can be identified in history as early as Plato (428-348 BC) and Aristotle (384-322 BC): whereas Plato regarded many aspects of an individual's nature to be formed in some way in the "heavens" prior to birth, Aristotle (Plato's own progeny) advanced a view of the human infant as a "blank slate" waiting for the mark of experience (which is to say that the identity, psychological attributes or personality[4] at birth were completely unformed). The Scientific Revolution begun, let us say, with Nicholas Copernicus (1473-1543) – and a narrow empiricism advocated in the behaviorist tradition, especially the "radical" one espoused by Burrhus Frederic Skinner (1904-1990) – have left us with these and other polarities intact. Science insists on observation, measurement, rule of mathematical law and falsifiable inductive reasoning; accordingly, any aspect of human nature[5] not amenable to such scrutiny and obedience has been sidelined. The behaviorists have squeezed "mind"[6] out of the equation altogether, leaving us with our disintegrated modern discipline.

Perhaps it is still possible to develop a "moral psychology" that recognises and facilitates the capacity of each person not so much to master their own destiny as to seek their own authentic "truth"[7]. In science, it is in digging and deducing that we discover: in psychology, surely, it is in seeking and yielding that one finds (this certainly seems true of the spiritual life, by all accounts). A "moral psychology" is not one that seeks to promote (far less impose) any particular moral agenda; rather, it represents an invitation to each person to identify and find the courage to traverse one's own basis for living. This process must begin with a brutal honesty because there is an enormous "spiritual blindness" that blights every human being. "Denial" (or "Don't Even 'No' I Am Lying"), is part of our nature – a block against living fully that prevails in all of us, in various ways, at various times and in varying degrees. To scoff at the existence of such blindness in oneself is the most natural thing in the world for us to do, and yet it is to exercise it. If we want to "get real" with ourselves, suddenly we find we need other people. The spectre of shame may send us scuttling for cover at the thought of revealing ourselves exposed – undefended as it were – in unchosen company; nevertheless, it is the very willingness to present one's "self" authentically (if prudently) in an assembly of equals that can catapult us into new realms of understanding, maturity and peace.

---

[4] Terms such as "identity", "psychological attributes" and "personality" are, of course, not necessarily those that would have been used in Ancient Greece. Here, they are simply intended to convey the gist of what modern psychologists still have not been able to account for "scientifically" – and about which they are somewhat divided.

[5] The looking glass holding these reflections images the modern Western world; however, it is hoped that the arguments, principles and optimism espoused throughout this book have the capacity to speak sufficiently well to the truly universal "human condition".

[6] The term "mind" is used to refer to those (especially human) attributes such as consciousness, conscience and capacity for "choosing", about which psychologists still fundamentally disagree: anything not amenable to direct measurement in the laboratory.

[7] Possibly inspired by Socrates (469-399 BC), in *Hamlet* William Shakespeare (1564-1616) has Polonius (who may have wanted his son merely to be careful of his reputation) exhort to Laertes, "This above all: to thine own self be true, And it must follow, as the night the day, Thou canst not then be false to any man." (Act I, Scene III)

If you consider such stuff the province of newfangled psychotherapy, think again. It is true that Carl Ransom Rogers (1902-1987) advocated a psychotherapeutic approach ("person-centred") that kept the psychotherapist's personal agenda out of the mix, and it is true that Sigismund Schlomo (Sigmund) Freud (1856-1939) and Carl Gustav Jung (1875-1961) identified ostensible components of "mind" inaccessible even to subjective experience – but no mainstream psychotherapeutic movement has yet appreciated the full impact of "spiritual blindness" on itself as well as its clients. The second striking deficit in contemporary "helping" approaches is the untapped resource of the "poacher-turned-gamekeeper" – people who have survived and emerged from their darkness (remarkably still drawing sacred breath in many cases given the depth of their traumas). Many such persons wouldn't take credit for their re-established lives, and may be willing to help others free of charge. Are the fees incurred in professional psychological helping – a particular motive-bound dance, or "racket" to (mis)apply the terminology of Eric Berne, 1910-1970[8] – merely fair exchange for services rendered, or is cash the mortal enemy of those pre-requisites for spiritual growth – humility and pure motives? Perhaps we enjoy good paid-for psychotherapy now; nevertheless, poor psychotherapy exists because agenda-driven governments create a climate of accountability geared more to political careers and "spin" than the betterment of an underclass too sick to speak for itself. Practitioners who do not conduct themselves apolitically, and solely for their clients' advantage (in so far as they can discern what that really is) can never discharge responsibility for assuring the mutual honesty upon which the legitimacy of their provision actually swings.

Mustn't we learn to recognise the difference between the parts of our "selves" which are somehow inherent, immutable or otherwise deserving of murmuring self-acceptance (especially when they are misaligned with external pressures or authorities), and those base and inferior dispositions (including toxic self-centredness) which hinder us (and harm others) yet are amenable to dissolution? We don't necessarily need science or formal psychology to do this – just open-mindedness. Whether we are partial to or disdainful of terms such as "scientific" or "God-given" should not distract us. Arguably, the business of trying to engineer the world (particularly its other inhabitants) through discharge of "will" is not merely dangerous, but lies at the heart of our species-bound malaise. Unreasonable expectations (which always *look* reasonable) are just disappointments and resentments waiting to happen. The impact of resentments on psychological health (sanity) shouldn't be underappreciated … but who is to say which of our expectations are unreasonable if we are blind to ourselves? This, surely, is why we need each other. Groups of people ("we" is any "more than one") afford their members not merely solidarity, but the reciprocal shared capacity of one member to permit another to hold up a "spiritual mirror". Categorically, "Now I see myself" is not the same as "You can write my moral agenda". Readiness to see oneself in a more objective light requires not just willingness and courage, but a certain measured discretion because of the lack of faultlessness inevitably found in others. Travesties of trust are neutralised when "spiritual equality" is first established for its own sake, and then rendered recognisable in the new discourse suddenly and brightly lit.

---

[8] Following scrutiny of all of the relevant threads in the modern academic discipline that is psychology (Part I), and the gamut of paid-for helping services hinged on its various tenets (Part II), Transactional Analysis emerges amongst all of the modern therapies as the front runner for achieving personal autonomy. In so doing, TA passes a most vigorous test. Eric Berne was heroic in expanding upon the forces underlying relationships as a source of personality development and psychological health. A whole new theoretical raft for the elevation of TA loveliness is depicted in *Nine Seahorses*.

In *Walden* (1854), Henry David Thoreau (1817–1862) wrote of *Life In The Woods*: of experiencing nature "transcendentally" (i.e., in some manner beyond sensory or empirical experience; shall we say, yielding to nature as it presented itself rather than as he would mould it). Thoreau, underappreciated in his day, stood for natural justice – especially against "expedient" administrations. In *Civil Disobedience* (1849) – a strong statement in defence of personal conscience – he advocated resistance (meaning jail if it came to it) against unjust governments and wars, especially any that condoned slavery. Although regarded a heroic figure amongst anarchists, he stood for improvement rather than abolition of governments. He was an idealist who realised that "when men are prepared for it", there will be no need for government at all. In these ways, Thoreau was an optimist who saw man's freedom in Polonius's exhortation "To thine own self be true"[9].

Nearly a century later (in 1948), and in quite some philosophical contrast notwithstanding its matched title, the arch-behaviorist Skinner (*supra*) wrote *Walden Two* – an imaginary society governed by behaviorist principles (i.e., the shaping of behaviour – and culture thereby – through "positive reinforcement" or incentives). A thinly disguised quasi-Marxist order – with self-government facilitated by unelected planners and community behaviour supervisors reminiscent of *Nineteen Eighty-four*'s dubious Big Brother (George Orwell, 1903-1950) – *Walden Two* features a planned economy, children conceived by teenagers and raised in the community (rather than a nuclear family), unconcealed eugenics and the Nietzscheian banishment of God (whose exclusive purpose ever was, according to Skinner, to allay anxiety).

We have proposed that the discourteous imposition of "will" accounts for all of man's inhumanity to man. *Nine Seahorses* is inspired by the spirit of *Walden* – constituting a respectful riposte to *Walden Two*. Wedded to neither Thoreau's "self-reliance" (in *Walden*) nor Skinner's "scientific determinism" (in *Walden Two*), and shunning an irresolute course between them, this *Plea For Sanity In Three Parts* aspires in a "moral psychology" to a profound appreciation of what it means for the "self" – for its own sanity and, so, for the sake of others' – to overcome its "self-centredness" through peaceable and co-operative engagement with its counterparts across all of humanity. In that way, *Nine Seahorses* is not about "self-reliance" *per se*, but assuredness derived from an openness that can be achieved only in community. It is thereby "collective", but so appreciative of personal freedom that it could not be considered Marxist. Immersed in "transcendent trust"[10] – each of us discerning and embracing our own authentic personality unencumbered by any human authority is the most freeing endeavour we

---

[9] Polonius to Laertes in Shakespeare's *Hamlet*, Act I, Scene III: see preceding footnote

[10] Having dispensed with the "wisdom" of older generations, Thoreau expands as follows:

I think that we may safely trust a good deal more than we do. We may waive just so much care of ourselves as we honestly bestow elsewhere. Nature is well adapted to our weakness as our strength. The incessant anxiety and strain of some is a well nigh incurable form of disease. We are made to exaggerate the importance of what work we do; and yet how much is not done by us! or, what if we had been taken sick? How vigilant we are! determined not to live by faith if we can avoid it; all the day long on the alert, at night we unwillingly say our prayers and commit ourselves to uncertainties. So thoroughly and sincerely are we compelled to live, reverencing our life, and denying the possibility of change. This is the only way, we say; but there are as many ways as there can be drawn radii from one centre. All change is a miracle to contemplate; but it is a miracle which is taking place every instant. Confucius said, "To know that we know what we know, and that we do not know what we do not know, that is true knowledge." When one man has reduced a fact of the imagination to be a fact to his understanding, I foresee that all men will at length establish their lives on that basis. (Walden; Or, Life In The Woods, 1854, "Economy")

can exercise - for the sake of our own liberation, the happiness of others and the integrity of the planet. A simple satisfaction with what comes our way rather than what we would grasp at, combined with a little faith in the natural order of things, ensures that nothing happens that is not for a fuller purpose in the end. An assimilation of this, and the optimism that accompanies it, is an important early step on the road to sanity, and also the one for re-iteration *ad infinitum*, even if *ad nauseam* on dreary days, if we are to achieve appreciable progress in the long run. "All for one and one for all!"[11]

Part I of *Nine Seahorses* is a considered overview of the discipline of academic psychology (at least, those parts of it that speak to the "human condition" or what we might refer to as personal sanity). Part II - which is a tour of modern psychotherapy more exigent yet fecund than the outline of modern psychology afforded in Part I - opens with consideration of the "moral environment" before proceeding to a more detailed account of what is meant herein by a "moral psychology". Pending development of these ideas - and anticipating favourable reports of "moral psychology" in action - Part III comprises a more figurative and elucidatory (still, necessary and integral) exposition of those principles upon which living out a "moral psychology" rests.

---

[11] Attributed, of course, to d'Artagnan and the three musketeers (Athos, Porthos and Aramis) who stuck loyally to and with each other through thick and thin in the 1844 novel *Les Trois Mousquetaires* by Alexandre Dumas (Dumas Davy de la Pailleterie 1802-1870), the expression "*Tous pour un, un pour tous*" was popular in various translations across 19th century continental Europe. In Latin ("*Omnes pro uno, unus pro omnibus*") it is occasionally quoted as the motto of famously neutral Switzerland. Concerned about divisions in the early Christian church in Corinth, an appeal for unity was conveyed powerfully by (Saint) Paul of Tarsus (*circa* 5 BC-67 AD) in 1 Corinthians 12: 12-26:

Just as a human body, though it is made up of many parts, is a single unit because all these parts, though many, make one body, so it is with Christ. In the one Spirit we were all baptised, Jews as well as Greeks, slaves as well as citizens, and one Spirit was given to us all to drink.

Nor is the body to be identified with any one of its many parts. If the foot were to say, 'I am not a hand and so I do not belong to the body', would that mean that it stopped being part of the body? If the ear were to say, 'I am not an eye, and so I do not belong to the body', would that mean that it was not a part of the body? If your whole body was just one eye, how would you hear anything? If it was just one ear, how would you smell anything?

Instead of that, God put all the separate parts into the body on purpose. If all the parts were the same, how could it be a body? As it is, the parts are many but the body is one. The eye cannot say to the hand, 'I do not need you', nor can the head say to the feet, 'I do not need you'.

What is more, it is precisely the parts of the body that seem to be the weakest which are the indispensable ones; and it is the least honourable parts of the body that we clothe with the greatest care. So our more improper parts get decorated in a way that our more proper parts do not need. God has arranged the body so that more dignity is given to the parts which are without it, and so that there may not be disagreements inside the body, but that each part may be equally concerned for all the others. If one part is hurt, all parts are hurt with it. If one part is given special honour, all parts enjoy it.

(*Jerusalem Bible: Popular Edition*. Darton, Longman & Todd)

As has been highlighted already in this Preface and shall be said again by and by, we should not let the jargon of specific disciplines (science, psychology, theology) distract us. Paul's analogies could be expressed another way - simply as the profound and remarkable proposition that all living things today have evolved for the same some thousands of millions of years (assuming a Darwinian "singularity" or "last universal common ancestor"), and can share a remarkable proportion of their genes. Whilst humans share about 99.5% of their chromosomal DNA with each other, they also share 98.4% of their genes with chimpanzees, 98% with rats, 70% with slugs and 50% with the banana. Such statistics as these, or approximations to them, are ubiquitous in popular science. Taking account of it all, according to one point of view, every contemporary living thing is rendered equal in nature. We must draw from what we see, what we will.

Part I

"It's An Inside Job"

Chapter 1

"Two-faced psychology"

Psychology has always had a lot to do with motives
Like prostitution and war, hasn't "psychology" been around in one
form or another forever? Throughout history, human beings have tried
to understand one another - whether sympathetically, for practical
purposes, or for reasons more akin to conquest. In subtle and not so
subtle ways, we have resorted to the most cunning and vile of tactics
in high-stake arenas such as the battlefield and the lovers' nest.
Put in such terms, psychology seems to have a lot to do with motives.

Linguistic roots
Psychology is a word which has roots in Greek[12] where it is spelt
Ψυχολογία. Translated it means "the study of the 'mind'" (or 'breath'
or 'spirit' or 'soul') and can be compared with another word "physis"
(spelt in Greek φύσις) which means "nature", implies the emergence of
light from darkness[13], and which spawned the modern word "physics"
used to describe the study of the natural world (and universe) today.

Human language spans human psychology
Our capacity for language is a species-specific and fundamental yet
mysterious phenomenon. Spanning the duality of modern psychology -
the tension between subjective "mind" and objective performance[14] -
language is clearly an observable and measurable instance of human
behaviour on the one hand. Nowadays there are sophisticated theories
explaining its development in children, and its reliance on certain
(physical) components of the human brain and central nervous system.
The sub-discipline of "human cognitive neuropsychology" relies on
intelligent interpretation of trauma following injuries. On the other
hand, there are still no complete (or better than speculative)
accounts of why human beings have this capacity and other species do
not (whether this is, in fact, true) and whether language is part of
a system of faculties that underpins a species-specific capacity for
consciousness, the subjective experience of pain, even "conscience"
and mutual love. An accessible philosophical treatise is provided in
Euan Macphail's incisive summary of *The Evolution Of Consciousness*[15].

---

[12] Ancient Greece spanned the period (approximately) from the "Dorian Invasion" around
1100 BC to the Roman conquest after the Battle of Corinth in 146 BC. The Dorians were
one of three Greek tribes inhabiting Crete in Homer's *The Odyssey*. Probably they were
responsible for (eliminating the old and) establishing an enduring culture (i.e., a
resilient set of traditions and dialects) which informed Classical Greece - vital in
history because the developments in language, philosophy, political systems, science
and the arts etc which took place during the 5th and 4th centuries BC influenced the
later Roman Empire deeply; in turn, shaping significantly the modern (Western) world.

[13] In *Walden*, Thoreau describes the seasons at Walden Pond (Concord, MA). His depiction
of Spring conveys an apocalyptic but existentially optimistic view of nature. Henry
David (born David Henry) Thoreau (1817-1862) was an American naturalist, philosopher
and writer who famously advocated, in one volume, *Civil Disobedience* against unjust
governments and wars, particularly if they supported slavery. The arch-behaviorist
Burrhus Frederic Skinner (1904-1990) carried a copy of Thoreau's *Walden* in his youth
and was inspired to write during the 1940s *Walden Two* - a fantasy about community
living based on behaviorist principles. Although referred to as an "individualist
anarchist", Thoreau favoured the improvement rather than the abolition of governments.

[14] The prevailing school of psychological thought in modern Western institutions,
especially universities, is still "behaviorism" which - focussing only on that which
is directly observable and measurable (i.e., what living things actually do), with its
predilection for controlled manipulation in the laboratory - somehow separates itself
from those who prefer to consider subjective experience - or, if you like, "mind".

[15] Macphail, E. (1998) *The Evolution Of Consciousness*. Oxford University Press: Oxford

Psychology becomes institutionalised
"Mind" and "behavior(ist)" strands of modern psychology can be traced
to Leipzig, in 1870s German Saxony, where Wilhelm Maximilian Wundt
(1832-1920) set up what is widely accepted to be the first psychology
laboratory. Apparently Wundt, the son of a Lutheran pastor, was most
cerebral – disposed to studying over stereotypical boyhood pursuits,
and later shunning physicianship in favour of vocational scholarship.
Serving an apprenticeship under Hermann Ludwig von Helmholtz (1821-
1894)[16] in Heidelberg, he became well schooled in the practice of
observation and experimentation in the laboratory. These principles
of approach to acquiring knowledge were highly regarded in their day
because of the massive impact that Nicholas Copernicus (1473-1543),
Galileo Galilei (1564-1642) and Sir Isaac Newton (1643-1727) had had
in generating the "Scientific Revolution" – in which many assumptions
about the nature of the world and universe that had been held until
then – i.e., throughout all human history – were suddenly overturned.

The psychological impact of the Scientific Revolution
One can barely imagine the psychological nature of this shake-up. Up
until the 16th and 17th centuries, and the fresh scrutiny of celestial
objects, star-gazing human folks understandably may have presumed –
unwittingly (since they had no reason to do otherwise) – that nothing
material existed beyond what they could see. Perhaps, moreover, there
was (and still is) an instinctual tendency to regard more proximate
objects as proportionately meaningful and religiously significant.
There are many examples of sun-worship in ancient history[17] – entirely
reasonable then – as anyone needed little evidence to appreciate how
light and heat emanated from that solar source, singularly sustaining
all living things including crops, domestic animals and humans
themselves. By the 15th century, Christianity was well-established in
Western thinking and, although it relegated the divinity of the sun,
there was nothing in scripture to contradict the supposition that the
sun revolved around the centre of the universe, i.e., the earth[18].

Science and religion are not natural bedfellows
Copernicus was responsible for introducing "heliocentrism" or the
notion that the sun (rather than the earth) is the centre of the
universe. Galileo famously incurred the displeasure of the Vatican
for maintaining that tradition. In those days (and, of course, for
centuries and millennia before) it was fashionable to kill people by
the most foul means for non-conformity, and the Roman Inquisition was
no exception[19]. Galileo, who in early adulthood had contemplated a

---

[16] Helmholtz was to become a prolific physiologist, arguably the greatest of all time,
developing theories in as broad reaching areas as hearing and vision in physiological
psychology; thermodynamics, electrodynamics and the conservation of energy in physics
(earning the admiration of Albert Einstein, 1879-1955), and aesthetics in philosophy.

[17] In Hinduism, the sun god is called "Prati-Aksh Devta" meaning "The Seen Divinity",
and in Sanskrit the sun is "Mitra" or "Friend". In Ancient Egypt, a progression from
multitheism towards quasi-monotheistic "Atenism" was encouraged by Amenhotep IV (aka
Akhenaten) in the 18th dynasty (*circa* 1350 BC). There are other examples of sun-worship
in ancient and not-so-ancient Africa – and in other places, e.g., amongst the Aztecs.

[18] There are numerous references in the Bible to setting the earth's foundations, the
earth's immovability and the sun rising and returning to its ordained place. We do not
have to look far for apparent contradictions and anomalies in scripture; however, we
might ask ourselves whether in doing so we are seeking out literal truths, a spiritual
message or simply seeking to scoff. Is it not our latent motives which are critical?

[19] Such brutality seems fundamentally at odds with the teachings of the most peaceable
figure in history – Jesus Christ – whose followers' own history is one of remarkable
received oppression (whether in the form of the personal vendetta of Nero in 67 AD, or
the "Great Persecution" by Maximin, Decius and Diocletian in the early 4th century).
Even the more "civilised" of their persecutors – such as Pliny The Younger – sought
"merely" position and empire – never committing atrocious carnage in the name of God.

religious vocation (as a Catholic priest), was spared execution –
being subjected only to permanent house arrest – but others were less
fortunate. Persecuted more for their views on religious matters,
proponents of heliocentrism such as Giordano Bruno (1548-1600) were
burned at the stake for holding a personal view of God akin to
"pantheism" (God and nature or the universe are equivalent). By the
time Sir Isaac Newton came to publish mathematical laws describing
the motion of the planets[20], his evidence was too incontrovertible to
permit charges of heresy and, in any event, the Roman Church had lost
its political foothold in England after the reign of Henry VIII.

Newton's humility
The date of Newton's birth (at the hamlet Woolsthorpe-by-Colsterworth
in Lincolnshire, England) depends on which calendar is invoked. At
the time he was born the "Old-Style" (OS) Julian calendar (introduced
by Julius Caesar in 46 BC) located his birth date at 25th December
1642. For some, it is strangely coincidental that Newton was born in
the same year that Galileo died. The "New-Style" (or NS) Gregorian
calendar (named after Pope Gregory XIII who decreed it in the papal
bull *Inter gravissimas* on 24th February 1582) was introduced only
gradually across parts of Europe, and locates Newton's birth date at
4th January 1643. Newton's father (Robert Newton, a farmer) died six
months after marriage, and three months before Isaac was born. When
Isaac's mother (Hannah Ayscough) re-married, the youngster was lodged
with his maternal grandmother (Margery Ayscough). In circumstances he
appeared to resent, he took a strong dislike to his stepfather (the
Reverend Barnabus Smith). In a confessional list of sins committed up
to the age of 19, Newton declared, "Threatening my father and mother
Smith to burn them and the house over them"[21]. Born prematurely,
Newton was a sensitive, private, humble man who wrote as much (if not
more) about religion as about science, having said in a letter to the
"father of microscopy" Robert Hooke (1635-1703), 6th February 1676,
"If I have seen further it is by standing on ye shoulders of giants".
We can see how Copernicus and Galileo must have figured tall amongst
Newton's lofty ancestors, but what of the evolution of ideas taking
place alongside these biographies? How did these translate to Wundt's
Leipzig and beyond – informing so essentially our modern psychology?

Self-indulgent philosophers
Once human beings start trying to engage with each other about what
is true and what is not true they (almost) invariably start arguing;
however, most people (with the exception of the most self-indulgent
philosophers) can agree that black is not white. It is this kind of
hard objectivity that is sought by those who follow in the empirical
tradition. In the example just given, we are referring to a stimulus
(light reflected to greater or lesser degrees depending on the light-
absorbent properties of an object) and a sensory experience (vision).
The philosophical tradition of empiricism considers that knowledge is
acquired only through experience. We can trace this sort of thinking
as far back as Aristotle (384-322 BC) in Classical Greece. Aristotle
occupies an elevated position in the known evolutionary path of ideas
stemming from Socrates (469-399 BC) about whom little is recorded
other than via progeny: from Plato (428-348 BC, of whom Aristotle was
a student) to Alexander the Great (336-323 BC, whom Aristotle taught,
and who expanded the Greek empire massively in his time). Aristotle's
view of the human mind at birth – as an unmarked tablet waiting to be
written upon by the mark of experience – was developed by Eastern

---

[20] Newton, I. (1687) *Philosophiæ Naturalis Principia Mathematica*. Samuel Pepys: London

[21] Cohen, I.B. (1970) *Dictionary Of Scientific Biography (Volume 11,* p.43). Charles
Scribner's Sons: New York

philosophers such as Avicenna (980 AD-1037) in 11th century Persia, Abubacer (1105-1185) in 12th century Arabia – and by Saint Thomas Aquinas (1225-1274), a Dominican priest who influenced not only Christian theology but all of Western philosophy to the present day. To those readers for whom the *tabula rasa*[22] principle seems obvious – a "no brainer" so to speak – it is as well to remember that Plato (Aristotle's mentor as we have seen) considered "mind" to be formed in the "heavens" prior to life[23]. Ideas are often as much reactions against what has gone before as they are novel or revolutionary. The Platonic view of a human mind that has the (intellectual) capacity for union with its maker was shared by Saint Bonaventure (1221-1274), a Franciscan contemporary of Saint Thomas Aquinas and, like him, one of only 33 Doctors of the Church. It is a corollary of empiricism that "innate" knowledge (revelation, inspiration, intuition, ideas – even reason) either doesn't exist, or is spurious (with the possible exception of "knowledge" transmitted through DNA). The extent to which one is "radical" about such matters is (inversely) proportional to the extent to which one tolerates exceptions to these strictures.

The founders of empirical psychology fall out with each other
Advancing in history to the establishment of Wundt's laboratory in 1879, we can appreciate better, now, how the empirical tradition and the Scientific Revolution shaped psychology as we know it today. From Helmholtz, Wundt inherited scientific skills in observation and measurement. Wundt was less interested in celestial bodies as he was internal machinations, or the contents of consciousness as it were. Wundt's typical approach to investigation of the psyche was to invite subjects (whom he introduced to the quiet and undisturbed environment of the laboratory) to contemplate the contents of their "minds"; i.e., to "introspect", as they experienced the ticking of a metronome (a device that clicks periodically, like the device a musician might use when a percussionist is not at hand). From the self-reports so generated, Wundt deduced a "Theory of Feeling" in which every internal state (for instance, the "anticipation" that preceded a forthcoming click) could be located in relation to three orthogonal dimensions: "pleasure versus displeasure", "excitement versus calm" and "strain versus relaxation". It is not so much true that Wundt's theories survived history as it is that his laboratory spawned a generation of influential theorists in their own fields. At Leipzig itself, Oswald Külpe (1862-1915) had abandoned his first subject – history – to study under Wundt, later becoming Wundt's assistant.

---

[22] The expression "*tabula rasa*" is attributed to "the first of the British empiricists" John Locke (1632-1704) – an Englishman who inspired the Scottish philosopher and fellow British empiricist David Hume (1711-1776), British philosopher and MP John Stuart Mill (1806-1873) and – abroad – French philosophers and Revolution protagonists François-Marie Arouet aka Voltaire (1694-1778) and Jean Jacques Rousseau (1712-1778).

[23] Reminiscent of Psalm 139: 13-17, thought to date from Old Testament David or later; i.e., written some time between 1100 and 400 BC, thereby preceding Plato considerably:

It was you who created my inmost self,
and put me together in my mother's womb;
for all these mysteries I thank you:
for the wonder of myself, for the wonder of your works.

You know me through and through,
from having watched my bones take shape
when I was being formed in secret,
knitted together in the limbo of the womb.

You had scrutinised my every action,
all were recorded in your book,
my days listed and determined,
even before the first of them occurred.

(*Jerusalem Bible: Popular Edition.* Darton, Longman & Todd)

These two fell out famously over "imageless thought". Unlike Wundt, Külpe argued that introspection could be used to study complex cognitive processes, coining the expression "imageless thought" to represent psychological processes that were not necessarily hinged on sensory information, or anything (figuratively) in the "mind's eye".

Equally diverse early progeny
The record of prominent psychologists who emerged from Wundt's Leipzig establishment is as diverse as it is impressive. Külpe's progeny included the Marxist philosopher Ernst Simon Bloch (1885–1977) and Henry Jackson Watt (1879–1925) – known for *Einstellung* or "mental set" in arithmetic. Aside from Külpe, Wundt's own students included: James McKeen Cattell (1860–1944), the first professor of psychology in the USA and whose work encompassed intelligence and mathematics in psychology; Granville Stanley Hall (1844–1924), the first President of the American Psychological Association (or APA); Charles Hubbard Judd (1873–1946), an educationalist who favoured empirical over theoretical approaches in schools; Charles Edward Spearman (1863–1945), known for the mathematical "rank" correlation and "g" (or a general factor in intelligence); Lightner Witmer (1867–1956), inventor of "clinical psychology" and co-founder of the first ever psychological clinic at the University of Pennsylvania in 1896 – and Edward Bradford Titchener (1867–1927), an Englishman who settled at Cornell University (New York). It was Titchener who brought the concept of "empathy" into modern psychology – translating from German the original *Einfühlung*, first used by Robert Vischer (1847–1933)[24].

The great brain-wash
Notwithstanding this august set of significant apprentices, Wundt's "introspection" was eclipsed by the tidal wave of behaviorism that swept America in the early-to-mid 20th century. Maintaining this spelling (without the 'u'), we acknowledge the nationality of its founder John Broadus Watson (1878–1958), and also its most well-known and enthusiastic proponent, Burrhus Frederic Skinner (1904–1990). Behaviorism, explicitly, is concerned with behaviour which – being measurable and amenable to controlled investigation, especially in the laboratory – is, according to behaviorists, more usefully the proper subject matter of psychology than "internal" states. In just this way, behaviour was suddenly divorced from "mind", a concept which the most radical behaviorists consider redundant (unnecessary). Still prevailing in contemporary British, European and North American universities, behaviorism has generated a large body of empirically-driven theory for its own scientific sake, but also in the hope of extrapolating its complex models of learning to humans which – for the most part – it recognises as a species instance of vertebrates.

Curiously unrecognisable "progress"
Would not our amateur "psychologist" – the one who throughout history played guessing games with his enemy in war, succumbed to treachery in "love", or stooped in compassion to assist a fellow human being in need when no-one was there to witness the beneficent deed (and, somehow, he knew that) – be somewhat disappointed about the shape of the modern discipline? Have not the Scientific Revolution and the limitations of a narrow empiricism (one that appreciates the value of experience only when it is so measurable that we can all see it) excluded the thinking "mind" whose focus the vernacular "psychology" ever was? The agnostic as opposed to the radical in behaviorist terms was thence to be discovered out in the ideological cold. In relation to our "minds" – in psychology – are we not now somewhat two-faced?

---

[24] Vischer's *Einfühlung* or "aesthetic sympathy" was also championed by Theodor Lipps (1851–1914) – a German philosopher-cum-psychologist greatly admired by Sigmund Freud.

"Rhubarb"
If Chapter 2 is difficult to digest try 32 times before Part II

Chapter 2

"Learning to 'control'"

Building blocks
According to the behaviorist tradition, the building blocks of all
learning are associative in nature. When animals (including humans)
are exposed to reinforcers; i.e., significant pleasant (aka
"rewarding") or punishing (aka "aversive") stimuli – in combination
with "neutral" ones such as a bell or a tone – links or connections
are forged between hypothetical "nodes" in the central nervous system
(or CNS) representing the elements in the learning environment. It is
worthwhile grasping the principles underlying these processes
because, intelligently interpreted, their capacity for understanding
and predicting human behaviour, including psychopathology (behaviour
needing treatment) and its "un-learning", is quite marvellously vast.

Scientific serendipity
Ivan Petrovich Pavlov (1849-1936) was a Russian physiologist awarded
the Nobel Prize in 1904 for work on digestion. With the dogs in his
laboratory already catheterised for saliva, Pavlov steered his
attention towards the systematic investigation of a rather curious
phenomenon: "anticipatory" secretion of saliva before presentation of
food, particularly when, for any reason, food had not been presented.

The classical unit of learning
The basic procedure in Pavlovian or "classical" conditioning is as
follows:

BASIC PROCEDURE IN PAVLOVIAN OR "CLASSICAL" CONDITIONING

"Trial"	Stimulus t1	Stimulus t2	Behaviour	Commentary
1	–	Food	Salivation	Food reliably elicits salivation. Because no learning is required, the food is referred to as an "unconditioned" stimulus or US and the salivation as an "unconditioned" response or UR.
2 + n as required	Bell	Food	Salivation	A neutral stimulus (one that is not particularly pleasant or unpleasant and which doesn't elicit a UR in its own right) such as a Tone or Bell is "paired" with the US by presenting it (immediately) prior to the US on several trials.
2 + n + 1	Bell	–	Salivation	After a sufficient number of trials, the previously neutral stimulus – now presented alone without the US – elicits behaviour that resembles or is identical to the UR. The change that has occurred is an instance of learning. The previously neutral stimulus is now referred to as a Conditioned Stimulus, or CS, and the elicited behaviour a Conditioned Response, or CR.

Essential principles of associative learning
Notes:

1. The US is known as "reinforcement", and is the driving force or "battery" behind learning (i.e., no reinforcement = no learning).

2. According to "stimulus substitution theory", the CS takes on the properties of the US[25], in which case the CR should resemble the UR.

3. Since the UR to pleasant USs generally looks like "approach" behaviour, the CS will also look like "approach". The reverse is true for "aversive" reinforcers – the subject will "avoid" the CS.

4. The emotional states that accompany CRs may be understood broadly as (biologically established) "hope" and "fear" respectively[26].

5. We can extrapolate out of the laboratory and to human beings: people will "hopefully approach" CSs previously paired with pleasant USs and "fearfully avoid" CSs paired with unpleasant reinforcers.

6. The number of trials needed for learning varies according to the "strength" of the US. In the case of "flavour aversion", where the US is an ingested toxin, only one trial may be necessary. Human beings learn quickly when the reinforcer is very powerful (or traumatic).

7. Learning is optimal when the CS precedes the US (i.e., forward conditioning) when it may continue with US onset (delay) or terminate prior to US onset (trace). In simultaneous conditioning, the CS and US occur at the same time. In backward conditioning, the US precedes the CS – intuitively a weaker case; after all, why would an animal learn about a stimulus that doesn't "predict" a significant event?[27]

8. The rate of learning may be affected by adjusting the inter-stimulus interval or ISI (time between CS and US which is optimal for a particular CS and US combination) and inter-trial interval (ITI).

9. The potential for explaining day-to-day human behaviour – particularly movement about the environment and emotional make-up (especially acquired disproportionate fear) – is virtually limitless, governed in scope only by the rich variations in the ways we encounter numerous motivationally significant stimuli in our routine affairs. As we all do this frequently, there is a great deal of reinforcement – and hence learning – happening all the time. The more one appreciates this, the more one can appreciate the "nurture" side of the "nature-nurture" debate (the other side being "inheritance").

---

[25] possibly accounted for by a link forged during learning between theoretical "nodes" (neuronal representations) for the CS and US. It is important to remember that physiological accounts of learning are at an early stage of development, and that the actual identities of CSs and USs in the CNS – and the neuronal and synaptic changes associated with learning – are not in the least fully understood. It is a giant leap of speculation to contemplate the emergence of consciousness (let alone conscience) from CNS activity. There have been valiant attempts at driving relevant theory – see, for example, *Journey To The Centers Of The Mind* by Susan Adele Greenfield (1950-). Adequate theories of classical conditioning need to address known difficulties for "stimulus substitution theory" – including anomalous conditioned responding (i.e., CRs which are vague – or partial instead of entire URs – or which resemble UR opposites).

[26] "Hope" and "fear" in non-human animals can only be imputed from observed behaviour – as non-humans lack the capacity for divulging verbal reports of subjective experience.

[27] It is also possible to establish complex permutations of relationship (contingency) between the CS and the US in order to investigate both theoretical and physiological explanations for conditioning (usually involving neurons and synaptic plasticity).

"Learning About The Environment"
Vicar Lane, Leeds, West Yorkshire

The sheer scope of ways we can learn about the environment

We can appreciate this even more fully by considering empirically-established variations within the classical conditioning paradigm.

VARIATIONS WITHIN THE CLASSICAL CONDITIONING PARADIGM		
Effect	**Description**	**Notes (for humans)**
Latent Inhibition	Serial pre-exposure to the CS slows the subsequent rate of CR acquisition.	"I might get away with ignoring an unreliable warning."
US Pre-exposure	Exposure to the US prior to learning can retard the acquisition of a CR.	"I get what I want anyway."
Context Pre-exposure	Pre-exposure to the learning context can enhance fear conditioning.	"I thought this place was safe … Get me out of here!"
Generalisation	A CR may be exhibited in some proportional way to stimuli which are not the CS but resemble it (possess overlapping characteristics).	"If it looks like a snake, and wiggles like a snake, it might be a snake."
Sensory Pre-conditioning	Two neutral stimuli are "paired" in several trials. One is then potentiated by pairing with a US, following which the other neutral stimulus elicits the CR even though it was never paired with the US.	"Don't tar me with the same brush!" and "I suspect a wolf in sheep's clothing."
Second Order Conditioning	Pairing of a potentiated CS with a neutral stimulus which then becomes potentiated in turn. The first CS has functioned as a reinforcer.	Fear spreads like wildfire. (Is it like this for hope … why not?)
Over-expectation	Reinforcement of compound CSs results in decrements in CRs which were acquired in prior conditioning with each CS alone (out of compound).	A given amount of predictive (US) power is shared amongst competing CSs.
Overshadowing	A stronger CR to a given CS presented alone than to the same CS presented in compound with a more salient one.	CSs can steal the predictive limelight from each other.
Blocking	Prior conditioning with a first CS prevents or inhibits acquisition of a CR to a second CS when both CSs are subsequently presented in compound.	"I already know all I need to know … Why should I take notice of an impostor?"
Conditioned Inhibition	The inhibitory effect on a CR of a second CS when reinforcement is withheld during compound trials.	"Two's company … Three's a crowd."
Super-conditioning	An enhanced CR to a given CS if it is presented in compound with a conditioned inhibitor (see above).	"Sorry, I took you for granted."
Extinction	Serial presentation of the CS without reinforcement results in diminution of the CR to pre-training levels.	"You've changed." (Why don't you love me like you used to?)
Extinction of Conditioned Inhibition	Pairings of the inhibitory CS with the US are required: presentation of the inhibitory CS alone does not produce Extinction of Conditioned Inhibition.	"A fly in the ointment must buy flowers."
Partial Reinforcement	Retardation of learning when the CS is not reliably paired with the US.	"You keep sending me mixed messages."
Recovery	Reappearance of a CR following its own Extinction in various circumstances, such as a novel context including presentation of a novel stimulus prior to the CS.	"I've forgiven, but I haven't forgotten." (There's always something there to remind me …)

"I Might Get Away With Ignoring An Unreliable Warning"
Singing Sands, Ardnamurchan, Scotland

Three simple but important statements
All of these observations, variations and notes can be distilled into three simple statements:

1. Animals, including human beings, "endeavour" to discern relationships between environmental events – especially in order to "predict" the occurrence of those with adaptive significance.

2. It is possible to "un-learn" or somehow compensate for at least some of these by exposure to alternative stimulus contingencies.

3. In humans, there is a corresponding subjective "emotional life" which is some complex of "anticipatory hope" and "avoidant fear".

An additional learning mechanism involving "agency"?
Now, behaviorists recognise another type of learning which, conventionally, they distinguish from classical conditioning. It is ostensibly different from classical learning because a response (R) seems to be involved in association formation (with corresponding implications for the putative underlying physiological mechanisms). Theoretically, one can assume that "operant conditioning" (synonymous with "instrumental learning") can, in all instances, be explained in terms of classical (S–S) associations, even though it is difficult to generate a convincing case in some scenarios. The matter hasn't been resolved at the behavioural level – let alone in the central nervous system. So, what is operant conditioning? And why isn't it classical?

Description of operant conditioning (aka instrumental learning)
In the Skinner Box[28] (or "operant conditioning chamber"), an animal (such as a rat or pigeon) is (usually) free to move about within its confines unencumbered; however, a variety of manipulations can be exercised by the (human) experimenter in order to investigate the set of principles that seem to underlie the subject animal's behaviour. The essential properties of the Skinner Box, aside from confinement, include its capacity for registering behaviour ("responses"), a means of delivering reinforcement (via a food box or a grid-floor through which electric current can be passed) and, optionally, administering "neutral" stimuli: "keylights" and sounds (bells, tones, buzzers). The experimenter determines a contingency between a response (usually a lever press) and the delivery of reinforcement. Whilst it may take some time for the lever to be pressed at all (since no motive already exists for the subject to do so), this eventually happens by chance (there being not a great deal else to do in a Skinner Box), and the recurrence of the same behaviour becomes more probable. In no time, our rat is pressing furiously. There appears to be (certainly as anticipated by the experimenter) a particular and necessary response (R) and the consequent occurrence of a reinforcer (S). The nature of the association formed or strengthened during operant conditioning is commonly considered to be R–S (implying a yet-to-be-discovered neural or synaptic change in or between "nodes" for a response on the one hand and the reinforcer on the other) and, thereby, distinguishable by category from classical conditioning (certainly as depicted in stimulus substitution theory where it is S–S). The associative nature of operant conditioning was formalised in an alternative way by Edward Lee Thorndike (1874–1949) in his "Law of Effect". Thorndike refers to reinforcers as "satisfiers" which strengthen associations between "situations" (in which the responses occur) and the responses themselves. This alternative interpretation may be expressed "S–R"[29].

---

[28] So named after B.F. (Burrhus Frederic) Skinner – the most archetypal, prolific and radical of behaviorists – to whom we have been introduced already. The Skinner Box was developed during his sojourn as a Masters / Doctoral student at Harvard in 1930-31.

[29] As an historical aside, Thorndike's Ph.D. mentor was James McKeen Cattell – an erstwhile student of Wilhelm Wundt (to both of whom we were introduced in Chapter 1).

"Consequences": a weathered, melting iceberg near Greenland
from an original photograph by Mila Zinkova (Wikimedia Mbz1)

Definition of operant conditioning
Operant conditioning may be defined as a change in the rate of a conditioned (i.e., a learned) response depending on the schedule of reinforcement that accompanies it. It isn't difficult to think of numerous examples in everyday human life. If some action on our part seems to result in an event, or series of events, which in our subjective experience is pleasant; we are, on the whole, more likely to repeat or increase the rate of the behaviour that "produced" it. The reverse is also true: on the whole we will cease or reduce the frequency of behaviour that leads to circumstances that we find unpleasant. Exceptions may come to mind, particularly the realisation that folks (perhaps including ourselves) have at times seemed bent on the pursuit of behaviour that could only ever have brought misery to themselves and others. Of course, this is of enormous psychological interest – and we shall revisit it later when we consider (in)sanity.

Still one basic unit?
Why is it apposite to contemplate an "S-S" account of operant conditioning? It is a matter of combining alternative interpretations of conditioned behaviour with the principle of keeping things simple – which insists that we should not permit sophisticated explanations when basic ones will do: we mustn't complicate matters unduly. This tenet of necessary parsimony is known as "Ockham's Razor" after the English Franciscan friar William of Ockham (1288-1348, contemporary with Saint Thomas Aquinas and Saint Bonaventure). The rule holds that as few assumptions as possible should be adopted when explaining anything. For modern psychology, the notion was embodied in a canon attributed to the British zoologist, Conwy Lloyd Morgan (1852-1936):

In no case may we interpret an action as the outcome of the exercise of a higher mental faculty, if it can be interpreted as the exercise of one which stands lower in the psychological scale.

Lloyd Morgan's Canon and Thorndike's "Law of Effect" both contest the notion that animals (human or otherwise) discharge any spurious mental faculty whilst exhibiting ostensibly "intelligent" behaviour.

How operant responses might be classical
Referring back to our rat in the Skinner Box, couldn't its lever pressing be a CR arising out of the S-S pairing of the lever itself (CS) with food (the US)? Protagonists who defend the proposition that operant conditioning represents a mode of learning in its own right say that if operant responses were really all classical ones, they should only ever (according to stimulus substitution theory) resemble the unconditioned response to the reinforcer. In support of their case, they cite numerous examples of conditioned operant behaviour that don't resemble the UR remotely. Most of such operant theorists favour a Skinnerian (R-S or response-reinforcer) interpretation over a Thorndikeian (S-R or situation-response) one because the latter – requiring only the learning of a relationship between the context, or at least some element(s) of it, and the response (albeit strengthened by the occurrence of the reinforcer) – does not permit subjective anticipation or "agency" (no matter how "mind"-like this word seems).

A learning scenario: it could be you
The reader is invited to reflect, in the context of a hypothetical vignette, on what kind of learning – expressed in associative terms – may be proceeding during the development of preferences for, or aversions to, stimuli that once had no particular significance. Suppose in crossing the road outside your home, wearing your dashing new red coat, you are knocked over by a bespectacled driver who yells rather aggressively from a speeding green car that the incident was entirely your fault. Simultaneously, the church bell chimes the hour,

and a party of curious schoolchildren passes by on the other side of the road. Having hobbled home, you realise you had forgotten your own spectacles, and had been preoccupied all along with a family illness.

A variety of elementary learning mechanisms
Selected instances of associative learning about this incident mapped to each of the alternatives we have outlined are summarised below:

SELECTED INSTANCES OF ASSOCIATIVE LEARNING ABOUT AN ACCIDENT

S-R (Thorndikeian)	R-S (Skinnerian)	S-S (Pavlovian)
You notice that you are hesitant crossing the road (R), but only outside your home (S). This is especially true if you are wearing your red coat, and when it's the afternoon – about the time when children leave school for home.	You notice that you hesitate more than usual when crossing the road anywhere (R). You have a vague (anxious) feeling that whenever you do this (approach the kerb to cross the road), something dangerous may be about to happen (S).	Abroad on holiday, you develop nausea (CR) when you see any green vehicle (CS) – even well away from public roads. It occurs to you that there isn't any rational reason for this: the nausea happens because of the accident (US).

Fear is a ubiquitous learning outcome
It is noticeable that all of these scenarios involve an unpleasant feeling (which we can approximate to fear), and the very way the circumstances in each case are expressed seems to reflect the various assumptions made about the learning experience; moreover, it is very difficult to tease out a Skinnerian account from a Thorndikeian one.

The adaptive significance of learning
Before leaving behaviorist accounts of learning, it is appropriate to pause briefly to reflect on their adaptive significance, and how conditioning might generate rogue emotional states. We can imagine readily how, in natural selection, developing approach and avoidance behaviour in relation to certain conditioned stimuli might improve an organism's chances of obtaining food or avoiding dangerous predators. This is to say, it is not difficult to see how evolution might have generated associative learning for survival purposes. This is not to go so far as to say that associative learning is, in fact, the outcome of an evolutionary process except in so far as all phenotypes are. Assuming, nevertheless, that there is a strong case, why would it generate emotional complexes common in humans that are, from the psychotherapist's side of the coffee table, irrational and crippling?

Summary of classical and operant conditioning
Further reflections on these problems feature in Chapter 9. For now, the main points (with ancillary notes) can be summarised as follows:

1. Classical conditioning looks like an adaptive asset in which organisms "endeavour" (within a reliable inter- and intra-species system incorporating a tendency to persist) to "predict" (anticipate in the future) the occurrence of biologically significant stimuli.

2. Operant conditioning refers to a change in the likelihood of behaviour depending on its outcome, appears to be designed to "control" the occurrence of reinforcers and is, at least in some cases, open to classical interpretation (S-S) as well as S-R and R-S.

3. Classical and operant conditioning generate conditioned emotional states; we may say "anticipatory hope" and "avoidant fear", a complex combination of each present in any individual's affective profile.

"No 'I Deer' How The Mind Works"

4. Via language, humans can express their subjective experience of conditioned emotional responses (CERs), but non-human animals cannot.

5. Using appropriate stimulus (and sometimes response) contingencies, conditioned behaviour can be "un-learned", "overwritten" or otherwise compensated for. (This is the basis for "behavioral" psychotherapy.)

6. Accounts of associative learning that have taken a century to build (and here we have outlined only the very elementary aspects) have adhered scrupulously to principles of parsimony in developing theory; nevertheless, it is still not known whether there is a single associative mechanism for classical and operant conditioning, or whether they rely on two or more fundamentally different processes.

7. The physiological plasticity that is assumed to underpin the behavioural changes seen in associative learning has been investigated in simple organisms[30], and some progress has been achieved in detecting matched behaviour-neurobiological alterations – particularly at synapses in the nervous system. To say that there is anything like a complete or even provisionally comprehensive account of the neural substrates of learning would be a gross overstatement.

8. Colloquially, most humans are happy with concepts such as "consciousness", "conscience" and "choice", and can describe these on both conceptual (everybody's got one) and subjective (this is what mine looks like) levels; nevertheless, we have come to expect radical behaviorists to be reluctant to acknowledge such phenomena as "real".

9. For B.F. Skinner, a "scientific determinist" as well as a radical behaviorist, there is no such thing as "free will": the movement of an organism about its environment can be accounted for fully and causally in associative terms; i.e., behaviour obeys scientific laws.

10. Whether Skinner is correct or not, any organism's subjectively experienced capacity for "controlling" its environment that arises out of conditioning processes may be illusory anyway[31], and this applies to humans. Aberrant CERs, such as disproportionate fear, are a specific case – not just because they are irrational – but because they have a counter-adaptive effect on functioning. Such modern heresy constitutes no argument against "consciousness", "conscience" and "choice" – which may rely on discriminable (or other) faculties.

11. If scientific knowledge about the neural substrates of learning is preliminary at best, it follows that theoretical approaches to any putative physiological basis for more elusive mental faculties such as "consciousness", "conscience" and "choice" are tentative at best.

12. Finally, the existence of the same mechanisms and processes for learning within a species doesn't necessarily mean that all members of that species will behave the same way in the same circumstances. There are individual differences in human behaviour that seem to hinge on resilience; in fact, we might justifiably say that modern psychology is pre-occupied with "toughness" of one kind or another. Which of these differences are genetic or otherwise "inherent", and which are "acquired" or otherwise amenable to modification – whether through psychotherapy or some less expensive route? Let's face it: "It's easy when you know how" and "The best things in life are free".

---

[30] A common example is a laboratory preparation of the sea snail *Aplysia Californica*.

[31] Chapter 9 features creative and thorough expansion of this and related propositions.

"Extravert"
Newquay Harbour, Cornwall

Chapter 3

"It's not what you do, it's the way that you do it"

"Too Much Information"
In 1924, an unusually severe breach of the River Neva inundated
Leningrad, including the cellar which housed Ivan Pavlov's laboratory
and kennels. The flood was so severe that access to those areas was
not possible for several days. On his eventual return, Pavlov noticed
two striking phenomena. First, it became very clear very quickly that most
(if not all) of his dogs had "forgotten" the conditioning to which
they had been exposed recently as part of the ongoing research
programme. As the days and weeks passed, moreover, some of the dogs
seemed to "bounce back" or be relatively unaffected – whereas others
seemed "nervous" and still traumatised. From this second observation,
Pavlov developed the notion of "Transmarginal Inhibition" or "TMI"
(humorously "Too Much Information") to describe the tendency of the
nervous system to "shut down" in response to overwhelming (traumatic)
emotional or physical stimuli (i.e., "stress")[32]. The "Threshold of
Transmarginal Inhibition" ("TTMI"), more specifically, refers to the
variation between individuals in the point at which TMI occurs: given
the same trauma, certain individuals "shut down" sooner than others.

Obsession with weakness
Pavlov seems to have had a predilection for descriptions of
psychological pathologies and their putative physiological substrates
(including schizophrenia and certain "cortical" cells) hinged on a
dimension of "weakness". For Pavlov, "strength of the nervous system"
was a fitting way of accounting for (canine) dispositional variations
following the 1924 inundation. In a model of the nervous system which
mediates learning[33], afferent stimuli – which have an "excitatory"
effect – are modulated (or dampened) by some "inhibitory" process in
order to avoid "overload". Whilst a general effect, its strength and
inertia varies between individuals. Where excitation and inhibition
are both "strong", TMI occurs late (i.e., there is high tolerance of
stimulation before "overload" and the TTMI is high), and vigorous CRs
are seen in classical conditioning. "Equilibration" is Pavlov's
expression for the way in which excitation and inhibition are
balanced (as a general phenomenon associated with stimulation but
also as a trait-like tendency between individuals), and "mobility"
describes the fluidity with which excitation–inhibition shifts occur.

An ancient taxonomy
Pavlov wasn't the first sharp observer to notice variations in animal
character (now the sub-discipline of human psychology known as
"personality" or "individual differences"). A taxonomy of four
temperaments that originated in Ancient Greece and prevailed for some
2,000 years (until the Renaissance) has been adopted by a plethora of
psychologists in the modern mould – as we shall see. Its survival
into contemporary psychological culture is rather surprising given
the system's simplicity, its superficial naïveté – and the extent to

---

[32] TMI occurs across three stages: "equivalent" when responses are, for the most part,
quantitatively proportional to stimuli; "paradoxical" involving a quantitative anomaly
in which strong responses follow weak stimulation and *vice versa* – and "ultra-
paradoxical" involving a qualitative anomaly in which "approach" behaviours towards
"aversive" stimuli and "avoidance" behaviours in relation to rewarding ones are seen.

[33] As in the previous chapter, our explanations of conditioning are founded on
conceptual models, not proven biological processes. These are framework theories
waiting for corroboration or otherwise. The point is, we don't know how the brain
works: we must be modest about the achievements of science in explaining human nature.

which we have become technologically sophisticated these days. But it is only in tracing the evolution and development of our present frameworks that we can come to appreciate what assumptions have been effected over time and, thereby, what preconceptions prevail today.

Love and strife
Our familiarity with the periodic table (of the elements) affords us a particular view of the physical world that renders almost impossibly difficult an authentic appreciation of the way sense was made of the world in pre-Socratic times (i.e., before 469 BC). In those days, according to Empedocles (490-430 BC), the "roots" of the material world were earth, water, air and fire. He accounted for the ways that materials behaved and morphed in terms of the unseen powers of "love" and "strife" (apparently attractive and divisive forces respectively). Plato was the first to use the term "elements" to refer to Empodocles' four material roots. In all of pre-Renaissance history, and arguably up until the present day - in, for example, "new-age" spirituality - a multitude of diverse global traditions has acknowledged a small number of material elements to which one or more "aethereal" ones have then been deemed ancillary[34]. The ancient four elements are readily identified as analogous to the *states* of matter recognised in modern science; i.e., solid, liquid, gas and plasma.

Greek sense of humour
In classical Greece, the ancient elements were associated with the four possible permutations of their two primary dimensions of "hot-cold" and "dry-wet" where: earth = dry and cold; water = cold and wet; air = wet and hot, and fire = hot and dry. Intuitively they were also identified with the seasons (autumn, winter, spring and summer respectively). This categorisation arrangement has come to be known as "humourism" (or "humouralism"), and is associated most commonly under this nomenclature with two seminal figures in the history of medicine - Hippocrates and Galen. Hippocrates of Kos (460-372 BC), aka the "father of medicine" (after whom the "Hippocratic Oath" is named) was a contemporary of Socrates. Bodily health in Hippocrates' understanding was contingent on the correct balance of four fluids (i.e., the humours) - each of which corresponded with an ancient element: black bile[35] (earth), phlegm (water), blood (air) and yellow bile[36] (fire). The humours wax and wane in the body according to diet, exercise, the seasons and so on. Medicine in those days amounted to corrective intervention: a compensatory diet, purging with laxatives, the application of leeches (in the case of "excess" blood), or other treatments intended to reverse the effect of the ascendant humour; e.g., cold and dry applications for mitigating a (hot and wet) fever.

Galen's medicine
Galen (129-200 AD) was a Roman physician known in his home country as Claudius (or Aelius) Galenus. More frequently he is known as Galen of Pergamum (or Pergamon, now Bergama in Turkey) where he discharged

---

[34] The word "quintessential" is based on the idea of a fifth, shall we say, *je ne sais quoi*. In Ancient Greece, the fifth element was "aether". In Hinduism it is "akasha". Whilst four of the seven (Hindi) chakras are fire, earth, water and air, the remaining three are non-material. The oriental concept of "void" traces its roots to Buddhism.

[35] Black bile, secreted by the kidneys and spleen (according to the ancients), was thought to be responsible for what came to be known as "melancholia" or "depression" (although the history of "melancholia" encompasses a broader range of psychological "disorders" - including what we now refer to as the range of "psychotic" illnesses).

[36] Yellow bile is a yellow-green liquid secreted by cells in the liver (hepatocytes). Stored in the gall bladder, or secreted directly into the duodenum, yellow bile aids digestion of lipids. The human liver can produce up to a litre of yellow bile per day.

duties as physician to the gladiators. During his latter days back in
Rome, Galen produced a large body of works – a significant proportion
of which survived to steer the development of medicine not just in
the West but in the world of Islam[37]. Always recognising and crediting
Hippocrates, Galen was responsible for projecting "humourism" into
nascent psychology as well as modern medicine. Following Hippocrates,
Galen believed that temperament, like health, was attributable to
humoural balance (*eucrasia*) or imbalance (*dyscrasia*): a preponderance
of black bile engendered a "melancholic" (dejected) temperament;
phlegm a "phlegmatic" (sluggish) temperament; blood a "sanguine"
(spirited) one, and yellow bile a "choleric" (volatile) disposition.

Pavlov projects his weakness onto the ancients
What, then, of Pavlov's dogs, the cellar-ravaging Neva and TMI? Why
not just two rather than four temperaments – "weak" (early onset of
TMI) and "strong" (late TMI)? Rather curiously, given Ockham's Razor,
Pavlov perpetuated the old system where: "choleric" corresponds with
"strong excitatory" (suggesting an imbalance of excitation–inhibition
with excitation predominating); "melancholic" matches "weak-
inhibitory" (suggesting a corresponding weak inhibition imbalance);
"phlegmatic" is "balanced" excitation–inhibition, and "sanguine" is
excitation–inhibition in equilibrium with "lively" characteristics.

Intuitively satisfied?
When we consider the possibility of four discrete temperament types,
are we intuitively satisfied that people can be partitioned in this
way? Certainly we could have fun trying to categorise our nearest and
dearest into these "square holes", but do they really fit? If not,
what (if anything) could be "true" about them, and in what ways ought
we to refine the basic propositions that they convey? Any significant
appreciation of modern physiology would render almost ridiculously
primitive Hippocratic explanations for illness; moreover, any kind of
corresponding psychological typology jars with our intuition about
the complexity of human personality. Many people find labels for
people pejorative, even those generated in formal, medical diagnostic
systems. Most folks don't like to be "pigeonholed" because, having
been "prejudged", they feel less "understood" as a unique individual.
Don't we, each of us, find other people intricate and unpredictable?
The Hippocratic scheme, nevertheless, has been invoked, harnessed or
modified by a multitude of figures who have shaped modern psychology
– particularly the sub-discipline of "personality" or "individual
differences". Amongst the most well-known and prolific of these was
the self-styled *Rebel With A Cause* – Hans Jürgen Eysenck (1916-1997).

Eysenck follows Newton
Born in 1916 Berlin during the Great – or First World War, Eysenck's
Thespian parents[38] separated when he was two. His mother re-married
but, being Jewish like her new husband, Max Glass, was forced to flee
to France during the political ascendancy of Hitler and the Nazis.
Hans Eysenck was lodged (cf. Sir Isaac Newton) with his maternal
grandmother, Frau Werner, who later died in a concentration camp.
Eysenck himself refused to join the Hitler Youth, rejecting a place
to study Physics at Berlin University. Eysenck sought exile in France
and then England in 1934. Obtaining his doctorate at the University

---

[37] Although many of Galen's works were lost or destroyed, a significant body eventually
was adopted by Islamic physicians, and later translated back into Latin. Galen's
investigations were confined to primates, dogs and pigs because of a trenchant taboo
surrounding the dissection of human bodies – and his records featured significant
errors as a consequence. This impediment to progress was dissolved during the Italian
Renaissance when Andreas Vesalius (1514-1564) published new work with human cadavers.

[38] Eduard Anton Eysenck and Ruth Eysenck (née Werner) aka Helga Molander on stage

of London, Eysenck established Clinical Psychology in Britain after World War II at the Institute of Psychiatry in the Maudsley Hospital.

No fan of "unscientific" psychoanalysis
No fan of psychotherapy, particularly of the psychoanalytic kind (Eysenck was quite vociferous in rejecting any "unscientific"[39] concepts such as an unconscious mind or "Id"[40]), Eysenck was an ardent admirer of Galileo because of his stature as a scientist, and because he was persecuted for what he discovered and stood for. We can see in Eysenck, then, continuation of the empirical and scientific tradition to which we have alluded often - one that could clash unpleasantly with alternative approaches within the same discipline (i.e., modern psychology) less geared towards direct observation and measurement. Eysenck's approach to psychological treatment in clinical settings was heavily reliant on the principles of conditioning that we reviewed in Chapter 2. Established under the behaviorists' banner - the techniques, referred to as "behavioral", are commonly in use now.

"Toughness" is really "softness"
Eysenck earned a reputation as a controversial figure, not just as a landmark psychologist. His positions on, for example, the genetic contribution to intelligence and "genius" (including sex and race[41]) - and the actual nature of the relationship between smoking tobacco and cancer[42], were as often misinterpreted as they were appreciated. Eysenck was an industrious publisher of books and papers (so creating an unmistakeable career yardstick for the trenchant empiricist). Most of these were concerned with the measurement of IQ ("Intelligence Quotient") and individual differences by questionnaire. The idea behind the use of questionnaires is that huge amounts of behavioural data can be garnered very quickly with no significant sacrifice of accuracy (compared with costly and time-consuming interviews) - provided people are honest in the way they respond. Disadvantages include the possibility that respondents lack the self-awareness necessary to answer questionnaires "truthfully"; alternatively, may be too keen to register answers they think the researcher is looking for - or just afford ones that make them feel good about themselves.

No casual scrutiny
Whilst questionnaire testing may seem rather "convenient", the statistical procedures applied to the data so obtained are typically rigorous, meticulous and painstaking (arguably too much so given the inevitable vagaries and "error" in human self-report). In a complex correlational procedure known as "factor analysis", the relationships between individual questionnaire items are evaluated in such a way that patterns of behaviour not amenable to identification by more casual scrutiny can be detected. Questionnaire data pertaining to a multitude of human dispositions ("lower order") have been, as it

---

[39] Ironically, Sigmund Freud (1856-1939) pitted the allegation "unscientific" against Carl Jung (1875-1961) for his breadth of appreciation of personality (see Chapter 8).

[40] It will be of great interest to any reader with a Freudian bent to know that, in the interview series "The Last Word" published in *The Guardian* newspaper on Saturday April 18th 1992 - when asked, "What is the trait you most deplore in yourself?" Hans Eysenck, the self-styled James Dean of psychology and "inventor" of the personality trait "Psychoticism" (equivalent to "tough- vs. tender-mindedness") answered, "Softness".

[41] Eysenck seemed satisfied to recognise that all geniuses are men (which is not to say that the average male and female scores on IQ tests are statistically different) and to engage in discussions about racial inequalities in performance on IQ tests - which have been highly modified since they were first produced - to eliminate cultural bias.

[42] The essence of Eysenck's position on the causal relationship between smoking and cancer is that it is non-existent or indirect; rather, a third factor - personality - is the causal agent for both (smoking and cancer, which only appear causally related).

were, cast into the statistical aether to see what ("higher order") dimensions draw these into some coherent picture. Theoretically, the most enduring have been the two primary traits of Extraversion ("E"), or outgoingness, and Neuroticism ("N") or emotional (in)stability. Most, if not all, "lower order" human tendencies fall under, and are statistically related to, one of these two overarching constructs.

Finding what you're looking for in science as in the spiritual life
Now, scientists are well known for despising "circular arguments". A circular argument is simply one that makes an assumption in its early stages of formation upon which a vital conclusion drawn later relies (very similar to the colloquialism "begging the question"): "When did you stop stealing from your employer?". The main problem with E and N is that they hinge on several circular (or quasi-circular) arguments:

1. As concepts, E and N are defined by what they measure. If someone were to ask the question "What is Extraversion?", the answer would be "Extraversion is what an Extraversion questionnaire measures".

2. "There are three kinds of lies: lies, damned lies and statistics" is attributed to Benjamin Disraeli (1804-1881), Prime Minister of the United Kingdom 1874-1880 and a friend of Queen Victoria (1819-1901) who reigned over the United Kingdom of Great Britain and Ireland from 1837 until her death (i.e., for over 63 years). The expression was made famous in North America by Samuel Langhorne Clemens (1835-1910) – otherwise known as Mark Twain – author of *The Adventures of Tom Sawyer* and *Adventures of Huckleberry Finn*. It is not so much that there is a deficit in the integrity of the statistics harnessed for the work on personality traits as that some of the mathematical processes involve a significant degree of subjective interpretation[43]. A researcher may focus on lower or higher order traits, and perhaps there are examples of both needles and haystacks in the literature.

3. The raw item material generated for the questionnaire study places limits on what can emerge during any data processing exercises that follow. At the very framing of a research question you are, to some extent, "begging the question". You can only answer the questions that you ask. If you are a dyed-in-the-wool empiricist wedded to the need for observation and measurement, you are going to look only for observable and measurable things. (Perhaps science is, after all, rather like the spiritual life – you find what you're looking for!)

Making do with "Stimulus Intensity Modulation"
To be fair to Eysenck and other personality trait advocates, you can only work with what is possible; i.e., it is not possible (for both practical and ethical reasons) to measure Extraversion across the surface of the brain with a "slipstick". The measurements can only be indirect. There is also significant mitigation that is afforded by invoking the principle of "validity"; i.e., the extent to which external evidence suggests that a personality questionnaire measures what it claims to measure. If a person obtained a high score on an Extraversion questionnaire, but was never to be seen at parties, you might question the validity of the questionnaire. The strongest case for a personality trait – in the eyes of the empiricist – is the biological one, and there is a substantial raft of research evidence suggesting that extraverts are "stimulus-hungry" (the reverse being true for introverts). For example, an extravert will produce less

---

[43] amongst which are the choice of technique for locating a reference factor in vector "hyperspace", the interpretation of Eigen Values (factor variance) or "scree plots" in deciding on an appropriate number of factors to extract from a correlation matrix – and the final method of rotation of factors for "best fit" (orthogonal versus oblique)

saliva than an introvert for a given quantity of stimulation (in the mouth with a fixed amount of lemon juice). Once into biology, the distraction of inheritance materialises, and the validity data for Extraversion (within the experimental category "stimulus intensity modulation") has been augmented with swathes of "twin" and "family" studies which – depending on how they are collapsed and allowing for biases in interpretation – suggest that the extent to which E is "inherited" (the "heritability coefficient") might be about a half.

A spanner (or two) in the works
The intrinsic nature of Extraversion has been modified since it was first established in questionnaire form. The Maudsley Personality Inventory (or MPI), published in 1959, was replaced by the Eysenck Personality Inventory (or EPI) in 1964. Both of these scales measure E, N and L, where L is a "Lie" scale included to detect false or improbable answers (of the "I never tell lies" kind). The MPI and EPI are, moreover, psychometrically equivalent – meaning that E and N in the two scales respectively measure the same thing (the questionnaire items aren't identical but they look pretty much similar in terms of what they are asking). The Eysenck Personality Questionnaire (or EPQ) published in 1975, however, threw a spanner in the works – well, actually – two spanners. The first spanner was the inclusion of a third "higher order" trait named "Psychoticism" or "P". If you look at the questionnaire items that make up this scale they have a lot to do with impulsivity – or acting hastily, and there's a mish-mash of other items to do with self-centredness – even cruelty[44]. The second spanner is that the E scale in the EPQ doesn't any longer look like E as it was presented in the MPI or EPI. It's changed from a mixture of sociability and impulsivity (in the EPI) to a more pure measure of sociability (in the EPQ) – the impulsivity items having migrated to P[45]. Similarly, whereas the N scale in the EPI measured both social sensitivity and hypochondriasis, the latter is missing from EPQ N[46].

A few indicative items from Eysenck's E, N and P are shown below.

SAMPLE ITEMS FROM EYSENCK'S E, N AND P

EPQ Extraversion (E)	EPQ Neuroticism (N)	EPQ Psychoticism (P)
Are you a very talkative person?	*Are you worried by awful things that might happen?*	*Would you take drugs that have strange effects on you?*
Would you enjoy a lively party?	*Do you suffer from 'nerves'?*	*Do you think insurance schemes are a waste of time?*
Do you like plenty of excitement going on around you?	*Are you often tired and listless for no good reason?*	*Did you tend to dislike your parents?*
Do you often do things on the spur of the moment?	*Would you describe yourself as 'moody'?*	*Do you sometimes tease animals?*

---

[44] Roger, D. and Morris, J. (1991) The internal structure of the EPQ scales. *Personality And Individual Differences, 12,* 759–764.

[45] Rocklin, T. and Revelle, W. (1981) The measurement of Extraversion. *British Journal Of Psychology, 20,* 279–284.

[46] Roger, D. and Nesshoever, W. (1987) The construction and preliminary validation of a scale for measuring emotion control. *Personality And Individual Differences, 8,* 527–534.

"Overarching Dimensions"
Fountains Abbey, North Yorkshire

A messy personality
Summarising questionnaire studies: (i) the individual items that
belong to personality scales speak loudest about what the scale
actually is - psychologically speaking; (ii) although there are
strong mathematical relationships between items within each scale,
the scales themselves are derived in subjective procedures; (iii)
although the hardest evidence that traits exist comes from biological
criteria ("stimulus intensity modulation" and heritability studies),
it is still difficult to draw concrete conclusions because there is
only a "weight of evidence", not incontrovertible corroboration, and
(iv) it is apparent, even at first hand, that whether you examine the
traits mathematically (with correlations) or behaviourally (looking
at what the actual questionnaire items say), even the "higher order"
dimensions appear "messy" (i.e., not entirely coherent internally).

Accounting for individual differences in "stimulus hunger"
Let's suppose that enough number crunching has been done in the past
few decades in favour of E and N. Do they tell us much more about
human nature than the ancient temperaments, or Pavlov's "excitation-
inhibition"? Is it possible to wrap up all of these approaches
(Ancient Greek, Pavlovian, Eysenckian) into one "stimulus hunger"
framework? The extravert has a lower "resting" or baseline level of
arousal than the introvert, this being determined at least in part by
genetic factors. Because we all function best (psychologically) at
some intermediate level of arousal; i.e., neither asleep nor super-
vigilant, we engage in dispositional behaviour strategies (reflected
in personality traits) to maintain this optimum. The extravert seeks
stimulation so as to increase arousal from baseline to ideal, whereas
the introvert avoids it for the same purpose. Traits are considered,
like "hard" phenotypes such as height, to be "normally distributed"
(compliant with the "bell-shaped curve") - most people falling around
the average - with fewer and fewer located towards the extremes.

Eysenck on the same page as Pavlov
Just like Pavlov before him, Eysenck mapped E and N onto the four
ancient temperaments with no apparent equivocation: the "melancholic"
temperament corresponds with unstable introversion (E-N+), the
"phlegmatic" is a stable introvert (E-N-), "sanguine" is equivalent
to stable Extraversion (E+N-) and "choleric" is unstable Extraversion
(E+N+). Eysenck's arousal model is strongly reminiscent of Pavlov's
TMI, where Eysenck's extraverts correspond with Pavlov's "strong"
(stimulus-tolerant) nervous system. Pavlov's TTMI could be regarded
as analogous to the various points at which stimulus-control or
emotionally avoidant behaviour "trips". Again we see the development
of ideas as evolutionary, with successive theorists building on (at
least recognising the relevance of) the models that have gone before.

Even more risk of misunderstanding
There are many variations on these approaches to understanding
individual differences across many walks of modern life. One of the
most well known is the Myers-Briggs Type Indicator (or MBTI) from the
1940s, based on the work of the Swiss psychiatrist who established
"analytical psychology" (as distinct from Freudian psychoanalysis) -
Carl Gustav Jung (1875-1961). The MBTI is an instrument for measuring
the four functions of the Jungian conscious psyche (sensation aka
"sensing", "intuition", "thinking" and "feeling"). The MBTI outcome
is allocation of a person to one of 16 types; however, we have
already addressed the problem of partitioning humans into categories.
The MBTI's psychometric properties have been challenged by academics;
nevertheless, it is widely used in the business world where there is
a huge risk of misinterpretation by non-specialists, and misplaced
discrimination against employees based on spurious test results.

Woven threads

The threads of human personality we have teased out can be woven back into "concentric temperaments" as depicted in the following diagram.

"CONCENTRIC TEMPERAMENTS" DERIVED FROM THE ANCIENT ELEMENTS AND HUMOURS, PAVLOV'S EXCITATION-INHIBITION, AND EYSENCK'S E AND N (PERIMETER DESCRIPTIVES ARE FROM A SEMINAL EYSENCK PUBLICATION)

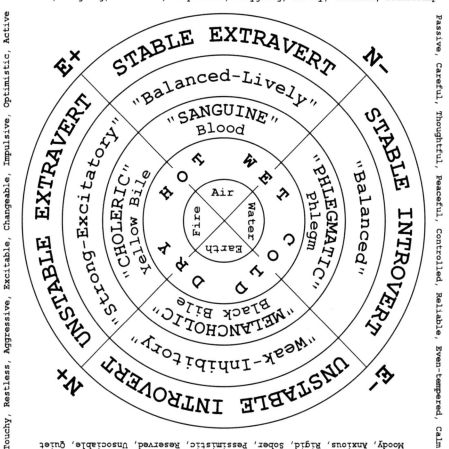

Sociable, Outgoing, Talkative, Responsive, Easygoing, Lively, Carefree, Leadership

Time for confession

Surely it is quite extraordinary, given the scientific age in which we live, with its consistent calls for "evidence" and "proof", that such primitive models of personality are still considered pertinent to modern psychology and all its attendant activities – including psychotherapeutic treatment. Could we not – in a burst of collective frankness – confess how much we don't know, as assert how much we do (whether about how the human brain works, and what it does or doesn't generate, or what the universe is made of and "where it came from")? It seems we would rather defer to small but empirically-derived tangibles than contemplate, in a spirit of epistemological humility, how precious little we really are able to establish about our mutual differences, and immeasurably how much more we *might* have in common.

"Mindless Egghead"

Chapter 4

"Inside the machine"

Enlightened teenagers and the behavioural abacus

Whilst there may well exist sizeable droves of enlightened teenagers amongst us, a significant proportion of undergraduates embarking on psychology courses in the Western world is shocked to discover that, far from having found a quick route to self-discovery (as well as, perhaps, some privately-yearned-for happiness), they are rapidly (and reluctantly) inducted into the obscure world of statistics. The undergraduate curriculum (determined in Great Britain by the British Psychological Society, or BPS, which accredits all serious university courses in the UK domestic countries and has counterparts in other nations) shamelessly forces the subject into the empirical mould. There is a very good, understandable and acceptable reason for this; but also a vastly underappreciated disadvantage that we mustn't talk about. The good reason is that without some means by which we can bring authority to argument other than sheer force of persuasion, we could be teaching the next generation of psychologists nothing more reliable than an anthology of subjective viewpoints. Since, moreover, even the most enlightened of professors can disagree on a matter, how would we ever resolve a difficult psychological issue? By harnessing the empirical tradition that we have outlined, the BPS considers that it can bring to bear a certain objectivity to the discipline. By insisting on observation, measurement and calculating everything psychological on the behavioural abacus, the BPS and its worldwide associates anticipate a scientific consensus accumulating with a rapidity proportional to the quantity of relevant research produced. The psychology research programme competes not only with other disciplines – but with all the contenders in our governments' coffers (the space and military programmes, as well as the health, social and education priorities of the day). It is, nevertheless, big business.

The scientific cart and the epistemological nag

Although it is, indeed, far better that academics and their students are facilitated to agree on at least a few things (goodness knows there are enough intellectual and other cul-de-sacs in a "typical" undergraduate life), we have hidden away what our intuitive students borrowed money for. As psychologists became compelled to observe and measure, thanks broadly to the 20th century behaviorist lobby, their subject had to become observable and measurable. They have redefined psychology for both the undergraduate and lay person and called it a "science of behaviour". The scientific cart has gone before the epistemological nag, and we have become somewhat dumbstruck by the brilliance of the "mindless eggheads". How could this have happened?

Understanding your own vitality

Philosophers have assumed that if we are willing to consider the existence of "mind" at all, it must be one of two things: either it is an epiphenomenon emergent from matter ("monism" or "materialism") – or it exists in its own right and does not rely on matter to do so (then known as "dualism"). It is one of the fundamental challenges of all psychology and, if we have taken our first steps in a spurious direction, we may need to start from scratch to get things right. The vainglorious tendency of philosophers to polarise and dogmatise was described in the very first paragraph of the Preface to this volume. As human understanding of its own vital subjects (let us say any philosophy of life – including psychology and psychotherapy) can be contaminated to the core by intellectual diversions and divisions, some examples of polarisation from ancient and modern history follow.

EXAMPLES OF POLARISATION FROM ANCIENT AND MODERN HISTORY

Position A	Position B	Exposing dogma …
The universe was created. ("Creationism")	The universe had no beginning. ("Hawkingism"[47])	Modern physicists, if pressed, will admit that their calculations pertain close to but not at or before a "big bang". They, like the Creationists, moreover, were not there to witness any such event.
God made the world in seven days. ("Fundamentalism")	There is no such thing as God. ("Atheism")	Protagonists on either side will not tolerate the prospect of a sane human adult combining a basic appreciation of Darwinian evolution with a personal, spiritual, even divinely-inspired basis for living.
"Mind" and matter are separate and mutually independent. ("Dualism")	"Mind" is an emergent and / or contingent property of matter. ("Monism")	As the true nature of matter itself let alone the constitution of the universe are barely understood how can we possibly say that mind is, or is not, a property of matter? A final "theory of everything" will be less about what humans measure than it will be "measurably human".
Human beings are masters of their own (and other people's) destinies via "free-will". ("Indeterminism")	Everything that happens is the outcome of one or more immutable natural laws. ("Determinism")	It has never been proven that human "free-will" is not an illusion – yet we haven't discovered all of the natural laws. Reason is not the only path to knowledge if you have experienced the effect(s) of faith which is also an act of "choice".
Right-wing politics rule OK. ("Fascism")	Left-wing politics rule OK. ("Marxism")	Any autocratic government generates gross travesties of "natural justice". Both over-regulated and under-regulated financial markets implode miserably sooner or later.
Men are better than women. ("Sexism")	Women are better than men. ("Sexism")	Biological sex is the nearest to a sharp duality, but even this is not universal[48]. Gender – which has personal and sociological identity connotations – is far less clear: you are what you believe you are.
White people are supreme. ("Racism")	Black people are supreme. ("Racism")	In less than a century and a half[49] (and but for the American Civil War) the USA has progressed from legal slavery to President Obama. Perhaps Barack Obama's inauguration and vision herald the human race's greatest hope for its own survival.

[47] We benefit realising that "beginninglessness" is Aristotleian in origin (at least), significantly preceding Stephen Hawking's popular (1988) *A Brief History Of Time*.

[48] The human Y sex chromosome affects male fertility and determines gonadal sex (XY is male and XX is female), but there are XY females and other permutations such as Klinefelter's Syndrome (XYY – with testes) and Turner's syndrome (XO – with ovaries) – as well as other chromosomal permutations (e.g., XXX or "supermale") and "intersex" physiological variations – rendering sex determination a grey area in certain cases.

[49] Legal slavery in the USA was only abolished in 1865 after the American Civil War (1861-1865) and the victory of the Union over the Confederacy of southern slave states which had declared secession in order to protect slavery-dependent economic interests.

"Rubin Vase": Polar opposites? Or something meaningful between?

"Spiritual blindness"
If there is any single principle running through examples like these,
it is that a polarised view rarely, if ever, embodies the whole story
- or represents any worthwhile "truth". We might also suspect that
the degree of fervour with which a polarised position is defended
(especially if violently) is directly proportional to the extent to
which its own protagonists may have personal misgivings about it.
This (distinctly) human tendency to refuse to accept some (especially
psychological) "reality" obvious to others is known colloquially as
"denial" or, "Don't Even 'No' I Am Lying". As the counsellor for drug
and alcohol problems often quips, "Denial is not a river in Egypt".
The helpee already "knows" that they are in trouble using their "drug
of choice", but hasn't yet discovered the willingness to assimilate
the depth of that "truth" unreservedly. Before the client arrived in
treatment, the anomalous nature of their behaviour may not have been
"visible" to themselves at all. (Anomalous here means that effects
harmful to both the user or misuser and others - disproportionately
deleterious compared with any anticipated - inevitably follow use.)
We may describe this inability to see one's own denial as "spiritual
blindness" (where "spiritual", as we have said before, simply means
"unseen"). Such "blindness of blindness" is not tautological because
we really do mean that its "victim" cannot see her or his own self-
deceit. This second order blinkeredness is reminiscent of the hidden
misgivings of the polarised philosopher who cannot see through his or
her own agenda. When one cannot see even the shadow-shape of the axe
one is grinding (far less admit to its ulterior purpose), one is also
"spiritually blind". Perhaps we will never know, under our own
auspices, whether as individuals or species of living thing, what
degrees or orders of blindness may lie beyond our "seeingness".
According to one philosophical position, mankind will never be able
to attain an objective perspective of the universe, whatever that is
- but which includes ourselves as perspective-takers - because of
"inbuilt" limits on our capacity for discovering and understanding[50].

A common-or-garden test of pulse
Taking common-or-garden human experience for a moment, let us test
our common-sense pulse, or ground ourselves in a broader empiricism[51]
- which is just to say rely on the subjective experience of life and
living that we all possess. Contemplate first, if you will, the human
child exploring the natural world with abandon. Is there anything in
that child's subjective experience that disposes her or him to
discern any separation between "mind" and body? In all probability
our child wouldn't be contemplating such matters at all: their

---

[50] The notion that humans will never be able to know everything, even allowing for the
eventual progress of philosophy and science, can be traced through characters with
whom we are already familiar - particularly Plato (428-348 BC), Aristotle (384-322),
Saint Thomas Aquinas (1225-1274) and John Locke (1632-1704). Today's philosophers may
draw upon any of several more newly mooted principles including "Bremermann's Limit"
which refers to the maximum processing speed of any self-contained material system and
is equal to 2×10^{47} bits per second per gram. Bremermann's Limit is named after the
German-American mathematician Hans Joachim Bremermann (1926-1996) and is derived from
both the energy-mass conservation principle ($E=mc^2$) identified by the German-born but
nationality-itinerant physicist Albert Einstein and the Uncertainty Principle (e.g.,
that both the position and velocity of a particle cannot be known with utter precision
simultaneously) espoused by the German physicist Werner Heisenberg (1901-1976). Unlike
the scientist, the ardent dualist (naturally) would neither subject their "minds", nor
correspond what they may "know", to the limiting parameters of any material system(s).

[51] Hardly heretical as the roots of the English word "empirical" are in the Ancient
Greek ("εμπειρικός" in modern Greek) translating to Latin as "experientia", meaning
"experience". A "broader empiricism" here just means a broader experience; i.e., not
limited to sensory experience alone. Folks can and do testify to and agree upon the
meaning of common types of experience as well as to the slide rule or yardstick.
Without such shared understandings human relationships would be dry if not impossible.

experience is simply a subjective enjoyment. If prompted by an adult to say whether "mind" and body are separate in some way, by even the most subtle of questioning, our child might well furnish a glance of disdain, bordering on contempt. Consider next the "typical" teenager. Perhaps now there might be some recognition by our subject of mental "angst", but would your burgeoning adolescent agree in no confused way that body and "mind" components of that subjective experience are discriminable? ("It is my mind's eye, even my soul[52], that sees and experiences dismay at my acne, but it is kinaesthetically a conjoined experience".) Finally, do most adult humans not just take for granted their moment—by—moment experience of "self in the world" unless it is interrupted by some intense attack of pleasure, pain, panic or existential *ennui*? Why is the "mind—body problem" of interest to anybody other than those with time to spend acquiring intellectual credit or grinding an ulterior philosophical axe? Taking account of the limited progress that the great brains of history have made resolving it across millennia hitherto, is it not a rather indulgent and vainglorious pursuit? Whether so or not, we are compelled to trace its trajectory historically (at least in outline) if we wish to understand its impact on modern psychology and, thereby, you and me.

Dualism and ultra-dualism

The supposition about "mind" that emanated from Ancient Greece and pervaded the modern world via some of the most famous thinkers in history, including significant figures in the Church, is that "mind" is not material. In Plato's *Phaedo* (who narrates to Echecrates) – a middle dialogue dating *circa* 380 BC – the logic of the condemned[53] Socrates regarding the afterlife is evaluated by friends in dialectic (a communication forum of at least some shared understandings in which protagonists are engaged in a tussle to convince each other of the superiority of a particular point of view). Cebes and Simmias find most cogent the "argument from form of life", or the notion that as the "soul" is the "cause" of earthly life it can never have been anything but alive itself, and will continue to be alive after bodily death. There are several possible counterpoints to the argument[54]; however, it is not so much the point whether Socrates was "right" to be existentially optimistic in his last moments as to appreciate that the earliest and greatest of all philosophers were "dualists". For Plato in Ancient Greece, "forms" were aspatial, atemporal and extra-mental blueprints of perfection: "universals" – such as love, truth and beauty – as well as everyday concepts such as roundness. Forms comprised the very essence (*ousia*) of and preceded material things which, in relation to the forms themselves, were mere "shadows"[55]. Although Plato and his protégé Aristotle differed regarding how, and the extent to which, mental assets were acquired – for both of them the intellect whereby forms are perceived was a metaphysical entity. In maintaining that "mind" and matter are of different "substance" – drawing upon the analogy of chariot and charioteer to make the point – Plato in particular is referred to commonly as an "ultra-dualist".

---

[52] Whilst "mind" and "soul" are often interchangeable and confounded in arguments about dualism, any useful distinctions would almost certainly rely on theological arguments.

[53] Socrates was executed by "forced" drinking of Hemlock – a plant poison – at the age of 70 for the offence of impiety against the gods and corrupting the youth of Athens. Contrary to the charge of his accuser Meletus, Socrates considered that his reputation had really been undone because of his challenging the wisdom of those in high office:

I found that those who had the highest reputation were nearly the most deficient, while those who were thought to be inferior were more knowledgeable. (Apology, 26)

[54] Interestingly, religious authorities hold that God creates man's soul "immediately".

[55] Seahorse Sam recommends a moment in the company of the front cover at this juncture.

"Doucement!" (Easy Does It!)
Post-Revolution France, near Place de la Concorde, Paris

Cogito ergo sum
A significant figure in the Scientific Revolution for his support of rationalism[56], René Descartes (1596-1650) argued that thinking was the only thing about which he could be certain. One could doubt that one had a body, but one could not doubt that one was thinking about whether one had a body and, so, thinking was in some sense more "real". Even to doubt that one thought or existed was evidence of thought or existence for Descartes[57]. He coined the expression *cogito ergo sum* which translates to English as "I think, therefore I exist". Like Plato, Descartes believed that "mind" was strictly non-physical in nature. Its essence was thought, and it was possessed only by humans. The primary theoretical difficulty for "substance dualism" (holding that "mind" is made of different "stuff") is to find a way to account for how "mind" and body interrelate causally (awkwardly assuming that "mind" exerts "will"). For Descartes, the exchange germane occurred at the pineal gland which he termed "the seat of the soul". Although Descartes supposed otherwise, the pineal gland does not exist only in humans; moreover, whereas for Descartes the pineal gland was undivided it is, in fact, hemispherical like the cerebrum. Of course, unlike "mind", the pineal gland is material like the rest of the body and, so, dualists in those days argued that God mediates all causal effects – not just at the pineal gland. Evidently, this is not the type of explanation that many modern thinkers will entertain.

Comte's "religion of humanity"
Positioning itself contiguous with but contrary to dualism lies a set of related philosophical traditions which, as a whole, sidelines any kind of subjectivity in favour of the supposed objectivity derived from constraining acceptable knowledge to that which can be known in some certain manner – particularly via the five senses. Although similar principles of approach can be traced further in history[58], "positivism" is generally attributed to the first sociologist, the French philosopher Auguste (Isidore Auguste Marie François Xavier) Comte (1798-1857). Comte's ideas thrived in the wake of the national malaise that emerged following the French Revolution (1789-1799). Setting aside all political considerations surrounding that historic event, it isn't entirely unreasonable to speculate that French people then (like humans everywhere in place and time who have preferred or submitted to leadership over autonomy), missed suddenly the monolith of authority that now had been dissolved along with the monarchy (Louis XVI). Alongside John Stuart Mill (1806-1873), with whom Comte developed a personal friendship, Comte argued for a "religion of humanity" – a clear precursor of modern humanism. Comte's notions regarding the evolution of human society through three stages from: (i) the theological (pre-Enlightenment) to (ii) the metaphysical to (iii) the positive (reverberating in both Marxism and psychoanalysis) betray a subspecies of atheism which – incorporated in his entire philosophy, apparently – did not save him from severe mental health problems and a suicidal disposition. It was Comte who coined the term

---

[56] Rationalism, being a philosophical rival of empiricism, holds that the intellectual power of reason (or deduction) is a more proper foundation for acquiring knowledge than interpretation of sensory experience. In its radical mode, it is the only way.

[57] René Descartes' "methodological scepticism", in which he advocated starting with the exclusion of doubtful propositions only re-embracing them if they could be established firmly – such as re-embracing "I doubt that I think" as it constituted evidence of thinking – can be regarded as breathtaking cleverness, or mere contrived and indulgent generation of nonsense for no useful purpose. If we apply the maxim "Keep It Simple" to Descartes, we might also regard his "Theory of Fallacies" in the same light. ("This statement is untrue" as a proposition is just tedious rather than simply marvellous.)

[58] notably the North African, Muslim, philosophical historian – Ibn Khaldun (1332-1406)

"altruism" to describe what he regarded as a pre-requisite for the evolution of human society to its pinnacle – that individuals should subjugate their personal rights in favour of service to others. We can easily imagine, nevertheless, how affording one's services to others can assume varying shades of psychological and relationship significance depending on the underlying motivating factor(s). Whether services are sold for money rather than given free of charge would seem to have the potential for generating ulterior motives (principally financial gain), and various other conflicts of interest can intrude (particularly diluting the principle that a paid-for service is geared towards the purchaser's best interests as a primary purpose). Even where there are no fees, perhaps the flavour of any service is at least partially coloured by professional ambition(s).

Difficulties of interpretation

An enthusiast for positivism like his fellow countryman before him, Émile Durkheim (1858-1917) transported Comte's ideas into the new discipline that we know today as sociology. Durkheim favoured the evaluation of human communities on a dimension of health, resorting – in a spirit of positivistic objectivity – to statistical data as preferred indicators. Naturally this provokes the question (in the same way that beauty lies in the eye of the beholder), "What constitutes healthy or unhealthy?", but also presents difficulties of interpretation. For instance, Durkheim argued that certain Catholic communities were more healthy than certain Protestant ones based on police suicide statistics entirely; however, how can we know that those Catholics were not less disposed to commit suicide for fear of spiritual damnation rather than because they were happier or otherwise more sane? This is not to say that Catholicism of itself generates fear or discourages confidence in a supreme power external to the "self" for, as an uncontaminated theology, it advocates the very converse. Many of today's Catholics, nevertheless, testify to dreadful and trenchant conditioned fear rooted in their upbringing. We would be foolish to overlook the fact that psychologically sick people are usually disposed to blame others for perceived wrongdoings (not yet having acquired the personal responsibility, autonomy and freedom that accompanies a morally realistic take on the world); nevertheless, it can be feverishly difficult to forget even having forgiven. It's no use a bishop as shepherd of his flock bewailing, in turn, the moaning of "recovering Catholics" outside the doors who cannot see how much God loves them; perhaps they can't see because they are "spiritually blind", and who is going to help them to become free to enjoy that divine care if there is no admission of responsibility or offer of help within the responsible establishment? Of course, to the extent that wrongs really have been done, the perpetrators have almost always been victims themselves in history. What does it take in matters cultural for one or more persons to stand up, break the mould and be counted in favour of recognising both the existence and actual nature of a chronic problem, expressing the willingness to move towards a holier alternative and future?

Am I OK?

For in the perpetration and preservation of religious dogma, the wielding and biographical injection of acquired fear – how it then feels subjectively, and how it colours a life – can be most insidious on several counts. First, traditionally the established Church has imparted its (interpreted) moral messages as catechistic authority which can be transmogrified into spiritual conscience from adult to child through instruction (as distinct from, say, personal guidance to be discovered as a quiet and gentle, divine or divinely inspired "voice"). Second, its catechism is directed at the spiritual core of each person where all of us can be and are occasionally vulnerable

(Who am I? Am I OK? Am I OK with other people? Do I belong in the world?). Third, the moral messages (usually aren't, however) can be anomalous regards "natural law"[59]. For instance, we can trace the sexual morality of the Church back to its most elevated thinkers such as Saint Thomas Aquinas – for whom the principles underlying proper sex conduct were governed exclusively by its "natural" purpose, i.e., procreation. We can all agree that a probable "natural" consequence of sexual intercourse (between males and females at any rate) is the creation of new human life and, perhaps, most of us would agree that that is a precious or sacred matter (at least ethically in relation to the life thus precipitated). Now, do we take the position that human sexuality (should such a notion be palatable at all) begins and ends there or; rather, is bound intricately with our overarching personalities and, thereby, is a complex arrangement in one person – let alone at the interface between people in relationship? If you take the former view, you may even identify with Aquinas's assertion that only the missionary position was aligned with God's will for sex relations because it was most likely amongst all other possibilities to result in a pregnancy. Aquinas's writings have been interpreted in different ways and means by different people for different purposes; nevertheless, over protracted episodes of history, Aquinas has been reputed to regard masturbation and oral sex, for example, graver moral offences than rape and incest – on the grounds that they are less "natural". You can see how the established Church has come to be more obsessed with sexual mores than with the human capacity for foul violence. If you prefer the latter (complex) view of human sexuality, you may be willing to contemplate in a broader fashion what is sexually "natural" amongst human beings and in human relationships. Even within the Church it is becoming common to distinguish between a homosexual disposition (with a hint of recognition that God created a person that way) and proscribed homosexual acts. Fourth, the language of the Church in relation to transgressions of its precepts has been and still is too vehement. Since the Scientific Revolution, let alone in medieval times and earlier, offences from the sexually minor to the intellectually aspirational have drawn public interdiction, threats of excommunication, execution by foul means and damnation to eternal hell-fire. Is it any wonder that some Catholics consider themselves "recovering"? It's no use denying that the Church has created a reputation for itself as much the harsh and scolding parent as the tolerant, accepting and endlessly forgiving lover. Today some people can be heard to speak of believing in "a *loving* God". What is that about? Have you ever encountered such a tautology in your life?

No balance in strategic atheism
Amongst those modern positivists for whom religion *per se* (all of it) constitutes anathema are such notables as (Clinton) Richard Dawkins (1941–). Dawkins rejected the Anglicanism in which he grew up favouring the evolutionary theories of the English naturalist Charles Robert Darwin (1809–1882) as a superior explanation for the natural order (especially over "Creationism" or "Intelligent Design"). In his 1976 publication *The Selfish Gene*, Dawkins revolutionised Darwinism itself by explaining that the gene is the unit of "natural selection" in evolution rather than particular organisms within a given species. In so doing he invited us away from a narrow, subjective and inflated view of our place in biology, helping us to realise that only genes

---

[59] "Natural law" refers to the notion that certain moral principles are endowed to the human species intrinsically from nature and, consequently, through "natural justice" should be adopted universally. Whether "natural law" is written upon human hearts by a Godhead is a matter of faith. Historic figures associated with "natural law" include Aristotle, Saint Thomas Aquinas, John Locke and Clive Staples Lewis (1898–1963). Lewis's *Mere Christianity* is a fascinating argument in favour of divine "natural law".

and not individuals survive passing generations[60]. Dawkins is credited with coining the expression "meme" to describe another unit of selection and evolution – in the world of ideas. This metaconcept has been fantastically helpful in facilitating the realisation that human "genius" never springs forth from nothing – or from only itself: it is always the product of both an individual's thoughtfulness and an evolving historical context. We have seen in Chapter 1 how Sir Isaac Newton achieved high standing by possessing this essential modesty. Dawkins is a fervent atheist, campaigning vigorously against religion in the modern world. His arguments are easily accessible online and can be evaluated on their merit by anyone who wishes to do so. As a positivist, Dawkins is an extremist, adopting a deliberate, terminal position on the broad religious spectrum. Dawkins picks his opposites carefully, employing calculated pillory to ridicule fundamentalist factions. The debate is usually with someone who rejects Darwinian accounts of the evolution of species, particularly humans. Dawkins recognises neither the possibility nor utility of a thinking person possessing a realistic take of their place in nature whilst simultaneously seeking religious or spiritual inspiration for living.

The example and "success" of non-human animals
As there has been no clear reconciliation of monism and dualism, where do these divergent viewpoints leave us other than suspended in limbo (if not confused)? Descartes' belief that "mind" was species-specific (to humans) led him to conclude that non-human animals do not experience subjective pain, and vivisection was prosecuted with abandon across Europe until the 18th century (Age of Enlightenment). One may or may not like Descartes' argument that non-human animals do not have the capacity for subjective pain, but it is a fact that non-human animals cannot tell us whether they do – or do not – because they lack the capacity for language. Now, it is not at all clear or resolved even these days whether there is, after all, a constellation of human attributes (language, conscious "mind", subjective pain, the capacity for producing and appreciating music and mathematics, romantic love, the capacity for moral selflessness, the capacity for monstrous cruelty, conscience and desire for justice, an intrinsic and immortal soul) that is simply absent in other species[61]. Our fundamental struggles with such matters, and also the questions posed by such polarities as were presented earlier in this chapter, are relevant because they sit right beneath much personal bewilderment[62]. Why are we here? How did it happen? How can we avoid misery and be happy? Is there an afterlife? If so, what is it like? Does its existence or pleasantness depend on how we live now? We have no way of establishing beyond personal sentiment whether such dilemmas are suffered by non-human animals, and whether non-human animals burden themselves with the same, senseless, questioning disposition. Nor do non-humans seem terribly concerned with the "mind-body problem", nor do they record their musings to impress, cajole and win over fellow members of their own species. What is the secret of their "success"?

---

[60] In the Preface, we were invited to consider how all contemporary living things have an equal status in nature; nevertheless, all this time after Darwin, many of us regard human beings as the superior apex, or even the end-point, of the evolutionary process.

[61] The reader who desires to reflect on the entire gamut of species-specific attributes and their implications is encouraged to read either of Euan Macphail's exceptionally thought-provoking and scholarly books: for all-comers, *The Evolution Of Consciousness* (1998, Oxford University Press: Oxford) and, for enthusiastic and diligent readers, *Brain And Intelligence In Vertebrates* (1982, Clarendon Press: Oxford).

[62] Readers wishing to scrutinise two mutually exclusive positions on organised religion could try *The God Delusion* (2006, Bantam Press: London) by Richard Dawkins (in favour of radical atheism) and *A Catholic Replies To Professor Dawkins* (2007, Family Publications: Oxford) by Thomas Crean O.P. (in defence of Roman Catholic faith).

"Careless Cow" apparently, with comparably nonchalant offspring

"Shared Understandings"

Chapter 5

"Towards a moral psychology"

A "shareable subjective experience" …
What human beings do appear to have, by all accounts, and because those accounts are mutually accessible amongst us because of our common capacity for language, is a "shareable subjective experience". That subjective experience is, seemingly, hinged squarely on our consciousness which, by ordinary understanding, is intimately bound with our very self-awareness and our awareness of other human beings. Now there is something "circular" in this way of looking at things, because we are proposing a set of inter-related concepts without trying to find an external aetiological origin or, necessarily, a "scientific" explanation (although we certainly wouldn't turn one down if it happened upon us serendipitously). To be quite explicit about it; moreover, if there is any such "first cause" for human consciousness, we do not have to assume that it has a material or biochemical nature for no such proof exists in philosophy or science. What's wrong with saying that whilst the jury is out developments in understanding would be most welcome? To do so defers to another sensible notion – also obscure in origin – which cautions us against "contempt prior to investigation"[63]. Given the inconclusiveness of the arguments for both "monism" and "dualism" presented in recent pages, it is reasonable – perhaps even wise – to sidestep if not abandon the "mind-body problem" as it has been presented traditionally entirely. We do not have to accept the Cartesian notion of an independent metaphysical intellect, nor the radical behaviorist assumption of automaton, in order to have a useful, pragmatic notion or concept of "mind" for the purpose of a meaningful work-a-day modern psychology. The title of the previous chapter is a tweaked version of an expression coined by the British philosopher Gilbert Ryle (1900-1976) who described (disparagingly) the dualist's assertion of a "mind" or "soul" separate from but governing its body "the dogma of the ghost in the machine"[64]. Ryle recoiled at the prospect of a Cartesian "mind" having the capacity to control the body when "mind" and "body" respectively belong to two different "logical categories". Whilst we could say in Platonic or Cartesian terms that mind and body are made of different "substance", Ryle is saying more: that the difference between the two is more than that between chalk and cheese, even chalk and moon dust: they are different types of "things" entirely. Dualism is both a myth and a red herring. "Mind" is just a set of behavioural dispositions, is descriptive rather than explanatory, and is sufficient to account for "higher" faculties, including language.

---

[63] The expression, "There is a principle which is a bar against all information, which cannot fail to keep a man in everlasting ignorance – that principle is contempt prior to investigation" has been over-attributed to Herbert Spencer (1820-1903) who coined the Darwinian phrase "survival of the fittest". The quote has not been traced reliably to Spencer's record; moreover, although the first misattribution probably occurred earlier, it was compounded in the First Edition (1939) of the core text (aka "The Big Book") from Alcoholics Anonymous. Strikingly similar instances have been attributed correctly to the British Christian apologist William Paley (1743-1805) in *A View Of The Evidences Of Christianity* (1794), and also in *Anglo-Israel Or, The British Nation: The Lost Tribes Of Israel* (1879) by the Reverend William Henry Poole (1820-1896).

[64] Gilbert Ryle, who was a student of the philosopher and linguist Ludwig Josef Johann Wittgenstein (1889-1951), coined the expression "the ghost in the machine" in his book *The Concept Of Mind* published by the University of Chicago Press in 1949. A related book *The Ghost In The Machine* (1967, Hutchinson) by Arthur Koestler (1905-1983) constitutes a theory of human self-destruction and, like Ryle's work, is contemptuous of both the ultra-dualist Cartesian "mind", but also of Skinner's radical behaviorism.

... upon which we may all agree?
Is there any good reason to pursue the matter further? Well, perhaps
there is one. It is likely that, even among behaviorists across the
spectrum from, let us say, radical to soft - or "hawk" to "dove" -
there will be a variety of views about what is meant by "mind", and
how acceptable or repugnant that proposition may be philosophically.
If there is a single thread or common denominator, it is probably
that behaviorists - as a pack - are simply "anti-Cartesian", or just
don't like "dualism" (or, as we have seen, the notion that there is a
mental entity independent of any physical substructure). The radical
behaviorist (aka "hawk") such as Burrhus Frederic Skinner may be a
"scientific determinist" - a person who considers that all behaviour
is accounted for by cause and effect relationships without needing to
resort to either the existence or effect of subjective human will. Is
"free will" a necessary and integral part of a "moral psychology"? If
it is, we must find and incorporate it. If it is real, but not
necessary and integral, we must say why we can discard it because the
word "moral"[65] certainly conveys a connotation of personal "choice".
Some folks are equally as wedded to the idea that everything we think
and do is "decisional", as others are to the notion that everything
that happens - including human behaviour itself - is "scientifically
determined" according to the same kinds of laws as those that govern
the behaviour of chemicals in a jar or the motion of the planets.
Amongst the latter belong people who will concede quite spontaneously
that not all of those (physical and) behavioural laws have yet been
discovered and, amongst those in turn, some will never concede that
such unrealised understandings might lie beyond the reach of science
(perhaps in the metaphysical or "spiritual" realm). We don't want to
return to Descartes' "seat of the soul" to re-open the point about
whether an invisible "will" can govern the material (body) and, so,
we will say something else: whether free will "really" exists or not,
human beings have a subjectively experienced and communicable sense
of both "self" and "other" which encompasses a whole or qualified
willingness to concur that what we do has consequences, that those
consequences can be pleasant and aversive to varying extents for both
ourselves and others and - that in human society - inevitably we find
ourselves accountable either in conscience or at law for what we do
or don't do. We are going only a little further than the principles
of conditioning that were outlined in Chapter 2, although suddenly we
have introduced the notion of "conscience". Let's examine it briefly.

Traversing irreconcilable positions
Now, suppose it is convenient, and may even be appealing to the
imagination, to take a hard-headed view of conscience, rather in the
same vein as Ryle has done regarding the "mind-body problem". After
all, there are (broadly speaking) two superficially irreconcilable
polar positions regarding conscience: namely, that conscience is
entirely metaphysical (say, the urging of the divine in personal
consciousness) on the one hand and, on the other, the psychologically
scientific (behaviorist) stance which is that conscience (assuming
one is not so hawkish as to reject the proposition that human beings

---

[65] As made explicit in the Preface (and elsewhere), it is not possible to emphasise
sufficiently that a "moral psychology" is not predicated on any authority external to
the individual unless that person elects of their own volition to embrace one. Nobody
is writing anybody else's moral agenda - but anybody is free to be guided as they
responsibly choose. Some people like to consider themselves morally self-sufficient,
and that is their prerogative. Others like to be guided by what they regard as human
wisdom, whether from an inspirational leader, or from some collective consciousness or
social conscience. Still others seek and find divine inspiration. A "moral psychology"
is accessible by all such persons. For some, if not most people, the source of their
inspiration (assuming they recognise one at all) can change over the course of a
lifetime. The relevant emphases will continue to be made throughout subsequent pages.

have one at all[66]) is the outcome of fear-conditioning[67] especially during childhood. Amongst those in the former camp are apologists (both ancient and modern) in the Church and well-known philosophers such as Immanuel Kant (1724-1804). The archetypal scientific psychologist in the matter of conscience is Hans Jürgen Eysenck whom we met in Chapter 3. Between these parade a range of morality theorists, some of whom have become famous in philosophical folklore: Karl Heinrich Marx (1818-1883), Friedrich Wilhelm Nietzsche (1844-1900) and Jean-Paul Charles Aymard Sartre (1905-1980) to name but a few. For present purposes, a brief résumé of the respective vantages is all that is required in order to establish whether it is feasible to proceed with an outline "conscience" that is sufficient for the "moral psychology" which traverses the apex of this constellation of preliminaries regarding sanity, insanity and the "human condition"[68].

A recognisable "conscience"

For Kant[69], humans are both rational and morally free, meaning that they can readily make choices about a universal and intrinsic sense of "right" and "wrong" determined by "natural law" (to which we referred in the previous chapter). According to Kant, we have the capacity – especially when confronted with, challenged or confused about a course of action – to evaluate alternatives against the "categorical imperative". The category here could be "all humanity", and the imperative is what the category tends to discharge (from conscience) as a class. In other words, it is like a person asking, "What would (indeed, *should*) most people do in this situation?" In Kant's framework for dealing with morality, there is clearly some choosing process obliged, say, to defer to some moral authority which is not identical to the choosing "module" itself. In their respective ways, Nietzsche, Sartre and Marx have all argued *against* "natural law", preferring a political or quasi-political view which emphasises in different ways the various interests of classes of individuals or individuals as a class. For Sartre, there is no objective morality, and no God. We are responsible for our own moral development and for becoming "authentic" in that undertaking; accordingly, to defer to an external moral system, particularly a religious one, is to act in "bad faith". In identifying himself thus with moral self-sufficiency, Sartre was aligning himself idealistically with Nietzsche who earlier had distinguished between "master" and "slave" morality. Whereas the former is fundamental, worthy and individualistic, the latter emerges from social prerogatives and is, thereby, arbitrary and subjugated. For Nietzsche, Christian values are examples of "slave morality". Although we have considered diverse, even irreconcilable views of the sources of morality, none of these contradicts the possibility that species-specific, subjectively-experienced, importunate intrapsychic tensions are recognisable by any "ordinary person" as "conscience".

---

[66] Even such a "hawk" may tolerate the provisional view of conscience assumed presently and the more detailed account of its formation, effect and lifetime-course in Part II.

[67] We have covered the enormous scope of conditioned "hope" and "fear" based on a few simple mechanisms in Chapter 2. It is better to avoid the term "negative conditioning" for aversive or punishing reinforcement, because "negative" can have other meanings in the same environments – such as the omission of a reinforcer during a learning trial.

[68] The expression "human condition" is widely recognised, and equally broadly invoked across a range of disciplines, to describe the experience of being human *per se* – as a lifecycle from cradle to grave – including intrapsychic experience. It fits the thrust of this volume which could be put another way as, "The pursuit of personal sanity".

[69] Immanuel Kant is regarded as a model philosopher of the Enlightenment, when "reason" was harnessed as the new keystone for human thinking and behaviour (as distinct from old traditions including religious authority). Usually associated with the mid-18th to early 19th century many of its roots lay firmly ensconced in the Scientific Revolution.

Conscience: "Weight Of The Heavens" or conditioned fear?
Salisbury Cathedral, Wiltshire

The passions (including resentment) can stifle creativity
Nietzsche's career – which was chequered with lurches and setbacks
including relationship challenges, domestic upheavals and mental
health difficulties – presents enthralling instances of how the
psychology of a person interweaves with the biographical course of a
life. Notwithstanding having been appointed a professor in philology
(the study of linguistic and literary meanings) at the age of only 24
(ironically, just as he was veering away from literature towards
science); some 14 years later, the University of Leipzig refused him
a tenure on the basis of his offensive mimicking and mocking of the
Bible (and, thereby, much of monotheistic religious tradition in one
fell swoop) in a series of publications under the inclusive title
Also Sprach Zarathustra: A Book For All And None (1883–1885). In his
own record, Nietzsche was stridently resentful about this rejection,
which is fascinating in at least two vital respects: first, the
relationship between resentment and insanity is critical as we shall
see later; second and ironically, Nietzsche regarded an individual's
creativity to be hostage to the passions (in so far as it was
necessary to sublimate the latter in order to release the former in
some kind of trade-off between base instinct and intellect). The
relationship between "repression–sensitisation" and health is another
story in the history of sanity, as also we shall see by and by.

Strangleholds on money and power
The key idea behind Marxism is that of "class struggle"[70]. For Karl
Marx, the whole of human history has been one in which material
wealth (particularly the means of producing goods and the markets in
which they are traded) has been controlled by a privileged few
(collectively described as the "bourgeoisie"). Organised religion is
indicted by Marx as an accessory in the business of oppression of the
common people (or "proletariat") – responsible for the "loss of man"
by generating a "false consciousness" of reality in institutional
ethics. Morality, according to such a radical view, is a tyrannical
counter-revolutionary device perpetuated to maintain establishment
strangleholds on money and political power. Perhaps ranking as the
paramount conspiracy theory of all time, it was Marx who described
religion in this way as a sedative, soothing "opium for the masses".
Would Marx, nevertheless, recognise the intrapsychic tensions that
can urge a person to favour one course of action rather than another,
generate conflict in some circumstances – and which potently shape
important consequences with which a person has to live depending on
the diverse courses adopted? An only cursory examination of his
biography suggests that he might. Like Albert Einstein (1879–1955)
and Friedrich Nietzsche (who foreswore his Prussian citizenship),
Marx became (and remained) stateless. Having been expelled at one
time from Paris, he failed against his expectations to secure British
citizenship. He had already moved to London where he lived in poverty
with his large family – which included a child by his housekeeper.
Marx's ideas have more to do with (uprooting) social structures than
individual behaviour – whereas we are concerned with developing a
psychology that helps any person to acquire and maintain sanity in
all conditions, including the world in its present parlous state, and
any other socio-political ideology that may hypothetically transpire.

---

[70] *Nine Seahorses* is reminiscent of Marxist ideals in that its underlying concept and
related principles (see Addendum) hinge squarely on equality and mature community;
nevertheless, *Nine Seahorses* is separated from Marxism fundamentally – by at least
emphasis and, substantially, in its ultimate objective – because *Nine Seahorses* sees
the human struggle (including the history of human malaise) as one of self-centredness
rather than "class struggle". *Nine Seahorses* anticipates personal liberation through
the practice of spiritual principles rather than the redistribution of material wealth
as a first ideal (whence "social justice" will proceed as an inescapable corollary).

Conditioned (secular) conscience

Then there are those "true" psychologists, eminent ones such as Hans Eysenck amongst them, who argue that conscience is a complex set of conditioned responses which, having been formed in that way, are amenable to reversal according to the same or similar principles. According to Jeffrey Alan Gray (1934-2004), a well-established psychologist colleague of Eysenck's at The Institute of Psychiatry:

What, then, is the conscience? We have already come across Eysenck's answer to this question ... conscience is a set of conditioned fear reactions. That is, in early life we learn to associate (by classical conditioning) fear of impending punishment with stimuli associated with the commission of socially disapproved acts. When in adult life we feel the impulse to commit such acts, the occurrence of a conditioned fear reaction prevents us: conscience. If we do succeed in carrying them out, we may nevertheless feel afraid of the consequences: guilt. It is difficult at the present stage of development in psychology to evaluate this suggestion with any precision; but there may well be much truth in it.[71]

Inspired (religious) conscience

Finally on this topic, an example of an establishment Christian's (i.e., a Roman Catholic's) position on conscience is best appreciated also by direct quotation. Here, Thomas Crean O.P. - a Dominican friar who responded directly to the attack on religion that was presented in Richard Dawkins' book *The God Delusion* (2006, Bantam Press: London) - writes conclusively towards the close of his argument[72]:

The human mind or soul is spiritual, therefore, and cannot share in the body's dissolution. It remains in perpetuity, with its power to know and to love, or also to hate. And though this cannot be verified by reason, the Catholic holds that the body will rise again, vivified by the same power that once created the world, to share in the immortality of the soul.

The atheist is logically obliged to reject free will. This is especially clear if he is, like most Western atheists, a materialist. Since every event has a cause, our bodily actions also must have a cause. But if all is matter, then our bodily actions are caused by matter. Now matter does not act for any purpose of its own, but by necessity: water does not flow downhill because it has chosen to, but because it must. Therefore, if all is matter, our bodily actions happen by necessity, and free will is an illusion. But if free will is an illusion, we need pay no attention to those who argue for atheism, since they cannot be thinking and writing as men guided by truth, but only as driven along by matter.

The Catholic, supported by the spontaneous consent of all mankind, holds that man is free. His actions therefore derive from some power within him that is not material but immaterial or spiritual, namely, his will. But if there were no God, I could not possess any such spiritual power. For my will did not exist before I did; nor, since it is not material, is it composed of pre-existing parts. It follows that a will, as also an intellect, must be freshly created for each new man who comes into being. Only God can do such a thing. If then we believe in freedom, we must also believe in God.

---

[71] Gray, J.A. (1971) *The Psychology Of Fear And Stress*. Cambridge University Press: Cambridge (1987, p.347)

[72] Crean, T. (2007) *A Catholic Replies To Professor Dawkins*. Family Publications: Oxford (pp.159-160)

Yet though man is free, he is not a law unto himself. God who makes his will has the right to command him how to use it. We must follow the law of good and evil that He has impressed upon our heart, and be ready to welcome those whom He may send to teach us about His will. And since no wise lawgiver promulgates a law without intending that its provisions be enforced, we shall be judged by God on the use that we make of our free will.

Common ground and a definition of "conscience"

Where does this leave us now? For the purpose of a "moral psychology" we don't wish to assume one alternative amongst these various views because: in the first instance and according to our stated view of extremes, it is unlikely that from one standpoint alone we will find a whole, incontrovertible and inclusive "truth"; second, if it is at all possible, we would like to find and build upon common ground, or at least the nearest we can find to something resembling it and, third, we need to take only what is sufficient for a "moral psychology". Accordingly, we shall just say that conscience is: a quiet strain, having the capacity to become psychologically "noisy", which has the effect of pressure to settle upon one or more beliefs, attitudes, intentions or behaviours (including not doing certain things as well as doing them) and which is experienced subjectively as psychological conflict – usually mild, but potentially deadly[73].

The abhorrence of "emptiness": a question

Before moving on to Part II ("You Can't Win A Bad Game") which is about psychotherapy (or professional psychological helping), it seems natural to pose one more question; admittedly rather a proposition, before drawing up a summary of what we have learned about personal sanity from our whistle-stop tour of modern psychology. The question is, "Does this tension that is conscience as we have just depicted it, along with any other psychological tensions that we may care to recognise[74], engender a kind of subjectively-experienced 'emptiness'[75] which, as fallible human beings, we are prone to fill with all kinds of distractions, some of which are harmful to ourselves and others?"

Downstream, at the heart of the matter

Ancillary questions at the heart of "moral psychology" flow from this primary puzzler: "What is the nature of this emptiness?"; "Does everyone experience it?"; "Under what circumstances are folks more or less likely to experience it?"; "Why do folks pursue certain rather than other distractions?"; "Do we have the capacity to observe it, evaluate it, effect or adopt alternative behavioural courses directed at filling or otherwise compensating for it?"; "Is there a moral quality to any such processes?"; "Can the 'nag' of conscience be disregarded, resisted, or modified by personal will or psychological therapy?"; "Can 'self' change 'self'?" and, if so, "Why are there psychotherapists?" … In the first instance, what is this "emptiness"?

---

[73] According to Matthew's Gospel in the New Testament, Judas Iscariot hanged himself after betraying Jesus. One can speculate easily about the role of conscience in the long list of suicides in human history without straying off-topic. Even where there are exceptional external pressures, there will always be a clash with the survival instinct. There are many suicides each day – each a tragedy – and each imbued with a cloud of indescribable psychic pain of which "conscience" comprises at least a part.

[74] probably recognisable as "cognitive dissonance". Widely acknowledged in psychology since 1957, cogntive dissonance was introduced by Leon Festinger (1919-1989) who described it as a cognitive discomfort accompanying two or more contradictory beliefs and which we are driven to mitigate by rationalising or changing the beliefs germane.

[75] The notion of "hole in the soul" is easily discovered in popular psychology, and is probably traceable to Carl Jung's *Modern Man In Search Of A Soul* (1933). An earlier, dreadful, identity is in *Dark Night Of The Soul* (Saint John of the Cross, 1542-1591).

"What Is This Emptiness?"

Existential despair, like depression, does not answer itself
One of the greatest collective disappointments suffered by those at the cerebral centre of the Enlightenment was the (seemingly unexpected) frustration experienced by its most ardent adherents (such as Immanuel Kant) in attempting to prove the existence of God[76] (or any other divine reality) based entirely on man's sweet "reason". As the Enlightenment was understood by (nearly) all accounts to have represented the intellectual vehicle by which man was to release himself from the shackles of historical parochialism, something now had to take the place of, or go somehow beyond, reason itself. This, approximately, is how existentialism emerged. Existentialism, as a school of philosophy, favours the scrutiny of subjective human experience within a particular milieu which may be understood as the dilemma that human beings may encounter when trying to understand why they exist at all – and how they might go about their existence in a personally meaningful way. In a terrible sense existentialism looks like, and may turn out to be nothing more than, a vocabulary for moaning about everything that we don't "know" for certain. The term itself may have been coined by Gabriel Honoré Marcel (1889-1973), a Catholic[77] playwright; however, the first momentum behind the movement is usually credited to Søren Aabye Kierkegaard (1813-1855), a Danish philosopher with broad interests (simultaneously, a theologian who promoted pursuit of religion as a response to existential despair).

All religions address existential questions
The struggle to find purposefulness, whether through religion or any other kind of personal philosophy or related endeavour, can be discerned in ancient as well as recent history. In Northern India (now the Republic of Nepal, home to the Himalayas and Mount Everest) the teachings of the Buddha (Siddhārtha Gautama)[78] were received by oral tradition for some four centuries after his death before being recorded in the Buddhist texts. The Buddha's life was spent in restless pursuit of "truth" (Dharma) or "enlightenment". He found it, as legend has it, under a pipal tree (Sacred Fig or Bodhi) by the River Nerenjana in the Indian state of Bihar. What today we might call "moderation" (somewhere between self-indulgence on the one hand, and self-denial or – more violently – self-mortification[79] on the other) is known in Buddhism as the "Middle Way" or "Noble Eightfold Path"[80]. The Middle Way involves right conduct in the domains of wisdom, ethics and concentration in order to achieve "self-awakening", liberation ("Nirvana") and alleviation from suffering[81]. Existential preoccupations – or the search for personal meaning with moral overtones – are central in all of the world's major religions: polytheistic Hinduism and monotheistic Judaism, Christianity and Islam; however, Buddhism is not usually considered a religion *per se*.

---

[76] Almost needless to say, atheism (the affirmation that there is no God) has not been established by reason either, and "open-minded" philosophers are usually amenable to conceding ground to any person who claims to have experienced the divine directly – because such subjective experiences lie outside the philosopher's familiar stomping grounds of sensory experience on the one hand, and reason, sweet reason on the other.

[77] actually a convert from atheism which ran in his family

[78] Estimates of the Buddha's dates vary between about 600 and 400 BC.

[79] perhaps more commonly associated with fervent Christians purging "desires of the flesh" – sometimes prosecuted to self-carnage using devices such as a cilice or crop

[80] Curling on to itself, the first element of the Noble Eightfold Path, "Right View" – which might also be regarded as a reality-checking endeavour – is an understanding of the "Four Noble Truths", of which the "Noble Eightfold Path" is itself the fourth.

[81] In Buddhism, "Dukkha", which translates as suffering, has its origins in ignorance – or an unclear mind – attachment to worldly things and cravings of the sensual kind.

Unsatiated existentialism
Notwithstanding the long history of such human longing, Nietzsche has
claimed that the "death of God" is well advanced socioculturally. God
has been a product of human imagination – albeit a most entrenched
one – and the inexorable dissipation of belief in all forms of deity
will eventually leave humans without excuse for knowing anything with
"certainty". In existentialism's darkest form, "nihilism", there is
no hope at all: the world is defined by its absurdity, and there is
no response for it. Nihilism's condition in active mode looks rather
like clinical depression: but surely, then, the existential moralist
like Sartre – preoccupied with "authentic" existence – is only likely
to "find himself" up a dead-end street literally (i.e., in an early
coffin), because he works a philosophy that asks too many questions
and delights in presenting no answers. Existentialism gives us a
compelling framework for describing the ache of human "lostness", but
its usefulness, quite sadly, ends there because, of its intrinsically
pessimistic nature, it refuses steadfastly to yield its own antidote.

When we stop arguing belligerently with the blindingly obvious …
If there are no answers in unsatiated existentialism, and we have not
embraced without any reservations or doubts a religion of choice –
or, even if we consider that we have, perhaps we have not always been
open-minded enough to consider ancillary ways to render easier our
days (for surely God has not prohibited us from enjoying creation) –
then, could a "moral psychology" fit the "search-for-happiness" bill?
If there is any pre-requisite at all for sanity, surely it is a very
simple "spiritual" yielding (where "spiritual", again, simply means
"unseen"). We all know what this penny-dropping experience is: it is
when one stops arguing belligerently with the blindingly obvious,
releasing oneself instantly into a "fourth dimension"[82] of alignment
with the universe into the bargain. We begin by desisting from
looking the gift horse of life in the mouth. Thankfully even the most
stupid or sick of us can start at that point. We all know about this
freedom from angst because of (at least occasional and small) doses
of personal, first hand experience. It is a question of recognising
and appreciating the precious phenomenon, and then working with each
other to produce larger measures of it. The behaviorists can't cage,
quantify or interpret them in the laboratory. Such realisations are a
private as well as a shared phenomenon. They happen in and belong to
you. Nobody can take them away from you. In you and others they can
change the world. If, from Plato until now, the central or consistent
focus of psychology has been the intellect, it is time to move on
quietly – for satisfaction and fulfilment are for *Everyman*[83], or they
are nothing at all (unless you are a bigot of the most ugly kind).
Psychology is no longer the playground of the *cognoscenti*. Let's
restate the focus of a proper and relevant psychology: it is the
yielding or submission of each spiritually equal human person to how
it actually is. Let's stop trying to be clever, and let's get real.

… suddenly we are in possession of an "unfair" advantage
We are now ready to consider the world of professional psychological
helping armed with: an understanding of the context in which such
professionals operate (which bestows upon us an "unfair" advantage);
a pragmatic (but justified) swerve around the "mind-body problem"
(but knowing fully why we have effected it); a working definition of
"conscience", and a preliminary appreciation of how compensating for
the "human condition" can land ourselves and others in hot water.

---

[82] For the physicists out there, we're just talking about a nice harmless feeling … OK

[83] derived from an unattributed 15th century play – *The Summoning Of Everyman* –
suggesting any unremarkable person with whom any other "ordinary person" may identify

"Psst! … Had Your Shirt-tail Tugged Lately?"

"You Can't Win A Bad Game"

Part II

"You Can't Win A Bad Game"

Chapter 6

"The moral environment"

Early definition and the first principle: appreciation
In a "moral psychology", the "moral environment", put simply, is the
context in which we must be sane[84]. In a purely physical and
psychologically facile sense, this "place" must be regarded as our
planet, for it is the only location which every human being inhabits.
In the West, we are heard to say colloquially, "I'm in a good place
right now"; or, "Mary and John have been in a bad place since their
cat died". This sort of terminology[85] suggests that people readily
embrace psychological analogues of physical locations as valid
representations of the complex and diffuse instances and episodes of
subjective experience – we might say "mind" – that pervade if not
constitute all of our waking and sleeping moments (including our
dreams). When we are happy, or feel sane or "together", we are apt to
agree that the world is a beautiful place, that we can't get enough
of living, that we are grateful for our lives and that we don't want
to die. We may even concede (subject in some cases to certain arm's
length or behavioural conditions) that its other human inhabitants,
with whom we must share the world's fresh air, are agreeable enough
for the exchanging of pleasantries. Although we all have "bad hair"
days, and sometimes days that are worse, this kind of sanity is
"easy" because it requires no special effort on our part to acquire.
All we have to do is wait till we appreciate. It is true that we can
short-circuit that waiting, "wake up and smell the coffee", but this
diverts our attention; after all, the world and its incommodious
occupants can be demanding. Seemingly there is a multitude of tedious
matters to which we must attend, not the least among them being where
we will sleep tonight – without an empty stomach to keep us awake.

The second principle: accepting that "it's an inside job"
But there is another level and quality of appreciation of our "moral
environment" that makes the difference between life as a struggle
interspersed with moments of relief and pleasure (assuming we make it
to a "threescore years and ten"[86] finishing line); and life as a
peaceful and satisfying undertaking (for we have all undertaken it no
matter whether we dwell on having chosen to be born). Another way in
which we can "wake up" is to realise – as a permanently assimilated
proposition – that no matter what happens or doesn't happen, and
notwithstanding any and all of our expectations – when life seems
rotten and we feel lousy about it, the source of our dissatisfaction
lies within our personal psychology, rather than in a flawed or
perverse universe (including its Creator should you believe in such)

---

[84] Pre-empting the next chapter – and as an indulgence to those readers whose personal
construct of "sanity" is confined to its dearth in certain psychiatric syndromes,
particularly those of a serious ("psychotic") nature and, as we know, catalogued in
certain medical diagnostic systems – the usage of "sane" and "sanity" here is broad
and hinged on its Greek and Latin origins where the suggestions are health and
wholeness as distinct from disintegration. Everyone wants this kind of sanity: it is a
universal human hunger – it is for you and your patients as well as a lay readership!

[85] "Being in a good place" is probably just hippy slang; however, there are more formal
and specific versions in modern psychology, amongst which is Mihály Csíkszentmihályi's
(1934-) notion of "being in the zone / groove" referring in his "positive psychology"
to "flow", or complete immersion in whatever one is doing now – in the present moment.

[86] Human life expectancy, according to Psalm 90 of the Old Testament (exhorting us to
count and be grateful for our days), is 70 years – or 80 if we are lucky. Although a
popular expression, it is only in the King James Version of the Bible (a 17th century
Church of England translation) that these 70 are stated as "threescore years and ten".

or an equally faulty, even vengeful, fellow human being. This is not to aver in the least that we are never hard done to, even in the most reprehensible ways; nor that other people weren't ever at fault in relation to what has happened (that shouldn't have) or not happened (that should have) in our lives. Certainly it is to posit, however, that it is in the very handling of such challenges that personal sanity stands, lurks invisible, remains unreachable or just fails us entirely. "Being in a good place" doesn't mean merely realising that the planet is green and blue and beautiful, but knowing that when it seems otherwise, it is we who make it ugly, and not the circumstances in which we flail about vainly. In other words, there is something about our perception that renders things awry, and it is to ourselves that we must look if we wish to put things right (for to attribute or engineer elsewhere only ever invites disappointment sooner or later).

Intermezzo: interpreting the "moral environment"
Is the "moral environment" that really matters, then, simply our "selves" (as far as we can perceive our "selves"), or the realm of subjective experience or "inner world" that we also all inhabit? No. It is more than that, because that realm is continually marked out and shaped and coloured by the way we process what we perceive. This is what makes us what we are and who we will become. Whether we start out with a core "mind" or soul — or neither but an Aristotleian blank slate — or don't start out at all but are always reincarnated — will be a very interesting concern indeed to at least some of us, and we may arrive in person at a more settled or even different position on the question in the course of developing our own "moral psychology". Meanwhile, and whichever our starting point (but shall we agree birth or conception at the earliest), how we array all that we perceive in our "minds", and the manner in which we call upon those records later in the same or on another day, has everything to do with whether we tiptoe merrily through life's tulips[87] as it were, or jump off bridges or out of windows, or somehow survive — crying with ulterior, silent and futile pleas of, "Help Me…!" to our fellow human beings, thereby creating trails of relationship and other wreckage through the course of unanchored and undisciplined lives. Each microcosmic and larger instance of our interpreting the "moral environment" represents a significant investment in — or withdrawal from — our sanity reserves.

The third principle: trusting the process
The third level of psychological responsiveness that we may bring to bear on our "moral environment" is a rather more mysterious and elusive one, but actually no less simple or accessible. To recap: suppose on an average day we forgot to be attentive — but in a sudden moment of clarity took in a view, or pondered with curiosity an example of non-human animal behaviour, or wondered what another person was really feeling — then, we have woken up to the coffee pot and obtained a little more of life. (Did we notice how much return we got on the effort and how scientifically measurable that return was?) Suppose on a difficult day we said to ourselves, "Ah well, that misfortune was down to me I guess, and I can let it go at that"; now, how much easier was it to obtain the first appreciation! (Did we realise quite how much the resentment of our troubles inhibited our capacity for free and easy living?) And now third, the more we became willing to awaken in these first two ways, the more the course of our lives seemed actually and reliably to improve. (Was this a trick of perception or some other enigmatic but ludicrously apparent reality?) Old dogs learn new tricks, but some things are easier said than done!

---

[87] The catchy and innocently romantic (now iconic) *Tiptoe Through The Tulips*, written by Joe Burke (1884-1950) and Al Durbin (1891-1945), was performed to appreciative audiences during the 1920s by Nick Lucas (1897-1982) in *Gold Diggers Of Broadway*.

"Wake Up And Smell The Coffee": Easier said than done?

Definition of the "moral environment"
For the sake of clarity and expansion of the argument, a working definition of the "moral environment" seems apposite and timely here. As far as the present *Plea For Sanity* in *Nine Seahorses* is concerned, the "moral environment" comprises the various "worlds" that all of us each inhabits: the "external worlds" of planet, nation, family and the various communities in which we elect to belong, and with which we engage – from work environments to social organisations to religious and spiritual fellowships, all of which are interpreted and processed from cradle to grave by our "minds" which certainly contain records of experience in traces whose exact natures are very far indeed from precisely understood in epistemological terms, but which we know mostly as the "inner world" of subjective experience … and it is the quality of that subjective experience that determines how others regard and how we ourselves experience and adjudge our sanity.

Recap of our position on "mind" and a definition of "conscience"
Our approach to personal sanity up to this point co-opted "mind" carefully, then recognised a rudimentary "conscience" ecumenically, and now we have introduced the "moral environment". We sidestepped the "mind-body problem" as history has precipitated it for reasons threaded through Part I, but we formed a definition of "conscience" because we need it for a "moral psychology". At the climax of Part I (a résumé of the modern discipline of psychology as it pertains to the "human condition"), and having considered alternative ways of looking at the concept of conscience from diverse positions in (chiefly) religion, philosophy and psychology – always seeking and having found at least some common ground – a pragmatic, working definition of "conscience" for a "moral psychology" was proposed:

a quiet strain, having the capacity to become psychologically "noisy", which has the effect of pressure to settle upon one or more beliefs, attitudes, intentions or behaviours (including not doing certain things as well as doing them) and which is experienced subjectively as psychological conflict – usually mild, but potentially deadly

Recap of questions posed by "conscience" in a "moral psychology"
Part I (Chapter 5) also indicated the variety of sanity-relevant questions this form of definition or model generates:

"Does this tension that is conscience as we have just depicted it, along with any other psychological tensions that we may care to recognise, engender a kind of subjectively-experienced 'emptiness' which, as fallible human beings, we are prone to fill with all kinds of distractions, some of which are harmful to ourselves and others?" … *"What is the nature of this emptiness?"; "Does everyone experience it?"; "Under what circumstances are folks more or less likely to experience it?"; "Why do folks pursue certain rather than other distractions?"; "Do we have the capacity to observe it, evaluate it, effect or adopt alternative behavioural courses directed at filling or otherwise compensating for it?"; "Is there a moral quality to any such processes?"; "Can the 'nag' of conscience be disregarded, resisted, or modified by personal will or psychological therapy?"; "Can 'self' change 'self'?" and … "Why are there psychotherapists?"*

Perseverance in the "moral environment"
Provisionally, it is in the perseverance of an "Accountable Self" in the "moral environment" that sanity stands or falls. By the close of Chapters 9 and 10 we shall have answered all of these questions systematically. Some of our standpoints will have been presented formally; nevertheless, it is in the acquisition and maintenance of a personal "moral psychology" that unstealable understanding resides.

The force of the "moral environment"
Now, what aspects of the "moral environment" lend force to this strain or pressure that can have such life-enhancing or deadly consequences depending on how we settle upon things? Among them can be counted: the "weight of human history"; the times in which we live (aka the *Zeitgeist*[88]); the circumstances in which we grew up as infants and children including our families (or whatever we had that was nearest to such), and what we have done with our lives as sentient[89] adults (in the personal narrative we ever create). Contiguous are the psychological structures and processes we possess and employ because we are instances of our species (a society, as it were, with no conditions for membership as long as we draw breath). Then there are also the variations amongst us described in terms of "temperament", "personality", or "individual differences" although – as we have seen in Chapter 3 – the best models are actually primitive and questionably relevant to any underlying and universal faculties.

The "weight of human history"
The "weight of human history" creates pressure on us as individuals in the here and now because, wherever in the world we reside, there are seen and unseen, spoken and unspoken, and formal and informal laws, customs, values, mores and traditions with which we are expected to comply. These are always eruptions of deep history; i.e., the evolution of culture. To appreciate the variety that abounds demands voyage, experience and understanding. Seasoned travellers may become more and more inured to "culture shock", but it is a very real phenomenon to anyone who has experienced it. We take our indigenous culture for granted. The impact of another is surprisingly great. We scuttle for cover. Perhaps those who ever successively navigated profound culture shock (compared with those who hadn't) somehow overcame an inner resistance[90]. Do we find it "natural" to comply with every one of these expectations wherever we are? To the extent that we don't, pressures of some kind on our "consciences" are imparted.

Lateral thinking and the unravelling of history
One way in which the diversity and richness of such variations in culture can be appreciated is to conjure by imagination any number of "parallel universes" that one can create, contemplating how things could have been in the past, and might be today. Far from mere idle or fantastic indulgence, this kind of recreation is the very stuff of growth and progression at the levels of both human individuals[91] and the various collective entities that wax and wane like the moon: nations, monarchs, governments, political factions, overarching civic regulators, commercial and other organisations with a specific motive, each of which combines with a superfluity of responses from individuals – and groups of people with whom they are intimately connected, including families – within pyramids of rich relationship.

---

[88] referring to the broad culture of an identifiable place and time in human history (its news, values, arts, achievements etc – probably best regarded as what comes to mind in the sense of nostalgia). It translates from German as "Spirit of the Times".

[89] "Sentient" here just means consciously thinking and feeling; with no apology for any suggestion of lifecycle acceleration. The capacity of non-human animals to report their subjective experiences to our own species has already been considered in Part I.

[90] What is the psychological nature of such resistance? Under what circumstances and in what manner might its hindering quality be dissipated or dissolved? What are the moral implications of such processes? These questions are like – and may be added by way of adjunct – to the ones about which we have already reminded ourselves in this Chapter.

[91] In *Walden; Or, Life In The Woods* Thoreau concluded, "I learned this, at least, by my experiment: that if one advances confidently in the direction of his dreams, and endeavors to live the life which he has imagined, he will meet with a success unexpected in common hours." (*Walden; Or, Life In The Woods*, 1854, "Conclusion")

"War Memorial": Supermarine Spitfire Mk IX
near Newquay Airport (was RAF Saint Mawgan), Cornwall

Vignettes from seven continents
One doesn't need to traverse much of history, or dig too deeply, to
unearth exemplars. A continent-wise set of notables from recent times
follows. Each of these individuals somehow survived the pressure of
hierarchical relationship - their personal sanity having been tested,
but having remained intact or otherwise got restored. No recognition,
approval or disapproval of their political or other views, positions
or causes are intended or relevant: the brief summaries are presented
only to illustrate the relationship between individual "conscience"
as it has been defined herein and the pressure of human history.
Although these figures are - for the most part - widely admired, the
vast majority of courageous cases in point, perhaps even the most
perfect instances, like The Unknown Soldier[92], remain utterly unsung.

In North America, Joan Chandos Baez (1941-) was born in New York to a Mexican
father and Scottish mother (she resides with her mother in Woodhouse, CA).
Religiously mongrel, her immediate ancestors between them having backgrounds
in or dedications towards Scottish Episcopal Anglicanism, Roman Catholicism
and Methodism, Baez herself still engages with Quakerism. Inspired by Martin
Luther King Jr. (1929-1968, with whom she developed a friendship) Baez has
campaigned courageously, unswervingly and sometimes ferociously for pacifism,
non-violence, abolition of the death penalty, anti-war positions (including
Iraq), tolerance of and equal rights for folks of diverse sexuality, various
other civil rights including anti-racism, employment rights and free speech.
Remaining party-apolitical herself until publicly endorsing Barack Obama in
2008 (backing him on the basis of his capacity to help the poor), she has
been peculiarly outspoken about abuses of human rights right across the
political spectrum, having experienced at various times surveillance and
death threats especially during visits to South America in the early 1980s.
Baez is reputed to regard her social causes at least as significant
personally as her track record in folk music. The young age at which Baez
first took a stand for what she believed in and the doggedness with which she
has maintained her dedication to such a wide variety of causes aligned with
the general theme of human equality, suggest that she didn't have to work too
hard at discovering who she was. Her campaigning right across the board was
not underpinned by powerful allies; rather, like-minded friends. Although she
has had a somewhat chequered romantic life, she seems secure and happy. Her
domestic arrangements are designed to facilitate her appreciation of nature.

In South America, María Eva Duarte de Perón (aka Evita or "Little Eva") died
from undetected cervical cancer at age only 33 in 1952. She was born out of
wedlock and in such obscurity that her surname is uncertain. She was probably
the illegitimate daughter of a wealthy man (Juan Darte) and a woman (Juana
Ibarguren) with whom he had an additional family but left without financial
support. Evita's baptismal certificate (as "Eva María Ibarguren") records
birth in 1919; however, the birth certificate prepared immediately prior to
marriage to President Juan Perón (1895-1974) of Argentina (as his second
wife) records birth in 1922. She had travelled to Buenos Aires from the
country in 1934 anticipating fortune as an actress. She met Perón in 1944 and
married him a year later. As Argentina's First Lady, she won the hearts and
minds of the nation, campaigning for charitable causes, employment rights via
the Perónist trades unions and - having formed an entirely female political
party - women's rights including suffrage and the availability of divorce.
Her candidature for Vice-Presidency in 1932 was thwarted by poor health but
also by resistance from the military and the social elite, an establishment
loathing she had endured over and over as the loyal wife of the President.

---

[92] There are many usages of the expression "The Unknown Soldier" in literature and the
arts; however, most often "The Unknown Soldier" refers to any grave or memorial
(typically inscribed "Known To God") dedicated to unnamed individuals lost in war -
especially the First World (or "Great") War in which many millions died - including
swathes of boys (not men) who fought each other in horrendous battlefront conditions.

There are suggestions of personal corruption in the record, possibly involving the diversion of monies associated with her enormous Foundation for which she undoubtedly worked tirelessly, and ulterior association with General Franco in Fascist Spain not long after the Second World War. On that European tour she was also received well in France, but less warmly in Rome. The British Royal Family would not receive her at all. Her visit to Switzerland was a disaster and precipitated her decision to head for home. Reports of her life suggest a dedication to the cause of the impoverished, unfortunate and oppressed that was not merely extraordinary, even fanatical, but somehow mystical. She is still known as "Spiritual Leader Of The Nation".

———

In Europe, Terry Waite (1939-), the son of a British policeman, seemed to have developed his Christian instincts somewhat independently of parental influence. From his early adult years he enjoyed a steady, solid series of posts in the Anglican Church – including several positions overseas – a great deal of travel and an enviable record in hostage rescue having negotiated: the release of Anglican Priests in Iran in 1980; British hostages in Colonel Gadaffi's Libya in 1984; moreover, having developed working relationships in the Lebanon from about 1985. By January 1987 he was "Special Envoy" to the Archbishop of Canterbury, then Dr Robert Runcie, but was *Taken On Trust*[93] in January 1987 in breach of prior agreement with the Islamic Jihad Organisation which had promised a safe passage to visit sick hostages. Waite was held for nearly five years, of which four were in solitary confinement. The subjective experience of that episode of detention is conveyed powerfully in his own writings – especially the autobiographical *Taken On Trust*. His experiences of separation, cultural severance, loneliness, beckoning hopelessness – the psychology of his survival of the entire ordeal – combined with his highly personable and affable nature, have made him an eminently impressive speaker.

The Foreword to *Taken On Trust* reads:

During my long years of solitary confinement in Beirut … I 'wrote' in my imagination … I always managed to return to my story and thus was able to preserve my sanity and identity … Now I can see that past, present and future are carried in the experience of the moment … We all suffer … suffering need not destroy; it can be creative … I would wish that for my captors … If you read this book as a captive, take heart. Your spirit can never be chained.

———

In Africa, Nelson Rolihlahla Mandela (1918-), having descended awkwardly from African nobility, developed political interests rather early in life. He qualified in law eventually, providing subsidised services to the otherwise legally disenfranchised in South Africa's apartheid system (i.e., segregation and other discrimination against black people). From about 1948, and the election victory of the Afrikaner National Party, he fought apartheid tooth and nail, rising to lead the armed wing (MK) of the African National Congress (ANC) from 1961. He was convicted of sabotage, and imprisoned from 1963 until 1990, many of those years having been spent in solitary confinement on Robben Island. His release came about because his reputation remained alive, carried by numerous individuals who remained dedicated to the cause of equality in South Africa. On his release, Mandela defended the use of violence as a last resort against violence, maintaining that the conditions for such violence still prevailed. He was, nevertheless, awarded the Nobel Peace Prize in 1993. South Africa's first truly multi-racial elections took place in 1994 and Mandela (as Leader of the ANC) became President by a clear majority, remaining President until 1999. Mandela insisted on conceding to the post-apartheid "Truth And Reconciliation Commission" that the MK had violated human rights itself during the anti-apartheid struggle. Nelson Mandela has been married three times altogether. He was reconciled with his second wife, Winnie Madikizela-Mandela (née Nomzamo Winifred Zanyiwe Madikizela, 1936-), on release in 1990 but they divorced eventually in 1996. Mandela, reportedly, began his autobiography called *Long Walk To Freedom* whilst still in prison.

———

---

[93] *Taken On Trust* is a Terry Waite autobiography (1993, Hodder & Stoughton: London)

"Impressive Speaker": A vintage woofer from the 1980s which,
pending redemption, remains connected to its power supply …
(this one, from a Snell AIII, has disintegrated foam surrounds)

▬ ▬▬ ▬▬ ▬▬ ▬▬ ▬▬ ▬▬ ▬▬ ▬ ▬▬ ▬▬ ▬▬ ▬ ▬▬ ▬▬ ▬▬ ▬▬ ▬▬ ▬▬ ▬▬ ▬▬ ▬ ▬▬ ▬▬ ▬

In Russia, Mikhail Sergeyevich Gorbachev (1931-) was the last President of
the Soviet Union until its (economic) demise in 1991. He was awarded the
Nobel Peace Prize in 1990 for his contribution to the end of the "Cold War".
A peasant by birth, he graduated in law in Moscow, rising rapidly through the
Communist Party under the patronage of Mikhail Suslov, then joining the
Politburo itself as its youngest member in 1985 at age 54. He was elected its
General Secretary almost immediately after the death of his predecessor
(Konstantin Chernenko who, like *his* own predecessor Yuri Andropov had held
office for only a short time before dying; accordingly, the need for a
younger leader had become pressing after the deaths of three Soviet leaders –
including Leonid Brezhnev – within about two years). A few Russian words
suddenly came into common use in the West, among them, *glasnost* – meaning
"openness" – and *perestroika* – meaning "reconstruction". Margaret Thatcher,
then Prime Minister of Great Britain, rather uncharacteristically expressed
publicly her confidence that she could "do business" with Gorbachev. Although
Gorbachev's reforms could only have taken the stagnant Soviet economy to a
better place, subjectively and privately he must have felt the weight of the
future of Communism on his shoulders as the Soviet Union's traditions – and
then entire political integrity – started to crumble during his leadership.
He maintained the confidence of the Communist Party nevertheless – in 1989
becoming President of the Soviet Union (a new executive post) in the first
elections in Russia since 1917. Soviet Communism, indeed, declined terminally
in 1989 as numerous (predominantly peaceful) counterrevolutions were effected
across Eastern Europe – after Gorbachev made it clear that any (hypothetical)
Soviet interventions would be "inadmissible". The process culminated in the
breaching of the Berlin Wall from within the GDR (German Democratic Republic)
on 9th November 1989. By 26th December 1991, the Soviet Union was finished.

▬ ▬▬ ▬▬ ▬▬ ▬▬ ▬▬ ▬▬ ▬▬ ▬ ▬▬ ▬▬ ▬▬ ▬ ▬▬ ▬▬ ▬▬ ▬▬ ▬▬ ▬▬ ▬▬ ▬▬ ▬ ▬▬ ▬▬ ▬

In Asia, more particularly Burma, Aung San Suu Kyi (1945-) as leader of the
opposition National League for Democracy (NLD) party won by an unequivocal
majority a 1990 general election called by the incumbent military junta. She
was placed under house arrest just prior to its occurrence, and has never
taken office having been incarcerated for many of the intervening years. She
barely saw her British husband (Dr Michael Aris who died of prostate cancer
in 1999) whilst he was alive as he was refused entry visas by the Burmese
authorities and Suu Kyi would not leave Burma (during periods between arrest)
suspecting that she would never obtain readmission to the country. Her
children by Aris live in the United Kingdom (where she pursued her university
studies) and she has barely seen them during their mutual separation. In 1991
(whilst under arrest) Suu Kyi was awarded the Nobel Peace Prize, her two sons
accepting it on her behalf. A committed Buddhist and advocate of Ghandian
non-violence, she is known for remonstrating that it is not power that
corrupts, but fear: the fear of those in power that they will lose it, and
fear of the scourge of power by those who are subject to it. Suu Kyi was
tried jointly with an American man of obscure motives (John Yettaw) for his
trespass onto her property in 2009. The extra sentencing she received
rendered her unavailable to run in the November 2010 election, only days
after which she was released once more (… as *Nine Seahorses* goes to press).

▬ ▬▬ ▬▬ ▬▬ ▬▬ ▬▬ ▬▬ ▬▬ ▬ ▬▬ ▬▬ ▬▬ ▬ ▬▬ ▬▬ ▬▬ ▬▬ ▬▬ ▬▬ ▬▬ ▬▬ ▬ ▬▬ ▬▬ ▬

In Australia, Neville Thomas Bonner (1922-1999) was the first indigenous
Australian to be elected to that country's Parliament. From impoverished
beginnings as an uneducated farm worker who never knew his father, his
inclination to stand ground for the rights of indigenous Australians combined
with a conservative political bent rocketed him through a variety of
organisations – culminating with his being elected to Parliament in his own
right (as distinct from representing a franchised organisation) from 1972. He
belonged to the Liberal Party from 1971 to 1983 after which he stood as an
Independent. He will be remembered in history most for the obvious political
first. What resonates here is his apparent resistance (if ever it were called
upon) against the conformity that might have made way for personal ambitions;
rather, he remained true to his "natural" self trusting in providence – just
what he seems to have shared most with our other six continental exemplars.

▬ ▬▬ ▬▬ ▬▬ ▬▬ ▬▬ ▬▬ ▬▬ ▬ ▬▬ ▬▬ ▬▬ ▬ ▬▬ ▬▬ ▬▬ ▬▬ ▬▬ ▬▬ ▬▬ ▬▬ ▬ ▬▬ ▬▬ ▬

Heroism in human history and Tolstoy's standard

These biographic accounts, depending on one's personal stance, may seem "heroic", and one might be tempted to regard these people as fundamentally significant figures in the shaping of modern history – even, perhaps, in the mould of the Egyptian Pharaohs[94], or Genghis Khan (1162-1227)[95], or Napoleon Bonaparte (Napoleon I, 1769-1821)[96]; however, this presents one or more new polarities. Whereas Thomas Carlyle (1795-1881) who, having written a passionate account of the French Revolution, developed a "hero" theory of history – holding that things today are very much as they are because of the measurable achievements of "Great Men" – Herbert Spencer (1820-1903) transposed horse and cart, or the cart and the horse, arguing that significant historical figures are, conversely, products of their times (equivalent to what was introduced earlier as the *Zeitgeist*). Inexorably and continually, the *Zeitgeist* is enmeshed with the "weight of human history" in that the former is, during any given episode of history, the natural culmination in time of the latter. Globally, there are many *Zeitgeists*, perhaps most easily envisaged as an evolving one per nation (although we may say just as plausibly per continent or family): the *Zeitgeist* is an (overlapping) unit of culture, so to speak. In the sense that the *Zeitgeist* is intangible, and not of itself material, it is like "mind" and it is like the "meme": you can't see one, but you certainly know about it. Of course it is beyond discussion that the "heroines" and "heroes" we have contemplated emerged (into global consciousness) and prevailed (psychologically and politically) in the context of their own times. Once again, whether one regards them as "hero" or "anti-hero" depends on where one stands personally on certain matters. What separates our chosen continent-wise characters from Khan, Bonaparte, and most leaders in history as it is recorded (including much of all religious scripture) is their promotion of peace and vilification of violence. Whether each matches Tolstoy's standard[97], the reader may decide:

Even if you are told that all this is necessary for the maintenance of the existing order of things … pauperism, famines, prisons, gallows, armies, and wars … that still greater disaster would ensue if this organization were destroyed; all that is said only by those who profit by this organization, while those who suffer from it – and they are ten times as numerous – think and say quite the contrary. And at the bottom of your heart you know yourself that it is not true, that the existing organization … must inevitably be reconstructed on new principles, and that … there is no obligation upon you to sacrifice your sentiments of humanity to support it.

---

[94] The Pharaohs of ancient Egypt are significant for many reasons, amongst which is their pre-eminence as iconoclastic rulers over several thousand years (approximately 3150 BC to the Roman invasion of 31 BC) – during the formation of civilisation *per se*.

[95] Founder of the largest unbroken empire in human history, Genghis Khan is associated with "hell-fire" invasions stemming from North-East Asia into Central Asia and Eastern Europe, as well as the promotion of religious tolerance within his territories! The Mongol Empire had been redrawn into smaller parts, including old China, by about 1294.

[96] Attributed to ingenious military accomplishments by historians, Napoleon Bonaparte established himself by *coup d'état* as First Consul and then Emperor of post-Revolution France, thence master of continental Europe until the invasion of Russia in 1812.

[97] Penned by Lev (Leo) Nikolayevich Tolstoy (1828-1910), who was more in favour of Spencer's view of history than Carlyle's, this quotation is from *The Kingdom Of God Is Within You* (1894, Bison Books: London, 1984, p.363). Tolstoy and Mohandas (Mohatma) Karamchand Gandhi (1869-1948) were of one mind as far as violence was concerned, both of them staunchly resolute that a human being had to be "intoxicated" or "hypnotised" – probably by corruption of power, or evil – to kill another human being. Tolstoy is known also for fiction in *War And Peace* (1865-1869) and *Anna Karenina* (1873-1877).

Tolstoy's standard as provocation

Tolstoy's provocation represents as perfect a model as it is possible
to imagine of staunch personal integrity in the "moral environment"
whether or not one is an apologist for violence even if conditionally
(like Mandela). There is an existing "order" that affects each of us.
We know it through first hand familiarity with our respective and
overlapping *Zeitgeists*. The formation of that familiarity in our
"minds" and how we respond to it (what we do, don't do, and how we
otherwise process and regard it), together with the consequences of
that response for ourselves and for others, are "moral psychology".

All of us are shaped by, and are now shaping history

Now, our seven exemplars: Are they products of history, or shapers of
history? Of course they are both. We all are. In every generation
there must be countless new "heroes" and "heroines" willing to stand
up counted on the grounds of some controversy or another in relation
to which it might seem "easier" to say nothing – thereby expending no
effort – and attracting no unwanted attention. Then again, perhaps
these people simply number among those who somehow discerned their
course, accepting and persevering with what they had to do. How many
others spend their lives waiting vainly upon a purpose or vocation?

Lardy stagnation

That feeling of drift and despondency (versus direction and purpose)
seemingly lies like solidified lard on the top of a jug of meat fat.
The richness and juiciness of the lives that we once knew as carefree
infants, children and young adults[98], stagnates suffocated and stifled
underneath, and we can't find any way – under our own auspices – to
warm ourselves enough to scrape off the crud, stir things up and get
going again. All that others can see of us is our pasty white surface
utterly lacking in sparkle, character or appeal. We feel as thick,
stupid and unappetising as we seem. Folks pass us by. We have lost
the confidence of spontaneity. We find ourselves churning quietly –
and then, at times, painfully and noisily – in a "descending vicious
spiral" of isolation, loneliness and inferiority. This "emptiness" is
ever more demoralising until it overtakes us on our blind side (no-
one told us about that …), and we seek help if we are still standing.

Dreadful infection

Dreadfully, according to ubiquitous literary and statistical sources,
such a phenomenon is happening at an increasing rate and is more and
more common at a younger age in most Western nations. It is probably
permeating the so-called developing nations and third world – even if
those places have their own toxic difficulties to redress as many are
taken over eventually by democracies[99]. In "developed" nations the
foundation for personal values has shifted from obedient religion[100],
fence-sitting agnosticism and atheistic "enlightenment" as variations
on one dimension; to deification of cash, celebrity-worship and
spiritual *ennui* on another. Alongside, we have been visited by the
descent of old vices taking form amongst us in deadly ways. If this
seems to you an exaggeration, consider getting out more – or visiting
your extended family soon. In recent decades, alcohol problems have
exploded, and the trajectory is still rising. Illicit drugs problems
accelerated more recently, but the same principles apply. Gambling is
just starting out, officially encouraged by tax-hungry governments.

---

[98] assuming we luckily enjoyed early lives unspoilt by existential or any other despair

[99] This is neither to endorse nor to denigrate democracy nor any of its alternatives –
mooted or unmooted; such reflections are outside the scope of the present argument.

[100] The received education in the established Church is catechistic, meaning it is
authoritative and imparted. Tolstoy preferred Christian inspiration by another route.

"Jug Of Meat Fat"

Rolling stones and runaways

The impact of such trends in the "moral environment", and the ways people are responding to them, shouldn't be underestimated – for in social environments as in personal lives, rolling stones gather moss. In addiction circles, the unfinished business of a declining life is often termed "the yets"[101]. An interrupted tragic social trajectory is better than an ignored one, and that is especially true for younger people because they have a greater stake in what is going on than everybody else on the grounds that they must endure more years of it. For reasons that may remain elusive to even the family, friends and educationalists in a teenager's life, some young people begin to drift away from the paths proffered by society (qualifications, training, routes into employment, responsible single or family life) turning to distractions (truancy, alcohol and drugs, dependent relationships) that look like recipes for unmitigated misery (police attention, the courts, prisons, hospitals and poor living conditions) and often become just that – not just for the distracted – but for those in their social vicinity – all those most loved and loving too.

Stand up if you sold out

Of course, this is not an entirely new phenomenon, but youth culture travels on sands shifting as quickly as time itself. Politicians and policymakers at least one and perhaps even three generations removed from the problem can be caught discussing whether "binge-drinking" is really a new phenomenon on consultancy fees more reminiscent of a final salary pension than a Job Seekers Allowance. Of course it is – but not for reasons that you imagine (else you would apply another remedy). Times are different. They are not the same as when you were young. Bob Dylan (1941-) told you[102] during your own salad days. You felt taken seriously, and you felt liberated. But the liberation didn't last, because it wasn't real. It certainly wasn't sustainable, even if it felt real. Look at the evidence. It was an illusion. You got tangled in the same trap as your career-bound predecessors, lured by the same ageless bait (money and status). A young person may drink or drug today as much to quench a thirst for fun as an "emptiness" entirely characteristic of his or her own place in space and time – their own "moral environment". We shall come eventually to the application of an "Accountable Self" in a personal "moral psychology" as an expression of social and civic responsibility. In the meantime, what shall *we all* make of *our* "moral environment"? For example, upon whom does or should responsibility fall in the hypothetical situation where a teenager incarcerated for an acquisitive offence (burglary) petitions successfully for personal injury or similar redress against a treatment system designed, implemented and funded by a government, arising out of failure to administer adequate substitute medication (more drugs – titrate yourself – but these have a longer half-life, keep you quiet and help you back on your feet – maybe – eventually) in time to head off the discomfort of withdrawal symptoms in the new temporary residence, the youth's prison cell? Having identified the respective parties in the scenario, including the ones behind the scenes such as the offender's family and the entire criminal justice system, one is compelled, unless beset by prejudice and knee-jerks, to ask in relation to each assailed party: "Why so?" and "How so?"[103]

---

[101] Whether or not one is convinced by "disease" models of such problems (and there are plenty of worthwhile arguments either way), they are "progressive" in the sense that, once they have set in, as long as a person continues to "use" their "drug of choice" (alcohol, drugs, gambling, sex, chocolate, shopping) life deteriorates mercilessly against any meaningful criteria one chooses (health, finance, relationships, sanity).

[102] *The Times They Are A-Changin'* is Track 1 on Side 1 of the eponymous 1964 album.

[103] The reader may care to revisit this scenario and its responsibility test(s) later.

Doing what you really want to do

Whilst there are significant ethical and practical implications of custodial sentences (because many incarcerated young people have experienced significant deprivation and poverty, a difficult family life, substance misuse and mental health difficulties; and because some young people kill themselves in custody; and because young people learn new tricks from old lags etc), a "moral psychology" is not directly concerned with whether it is "right" or "wrong" to lock up young people (whatever thresholds one might set for seriousness of offence, circumstantial culpability and so on)[104]. The central point so far as a "moral psychology" is concerned is the discrepancy between what young people say they want for themselves and what they actually do. In the UK there are thousands of young people serving custodial sentences including a significant number of children (under 18s); some of whom, because of resource problems, may be incarcerated with adults. The precise figures vary according to source and date – but the drift is that some 70-90% of young people leaving custody say that they do not want to re-offend, but a significant majority do. This gap, whatever its percentage or scale in reality (with hindsight in a "moral environment" defined in an offender's difficult existence by whether they end up back in the Courts) represents precisely the scope for "moral psychology" to endow its beneficence to young lives. Whom amongst us would not wish all criminal justice short-circuited, rendered to oblivion, because nobody had recourse to it any longer?

Collective responsibility in proportion

Should young people (or anybody else for that matter) be left to establish a "moral psychology" under their own auspices and resources however scant those might be at a time of special need? Can "self" heal "self"? Has it done so successfully in history to date? If it has, in whom has it done so, what was their secret, and may we share it? What is obstructing that process happening now? If something else is called for, would we recognise it if it presented itself? Does society have a role to play? This is just where the line between "moral psychology" and "moral agenda" will ever be most blurred. Not many of us would discount entirely the role of the family (howsoever defined or conceptualised but we are talking for the main part about parents) in the child's psychological development, and some would let it remain there to venture nowhere else. Still others prefer to exercise a "social conscience" and we may – in deference to political tradition – envisage a dimension from zero involvement of government or any social agency (*laissez faire*) on the one hand to the formal provision of psychological safety nets – even compulsory education and community service – on the other. Putting aside other political (including economic) arguments for a moment, the balance to be struck is one that takes account simultaneously of the social drift that we all know about[105] and the requirement to promote psychological autonomy for – as we shall see if we don't know already – there is no authentic independence without it. Perhaps the ideal scenario is one in which folks have found a way to help each other of their mutual appreciation of honest need and harmonious co-operation – to such an extent that argument about government involvement becomes irrelevant.

---

[104] Such a judgement would establish a moral agenda, whereas we have made it clear that in a "moral psychology" each person establishes their own identity, with its various positions and values, drawing then on the "natural" source of courage that accompanies discovery of the "authentic" self in order to live out a personally meaningful life.

[105] Without wishing to labour a point, sociologists (correctly) have been bewailing accelerating social disintegration ever since they got their feet under university desks. Problems of disaffection and alienation are very much with us and burgeoning at an armchair-rocking rate. A plethora of data support the general point that humans prefer healthy mutual engagement to isolation. This is discussed fully in Chapter 8.

"Pig Philosophy"
Gyrwe Anglo-Saxon Demonstration Farm, Bede's World, Jarrow

Probing between polarities for joy
The notion that collective experience and wellbeing (as opposed to religious authority whether in ecclesiastical law or "natural law"[106]) should constitute the proper basis for morality in society effervesced during the Enlightenment in the "utilitarianism" of Jeremy Bentham (1748-1832). "Happiness for the greatest number" was promoted over the interests of the individual wherever conflict arose; however, anchoring morality in "happiness" was interpreted by the refined John Stuart Mill as "a doctrine worthy only of swine"[107] unless it took account of "higher" (or "morally elevated") pleasures. For Thomas Carlyle, all utilitarianism is "pig philosophy"[108] on the grounds that mere pleasure and pain (no matter how noble) inform its thesis. Well then, to what extent has our experience of "obedient religion, fence-sitting agnosticism and atheistic 'enlightenment' as variations on one dimension; to deification of cash, celebrity-worship and spiritual *ennui* on another" over past centuries set us upon firmer[109] moral ground? Apparently, it has not. Neither dogma nor hedonism has precipitated favourable moral trajectory – whether we go by contemporary mental health and social statistics – or just what we see around us. As ever – we must search between polarities for joy.

Venturing "headshrunk" into psychotherapy
The ways in which we shape our own "minds" – our personalities and value systems, the foundations of all our day-to-day behaviour – or the ways in which they are shaped (depending on whether the relevant factors and processes are passive rather than active), is discussed throughout this volume hither and thither (especially as we proceed towards the close of Part II in Chapters 8, 9 and 10). In Part I, we had to determine our position on "mind" in deference to philosophical tradition, and practically all of serious 20th century psychology. The very discussion illustrated how mightily (and severely) mainstream human history has shaped our thinking in matters psychological today; in particular, the Scientific Revolution grips the moral *Zeitgeist*. The argument for a "moral psychology" could not have proceeded beyond that impedance without nailing down a consensus on "conscience" and demonstrating the significance of the "moral environment". We are about to go "headshrunk" into a detailed consideration of sanity and psychological helping as it has ventured out into the 21st century; absolutely, as with psychology itself, a product of its own history.

Visiting smaller "worlds" . . .
The journey throughout the next two Chapters is rather like taking a magnifying glass to the "moral environment". We shall zoom in from the planet, its continents and their political trials; from modern nations and their difficult struggles to manage social disintegration by juggling social fairness with social resources; to the smaller "worlds" in which we are touched – and from which we reach out from ourselves to touch and connect with others in our immediate "social environments". These are the things that people talk about when they present for psychotherapy: the "self", "others" and "relationship". The touching can feel at once as if it is life-enhancing, and just as immediately as if it is persecuting us. We can get very confused. What happens when a confused person meets a confused response? What happens when someone who has lost internal congruence, unable to see themselves objectively, descending into an almighty mess, meets . . .

---

[106] to which we have been introduced in Chapters 3, 4 and 5 of Part I

[107] *Utilitarianism* (1863) – see also J.S. Mill in footnote to Chapter 1 and Chapter 4

[108] *Latter-day Pamphlets* (1850)

[109] not "higher" … if you please

"Old Ways Of Thinking"
Statue of Galen (129-200 AD), Fountains Abbey, North Yorkshire

Chapter 7

"Sanity and contemporary psychotherapy"

. . . psychotherapy as the response to psychology
. . . psychotherapy which, in a sense, is the response to psychology? After all – if we all exist, learn, think, feel, behave, hope, suffer and eventually die, then we all inhabit the "world" of psychology. If as individuals our existence, learning, thinking, feeling, behaving, hoping, suffering and dying remains quiet and peaceful, internally congruent and aligned without oxymoronic conflict; moreover, presents no subjective experience of distress, then not only have we been fortunate beyond credibility, but we have also been permanently sane. This is another way of saying that we are all "nuts"[110]. It's just a question of when and where we hit the buffers – and how noisily. For most people, most of the time, all this is an unnoticed phenomenon – unnoticed even by ourselves. (Sometimes we seek a little comfort here and there.) For others, the elements of sanity have gone so awry, and the accompanying distress become so intense, that the illusion that one can fix oneself unaided has all but evaporated, dissolved or retracted to the point of unreachability; then, the psychologically agonised person reaches out for help (assuming that the reaching out hasn't already been done by enforcement of civil or criminal law). The response may come unpersuaded from intimate community. Then again it probably won't, if for no other reason than because we don't organise ourselves that well. Besides, folks understandably get to the end of their tether with sick people. Arguably they should.[111]

Patient "readiness" and response "relevance"
So what happens next? Well, it depends on two main things. The first and most pivotal is the internal readiness of the distressed person to go about things in a different way, or to move in a different psychological direction, and the effect is proportional; e.g., total readiness invites total change of habits – and total change of psychological direction[112]. The second is the relevance of response from other people, and "relevance" is a most encompassing word. These two factors in the trajectory of a needy person's psychological health are revisited over and over from here onwards, beginning with consideration of how compromised sanity tallies with this framework.

Our shameful prurience
We all have heard of the old asylums in which poor unmedicated souls, no longer a fit in their communities, or whose behaviour had become so unmanageable that they had to be contained securely, were locked up hidden away "out of sight, out of mind"; alternatively, paraded as it were *in situ* for visitors eager for experience of the grotesque and the awful. In the same prurient manner, ancient audiences would flock to consume the spectacle of Roman gladiators, or medieval pillory, or pyromaniac execution. Happily, in these times, we confine our predilections to exuberant gossip about contestants on talent show TV. What is it about us that enjoys, without sufficient shame, the tribulations of our fellow men, women and (especially) children?

---

[110] OK – not you

[111] It is a question of resisting the inevitable "game playing" (see Chapter 8) that accompanies insanity; thereby helping people towards independence and personal responsibility (with which we need to combine compassionate recognition that insanity depletes all sorts of resources, so taking us back to our collective responsibility – see Chapter 6 – and the case for a "moral psychology" class of insurance if you like).

[112] rather suggesting that a perfect psychotherapy could be nearly infinitely cheap

Tolerance for our own hypocrisy
Perhaps it is just that we are selfish creatures who prefer to live
personally in matters of pleasure, and vicariously in matters of
pain; whether of the body, or of the mind. Perhaps there are perverse
mental processes of which we (all) are capable by which we convince
ourselves that – whilst our own suffering must be avoided at all
costs – another's may be tolerated as long as (by our own assessment
of course) they brought it upon themselves; or it is not so close to
us that we feel it literally because of its contiguity; or it is not
so near that we cannot "pass by on the other side" onlookers unaware,
but must stoop to ask what is wrong. And then later, when we became
incapacitated ourselves, what did we remember of our behaviour and
our values? What kind of response did we expect or now humbly hope
for at our own buffers? What was our tolerance for our own hypocrisy?

Two sides to every coin
Perhaps these kinds of psychological anomalies generate the worst
kind of intrapsychic conflict; for, if we become "too" honest with
ourselves, we cannot bear the "conscience–weight" of our own
irresponsibility. The phenomenon is an everyday one. We know it from
childhood. We stole sweets, or hit our sister in frustration, and
felt "bad". It was the same feeling then as the one we know now when
we scrape a car and don't leave a note, or stray into the more
dangerous territories of property misappropriation and selfish "love"
affairs. If we haven't yet grown up, we live a life of chronic
burden, always under the suspicion of our own lurking moral gaze, let
alone the scrutiny of law. Whichever way you look at it, it is of no
use making excuses for self-betrayal. There are two sides to any
coin, and we can flip any situation over to look at it another way.
We credit ourselves with guile; in fact, it is denial. How do we know
it is denial? Because if you hold out playing a "bad game", you find
yourself on a losing wicket sooner or later. Ask anybody who has
tried it in the long run. As a theory this assertion goes a long way
as we shall see in Chapter 8. Fortunately there is a solution, and it
is outlined in Chapter 9. The whole of Part III is a testimony to
that solution in action – albeit founded in allegory rather than in
the laboratory. No matter. It has to be only convincing enough. What
you believe matters. You have the precious and unique "laboratory" of
your own life in which to work. You don't need to exclude from your
own "moral psychology" any first cause of "conscience", and you need
admit and afford hospitality only to those that you choose to invite.

The extent to which the blind lead the blind
What parallels of our personal discomfiture exist in any treatment
system at any one time? In what ways and to what extent are responses
confused, incoherent, uncoordinated, misaligned through internal
conflict; even perhaps in certain ways irresponsible, beset with
ulterior motives and lacking in integrity; above all, self-deluded by
excluding authentic sources of "conscience" and unwilling to change?
To the very extent that these prevail do the blind lead the blind? If
we take a view of the entire need (personal disintegration) and
response (psychotherapy in all its guises) for psychological helping
in one bird's eye view; have we not, as a human family so to speak,
sub-contracted it out (in most civic arrangements) so that we need
never look at it, nor examine it, nor fettle it, unless we have need
to use it? And then, if we have need to use it, do we not number
either among its clients, in which case we are too sick to see and
speak for ourselves (until our condition improves); alternatively,
among its designers, administrators and practitioners who are liable
to get bogged down – then having a vested interest in careers and
technicalities, salaries and familiarities; and who (juxtaposed with
suddenly honest clients) may be dismally qualified by (in)experience?

Psychotherapy needs self-examination as much as its clients
Surely what is true of me as an individual (and, very possibly, you)
is also true of the psychotherapeutic industry (for that is what it
is): if I seek self-knowledge for the worthwhile sake of acquiring or
maintaining personal integrity or vigour, I must be willing to
scrutinise my past. If I don't do this on (and with) purpose I am
liable to persevere with living (and meeting trouble unless I have
redirected psychologically or spiritually) never having to confront
my history. A client in psychotherapy (as indeed in all their other
relationships) may be afraid to tell the whole truth (and nothing but
the truth) about themselves (i.e., to shed all forms and degrees of
psychological defence) for fear of exposure, shame and intimacy –
whereas the professional psychological helper may be unwilling to
open up in a similarly "unprotected" vein because there is much else
to defend. But, surely, psychotherapy needs as much self-examination
as its clients. If it doesn't appreciate this – whether as an entire
professional domain, or within its constituent silos (pending the
kinds of reconciliations between them that can only bode well for us
all as we veer away from polarities and steer nearer to "truths") –
it risks the same consequences as the avoidant individual – in denial
and still belligerent to wisdom; i.e., eventual self-destruction.
Self-examination and reflection evidently yield shifts in thinking.
If the self-examination is earnest, the redirection is bound to be
favourable. Favourable trajectory promotes favourable circumstances –
sometimes quickly, sometimes slowly – but inevitably all the same.
Like everything that mutates into something better, psychotherapy
need never be called upon to leave behind its better "self". But does
it know what that "self" is or how to set about discovering it?
Whilst conflicts within a discipline, as within an individual, tend
to undermine integrity, effectiveness and reputation – ameliorations
of internal dissonance promote direction, satisfaction and peace.
There is also a tendency for relationships to change for the better.

"Unusual affect" and "layers of defence"
There are any number of useful yardsticks, apart from patent denial,
by which we can discern a poor condition – whether in a client
presenting for psychotherapy, or in the psychotherapeutic response.
Included among them are "unusual affect" and "layers of defence".
Unusual affect in the context of (in)sanity refers to, shall we say,
unfamiliar or giddy thoughts or feelings that are unpleasant to the
person experiencing them, may interfere with the free and easy living
of the sufferer and others in their psychological vicinity, and which
cannot be banished easily by discharge of "will". In some persons, at
some times, "unusual affect" can assume a serious form which, as it
features unmistakeable disturbances of reality-perception in the form
of delusions or hallucinations[113] – yet may be amenable to effective
pharmaceutical intervention – is likely to require remedial attention
urgently. In the (limited) present state of medical and psychological
technology, such problems lie fair and square within the province of
psychiatry. We are well advised to appreciate the competence of
suitably trained professionals in the treatment of such grave
conditions because no-one else has ever made a more convincing pitch.
At the same time, we would not wish to dismiss the seriousness of
"non-psychotic" disturbances which can be similarly debilitating and
sometimes fatal – usually in the shape of self-sabotage or suicide.
This is where the rightful implementation of interventions in the
medical mould are more blurred and controversial. The "medical model"

---

[113] Delusions are false beliefs. Hallucinations are quasi-sensory aberrations. Both are
instances of reality-distortion. Esoteric philosophical arguments about reality may
not interest the sufferer or the family, and are beyond the scope of this book anyway.

is characterised by two primary attributes: scientific (or empirical) method, and an identifiable professional culture. Even within it there are divergent approaches to psychotherapy, and sometimes these cross their arms and don't talk to each other. Blended in with them is a broad spectrum of other helping approaches and practices, and most of the time they aren't on speaking terms either. How, then, can a psychologically sick person (and sometimes people are very confused and vulnerable indeed when they present for help) effect a sensible choice about where to turn, assuming they have any choice at all?

Capacity for empathy
Now, according to one point of view, it takes a well-trained practitioner to discern insanity, but this stance barely scratches the surface. Putting aside denial, an insane person knows a great deal about insanity because of subjective pain – but their expertise cannot be harnessed usefully in a state of personal disintegration. Isn't the most sensitive monitor of another's insanity someone who has traversed and survived the same stony journey or, at least, one like it? Doesn't survival of insanity implicate development of honesty, even if only in overcoming denial? Don't we all experience goose bumps when we see or hear truth or beauty? Don't we all recoil consciously, or even beyond our awareness, from cant and clamour? Some people don't like this kind of questioning, but you must always ask yourself why they might resist it. It is patently obvious that someone who has similar experience to another possesses the greater capacity for empathy[114] and, so, someone who wishes to step into the helping shoes of one so qualified must be at least one of: virtuously willing when no-one better placed will do it; better qualified on a net basis by other assets, or representing a response system that is protecting its own power or financial interests on unethical grounds.

"Expert patients" …
In health care systems in the West (Great Britain anyway), there is a personhood known as the "expert patient". Applied to insane people such nomenclature borders on mockery with reckless irresponsibility. Compromised people lack "expertise" to the extent that they are laden with ignorance about how the treatment system works – doubled once with mental confusion – and twice with their own denial. Susceptible people who can't see the woods for the trees don't know which route away from insanity they might pursue because they don't know what it looks or feels like. If they did, chances are that sooner rather than later they would have adopted it, so dispelling their discomposure. Their appreciation of options, even supposing that these were clearly explained and the relevant services freely available, may be severely curtailed and, in any event, neither of these conditions is reliably satisfied at the front line. Such obfuscation may be exacerbated when prospective clients are active in addiction, in crime, or any other category of disorder especially contaminated with dishonesty. Whether offenders have complete, partial or no aforethought of misdemeanours (known in France as *"crime passionnel"* and in the USA as "temporary insanity"), people say and do things whilst psychologically afflicted (especially if under the influence of alcohol or drugs; even more so if addicted), which they would hardly perpetrate when psychologically healthy (sane), sober or recovered. All the same, although a person's criminal intent may be distilled from psychological vulnerability, raw accountability for social misdemeanours (the need for making amends) does and should remain regardless of "moral responsibility".

---

[114] having its roots in the German *Einfühlung* as we saw in Chapter 1. "Empathy" – which is mutual and shared understanding – is not equivalent to "sympathy" – which has far less (even negative) value in psychological helping as it fuels self-pity dangerously.

(Very) "Unusual Affect" (when lit)

"Layers Of Defence" can make us 'spiky'
Duart Castle, Isle Of Mull, Scotland

… or "competent coxswains"?
Ignorance, cerebral fog and personal denial render self-diagnosis and
self-treatment impossible or, at best, challenging to say the least.
Does each practitioner the suffering person encounters once the
(sometimes very slow) process of capitulation has started possess a
capacity for immediate and accurate diagnosis? No. We know this from
collective experience of the "revolving doors" syndrome[115]. Well then,
is there some unheard "voice in the wilderness"[116] whom we have not
heard above the clamour? No. No-one has rendered a one-size-fits-all
cure for insanity. Each response must be tailor-made, as bespoke as
the personality and history of the individual, else it is shoddy. And
if the afflicted person doesn't know what style to wear, or doesn't
appreciate the latest fashions, who will help in the bustling market?
What happens when they find themselves cast centrifugally from the
mall doors, returned on their backsides to the street – over and over
again – each time a cap doesn't fit? Any family they ever knew has
flown. Any money they never had is spent. Any hope they ever had has
gone. They start to die, inside out. There is a *prima facie* case for
"competent coxswains" (see Chapter 9) to steer these distressed
vessels into a well-fitting berth in a safe harbour; to explain what
can't be appreciated unaided; to afford temporary assistance with
navigation, and to defend against misunderstandings and inattention.

Maintaining optimism
Well – let's be optimistic. After all, where there is life there is
hope – and hope is reflected brightly in subsequent Chapters. In the
meantime, let's look at what might happen when someone who is "all
knotted up"[117] presents somewhere where there is a helping hand who
has a matched response – or who knows how to effect a good referral.
How "relevant" is the range of psychological help that is out there?

Understanding the evolution of silos
A (very old, possibly Chinese traditional) definition of insanity
expressed in terms of doing the same thing over and over – but each
time foolishly expecting a different result – is often attributed to
Albert Einstein (somewhat mysteriously given his association with
physics rather than psychology – although many of Einstein's humorous
quips regarding human vanity are registered in the various catalogues
of after dinner speech writers' guides). Now, as Sir Isaac Newton
knew (see Chapter 1) – and now we do – great scientists do not spring
from nowhere, but emerge from history standing on the shoulders of
"giants" (and lesser ancestors). The same is true regarding concepts
of insanity in psychology and, so, we might wish to traverse today's
silos in the context of their chronological evolution so as to
appreciate their gradual formation and interrelatedness. Whilst we
can refer to material already presented for much of this perspective,
we will be assisted in our appreciation by reference to a timeline
around which can be constructed a brief historical narrative. Against
such a backdrop, we will develop a discussion of various dimensions
against which any response to the challenge of (in)sanity may wish to
evaluate itself; following which (in Chapter 8) we may consider human
relationships, appreciated by none so much as Eric Berne (1910-1970).

---

[115] referring to the unmitigated phenomenon whereby clients turn up at services, only
to find themselves through lack of personal readiness, or response "relevance", cast
exterior, simply to return at another entry point further down the road … *ad infinitum*

[116] in the New Testament, the remote John the Baptist preparing the way for the Messiah

[117] an expression we will coin to represent the miscellaneous ways in which the various
schools within psychology and psychotherapy present barely convincing explanations of
everybody else's psychological problems. Perhaps we all need some "straightening out".
None of us has all the answers – but many are doing a great job with what they've got.

(NON-LINEAR) TIMELINE SHOWING EVOLUTION OF MODERN PSYCHOLOGY

Religion	Philosophy	Medicine	Scientific Psychology	Analytical Psychology

Hinduism from c.5000 BC

Judaism from c.2000 BC

Buddhism from c.500 BC

Empedocles (490-430 BC)

Socrates (469-399 BC)

Hippocrates of Kos (460-372 BC)

Plato (428-348 BC)

Aristotle (384-322 BC)

Christianity from c.30 AD

Galen (129-200 AD)

Islam from c.600 AD

Saint Bonaventure (1221-1274)

Saint Thomas Aquinas (1225-1274)

William of Ockham (1288-1348)

Nicholas Copernicus (1473-1543)

Galilei Galileo (1564-1642)

René Descartes (1596-1650)

Sir Isaac Newton (1643-1727)

Immanuel Kant (1724-1804)

Jeremy Bentham (1748-1832)

Auguste Comte (1798-1857)

Søren Aabye Kierkegaard (1813-1855)

Hermann Ludwig von Helmholtz (1821-1894)

Lev Nikolayevich Tolstoy (1828-1910)

Wilhelm Maximilian Wundt (1832-1920)

Friedrich Wilhelm Nietzsche (1844-1900)

Ivan Petrovich Pavlov (1849-1936)

Conwy Lloyd Morgan (1852-1936)

Sigmund Freud (1856-1939)

Émile Durkheim (1858-1917)

Carl Gustav Jung (1875-1961)

John Broadus Watson (1878-1958)

Martin Heidegger (1889-1976)

Gilbert Ryle (1900-1976)

Carl Ransom Rogers (1902-1987)

Burrhus Frederic Skinner (1904-1990)

Jean-Paul Charles Aymard Sartre (1905-1980)

Eric Berne (1910-1970)

Hans Jürgen Eysenck (1916-1997)

FROM AND WITHIN A "MORAL ENVIRONMENT" TOWARDS A "MORAL PSYCHOLOGY"

"Einstein's Insanity"
(A grate physicist with a quirky appreciation of human vanity)

From diverse ancient religions to disintegrated modern psychology
Older history, prior to recorded human civilisation, is added by way
of context to an ancillary argument at the beginning of Chapter 8.
Hinduism, traditionally, has recognised many deities and stands in
contrast to the monotheistic approach common to Judaism, Christianity
and Islam. The Old Testament, for many readers, is a ferocious
territory as much as it is an inspiring one: the fear of an exacting
God and the scything edge of the human sword permeate its cultural
narratives, practical wisdom and religious assurances. Recognising
exceptions such as Kierkegaard, Tolstoy and Jung — religion and
psychology are discriminable pursuits now although, naturally, they
share common interests — not the least among which lies the personal
integrity (and spiritual salvation) of their charges. In two-and-a-
half millennia of "rigorous thinking" beginning with Socrates (in the
West at any rate but we may care not to forget the Biblical prophets,
the Buddha and Confucius) neither philosophers nor scientists have in
any conclusive manner accounted for or dismissed human consciousness.
One of the main tensions within classical philosophy in relation to a
"moral psychology" has been "dualism" (or the "mind-body problem")
from which, actually, behaviorism and scientific psychology drew
their seminal momentum by way of reaction (see Part I). Explanations
of associative learning (classical conditioning and underappreciated
variations within that paradigm) in physiological terms have barely
transcended the interpretation of laboratory preparations of simple
invertebrate neuronal systems (see Chapter 2). If "consciousness"
hasn't been realised from known neural or synaptic morphology — far
less have language, all first causes of "conscience" and human
subjective pain (physical or psychological) been accounted for in the
realms of classical philosophy and science as we have known it since
Copernicus and the Scientific Revolution. "Scientific Psychology" and
"Analytical Psychology"[118] are represented in the timeline (columns)
as discriminable traditions; indeed, there is little actual crossover
institutionally. They are probably best characterised as "bottom up"
(anticipating accounts of phenomena from first principles) versus
"top down" (iterative refinement of models) approaches respectively.

Recap of lateral thinking in the unravelling of history
This timeline is just one way of drawing up history; however, it is
coherent with earlier Chapters and represents the "moral environment"
relevant to a "moral psychology". Like all human history, admittedly,
it is written up in a particular way for a particular purpose. It is
said that Martin Heidegger (1889–1976) died before completing a
Destruktion ("re-enactment") of philosophy — a perfect illustration
of the breadth of imagination that was recommended in Chapter 6:

*One way in which the diversity and richness of such variations in
culture can be appreciated is to conjure by imagination any number of
"parallel universes" that one can create, contemplating how things
could have been in the past, and might be today. Far from mere idle
or fantastic indulgence, this kind of recreation is the very stuff of
growth and progression at the levels of both human individuals and
the various collective entities that wax and wane like the moon:
nations, monarchs, governments, political factions, overarching civic
regulators, commercial and other organisations with a specific
motive, each of which combines with a superfluity of responses from
individuals — and groups of people with whom they are intimately
connected, including families — within pyramids of rich relationship.*

---

[118] Whilst "analytical psychology" is an expression sometimes reserved for the Jungian
approach to personality and psychotherapy (indeed the expression was coined by Jung to
differentiate his approach from Freudian psychoanalysis); here, it encompasses those
evolutionary threads within all the diverse schools whose devotees descend from Freud.

Unfinished business and "moral conflict"
We saw in Chapter 4 that human beings have always had a tendency to "polarise" – or assume black-and-white positions on fundamental matters. Modern psychology and psychotherapy are disintegrated and unfinished pursuits, largely because of this disposition. Trenchant positions on deep-seated difficulties (un)naturally create tensions within a professional discipline as much as intrapsychic conflict does in persons. Such internal misalignment, arguably, is one way of conceptualising "insanity" *per se*[119] (which is to suggest that some spurious partitioning of beliefs and values – or "moral conflict" – lies with deleterious effect, lurking invisible unless exposed, behind every instance of experienced distress). In professional environments, the resolution of conflicts isn't merely a matter of trying to achieve "occupational sanity" (or feel comfortable about one's professional identity or what one collects money for): the philosophical assumptions that one retains as both a private individual and a therapeutic artisan inform the very ethical basis of one's professional practice. Perhaps it is more important than many practitioners have realised to know who they are philosophically.

Having your philosophical cake and eating it
As a professional category, psychotherapy wants to have its cake and eat it. On the whole, it tends to assume that its clients must "decide", "redecide" or at least gradually embrace personal responsibility – apparently implicating Cartesian "free will" (in which mind doesn't need matter to exist). As we saw in Chapters 4 and 5, this position is favoured by religions which consider "mind" and "soul" synonymous, and "conscience" as spiritual or divine prompting. On the other hand, many psychotherapists in cultural terms identify themselves with the "religion of humanity" espoused by Auguste Comte who also pioneered positivism (see Chapter 4). Positivism holds that we can know only what is perceived (through the senses). As a philosophical tradition, it is aligned strongly with both materialism (holding that everything including "mind" can be explained by "matter in motion") and scientific determinism. Although not necessarily true of each individual practitioner keeping a personal view within the domains germane, most psychotherapies claim or aspire to a scientific – or pseudo-scientific – basis for the efficacy of their treatments.

The importance of shared assumptions about "mind"
As modern psychology doesn't "know" a proven position between dualism and materialism, it follows that psychotherapy doesn't either. It is not so much the point whether there are right or wrong answers to be had, as it is that practitioners might oblige themselves to promote awareness of the issues amongst themselves, reflecting on how the assumptions they unwittingly bring to bear affect the ethical quality of the treatment they deliver. The profession-wide presumption of "personal responsibility" may be acceptable even if "free will" is an illusion; nevertheless, psychotherapists mustn't render helpees more "helpless" than when they arrived because they somehow failed contractually to rework their destinies through "redecision". The therapist needs to maintain or effect with the client a compatible set of assumptions about "mind" and the manner whereby the client's psychological future is "co-created". As we shall see without too many more preliminaries, it may be possible to supersede "free will".

---

[119] In the USA "radical psychiatry" refers to the political issue of oppression through alienation. The "hero" of the "anti-psychiatry" movement in the UK was the Scottish psychiatrist Ronald David Laing (1927-1989), author of *The Divided Self* (1960) and architect of the expression "double bind" referring to the "mixed messages" that supposedly generate confused children and, later, sick adults. Whilst the roots of the linguistic form "schizophrenia" suggest a divided personality, psychiatrists are more disposed to recognise constellations of symptoms as criteria for diagnostic syndromes.

Varieties of "knottedness" and matching the response
A singularly significant factor in the "relevance" of a treatment
response has to do with the assumptions that are made by the
therapeutic agency about how and why – precisely – a person is "all
knotted up". The problem, really, is one of proportionate humility on
several counts. First, the reason why there are still so many diverse
treatment silos in psychological helping is because explanations for
how the "knots" got formed (or whether and how they were congenital)
are equally disparate: the various traditions and philosophies are
just alternative ways of looking at the same problem, and none of
them is entirely right; after all, none has furnished a complete
explanation, and none has produced any universal "cure". A realistic
appreciation of the limits of psychological technology is apposite
(see Chapter 2, "Learning To Control"); in particular, the scientific
community, if it is honest with itself, has very little 'I Deer' how
the mind works (especially how subjective consciousness is generated,
how we are endowed with our species-specific capacity for language,
whether these things are bound up with or even occasion in some
manner a peculiar or mutual capacity for experiencing pain – whether
physical or purely psychic – and how human "conscience" arises and is
despatched, especially in relation to dispensation of that pain). You
can discern proportionate humility in a psychotherapist by how much
they admit what they don't know – whether about what "mind" may be
(other than "shareable subjective experience"), and how science fails
to afford complete explanations[120]. Second, the therapist requires an
appreciation of the extent of match or fit between their available
response and the true nature of the presenting problem as far as that
can be discerned authentically; i.e., without the constraint of
conflicting interests or contamination with an ulterior motive. It is
not just a question of fixing statistics, or securing fundamental and
recurring income streams, or harvesting a misplaced sense of personal
efficacy; it is a question of corrupting temporarily feeble minds
with a false sense of hope. Far better, "I doubt my capacity for
helping you, but I may be able to find a (wo)man who can". Third and
pivotally, as already noted, the client needs the humility that is
readiness to change. This condition includes openness to recognising
the direction one must go – a highly personal undertaking in every
case (inevitably transpiring to have been the easier path after all).

Mainstays and gaps
One of the most popular contemporary psychotherapeutic modalities is
"behavioral" therapy, which is hinged squarely on the principles of
conditioning described in Chapter 2. It is known as "cognitive-
behavioral therapy" or "CBT" if combined with theory and research
associated with the "cognitive" sub-discipline of modern psychology.
Cognitive psychology does what it says on the tin: it identifies,
challenges and remedies "distorted" thinking (whilst such language
begs qualification, the trick in CBT – as in all psychotherapy – is
to win round the client to a new way of looking at things). CBT is
popular (with governments) because it has promised short, sharp and
cheap results: the jury will let us know of its deliberations in due
course. Medicine, by contrast usually quite expensive to administer,
performs its psychotherapy – for the most part – via pharmacies and
from the Freudian couch. The latter route, certainly, is a shared
road these days with non-medicinal psychology. Freud, to be fair,
must count among the most imaginative figures in the history of
sanity and psychotherapy. We still don't know whether his theories
will stand the test of time. Psychoanalysis and Jungian psychology

---

[120] Whilst science may well answer thorny questions, it is best grounded in a realistic
appraisal of how short it is of such finishing lines, assuming they will ever exist.

have spawned goodness knows how many varieties. The "relevance" of
all of the available responses in psychotherapy today has everything
to do with their history, but then so do the precise shapes and forms
of insanity with which they are confronted. But this is not to say
that today's insanities and today's psychotherapies are a match made
in heaven. Patently they are not, because so many besieged folks fall
through the fissures in the floor boards. A significant advantage of
taking the present perspective on psychotherapies (i.e., one which
recognises through history what they have and have not become) is to
create opportunities for re-establishing them – especially if their
inadequacies can be identified readily enough. If they are relatively
inexpensive to remedy, all the lesser any excuse for procrastination.

A "self"-perpetuating industry?
Inspection of an inventory of psychotherapies (on the following page)
– having appreciated already how they emerged in a timeline of
psychological history, and now seeing how respectively they perceive
"knottedness" – one of the most ungainly ways in which they wander
like unherded cats is in their appreciation of the human "self".
Radical behaviorists probably wouldn't recognise such a thing at all.
Psychoanalysts and analytical psychologists elevate it above all; yet
claim it is hidden and inaccessible except through perspicacious use
of their incisive professional instruments. Even amongst those that
possess an enlightened understanding of an evolving "self", how many
in psychotherapeutic practice explicitly and successfully lead
clients away from self-centredness as opposed to unwittingly
perpetuate the reverse with well-meaning encouragement to mitigate
personal anxieties at any cost? To what extent has psychotherapy
become a "self"-perpetuating industry – literally – because it has
failed to realise what it means for the "self" to become free of its
own burdensome shackles? We shall discover more of this in Chapter 9.

It's good to talk
As the author's primary hope for *Nine Seahorses* is that it strikes up
conversations about "moral psychology", it is not necessary here to
exhaust all the theoretical alternatives, nor defend a particular
domain of psychology, nor any particular psychotherapeutic approach
(except any that stands on its merits during scrutiny or contention).
The reader can find both received and critical accounts of the
psychotherapies – along with their merits and limitations (the latter
of course in far more smidgeonly proportions) – elsewhere in books
and journals; in libraries; in conference proceedings and workshop
papers; in public sector policy and strategy documents; from private
and voluntary sector organisations; in the yellow pages, and online.

If lucky stars be the food of sanity …
The remaining objectives within this Chapter are to illustrate very
briefly the diversity of the psychotherapeutic response and to resume
our discussion of "relevance" with supplementary reflections on
"scientificness", "mastery", "toughness", "empowerment" and so on.
The summary on the next page is not an exhaustive inventory;
nevertheless, it encompasses the mainstream, and includes short notes
on "knottedness" and "relevance". If you have the wherewithal to
peruse these details on the basis of possessing the clarity of mind
for their appreciation (for what they are and for what they are not);
the "head space" for making comfortable decisions about them; a car
for driving to the consulting rooms or the physical health to walk to
the bus stop, and you possess the financial resources to pay for them
– then you have the advantage of a very significant head start when
it comes to feeding your sanity by counting your lucky stars. If you
are just hoping for any response that might make things better, your
"family doctor" (or anyone else you can trust with some confidence)
is as good a place to start as any. You can let yourself be guided.

PSYCHOTHERAPY TYPES WITH NOTES ON "KNOTTEDNESS" AND "RELEVANCE"

Type	"Knottedness"	"Relevance"
Prescription Drugs	Psychiatry may understand "insanity" as "severe" mental illness only; nevertheless, it is a broad discipline. In pharmaceutical therapy, a biochemical imbalance or other deficit in the central nervous system is known, suspected or assumed (a psychological "cause" may never be identified).	Prescribed by a medically-qualified doctor, therapy involves drugs such as lithium for bipolar disorder, antidepressants, anxiolytics and anti-psychotics along with others for a variety of diagnosable conditions including Alzheimer's disease, epilepsy etc. Non-chemical psychotherapy may be harnessed adjunctively.
Behavioral Therapy	Chapter 2 presents classical and instrumental associative learning. The assumption is learning on a *tabula rasa*: the implication is "un-learning".	Behavioral therapy involves principles described in Chapter 2; e.g., flooding, desensitisation, aversion therapy etc – often for specific problems such as phobias.
Cognitive Therapy	Old faulty thinking occasions distressing feelings in the now. A cognitive psychologist works within testable, theoretical, rather than bottom up frameworks.	Cognitive therapy exploits sample situations – intervening within a thoughts-feelings-behaviour cycle, modifying self-defeating and unrealistic thought patterns.
Cognitive-Behavioral Therapy (CBT)	CBT draws on principles from both "cognitive" and "behavioral" approaches. CBT practise promotes "re-learning" at the level of situational thoughts and feelings ("cognitive") on the one hand and behaviours directly on the other ("behavioral"). The question, "Which of thinking or behaviour needs to change first?" is circumnavigable on the basis that either can and does work: efficacy is a question of trial and error for a given person.	CBT is widely recognised within psychiatry as well as mainstream psychology where it is believed to be (cost-)effective against a broad range of problems: "anxiety, depression, panic, phobias (including agoraphobia and social phobia), stress, bulimia, obsessive compulsive disorder, post-traumatic stress disorder, bipolar disorder and psychosis … anger, a low opinion of yourself or physical health problems, like pain or fatigue" (RCP online).
Freudian Psychoanalysis	Identifies conflicts in the unconscious mind or "Id" (presumed to occasion emotional disturbance in the analysand) by exploring "free association", fantasies, dreams etc. "Psychodynamic" involves the same principles, but the connotations are: briefer, shallower, smarter.	Traditionally a protracted relational process carried out at depth. Relies entirely on the Freudian theoretical approach to the structure of "mind" and how psychopathology arises. Has drawn criticism for being "unscientific" and "unproven" as much as it has admiration for its originality.
Jungian Psychotherapy	Deepens awareness of the unconscious mind in the conscious mind – especially via dreams.	A psychotherapy balancing unconscious and conscious "mind" – so facilitating "individuation".
Transactional Analysis	The decisional "life script" formed during childhood as a survival mechanism is no longer a useful basis for daily living.	TA defeats the "life script" via behaviour analysis – facilitating client "redecision" – thereby "putting a new show on the road".
Humanistic Therapy	Presumes a therapeutic trajectory involving "self-actualization". Implies a stifled life that has limitless potential now unbound.	Being neither "behavioral" nor "Freudian" but a "third force" promoting personal growth in a conducive relational environment.
Person-centred Counselling	Assumes psychological tensions arise when perceptions of the world including its "others" threaten the structure of "self".	Founded by Carl Ransom Rogers, therapy relies on facilitating the inherent self-healing tendency through non-directive counselling.
Gestalt Therapy	The client is distracted from the here and now – and relationships.	A humanistic therapy promoting self-awareness in relationship.
Existential Therapy	Assumes an "emptiness" of the variety described in Chapter 5.	Helps a client find personal sense and meaning in an absurd world.
Drama, Music, Art etc Therapy	The mode (drama, music, art) is an alternative to conversation for drawing out the personal narrative. Endlessly subtle.	Activities may seem more just recreational than therapeutic. It is a question of demonstrable efficacy, especially if paid for.

"Knottedness"
Studley Royal, North Yorkshire

Which psychotherapies are scientific from the tips of their toes?
There are a few dimensions within all of these treatment modalities
that bear teasing out and rendering explicit, because they have much
to do with the "relevance" of all common psychotherapeutic responses.
First, consider how many psychotherapy modalities rely entirely on
truly scientific grounds for their design, explanation or evaluation.
Barely any do (although many consider themselves scientific anyway).
The exceptions are pharmaceutical interventions and the valiant
attempts by scientific psychologists (behaviorists) to nail down the
learning traces that underpin conditioned emotional responses (CERs).
Such approaches are sometimes referred to as "bottom up" because they
pursue explanation at the level of physiological or mechanical cause
and effect (as we have said – from first principles). The reverse of
this approach is "top down", or the testing of putative models of
personality or psychopathology which are then evaluated in practice,
adjusted as required and retested in an iterative process (until – in
some scientific or other theoretical utopia – the top down and bottom
up tunnel burrowers meet head on, squarely, without missing one
another). The main point here is not so much to do with which
approach is more commendable as it is that psychotherapy is more
hunch than gospel. This is why the friendly folks in psychotherapy
say with a reassuring smile, "If it works for you, it works for you".
Whereas science and medicine favour the identification of specific
patterns of disorder (constellations of symptoms), matching them to
formal diagnostic criteria (the establishment and classification of
syndromes) upon which the therapeutic response is then designed;
everything else is a matter of trying something out to see whether it
works. If it does, well that is great news, but it can leave the more
curious and intellectually masterful amongst us scratching our heads.

The misplaced assumption of mastery
Second, curiosity and mastery – particularly the conceited latter –
deserve thoroughgoing discussion because there are poorly appreciated
paradoxes and anomalies in relation to "toughness" and "empowerment"
that may in certain (even many) instances occasion more confusion and
antagonism than reconciliation and resolution in relational contexts.
The problem is one of control. In Chapter 2 we learned how animals,
including humans, endeavour to "predict" reinforcement (pleasant and
unpleasant events) in the environment through use of external cues
(classical conditioning), and by adjusting behaviour (instrumental
learning). The theoretical environments that matter emanate from the
behaviorist tradition which supposes a "bottom up" explanation for
all human behaviour according to known or yet-to-be-discovered laws.
This paradigm or domain is a specific instance of raw or diluted
"scientific determinism" depending on how radical a position is
assumed by its adherents. The inferred subjective experience of the
learner is some complex of conditioned "anticipatory hope" and
"avoidant fear" in a given individual according to unique biographic
history. In Chapter 5 we saw how Hans Eysenck and Jeffrey Gray viewed
"conscience" as the product of conditioned fear, particularly during
childhood. We may impute from such assertions that subjectively
unpleasant CERs are experienced because of personal histories, and
that people will tend to avoid situations (classical conditioning)
and behaviours (instrumental learning) that generate aversive CERs.
Now, radical behaviorism and its corollary, "scientific determinism",
is a discovery of Western civilisation, more particularly an American
one, yet we all know that North America is the "land of the free",
and that everyone there has the capacity for realising their own
fortunes wilfully. How could this have happened then? Is everything
psychological determined? Or is nothing determined except that which
we impose masterfully on patiently waiting destiny? Or is neither of
these verifiable but rather there is something of "truth" in between?

Even if we fail to answer the question convincingly, we shall have
undertaken a serious attempt by the close of *Nine Seahorses*[121]
(although we rather gave the game away somewhere between the lines of
the three principles outlined during the preliminaries of Chapter 6).
In the meantime, let's keep our focus on one or two distinctions
regarding "empowerment" in order to minimise the risk of wasting our
time by pursuing red herrings relentlessly; who knows, by the close
of Part II we may have realised a dividend worth the effort expended.

The Western obsession with "toughness"
Apparently, modern psychology's unfounded and misplaced faith in
"free will" (see also Chapter 9) rides tandem with its equally wrong-
footed obsession with "toughness". Whilst the notion of resilience
must be real in the sense that we see variations in sanity for what
looks like the same dealing of the deck or throw of the dice[122], too
many presumptions are made about what the nature of those ostensible
individual differences really is. This assumes they exist at all, for
if scientific determinism holds sway, then the point is academic at
best: the universe yields and then takes its inevitable toll on a
life with the passage of time until it is dust (no exceptions). If
determinism can be rebuffed successfully, then it is still unclear –
even in the 21st century – whether conceptual "toughness": (i)
protects or buffers a "tough" person against the more demanding of
the events that unfold in a person's life, (ii) actually affects what
happens through, e.g., "positive mental attitude" (aka "PMA") or
(iii) is a descriptive indulgence, merely affording an illusion of
control in favourable circumstances tantamount to a personal vanity.

Seven significant domains in which "toughness" may be spurious
Demonstrations of the patently erroneous – or at least potentially
misleading – concept of psychological "toughness" are to be found in:

... interpreting "drive"
1. ... reports of associative learning which are constructed not just
around the formation of associations between environmental events, or
responses and reinforcers[123], but are presented in such a way that a
socioculturally-hinged "desire for control" element is also present –
especially if implicated as a meritworthy motivating factor (say,
macho bluster versus biological "drive"). Even fantasising that such
(especially Western) norms are scientifically rather than ethnically
plausible, the bottom up accounts that would lend standing to them
are not available at all. In any event, there is a difference between
"biologically necessary control" and "frustrated control fulfilment"
– or any other way you like of describing social "controlfreakery".

... "desire" versus "expectancy"
2. ... perspectives on "locus of control" that fail to take account of
the fundamental difference between "expectancy" and "desire". The
distinction between "perceived control" (expectancy) and "desire for
control" (potentially leaning towards pathological controlfreakery)
as discriminable psychological constructs has been effected neatly in
the literature[124], but pretty much missed by a significant proportion
of the psychological community which remains focussed exclusively on
a superficial interpretation of the original concept developed by

---

[121] Please don't cheat by peeking at the Epilogue: The conclusion of the wise seahorse.

[122] i.e., all exterior circumstances (measurable events etc) apparently being equal

[123] The Skinnerian view of instrumental learning as we have seen in Chapter 2 is R-S.
Thorndike's model for the same learning phenomenon is Situation-Response, or S-R.

[124] e.g., Burger, J.M. (1992) *Desire For Control: Personality, Social And Clinical
Perspectives*. Plenum: New York

Julian Rotter (1916-)[125]. According to Rotter, locus of control is a unidimensional and normally distributed (i.e., conforming with a Gaussian distribution or "bell-shaped curve") quantitative index reflecting the extent to which an individual attributes (by way of subjective belief reflected in predictable and measurable behaviour) the likelihood or probability of the occurrence of reinforcement not just to personal factors (such as intelligence, skill, aptitude, diligence) – aka "internality" – but also social (powerful others) and entirely external ones (luck, chance, fate) – aka "externality". In this way, "internality-externality" transcended the framework of classical cues and operant behaviour that the behaviorists had expanded upon as generalisable phenomena in the laboratory, but had not yet fully appreciated in terms of the accumulating biographical associative learning history of a human being living in the "real world". In practice, most people will score around the middle of the Gaussian distribution, with a sense that they can control many but not all of the motivationally significant events that happen in their lives. Failure to appreciate the distinction between "expectancy" and "desire" is failure to realise that the most stressful experiences are associated with the greatest discrepancy between the two; i.e., when "desire for control" is maximal and "perceived control" minimal. To portray an extreme example, earthquakes are stressful because the extent to which one comes to realise that one controls a significant event is vastly different to the extent to which one would like to.

… turning a negative into a positive

3. … psychological theories of depression which assume that remedial learning must establish or restore "perceived control". During the 1960s and 1970s, based vertically on behavioral foundations, Martin Elias Peter Seligman (1942-, now extremely well-recognised in North America as a founder and proponent of the new "positive psychology") developed a popular "learned helplessness" theory of depression. Serendipitously, Seligman discovered during experiments using dogs harnessed in controlled environments equivalent to a Skinner Box (see Chapter 2) that, unlike other dogs who had benefited from having had an opportunity to terminate electric current by pressing a lever, those who didn't developed, seemingly, a disinclination to engage in escape behaviours in new environments. Seligman was inspired and deeply influenced as a psychologist by Aaron Temkin Beck (1921-) after whom one of the most widely used questionnaires for measuring psychopathology – the Beck Depression Inventory or BDI – was named. It would be fair to say that Beck and Seligman have steered psychological (as distinct from biochemical or neurotransmitter) theories of depression significantly in the last half-century. Whilst "learned helplessness" may serve as a fitting description of what human folks look like when they are miserable, it doesn't follow that an impoverished operant history must be re-fettled in order to put things right. Problems for positive psychology do not so much stem from its promotion of optimism as from its potential for raising and sustaining unrealistic expectations. If optimism is like spiritual (as distinct from biological) hope – to be valued and nurtured under all circumstances – well then any framework that permits a sense of unconditional entitlement to personal happiness, or constrains the capacity of a person (especially if sick from covert resentments) to accept "life on life's terms", may be rendering quite a disservice; for just to the extent that any person chronically regards themselves, others, or the dealing of the deck as falling short of unretracted imaginary yardsticks do they remain unremittingly insane.

---

[125] Rotter, J.B. (1966) Generalised expectancies for internal versus external control of reinforcement. *Psychological Monographs, 80: Whole No.1.*

… resisting the tide of madness

4. … Ivan Pavlov's "strength of the nervous system" (see Chapter 3). This rather different approach relies less on learning history than on individual differences in inhibition raised in the central nervous system against afferent stimulation. Although Pavlov described excitation–inhibition in the context of all the four Ancient Greek temperaments, the elementary idea is that the greater the amount of inhibition generated, the greater the tolerance for stimulation – and the greater the corresponding "toughness". Doubtless certain of Pavlov's dogs rode out the Neva flood more psychologically intact than others, a tidy example of individual variations in "sanity" for that same roll of the dice (moreover, perhaps Pavlov's model of "excitation–inhibition" confers other theoretical advantages); nevertheless, the meaning that human beings attach to their lives is not hinged just on their capacity to remain undisturbed following the occurrence of what the insurance industry knows as "major perils".

… satisfying superiority

5. … Hans Eysenck's "Extraversion". An extension of Pavlov's ideas, Eysenck fitted "Extraversion" within a framework of "stimulus intensity modulation" in which extraverts – having a lower resting or baseline level of cortical arousal compared with introverts – require more stimulation in order to reach the same optimal level between sleep and hyper-vigilance. Mediated through the Ascending Reticular Activating System (ARAS), variations in the underlying biology may be significantly genetic with a heritability coefficient of about 50%[126]. Eysenck was preoccupied with other dimensions of "toughness" too: "Neuroticism", or emotional instability (associated inversely with "stress tolerance"); "Psychoticism" (actually a heterogeneous construct comprising mainly impulsivity but also irresponsibility and cruelty), and indices such as IQ (intelligence quotient) in relation to which he attracted pillory because of allegations of racial bias.

… letting it all hang out

6. … "repression-sensitisation" (R-S) models of emotional inhibition. According to Donn Byrne (1931–), individuals vary along a bell-shaped continuum (like any personality trait including Extraversion and locus of control) according to a disposition to "approach" or "avoid" threatening stimuli or, similarly, confront everyday situations that might present a challenge to one's psychologically defended "self". Repressors are avoidant and "bottle things up", whereas sensitisers are inclined towards approach behaviour and the release of stress-associated emotion. Approach is reminiscent of "hopeful" conditioned behaviour (see Chapter 2), whereas "avoidance" is reminiscent of conditioned fear. Hans Eysenck's concept of Extraversion suggests a positive relationship between E and sensitisation because of stimulus toleration and "sensation-seeking", but the evidence is ambiguous, largely because the questionnaire that measures repression-sensitisation – the R-S scale[127] – has weak psychometric properties[128]. The habit of withholding rather than expressing feelings is regarded as significant psychologically – not just in psychotherapy, but in physiological health – on the basis that sensitisation (its reverse)

---

[126] The extent to which psychological constructs may be inherited is notoriously difficult to establish. Formally, heritability is the phenotypic variance attributable to genetic variance, but can only be approximated roughly in most studies. The best examples in psychology are twin and family studies where the genetic relationship can be established with confidence, thus exposing variation due to environmental factors.

[127] Byrne, D. (1961) The repression-sensitisation scale: rationale, reliability and validity. *Journal of Personality, 29,* 334-349.

[128] Roger, D. & Schapals, T. (1996) Repression-sensitization and emotion control. *Current Psychology, 15:1 (Spring 1996),* 30-37.

short-circuits the "fight or flight" response to stress and its potentially damaging effects on the cardiovascular system if elevated over a sustained period because of consistent "emotional style"[129]. Whilst venting uncomfortable feelings might afford transitory emotional relief, the evidence that it promotes sanity or militates against heart disease and related conditions is not clear. There are better theoretical frameworks and psychometrics for conceptualising "Emotion Control" (see note to Chapter 14, "Learning to 'Let go'").

... tough by any other name

7. ... Suzanne Kobassa (aka Ouellette)'s (1948–) notion of "hardiness". Conceptually independent of the coronary-prone "Type A" personality, hardiness comprises three attitudinal components that reportedly buffer an individual against the deleterious effects of stress: "Commitment" is an attribute of hardy people because they "sign up" to life rather than dither; "Control" represents internality as meant by Rotter, and "Challenge" is the disposition to regard the rigours of life as a plate to which we may step up, rather than as uninvited woes which can overwhelm us. Although hardiness seems aligned with "positive psychology", their desirability therapeutically must rely entirely on whether such "toughening up" is an achievable aim, right for everybody and represents a true pathway to any worthwhile sanity.

Drawing satisfaction from what is rather than how "tough" we aren't
The jury is out on "toughness", and the verdict may be delivered by any number of routes; however, we can imagine two for the sake of present argument. As psychology is big business (see Chapter 4), in some eventual technical *coup de théâtre*, we may be afforded irrefutable demonstrations from first principles of precisely those individual differences that discriminate between the healthy and unhealthy (including the sane and the insane), thereby identifying those fortunates who can choose, through sheer application and force of personality ("will"), to carve and etch out especially purposeful, meaningful and satisfying lives for themselves. The technological gap between such an accomplishment and the contemporary "top down" models and more informal portraits of "successful" people that we know today is so yawning that the putative revelation would have to materialise in some dramatic setting we can barely imagine now. The second route is, naturally, the neat sidestep. How many clients presenting for psychotherapy are melancholic and maudlin from not measuring up? How many could depart from their first consultation happier (w)armed with a simple exhortation to draw satisfaction from what they actually are rather than what their culture apparently expects of them; from whom and what others unconditionally are; what is more, from how the world actually presents itself – with all its prejudices and intolerances – rather than how it might be engineered to avert disappointments? Far from defeatism, this is reality-checking – and it is also maturity.

---

[129] The putative impact of chronically elevated levels of activity in the hypothalamic-pituitary-adrenal axis on both the cardiovascular and immune systems has been well rehearsed since the 1980s and stems from earlier notions of personal vulnerability or "diathesis". The "Type A" personality, reportedly susceptible to both "hurry sickness" and cardio-vascular diseases, was identified as early as the 1950s, and has formed the basis for research on models of psychosomatic illness ever since. Neither cause-effect mechanisms nor a firm diagnosis of the "toxic" elements of the Type A complex of chronically agitated behaviour have been unambiguously established. In contrast to Type A, the "Type B" possesses, subjectively, sufficient time in everyday life and is healthy in matters cardiovascular and, apparently, psychological. There is also equivocal evidence for a "helpless-hopeless" cancer-prone "Type C". Impaired immune functioning arises from cortisol, a glucocorticoid secreted from the adrenal cortex which, in large and sustained concentrations, diminishes the number and effectiveness of white blood cells. Sustained levels of adrenalin, secreted from the adrenal medulla, promote injury to the endothelial lining of arteries and the development of artheromatous plaques. Its effects may be mechanical (exacerbated by hypertension) and through the mobilisation of levels of free fatty acids beyond metabolic requirements.

Social (in)justice and standing ground

A clarification about personal "empowerment" and social justice seems apposite here. Embracing the world as it really is, including "all its prejudices and intolerances", our unmanufactured selves and its other inhabitants as they really are, is not at all equivalent, even tantamount, to resigned reconciliation with inequality or injustice. Quite the contrary. The integrity ("moral alignment") of the "self" and the personal reparation that "moral psychology" affords are the very resources that underpin any person's desire to contribute to making the world a better place. The process of acquiring and maintaining a worthwhile personal sanity in the framework of a "moral psychology" involves, as we shall see in Chapter 9, a deeply personal self-appreciation hinged on preservation and augmentation of those parts of our identities that are immutable or otherwise valued in our own estimation, and the dissolution (even if gradual) of those that we recognise as dispensable diversion or personal rust. Once we have begun this process, the confidence to exercise the authentic "self" flows in automatically, as does the promise of comfort in our skin. If we want to campaign on behalf of an issue, or stand up and be counted, how much easier is that pursuit when we can see clearer where we stand in relation to all matters? Since "moral psychology" engages others, often we are situated to draw strength in numbers.

Winning the game of life

Stereotypically, psychotherapy is a horizontal, hypnotic experience, with a focus on one "powerful" other, even if that "power" is only inferred by the capacity for restoring sanity that is implicit in the payment of psychotherapy fees. In everyday life, the majority of us must encounter and engage with at least a modicum of alertness, fluidity and seeming purpose with our fellow human beings in all sorts of contexts. The usual ones are family (the home), friends (our social lives), work colleagues (employment environments) and service agencies (the entire range of organisations that provide a service, many of which are pretty much inescapable: central and local government, education and health care professionals, banks, shops). Whilst much of our business with others is commercial in nature, those contexts are the ones least likely in our personal histories to have laden us with emotional "baggage". Instead we must consider the unremunerated relationships with family, with friends, and with other persons and agencies in whom we must trust – to go about their business with us according to both explicit and unspoken traditions, codes and rules. These are the ones, if any, that have informed our sanity in the past and continue to do so now. In the same way that the best kind of practice or rehearsal a *Tour de France* hopeful can obtain in preparation for the "real thing" is road-racing, so must we embrace psychotherapy immersed relationally. We have to make ourselves accountable to the psychotherapeutic "other" in order to invest in our own progress meaningfully else we hide and get nowhere. There is a dimension of cogency in that "other" relationship which is at its most potent when it resembles closely the circumstances in which we must discharge our sanity to the fullest. With the exception of certain modes of counselling, we don't have psychotherapy with family and friends: we have real life. But we can approximate those contexts in psychotherapy – in *groups* – if we are ambitious, brave and willing. This means taking on people without telling them who or what they must be; moreover, what they can or can't say to us about ourselves. The *quid pro quo* prevails, of course, and we need take home only those messages that are truly meaningful to us. If we are loving, the messages we impart will be delivered in a similar spirit. This is how trust is sown and begins to flourish. When it becomes second nature, and we believe in it more than we believe in doubt, we have rendered it transcendent and have begun to win the game of life.

"Transcendent Trust"
Ethnic dancers at the Alnick International Music Festival

Chapter 8

"Good relations"

Food for thought

Now, what exactly of sanity is portended by the presence and by the absence of trust amongst human folks? Are we now so deeply lost in the forest of social alienation that the whole planet – us humans – has forgotten its sense of togetherness? Upon what else can we rely? Picture in your mind's eye, if you please, a world of 6,800,000,000 (6.8 billion) people. This is the world that is on your doorstep, and which is also your oyster should you prefer to digest it that way.

An explosion of life

At the turn of the 18th century, the world's population had reached a billion. By 1920 it was 2 billion. We numbered 3 billion by 1960 and 6 billion 40 years later. In Chapter 4 we appreciated that neither scientists nor creationists were around at the time of the so-called "Big Bang" to garner first hand accounts of it (far less account for how and why it happened at all, and what if anything preceded it[130]). A similar principle applies to how humans got to exist *per se* and then number nearly 7 billion in history. In simple terms, scientifically speaking and for the sake of argument, the universe is about 13-14 billion years old. Our solar system was formed from a molecular cloud about 4.6 billion years ago. There may have been a "last universal common ancestor" from which all existing life on earth descended (by natural selection and evolution of what came to be the gene pool) estimated to about 3.5 billion years ago. The first simple cells (prokaryotes) date from around this time. The first complex single cells (eukaryotes) date from around 2 billion years ago. Multi-cellular life forms date from around 1 billion years ago. Simple and then complex animals evolved some 600-550 million years ago. Land plants date from 475 million and amphibians from about 360 million years ago. In the last 300-100 million years our planet has been populated by reptiles, mammals, birds and flowers. The (non-avian) dinosaurs disappeared about 65 million years ago. The "last common ancestor" that today's humans share with one or more other species dates to somewhere around 3-7 million years ago, but modern humans, as we recognise each other today, did not evolve until about 200,000 years ago. We may say that human language – being species-specific – can be located to approximately this point in evolution, and almost certainly (and curiously) emerged (in anything like its present sophisticated form) after and not before the practice of religious and quasi-religious rituals. Indirect evidence from fossils, mitochondrial population genetics etc suggests modern humans migrated "Out of Africa"[131] somewhere around 50-70,000 years ago replacing other hominids (now extinct) in Europe and Asia. The entire human population at this time, or at least that from which modern humans evolved "Out of Africa" may have numbered only a few thousand.

---

[130] Whilst *prima facie* these seem reasonable questions, they are very human questions, and we must permit that even if humans have the capacity to eventually discover, understand and explain "everything", we are simply nowhere near the vicinity of such a destination. The chances are, moreover, that if "we" (are still human beings and) ever approach that place, the very language or other framework(s) invented, inherited or required to address such matters will be leagues beyond our imagination and reckoning. If you consider otherwise, what grounds or basis have you for estimating the unknown?

[131] "Out of Africa" competes as a theory with its next most regarded alternative which holds that modern humans evolved more independently and diffusely across the various continents from a common African ancestor – dating to as many as 2,000,000 years ago.

"20-20 Vision" (requires hindsight in *homo sapiens*)

It is not written that we must be alone
When we assimilate, moreover, the unfathomable perspective that our sun (and its planetary system including our earth) counts as but one star amongst about $3-7 \times 10^{22}$ (30-70 sextillion) in the scientifically known universe (calculated at the rate of a "typical" 2-400 billion stars in each of 80 billion or so galaxies arranged in clusters and superclusters), we can hardly avoid the conclusion – even sentiment – that we are small in every respect, even psychologically. But nowhere is it written that we must be alone – or separated from each other.

Limits on self-reliance
Modern psychology, gradually, has funnelled our attention towards the "self" (and, thereby, its indulgence); undoubtedly because, in each of us, it is our foremost preoccupation[132] (our favourite subject if you will). Since Ancient Greece we have been obsessed with dialectic ("cleverness"), and have remained so through the Enlightenment to the present day. But can there be any meaningful psychology that is not for *Everyman*[133] including the least intellectually agile? How far does our over-indulged capacity for constructing hypothetical futures obscure a proportionate appreciation of the world as it naturally presents itself, rather than as we might engineer it through discharge of human "will" (with all its attendant exaggerated and thwarted expectations)? Since Pavlov and Eysenck (in physiology and scientific psychology) especially – but also Freud, Jung and others (in humanistic and analytical psychology), we have become obsessed with "diathesis" (weakness). If cleverness has not spawned universal sense, and "toughness" represents nothing more significant or helpful than a conceited 20-20 hindsight view (of psychological endurance); we must seek sanity deeper within ourselves or reach farther out to others for it. Since Darwin and Huxley on the one hand, and Watson and Skinner on the other, we have been preoccupied with *Man's Place In Nature*[134] to the point of eliminating her and his "mind" from our enquiries. But restoring my "mind" is not the same as promoting my "intellect" for; as applies to anybody else, I can acquiesce with my "mind" to any amenable invitation – including one to authenticity – without recourse to sharpness or guile: the prefecture of a minority.

Feigning unselfishness
Reverting to our introductory gambit (Chapter 1), and fortunately for all of us other than Adam and Eve, humans have had a longstanding knack of feigning unselfishness if ever there was a sexual union in prospect. At the culmination of some fantastic number of generations there is now a barely reckonable swarm of us, and the world's human population, having expunged countless thousands of other species, may at last be peaking as bacteria in a crowded Petri[135] dish. We are having to resort to contrived means of food production – moving from ancient and motivationally innocent local agriculture to the global distribution of synthetic commodities – the cost of which can be measured in contamination of the planet's ecosystem and potentially catastrophic climate change, as well as traditional economic metrics.

---

[132] OK – not you

[133] See footnote to Chapter 5.

[134] *Evidence As To Man's Place In Nature* (1863) is the title of the volume by Thomas Henry Huxley (1825-1895) in which the notion of a "common ancestor" (for *homo sapiens* and other primates) was first presented. Then, the idea that "man is an animal" was a shock to the (especially religious) establishment and there was much convincing to be achieved in contemporary Oxford circles. The book spanned *On The Origin Of Species* (1859) and *The Descent Of Man, And Selection In Relation To Sex* (1871) in which Charles Darwin presented similar ideas about the evolutionary origins of human beings.

[135] after Julius Richard Petri (1852-1921), the German microbiologist

"Swanning About" (more graciously than a mounted bishop)

Alternatives to self-poisoning

Can we help it? Is it inevitable that humans sooner or later poison themselves to extinction? Or may we settle upon alternative ways of carrying on … in which case, how on earth might that be achieved? Dare we ask whether our problem is one of self-centredness? Can we examine ourselves without getting all upset and defensive about it, i.e., without despising the worth of personal moral inventory on the grounds of old prejudices about pontificating bishops swanning about on horseback (so to speak)? The Scientific Revolution and the Enlightenment have demonstrated in history that nobody likes being told what to do, especially by a hypocrite. Perhaps the established church(es) will recover in the centuries to come as, inevitably, all vestiges of human authority and intolerance are finally usurped by universal charity and mutual affirmation combined with faith in the divine rather than geopolitical influence. That is not our business unless we choose to make it so by becoming part of the holy process.

Living simply

Perhaps there are two ways of looking at our selfishness as a physician might try to understand the respective factors implicated in the progression of any observable pathology. The first is sheer and unnecessary consumption. The arguments are "out there". The whole of the new "Green" and "Environmental" political movements exhort us to "live simply". If we were not so obsessed with economic growth the pollution of the planet would be mitigated in direct proportion. The consequences of our lifestyles today will be borne by future generations, but we will not be there in the dock to answer to them. Is that OK with us (never mind them)? It's no use leaving it to the politicians for they like influence and power and economic niceties too much: they will not listen and act unless their holding office is rendered contingent on compliance with the sense of the wider world.

Demoting self-interest

The second is to resolve seriously the question whether abiding by self-interest is the most useful rule-of-thumb in all human affairs. We can explore the pros and cons with real and hypothetical examples as individuals and as families; as towns and as nations. A toddler might scream down the house for a bar of chocolate, not contemplating for a moment the capacity of the parents to provide shelter tomorrow; whereas the teenager may have settled upon lesser strategies for larger stakes (sulks for stipends). Eventually we won't have to reflect, because we will have adopted such stock-taking (of our own selfishness) as the most natural thing to do in the world (and beyond depending on the force and velocity of our warp-drive[136] technology) wherever we find ourselves as "more than one" (i.e., wherever there are two or more of us jointly occupying any conceivable location in space-time). The greatest challenge (and the "elephant in the room") for our most mature political forum – the United Nations – is to transcend the competing interests of its constituent members (i.e., nations) in favour of net benefits for the (human) world as a whole. The single greatest obstacle to such utilitarian co-operation is not so much the competing cultural, economic and military priorities of some 192 jostlers; it is, rather, the hands-tied capacity of national representatives to apply common-sense to mutual decision-making because of the domestic accountability of politicians at home (to the ballot box in democracies, or the "might is right" clout of juntas).

---

[136] "Warp-drive" will be familiar to Star Trek devotees as the means by which travel at or beyond the speed of light is achieved. We have been told by Albert Einstein that such movement is impossible because any material object becomes infinitely massive as it approaches 'c' – or 186,000 miles per second; but that hasn't prevented scientists (e.g., Miguel Alcubierre Moya, 1964-) and many others imagining it in science fiction.

"Shocking Family Relationships"

Political challenges are really psychological ones …

We can begin to see how our challenge is less a political one than a psychological one; which is to say, hope for our future lies in our own hearts and minds, and that personal change is possible. If we are to appreciate this better, we need to continue to try to understand how everything got to be as it is (how history brought us here) and how history may be shaped henceforth. This is where we must exercise great caution about the assumptions we bring to bear on how "things" (the ongoing unravelling of history) are "shaped". We have considered the "moral environment" with sincerity and application in Chapter 6. The mainstay of the argument has been that our personal sanity is contingent on the manner in which we process the various "worlds" we inhabit – from the planet through to the smaller domains of nation, town, family and so on – and that there are collective as well as personal responsibilities involved in "getting real" about our social problems (including those that impact on the young especially). We are about to become very specific about how all this happens, and it is pertinent to consider how all of what we "know" already might be reassembled and re-interpreted, if for no other reason than because modern psychology is unfinished and divided or "two-faced" (see Chapter 1). For inspiration in Chapter 6 we presented instances of admirable figures in recent history from each of the seven continents (although we were reluctant to regard them as heroines and heroes) who somehow, or perhaps inevitably, met Tolstoy (and his provocative standard of personal integrity and social courage) at least half way.

… and some of our political challenges are momentous

Now, in the dangerous 21st century, it might well be as much pure and reasoned strategy as hopeless idealism to posit that abandonment of self-interest is the only way we can save ourselves from each other – as long as weapons technology outstrips our capacity for *entente*. After all, the whole of human history is an account of unspeakable violence (as well as the far less frequently recorded but also far weightier instances of simple lovingness that have woven their way through exactly the same chronological accounting period, and which all of us have witnessed). We all benefit from connection and belongingness, and just about anyone who has been in one will testify that everyone loses a war. What human "win-win" constitutes the moral (i.e., having foundation on a principle) reverse of war? Ordinary association underpinned by simple purpose? Even if we are adept at discerning them in others, how well can we discover and remedy madness-inducing ulterior motives in ourselves? In the sense of truth between polarities (Chapter 4) – and psychological place (Chapter 6) – What is the "self"? … What is the "other"? and, What is in between?

Beginning a developmental account of togetherness

Invariably, each of us has had a mother and father (even if *in vitro*) and – in this respect if no other – we have not been entirely self-sufficient (for we did not imagine, design or create ourselves in the first instance). As a matter of fact, and for better or worse, humans somehow have managed to sexually conceive and raise their children in a fairly uncomplicated and unrehearsed way until Sigismund Schlomo (Sigmund) Freud (1856-1939); which is to say, we (*homo sapiens*) got by fine without him from about 200,000 BC (Darwinian Adam and Eve), or 50-70,000 BC ("Out of Africa"), until the turn of the 19th century in Vienna. How and why did Freud stick in his oar with such overstated impact? Whereas Newton's prominence in history was (in his own words as we have seen) attributable to standing "on the shoulders of giants", Freud knew instinctively that to make a splash in the modern world you have to promote sex. Freud's notions of infant sexuality and family relationships were (still are) shocking, but it is his proposed structure of "mind" that we will take most seriously.

From cure to quackery
Freud was a medically trained neurologist. As we have considered, the mores within (Western) physicianship are an enduring legacy from Ancient Greece (Hippocrates of Kos, 460-372 BC) and the Roman Empire (particularly Galen 129-200 AD). Freud was an academically precocious child and adored as the eldest of eight children by his parents (his father having sired two yet older children in an earlier marriage). As Wilhelm Maximilian Wundt (1832-1920) was conceiving experimental psychology in Leipzig in 1879 (see Chapter 1), Freud was approaching graduation as a medical student in Vienna (where his parents had settled after passing through Leipzig from Příbor[137] where Sigismund had been born). In his first training year, Freud was taught by Ernst Wilhelm (Ritter von) Brücke (1819-1892), a physiologist-colleague of Hermann Ludwig von Helmholtz (1821-1894) who, as we saw in Chapter 1, inspired Wundt in matters of science and technology directly. It is at this point that we may, with reasonable assuredness, attribute a "last common ancestor" to the scientific (behaviorist) and analytical traditions within the split and "two-faced" (see Chapter 1) modern discipline that underlies contemporary approaches to psychotherapy. The behaviorist tradition emerged in deep deference to Lloyd Morgan's Canon (see Chapter 2), and may be regarded as "narrower" empirically.

Freud smarter than Newton?
Without adequate scrutiny of history, Freud seems to have emerged from "nowhere" with his beguiling and fascinating model of "mind". His ideas are not attributed retrospectively as we know they should be; indeed, we do not have to delve far to find modern and ancient sources of inspiration for the "Id" (Unconscious), Superego and Ego. Parallels of the three Freudian components of "mind" are seen readily in the "tri-partite soul"[138] of Plato (428-348 BC); whilst the notion of unconscious (or subconscious) psychological "life" was new but common in the 19th century, as evident from William James's reviews[139].

Screwing down the lid
The essence of Freud's ideas about psychopathology is that there is an unconscious component of mind (or "Id") which generates subjectively unacceptable impulses — particularly sexual ones — which are then repressed[140] (or pushed back "down" where they do not have to be recognised or experienced[141]), so creating something of a pressure cooker effect (with the suggestion of strain and the potential for eventual explosion). Another hypothetical component, the Superego, represents the conscience-weight[142] of norms, rules and strictures inculcated in all but feral humans because of culture and upbringing.

---

[137] Příbor was then part of the Austrian Empire, and is now part of the Czech Republic.

[138] Elements of the "tri-partite soul" as presented in *The Republic*, and their Freudian counterparts, are: "Appetitive" (Id), "Rational" (Ego) and "Spirited" (Superego).

[139] *The Principles Of Psychology, Volumes 1 & 2* (1890) by William James (1842-1910)

[140] Repression is a classic ego defence phenomenon along with denial and displacement.

[141] After much navel-gazing in his 40s, Freud is reported to have "uncovered" (in self-analysis) sexual feelings during childhood for his mother and a matching jealousy of his father. Which is more disturbing? Freud's sexual pre-occupation? His insistence that the "Oedipus complex" (corresponding to an "Electra complex" of "penis envy" and father idolation in women) is universal in human childhood? Or that Western society has swallowed that contention hook, line and sinker? What is human prurience actually: has it more to do with the actual or vicarious use of power than sex (see Chapter 7)?

[142] The "weight of human history" (on "conscience") as we have portrayed it hitherto — especially in Chapter 6 — has not (yet) presumed any particular structures of mind for its formation or perpetuation (whether conceptual or physiological). The remaining two Chapters of Part II present further material on such possibilities, including due consideration of how any existing and new propositions may be supported empirically.

Do Freud's progeny attribute their thinking to a "Roman Legacy"
The Roman Baths, Bath, Avon (was Somerset)

Relieving the pressure
As those strictures typically moderate or censure instinctual drives
– particularly the sexual imperative – the Superego plays a crucial
role in repression. Freud's "psychoanalysis"[143] relied on interpreting
the (inaccessible) contents of the Id by indirect means: dreams,
hypnosis and "free association" (from the psychiatrist's couch). The
more these could be brought into the conscious mind (Ego), the better
the psychological prospects for the patient because of the
opportunities thereby presented for achieving intrapsychic alignment
through conflict-resolution and alleviation of emotional constraint.

Poetry, not science
Although Freud sought scientific corroboration for psychoanalysis,
strictly it is not scientific at all. It is exceptionally "top down",
and extreme in its abject powerlessness to attract concrete evidence
– whether for the existence of inaccessible components of mind *per
se*, or, for the efficacy of psychoanalysis in promoting personal
sanity[144]. We shall see that parsimony may guide our footsteps nearer
to a simpler and more satisfying account of the pressure cooker we
all know. Although successful (seemingly having acquired both
reputation and significant wealth) during his own lifetime, Freud
suffered dreadfully during the rise of the Nazis in the 1930s, and
later with oral cancer because of heavy use of cigars. His eventual
suicide in 1939 was "assisted" by a friend, Max Schur (1897-1969),
who administered fatal doses of morphine in London where Freud had
settled in 1938 having escaped persecution by the Gestapo. All of
Freud's several sisters were killed in the Holocaust. Freud's views
of family relationships – particularly incest – and his insistence on
the formation of "neurosis" during the developmental years (including
early infanthood, i.e., "pre-verbally") – have precipitated a deep
vulnerability in modern psychotherapy itself. This is its capacity
for sustaining psychological sickness in patients (for that is the
correct term for any helpee in any "medical" setting) because of the
distressed person's capacity for blaming parents when – even if such
blame be quite deserved in some cases – the analysand's worst
psychological enemy may be entrenched resentment or hatred fuelled
and protected by the doctor. Freud was less a scientist than a poet.

Doctor-disciples
Freud's most renowned doctor–cum–disciple was Carl Gustav Jung (1875-
1961). We shall consider key features of this man's particular stance
on human personality prior to detailed consideration of another
underestimated physician–psychoanalyst. Eric Berne (whom we shall
consider shortly) was an extraordinarily insightful psychiatrist who
claimed relationships as his speciality – including their deleterious
contamination with ulterior motives and "games". Unjustifiably
oblique amongst the ancestors of modern psychotherapists, none stands
quite as tall as Berne in his appreciation of what psychology is
really about (the first and closing sentences of Chapter 1 refer);
nor what lies in the psychological space between individuals engaged
with each other in our personal tussles for survival, reproduction
and individual purposefulness (necessarily counterbalanced with our
equally natural propensity for amenable engagement with each other).

---

[143] Although Freud's "baby", psychoanalysis was developed originally by a friend, Josef
Breuer (1842-1925), as a "talking cure" for "Anna O" (Bertha Pappenheim, 1859-1936).

[144] There are protagonists both for and against Freud. Scientifically speaking, and
according to Sir Karl Raimund Popper (1902-1994 – also an Austrian by birth and a
refugee from Nazi persecution just before World War II), Freud's ideas are not truly
testable; e.g., the Id is not falsifiable. It can hardly be any surprise, then, that
any favourable effects of psychotherapy may be accounted for by some other phenomenon
– especially the power of suggestion (confidence-trickery), and spontaneous recovery.

"Tall"
Eric Berne (1910–1970)

Freud and Jung tête-à-tête like Wundt and Külpe
Carl Jung, based at the Burghölzli University Hospital in Zurich[145], had heard about the new (Freudian) psychoanalysis from another Swiss psychiatrist, Paul Eugen Bleuler (1857-1939)[146]. Bleuler had taken a keen interest in Freud's work because of the supposed relevance of intricate machinations of the unconscious mind in mental illness – an instance of how the "hidden mind" was then fashionable amongst Freud's contemporaries. (Although Bleuler helped spread the tidings of psychoanalysis, he was later to reject it.) Jung and Freud corresponded intensively for some six years after exchanging notes and essays in the early 20th century when psychology (and hence psychiatry) was as yet an undeveloped discipline (for psychoanalysis had not yet acquired roots, let alone spread culturally the way it has today). Although Freud and Jung travelled to the United States of America together (with Sándor Ferenczi, 1873-1933) to spread their nascent gospel of the unconscious, they fell out[147] over religion and sex or – more correctly – the matter of "libido" (generalised psychic energy, originating in the Id according to Freud, and underpinning Jung's theories of personality development). But it was Jung's open-mindedness in matters beyond the immediate medical environment, across the arts and culture broadly (encompassing Eastern mysticism), that marked the greatest difference with Freud who incidentally, like Bleuler, considered Jung's recognition of a religious or "spiritual" dimension in human psychology "unscientific"[148]. Freud and Jung met hardly at all after the onset of the Great War. Both were somewhat preoccupied with their own emotional conflicts and traumas during their lifetimes: Freud with psychosomatic (digestive) ailments and his own mortality; Jung with identity partitions during childhood, extra-marital affairs (involving patients) and late-life isolation.

Physician, "Heal thyself"[149]
Whilst the disinterment of our dear ancestors' foibles could betray "moral error" (on the grounds that it could serve no purpose other than to reinforce, possibly by "projection", the "moral inferiority" of the prurient inquisitor), it should escape neither our notice – nor explicit noting for the record – that these physicians were quite unable to "fix" themselves armed with the new emotional "science". Psychoanalysis has never achieved, as a theory of (psycho)pathology or (psycho)therapy, anywhere near the impact of analogous discoveries in non-psychological medicine; e.g., "germs" in pathogenesis (Jaques aka Louis Pasteur, 1822-1895); inoculation in acquiring immunity (Edward Anthony Jenner, 1749-1823), or penicillin in remedy or "cure" (Sir Alexander Fleming, 1881-1955). We must not assume, merely because psychoanalysis has become famous, widespread – or very well-established as a professional industry – that it actually "works".

---

[145] Associated with several auspicious names in psychological medicine, the Burghölzli was well known to a patient, Eduard Einstein (1910-1965), son of the famous physicist.

[146] Bleuler is known for having coined the term "schizophrenia" as a replacement for *dementia praecox* on the basis that what we now refer to as psychotic illnesses (characterised by reality-disturbances in the form of hallucinations and delusions) were neither dementias (cognitive deficits with the connotation of brain erosion) nor confined to young people (although modern psychiatrists focus on "early intervention" – or treatment as soon as possible after identification – especially in young adults).

[147] reminiscent of Wundt and Külpe's divergence over "imageless thought" (Chapter 2)

[148] ironic given the basis upon which Freud has been regarded with contempt by certain psychologists closer to the positivist tradition – notably Hans Eysenck (Chapter 3)

[149] Often interpreted as an exhortation against hypocrisy – to "remove the plank from one's own eye"; indeed, the expression is New Testament in origin, and prophetic from Jesus Christ regarding his own crucifixion when he would be taunted, "Save yourself". Colloquially the medical profession has too much of a tendency to play / act like God.

"Taunted": an early 18th century gravestone located at
Camas nan Geall burial-ground, Ardnamurchan, Scotland

Templates for the organisation of experience
Whereas, for Freud, the volcanic pressure from the unconscious mind
threatens eruption of all that is psychologically smouldering and
dark, for Jung the unconscious mind possesses another altogether less
sinister set of attributes. In it (at some unidentified location,
scientifically speaking) resides the repository of "archetypes", or
latent templates that afford structure to empirical experience.
According to Jung, these archetypes are inherited in all creatures
with a nervous system (implying a substrate involving neurons – even
synapses). They are, thereby, universal in humans; although latent in
the sense that they require (personal and biographically unique)
experience for their functional expression. These archetypes are
known as the "collective unconscious", and may be disambiguated from
the "cultural inheritance" specific to a place and time in history
(broadly the "moral environment" discussed in Chapter 6, although we
have not yet said very much about its chronological transmission) and
also the "collective consciousness" of Émile Durkheim (1858–1917);
i.e., the shared and unifying standards of a contemporary culture.

The Jungian "self" and "individuation"
The Jungian "collective unconscious", in combination with the
"personal unconscious" (biographically repressed material), finds
expression in the conscious mind (I, Ich or Ego) in the form of
fantasies and dreams, and may be probed (as in Freudian
psychoanalysis) with "word association" prompts and other indirect
techniques for detection of its contents and psychological motility.
The "collective unconscious" includes an opposite-sex archetype known
as the anima (inner feminine identity) in males and animus in women
(inner male identity)[150]. It also possesses a (creative) layered
"shadow" which is close to the Freudian concept of psychological dark
matter. Whereas the shadow's upper strata are recently recorded and
personally unique, the remainder is ancient (in evolutionary terms)
and inaccessible. For Jung, the process of attaining maturity – or
"individuation" – involves the recognition and assimilation of all of
these elements of the unconscious, blended with the conscious mind,
into the overall archetype which is the "self"[151]. Thus, whereas for
Freud the foreboding and murky unconscious mind is made of repressed
and undesirable detritus, the entire Jungian identity is like a
sophisticated, sagacious benefactor, prompting its subject towards
ever-expanding possibilities of personal and "spiritual" growth.

Still not convinced of personality "types"
If Freud was more poet than scientist, Jung was more soothsayer than
poet, in that his ideas speak more chimingly about the "inner world"
of subjective experience to a wider human audience. Jung's version of
the analysable "self" is barely more testable than Freud's – just
more compelling. Unfortunately it loses its technical appeal in its
promulgation of a new hierarchy of personality "types" which we first
encountered at the end of Chapter 3 in the form of the Myers-Briggs
Type Indicator (or MBTI). The pigeonholing of our fellow human beings
may afford temporary intellectual satisfaction, but no-one really
believes in such compartmentalisation of ourselves (or our nearest
and dearest). In health and occupational screening environments, it
can be positively misleading. This is not to say that people can come
to very sensible (categorical) conclusions about themselves: "I am
quite sun-kissed enough, and should spend no longer tanning myself
unless I wish to court skin lesions or other nasty health problems."

---

[150] Although translating loosely as "On The Soul", in *De Anima*, Aristotle (384–322 BC)
wrote of the "essence" of various living things based on their particular functions.

[151] The accessible and salient archetype, "Ego", may also be referred to as the "self".

"Smouldering, Dark And Volcanic"
Ben Hiant, Ardnamurchan, Scotland

The "intuitive" Eric Berne: son, psychiatrist, soldier
In the opening remarks of Chapter 1, psychology was introduced as an ancient human undertaking or pursuit in which motives surely played a central part. Eric Berne's Transactional Analysis (TA) is the closest there is in modern psychology to a formal theory of ulterior motives. TA is a spin-off from or heir to Freudian concepts of human "mind"; in particular, its inaccessible (and untestable as we have seen in a recent footnote) structures. Eric Berne was a psychoanalytically-trained physician-psychiatrist like Sigmund Freud and Carl Jung; moreover, his inspiration seems clearly attributable to this heritage combined with his own imagination. How far was the development of TA coloured by its founder's own personality and biography? Eric Lennard Bernstein (1910-1970) was born in Montreal, Canada to a physician (David Hiller Bernstein) and a writer (Sarah Gordon). Eric's father died of tuberculosis in 1921 – before Eric was a teenager – and, seemingly, the boy took it hard. Following in the paternal footsteps, Eric went up to the Faculty of Medicine, McGill University, Montreal. After medical training he migrated to the USA in furtherance of his career. Having changed his name from Eric Lennard Bernstein to Eric Berne at around the outbreak of hostilities (World War II), he rose to the rank of Major in the US Army's Medical Corps where he was employed as a psychiatrist. Now thricefold imbued with presumptions of human authority from medical training, military culture and connections with the fast-travelling edicts of Freud, Berne developed a theory of "intuition" based on his knack of being able to discern the civilian occupations of soldiers returning home from war within a moment or two of a first encounter. Relying on a couple of sharp prompts: "Are you nervous?" and "Have you ever seen a psychiatrist?", Berne racked up confidence in the accuracy of his interpretation of subtle, non-verbal cues – corroborated following triangulation with the Army troops' medical records to which he had legitimate access. Today's TA practitioners place significant store on the "diagnosis" of "ego states" in their clients – founded on their sharply-honed capacity for interpreting subtlety – as we shall appreciate shortly.

Eric Berne's other relationships: analysand, husband, father
During the Second World War, from about 1941, Eric Berne had been an analysand of Paul Federn (1871-1950)[152], a famously loyal devotee of Freud's in Vienna. Around this time Eric was newly married to his first wife, Elinor, with whom he had two children. After the War (for about two years from 1947) Berne resumed analysis under Erik Erikson (1902-1994 – famous for having coined "identity crisis") at the San Francisco Psychoanalytic Institute (SFPI). It was Erikson who refused to "give Berne away" to his second wife (Dorothy de Mass Way) until Erikson deemed Berne ready in 1949. Eric and Dorothy had two children of their own to add to the three older children Dorothy brought to the marriage. Having wed and divorced three times by the end of his life, Berne eventually succumbed to several heart attacks in his 61st year. As we saw in (a footnote to) Chapter 7, Coronary Heart Disease (CHD) is the pathological hallmark of the overdriven workaholic, all at once compensating for an inferiority complex and striving for a sense of place in the world. Transactional Analysis would never have existed but for Berne's rejection by the SFPI who, in 1956, refused his membership application on the basis that only in further years might he be ready for it. Berne's response was to develop a theoretical approach of his own. This triumph was a manifest-instance of the "recognition-hunger" he experienced and wrote about so well.

---

[152] Having both published an article (*Narcissism in the structure of the ego*, 1928) and accused post-war America (after his emigration there in 1938) of "parricide" for its rejection of authority in society – the Austrian psychoanalyst and Freud-devotee Paul Federn committed suicide in 1950 after what he believed was a recurrence of cancer.

What did Eric Berne mean by "ego states"?

Eric Berne's legacy from Sigmund Freud was inherited via Paul Federn; as we know, Eric Berne's analyst for two years from the time that the Second World War commenced from an American standpoint (1941) until Eric's sojourn in the US Army (1943-1946). It is only in tracing this lineage that we can appreciate conceptually how the ego states - the very foundations of TA theory - came to exist in Berne's mind at all. First, consider the "Ego" from Freud's standpoint. Absent at birth, it develops like a protective skin around the Id from, say, about the third year of life whereafter it becomes an agent of repression - diverting and redistributing libido ("cathecting" and "re-cathecting" psychic energy). Its role is to "deal with" reality (a task whose value the Id fails to appreciate with any kind of deference at all). In this activity[153] it is assisted by safe and guiding environment of the relationship with the primary caregiver[154] - but compromised by (on the one hand) the instinctual, demanding and amoral substructure of the personality (the submerged part of the iceberg that is the Id) and the precepts of the (morally superior) Superego (on the other). In this conceptual arrangement a variety of "ego states" are possible depending on the maturational experience of the child, and how the person in question winds up relating to the outside world and its other inhabitants over the developmental years to come. In "ego[155] psychology", the condition of the ego thus emerging may be expressed along such dimensions as: strong versus weak; reaching out versus reaching in, and strength of binding to the Superego. An individual who had learned emotional self-reliance because of lack of nurturing in the early years - but had maintained a robust inner conscious life having exercised a distinctive personal ambition - may have been described as having had a "narcissistic" ego state or personality. Paul Federn's approach to ego psychology may be contrasted with that of Heinz Hartmann (1894-1970)[156] who was disposed to consider the ego in terms of its "adaptation" during maturation on a dimension from conflicted to unencumbered (by the Id) or autonomous. Paul Federn was more concerned with the ego's essence, defining it in terms of its own sense of self: *Ich bin Ich selbst* (I am I myself)[157]. Expressed as idiosyncrasies amongst Sigmund's disciples, the emphases on the ego's reality-testing function, its "ego feeling" and the "ego states" were Federn's work rather than Freud's. As we have intimated, Federn was loyal - prepared to hide his light under a bushel for the sake of the master's reputation (although it seems just as likely, given Freud's opinions of his apprentice's heresies, that he may have been just as anxious to avoid Sigmund's disapproval). We can only imagine the interplay of biographies and personalities that must have taken place between Federn and Berne during Eric's analysis (not forgetting Erikson in the mix); however, we know that the real impetus for the development of TA came from Berne's rejection by the SFPI. At this point, Berne's creative energies must have been provoked to a pique. What has become of TA since? Would Eric recognise his own TA "baby"?

---

[153] True to Freud (as distinct from alternative approaches), we are correct to consider the Ego as a dynamic agency rather than as merely a sitting, passive mental structure.

[154] usually, of course, the mother because of the bond established prior to parturition - and its continuity by dint of her capacity for feeding the infant from her own body

[155] As soon as it becomes possible that Freud would no longer recognise his own concept, we drop the capital letter to denote the variant (i.e., now ego versus Ego).

[156] like Eysenck, Freud and many other Jews - another unfortunate who fled continental Europe to escape Hitler (having left Austria in 1938 - arriving in New York in 1941)

[157] see also Federn, P. (1929) Das ich als subjekt und objekt im narzissmus. (The ego as subject and object in narcissism.) *International Journal Of Psychoanalysis, XV*, 4.

Formal definitions of the TA ego states
According to Ian Stewart and Vann Joines (1987)[158]:

An "ego state" is a set of related behaviors, thoughts and feelings. It is a way in which we manifest a part of our personality at a given time …

If I am behaving, thinking and feeling in response to what is going on around me here and now, using all the resources available to me as a grown-up person, I am said to be in my Adult ego state …

At times, I may behave, think and feel in ways which are a copy of one of my parents, or of others who were parent-figures for me. When I do so, I am said to be in my Parent ego state …

Sometimes I may return to ways of behaving, thinking and feeling which I used when I was a child. Then I am said to be in my Child ego state …

The ego state model is often known … as the P-A-C model, after these three initial letters …

When we use the ego state model to understand various aspects of personality, we are said to be employing structural analysis.

Structural model of the TA ego states (first order)
The basic (first order) structural model is one that simply shows the three ego states. In TA they are usually shown as stacked circles.

STRUCTURAL MODEL OF THE TA EGO STATES (FIRST ORDER)

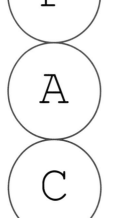

PARENT EGO STATE
thinking, feeling and behaviour imparted
from parents and other authority figures

ADULT EGO STATE
thinking, feeling and behaviour relevant to
solving problems rationally here and now...

CHILD EGO STATE
thinking, feeling and behaviour reiterated
from childhood, as if we were children now

---

[158] Stewart I. & Joines, V.S. (1987) *TA Today: A New Introduction To Transactional Analysis.* Lifespace: Nottingham (Chapter 1, p.4)

No deliberate fugues
Now, it is crucial (unless we wish to run away with ourselves) to appreciate that the TA ego states are merely inferred from behaviour, which is to say that they are not "real", except in so far as we may (in some or other future) discover them materialised in some identifiable and intractable component(s) of our mental structure, or it becomes blatantly churlish to resist an entire raft of behavioural evidence. In TA, the ways and means of "diagnosing" ego states are stated formally[159], and include: observable behaviour (what is said and how it is said along with non-verbal indications such as posture, gestures and facial expressions) together with – for corroboration – social cues (scrutiny of styles of interaction); historical data (exploring situations in which ego states were supposedly fashioned), and phenomenology (rehearsal of those old scenarios in the present).

Check-up from the neck up
The reader is quite capable of evaluating the nature and relevance of these fundamental TA concepts. Check yourself several times in the next few hours (assuming you have the benefit of human company and the inclination): can you readily establish that your mindset at any given moment (especially in relationship with another person), and the behaviour that accompanies that mindset (especially the style of your engagement with someone else) matches one of Parent, Adult or Child? Try to avoid contempt prior to investigation (see Chapter 5).

Health warning
Clearly, there is no such thing as a literal (biological or any other strictly "scientific") account of the formation of the ego states; nevertheless, a great deal indeed is assumed in TA about the way they are formed developmentally. This is where, juxtaposing wet metaphors (but we may avoid a watery grave in the process), TA simultaneously:

sails uncharted seas – and very elegantly too – because it generates explanations of behaviour patterns (including thoughts and feelings) unmatched in any other paradigm including "narrowly" empirical ones;

yet,

skates ambitiously on shimmeringly thin ice – especially in its psychotherapeutic mode – because, like psychoanalysis before it, it too easily attributes psychopathology to the impact of significant others (parents), when no such influences may have prevailed *de facto* (in "science" as it were). Even supposing they did, there are always (as we suggested earlier) two sides to every coin; i.e., the parents' version of expired "reality" to take into account. Finally but most importantly of all as far as the sanity of the client is concerned – the interpretation of problems based on the family history serves to perpetuate emotional sickness exactly to the extent that resentments (especially if founded on denial – or "discounting" in TA) are left unneutralised or (worse) fed with milky tea and misguided sympathy. A reassuring majority of TA practitioners (as well as counsellors, psychotherapists and psychological helpers in other specialities) will claim an adequate appreciation of (if not a deep identification with) the avoidance, at all costs, of self-victimisation in clients; nevertheless, how many of these as a first resort seek to eliminate resentments and hatreds as a foremost probable source of insanity[160]?

---

[159] For a formal (and accessible) account of Transactional Analysis as it has navigated from the 20th to the 21st century the reader is referred to Stewart I. & Joines, V.S. (1987) *TA Today: A New Introduction To Transactional Analysis*. Lifespace: Nottingham.

[160] Already a well-established position in certain quarters of thinking about emotional health, the case continues to be made – especially in Chapter 9, "A moral psychology".

A word to the wise
In matters psychological and psychotherapeutic, it is both judicious
and prudent to pre-empt any serious misunderstandings that may arise
about the relationship between personal sanity and personal
responsibility. There is always a tendency for psychologically sick
people to blame others, for inevitably there is a distortion of
perception around personal responsibility in any psychopathology. A
sense of persecution or victimisation is always accompanied by the
comforting and thumb-sucking tendency towards "self-pity". This is a
most useless commodity as no benefits may accrue at all from its
examination or analysis. It is worthy only of abandonment, and can be
"kicked into touch" quite easily by anybody willing to administer the
punt. This doesn't mean that an insane or sick person has never been
hard done to; nor that other people weren't ever at fault in relation
to what has happened (that shouldn't) in their lives; indeed, not
happened (that should). It doesn't mean that living isn't in some
ways and at some times a harsh and "unfair" undertaking (for we all
have undertaken it even though not one of us chose to be born). In
many cases of mishandling by others, we may relieve ourselves of much
of our sense of engulfment or grievance by realising that our
persecutors were probably once treated that way themselves - perhaps
even more harshly - and simply have not managed to break the spell.
Perhaps they were sick themselves. Perhaps they were provoked by us.
We shall revisit all of this on later pages. True evil is rare in
humanity, although it does happen, and it *is* recognisably terrible.
But it *is* in the very handling of all such challenges that personal
sanity stands, becomes unreachable or fails us altogether. By all
(TA) accounts, this is a process that begins very early in a life.

Give the bottle to the baby: the TA "life script"
Now, our basic instincts confer upon us (at no matter what age) an
immense intrinsic pressure to seek out and establish those things
(including intangibles such as psychological security, or freedom
from fear) which we know intuitively we must have to survive and
thrive. TA refers to all these things as "survival needs", and the
infant is "powerless" in that it relies on significant others; i.e.,
parents and other authority figures, to satisfy them. The infant also
"realises" that there is a complex of laws, rules or principles "out
there" which seems to govern whether it does or doesn't get what it
thinks it needs (and whether it doesn't or does get what it thinks it
doesn't need). The infant also has, seemingly, an innate capacity for
discerning (in at least a diffuse manner) a relationship between its
own behaviour and all of those vital happenings. Accordingly, the
infant makes "early decisions" that it perceives to be favourable
regards acquiring what it wants (and avoiding what it doesn't). This
amounts to a compulsion to match personal behaviour to conditions
laid down explicitly or implicitly by caregivers such as parents and
other significant authority figures. The infant decisions are always
self-limiting and involve the yielding of small and larger measures
of what TA refers to as "autonomy" (shall we say, the free and
unconstrained expression of "self" in subjective experience, desires,
fears and behaviour). The aggregate of these trade-offs is the "life
script" and, whilst it is formed in the same way for each person, it
tells a different story according to each infant's early biography -
particularly its exposure to parental "injunctions". These are those
emanated implicit and explicit "pre-verbal" (referring to that period
prior to which the child has the use of language - typically the
first year or two according to interpretation), verbal and non-verbal
messages which are assimilated by the infant as relevant to its
safety and care. Although the parents emit "permissions" ("It's OK to
…") as well as "injunctions" ("Don't …"), it is the injunctions that
hold sway because they have the greater perceived effect on spoils.

Twelve injunctions from Bob and Mary[161]
The 12 injunctions recognised in TA theory are:

Don't be (or exist)

Don't be you (or who you are)

Don't be a child

Don't grow up (or be sexy)

Don't make it (or be successful)

Don't (do anything)

Don't be important (or ask for what you want)

Don't belong

Don't be close (or trust)

Don't be well (or be sane)

Don't think

Don't feel

There are 12 injunctions because TA, as a body, is assumed to agree on the number consensually after Bob and Mary Goulding (née Edwards) who first presented them based on experience in therapeutic practice. The number has not been determined empirically; e.g., statistically. We might infer that these represent 12 typical ways in which clients in TA psychotherapy felt imposed upon in their younger lives as far as they can remember. Perhaps they also represent ways in which – stereotypically – we boss each other about in our adult lives now.

Inheritance: Claude Steiner's script matrix
TA aficionados would be unsurprised by such a notion, because they consider that the injunctions that they received as children emanated from their parents' Child ego states, and are stored faithfully in their own to be imparted to future generations (as, too, were the permissions; however, as we have intimated, these have less force generating emotional disturbance, and may even be employed remedially in TA psychotherapy). In TA theory, the parents also "transmit" from their Adult ego state to their offspring a host of "Here's how to …" modelling behaviours. TA supposes that these will be good examples because the Adult ego state is rational – unless the transmitting Adult is "contaminated" by the parent's Child or Parent, in which case the "Program" can be faulty (rendering the disadvantaged offspring a candidate for TA psychotherapy in the years to come). Counterinjunctions are the Parent ego state messages assimilated by the developing child to manage the injunctions with which it is already familiar. Because in early TA it was supposed that these are harnessed by the script-authoring child to manage the injunctions – in some manner functioning as their counterpoint – they were mooted as "counterinjunctions". In practice, they tend to be semantically aligned with the injunctions themselves; for instance, the injunction "Don't think" when it is accompanied by counterinjunctions such as "Hurry up" and "Do as you're told". This entire process is represented in the "script matrix"[162] attributed to Claude Steiner (1935-, probably Eric Berne's principal disciple and personal fan).

---

[161] Goulding, R. and Goulding, M. (1979) *Changing Lives Through Redecision Therapy.* Brunner-Mazel: New York

[162] Steiner, C. (1966) Script and counterscript. *Transactional Analysis Bulletin, 5:18,* 133-135.

CLAUDE STEINER'S SCRIPT MATRIX

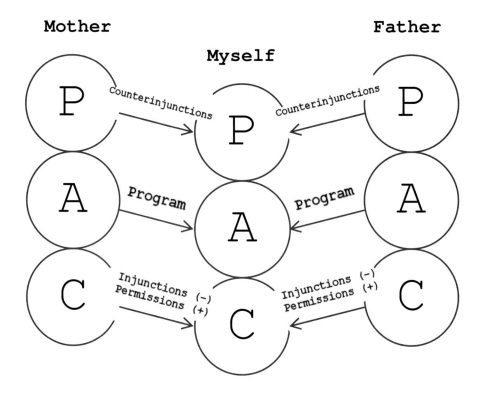

TA baby and TA bath water
TA protagonists are not wholly reconciled on the developmental point
at which Parent comes into existence, from which it follows that they
do not know what it is made of in biological terms, whether it is
physiologically as well as conceptually discriminable (from Child and
Adult), and therefore cannot determine whether it is pre-formed by
way of template or "archetype" – whether biologically via DNA, or in
any other conceptual or spiritual manner. Eric Berne was clear that
the Parent and Adult ego states come into existence after the first
few years of life (like the Ego in classical Freudian theory of
development of the personality structure), whereas "newer" TA
theorists (such as Tony White) have defended a two ego-state model in
which: (i) Parent exists early like Child; (ii) the Adult ego state
is incorporated within Parent, and (iii) instructional "tapes" are
lodged within Child as well as Parent. Without getting bogged down in
intra-discipline differences of viewpoint (which are merely *bona fide*
efforts to project TA forward usefully) we may note that Claude
Steiner, at his personal online resource, anticipates as "sweet news"
the possible eventual mapping of TA ego states onto phylogenetically
identifiable components of the central nervous system (which he
refers to as the "triune brain"). It may not be necessary to effect
such an accomplishment to establish TA's empirical credentials, as we
shall see. We discard the TA baby with the TA bath water (various
ambiguities) at our own cost; moreover, by the close of Part II, we
shall have hung many of ours and TA's hopes on one testable coat peg.

Structural model of the ego states (second order)
The mechanics of script formation are appreciated even more fully
with reference to a second order structural model of the ego states.

STRUCTURAL MODEL OF THE TA EGO STATES (SECOND ORDER)

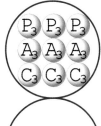

PARENT EGO STATE   (P_2)
assimilates parents and significant others as
introjects on the basis of counterinjunctions

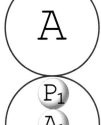

ADULT EGO STATE   (A_2)
thinking, feeling and behaviour relevant to
solving problems rationally here and now...

CHILD EGO STATE   (C_2)
processes injunctions and permissions early
(pre-verbal) and later (verbal and non-
verbal), effecting "early decisions" (in A_1)

Penetrating, mordant and caustic swine
In TA, the "script proper" is the overarching term for the "life
script" together with all of the parental injunctions and permissions
- transmitted as we have seen from the parents' Child ego state to
the offspring's own Child. The "life script" is formed from birth to
around two years - when injunctions are "pre-verbal" - and then up to
age around seven[163] when the counterinjunctions are well in play. This
coincides with P_2 formation in the offspring, and the experience of
significant others is recorded as a set of P_3, A_3, C_3 stacks in P_2.
The term "introject" is used to describe the "swallowing whole" of a
significant other, after which the subjective mental experience of
that person will be integrated and salient. In the early years, the
parental influence is confined to P_1 in C_2 (i.e., it represents the
pre-verbal injunctions). P_1, which endures throughout life, is known
as the "pig parent" as it is more penetrating, mordant and caustic
than P_2. Clients in TA psychotherapy report that P_1 is powerful, and
felt "corporally", as distinct from the "verbal" messages emanating
from P_2 which are readily experienced "aurally", as a critical voice.

---

[163] Jean Piaget (1896-1980) described the developmental phase up to two years of age as
"sensori-motor", and from two to seven years as "pre-operational". The expression to
the effect, "Give me a child until he is seven and I will give you the man" -
attributed to the Jesuits in general and occasionally to Saint Francis Xavier
(Francisco de Jaso y Azpilicueta, 1506-1552), co-founder of the Society of Jesus with
Saint Ignatius of Loyola (Ignacio López de Loyola, 1491-1556) - is widely regarded as
a truism, even if an uncomfortable one for one reason or another. Actually, Jesuits
historically have regarded children fit for schooling only from the age of about seven
prior to which they are better raised by nannies than schoolmasters (*Ratio Studiorum*).

The TA Parent ego state as "conscience"
As the authority figures' messages are usually imperative – and often powerful – they create subjectively-experienced, intrapsychic tension which is typically towards compliance. We have said that P_2 is an "aural" experience, and you can test yourself regarding whether it is not difficult to "replay" such critical voices in your imagination[164]. If this is a struggle, try it again when next you are confronted with any dilemma, when you may not have to try at all, merely recognise. The Parent "nag" addresses the Child ego state and invites a response. It is thus an intrapsychic form of address, and we see at once how "talking to yourself" has the proverbial distinction of indicating "the first sign of madness". In the TA second order structural model – which, we do very well to remind ourselves, is "top down" in the empirical sense (i.e. poetry awaiting corroboration scientifically) – the offspring already possesses an "electrode" of the parents' injunctions represented by the P_1, A_1, C_1 stack. P_1 is of significant interest here. In TA this "pig" or "witch" parent has the faculty of "magical thinking". It does this as if to "rationalise" the wordless, imperious, motivational harrying that billows from the stored injunctions. The magical thinking thus takes the form, "I'm not at all sure why I have to obey this command but if I am sane I will have a rationale for my actions and here it is …". One can see here the scope for children "inventing" fantasies of parental abuse – whether verbal or non-verbal – and whether trivial or more serious[165]. The matter raises again the importance of triangulation with parents' accounts of history wherever objectivity is called for. The pressure of TA "conscience" may have force through the combined effect of both P_2 and P_1 (the latter experienced more as a kinaesthetic nudge as we have suggested). The TA Parent ego state (P_3 in P_2, with or without P_1) is now not just reminiscent of Freud's Superego, but is another way of understanding "conscience" in addition to the ones already presented in Chapter 5 (where the behaviorists' view of conscience as juvenile conditioned fear and the religious view of conscience as the metaphysical guidance of the Cartesian mind or soul were presented).

The (re-)formation of TA conscience with the passage of time
At any given moment (t1), biographically speaking, the Parent ego state (P_2) may address Child (C_2) where Child "decides" what to do with that message. The subject may also endeavour to assimilate (and make sense of) the conscience-pressure P_1. By a subsequent time (t2), P_2 has been updated to accommodate new experiences (including fresh counterinjunctions), whilst C_2 has updated itself with "decisions". Allowing the possibility of C_2 having the capacity for "dialogue" with P_2 (as distinct from mere exposure to "monologue" from P_2 to C_2), P_2 will be updated intrapsychically. Throughout the whole (iterative) process, monitoring and reality-testing is at A_2, whose efficacy will be determined partly by its capacity for remaining independent of (or uncontaminated by) Parent (P_2) and Child (C_2). (Contaminations may be represented by overlapping ego states diagrammatically, and can be diagnosed and treated in therapy.) Now, the extent to which Child (and Adult) "decisions" can "re-write" (or otherwise compensate for the now disobliging effects of) the Parent ego state (whether P_2 or the electrode P_1) is a pre-requisite for restoration of personal sanity within a TA framework, and beseeches empirical confirmation.

---

[164] See also the Table "Variations within the classical conditioning paradigm" on p.12.

[165] The interested reader may wish to pursue Freud's "seduction theory" of hysteria and obsessional neurosis. Early in his career, Freud claimed that all such emotional conflicts arose out of repressed and actual experiences of childhood sexual abuse. Later he was to retract this position conceding that such experiences, although real psychologically (repressed), could be imagined. The issue was to divide his followers.

Existential "OK-ness"

In Chapter 5, we encountered existentialism – which may be regarded as a school within philosophy that recognises humankind's struggle to meet the absurdity of existence and find personal meaning and purpose within their own (a post-Enlightenment supposition that one cannot "reason" one's way into meaningful engagement with life as it presents itself or really is, nor towards a rational belief in or relationship with God). In TA theory, the laying down of the "life script" is associated with an "existential life position", speaking to the extent to which a person perceives themselves and others as "OK". TA "OK-ness" resembles classical definitions of "attitude" in the psychological literature[166] which invariably include a reference to the favourability or unfavourability of the object about which an attitude is held. Whether I am OK, and whether you are OK, matters to me because my position affects my psychological quality of life. Without generating complex alternatives, there are four permutations of personal and interpersonal OK-ness denoted as follows: the healthy I+U+ (I'm OK and you're OK); I+U- (I'm OK, but you're not); I-U+ (I'm not OK, but you are) and I-U- (I'm not OK, and neither are you). TA has not aligned itself internally on whether the basic life position that a person possesses precedes and informs the infant early decisions, or whether the early decisions inform the life position[167].

Conditional "OK-ness": driven to distraction

When things are not "OK", humans are driven naturally to remedy their condition by behaving in ways that restore OK-ness. Now this looks much like classic "drive"[168], and is also reminiscent of the manner in which we have depicted (existential) "emptiness", and the ways in which we may compensate for it. We shall reconsider this fully in the next chapter ("A moral psychology"). In the meantime, we may note that TA has identified in the same way as it has the injunctions (i.e., on the basis of experience in clinical practice rather than empirically) five "drivers" that can be discerned readily by anyone with a TA-conditioned eye. These drivers may be considered as the behavioural response to the tonally urgent counterinjunctions stored in the offspring's Parent ego state (the P_3, A_3, C_3 stacks in P_2) and which bear the effective message, "You are not OK unless you …":

Be Strong
      Be Perfect
            Try Hard
                  Hurry Up
                        Please Others

Whilst all five of the drivers can be experienced by any one person depending on the stressors present in a situation, an individual typically displays a "favourite" two or three which compete for prominence. They can be discerned in microcosmic instances of the script; aka the "miniscript" – a person's moment-by-moment behaviour.

---

[166] e.g., Fishbein, M. and Ajzen, I. (1975) *Belief, Attitude, Intention, And Behavior: An Introduction To Theory And Research*. Addison-Wesley: Reading

[167] Whereas Eric Berne considered the early decisions primary, and the life position assumed later, Claude Steiner sees the life position assumed as early as (feeding at) the breast. To demonstrate that the existential life position precedes the early decisions it will be necessary to demonstrate that some other discriminable and non-decisional neonatal psychological process or shift establishes the existential default (assuming that the life position is not wholly genetic). Accounting for the life position on the basis of a non-language-contingent facility with no other defining properties may not cut the mustard since early decisions themselves are "pre-verbal".

[168] An old notion in psychology related to the principle of homeostasis, "drive" is the tension that motivates an organism to restore imbalances in its (biological) systems.

An idiosyncratic control complex
In the aggregate, a person's drivers fuel an idiosyncratic control complex in which the subject is compelled to satisfy the conditional "OK-ness" determined by the counterinjunctions (stored in P_2). This inevitably involves the experience of unpleasant or aversive feelings matching those spawned during all the historic instances of autonomy-yielding during script formation. The problem with this (driver) process lies in the extent to which the person at the centre of things falls quarry to their own character formation, because they cannot "see" how their own driver behaviour, experienced as emotional tension, is not *bona fide* (associated with autonomy and an "OK" life position) but, rather, spurious in the sense that its very existence is for conformity with an old compromised (or "not OK") existential footing. Of course, in the present, we rationalise and justify our every move. This is how character defects (psychological mutton) may be very eagerly dressed as virtues (lamb scented with self-effacing rosemary); e.g., impatience attributed to ambition and determination. Now, this is most reminiscent of the concept of "spiritual blindness" introduced resolutely in the Preface and expanded upon in Chapter 4 ("Inside The Machine"). If we can't see ourselves transpicuously and modestly, or don't always have the willingness to do so, we may need others to hold to us a "spiritual mirror" for our own elucidation[169].

Layers of obfuscation
Ironically, in TA, these inauthentic feelings are called "rackets", and they rest on the bedrock of our untrammelled selves in layers of behavioural obfuscation. Skilled TA practitioners are equipped with mighty tools and machinery for penetrating these to get to the heart of your problems, but you may be wary of soliciting the process as it may feel quite raw at the roots. Therein lies a secondary (to the "spiritual mirror") rationale for sensitive but robust community; i.e., the protective "buffer" of "social support"[170]. In a practical sense, such solidarity is a first necessity, for no tightropes should be attempted without the safety nets rigged. Look around you. Where are these? They are rarely to be found, whether in psychotherapeutic environments or in society at large. This is our greatest collective shortcoming. We don't provide sanctuaries within spitting distance of park benches, and we permit individual rather than group therapy with the "appropriate" time boundaries effected at professional behest.

Off your chest and desk but still on your "to do" list
Who lives longest (counted in hours) with our drivers? Why, we do in person of course: we must live with ourselves at the end of each day. Whilst drivers may command our own insomnia, they may also occasion cervical or posterior discomfort to those in our relational vicinity. We all like to have a "listening ear" – someone who will let us get things off our chest – but if we don't change our personalities, letting off steam will only ever furnish fleeting respite and permit fleeting friendships. Accumulated rackets, especially unexpressed ones, are known in TA as "stamps". If the collector has been burning the midnight oil, we had better watch for the conflagration. When it comes (and in TA come it will, whether as seepage if "brown" stamps, or as a torrent if "gold"), it contributes measurably to the losing script "payoff", with consequences that rank according to its degree.

---

[169] unless we wish to stay stuck. Some of us, apparently, can afford to do just that. Times come, however, when some of us can't. It seems that each (especially adolescent) generation inherits – through some irregular mechanism or another – the bad habit of having to learn to choose the right company the hard way. What can we teach the kids.

[170] "Social support" works especially well when stress is high (e.g., Cobb, S., 1976, Social support as a moderator of life stress. *Psychosomatic Medicine, 38,* 300-314).

"Self-effacing Rosemary"

Fleeting leaning
The most fleeting "friendships" of all are sometimes the most symbiotic ones. We know from nature and biology that symbiosis is defined by mutual compatibility (capacity to meet a "survival need") and helpfulness or co-operation; however, with human beings symbiosis is like a tinderbox - meaning it has limited endurance prior to its conversion into something quite explosive. The problem is that, although some people quite like the reciprocated leaning, sooner or later one party gets fed up with a situation and changes their mind. That's when the trouble starts. Eric Berne knew a great deal about this sort of thing and we shall revisit it when we consider "games".

The ego states in functional mode
Meantime, we need to appreciate the difference between the structure of ego states and how they function in transactions. This interplay is as often as not devised (unknowingly) so as to precipitate (in others) responses reinforcing the (spurious) "truth" of the trenchant and prophetic "life script" (generating "rackety" feelings into the bargain). The Parent ego state (we are reassured to hear) is capable of "Nurturing" as well as "Critical" or "Controlling" behaviour. Although Child stores injunctions and permissions, and makes decisions about these, it also possesses an uncontaminated or spontaneous, fun-loving quality known in TA as one's "Free Child"[171]. The "Adapted" Child is the one that is conditioned by experience, and is manifest in two modes: "Compliant" (responding harmoniously with the Controlling or Critical Parent) and "Rebellious" (antagonistic).

FUNCTIONAL MODEL OF THE TA EGO STATES

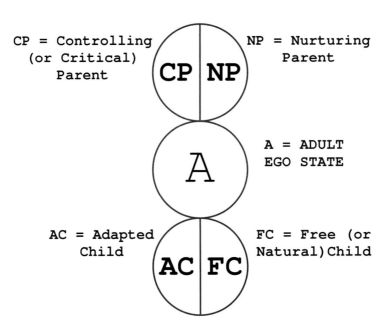

CP = Controlling (or Critical) Parent

NP = Nurturing Parent

A = ADULT EGO STATE

AC = Adapted Child

FC = Free (or Natural) Child

---

[171] When recreational with "brain power", Child may be known as the "Little Professor".

Interpersonal transactions: preliminaries

For Berne, the unit of interpersonal recognition is a "stroke"[172], and we are constantly engaged in affording these to each other in the transactions[173] that take place between us. Transactions are always "invited" by one party, and accompanied by an expectation (whether deliberate or unwitting) of a particular type of response. Much of the time we are mutually co-operative, and our codified transactions oil the hub-bub of work, family, friendships and human intimacy. Sometimes, however, these transactions turn awkwardly – precipitating high jinks – even (potentially) catastrophe if people are "playing" for whopping enough stakes. Although Eric Berne's theories of how this happens were engineered in the context of early post-Freud psychotherapeutic treatment, and conceived with the psychology of the individual very much in "mind", his ideas can surely be extrapolated to the ways in which we engage with each other on a much larger scale – through all the layers ("worlds") of the "moral environment"[174] – even to national and global affairs. It is quite possible to imagine international diplomacy – including its outcomes – progressing on the basis of the same principles underlying the examples that follow.

Interpersonal transactions in more detail

Each transaction is made up of a stimulus and a response, and transactions proceed from the Child, Parent or Adult ego state of one person to the Child, Parent or Adult of another. The three types of transactions recognised in TA are complementary, crossed and covert.

Complementary transactions

In a complementary transaction, the ego state addressed is the one which responds, and communications may continue smoothly:

Husband: *Can you help me find my shoes?*

Wife: *Oh! You haven't lost them again have you?*

Husband: *Yes! Silly me. I keep losing them don't I?*

Wife: *What will I do with you? Are they in your wardrobe?*

Husband: *No – I can't find them there.*

Wife: *Have you looked by the back door?*

Husband: *Oh yes! Here they are! What would I do without you?*

Here, Husband is in Child throughout, compatible with Wife's Parent.

Crossed transactions

In a crossed transaction, the ego state that responds is not the one that was addressed. A primary communication rule in TA holds that disruptions are always caused by crossed transactions (including "discount transactions", in which the transmission is ignored):

Husband: *Can you help me find my shoes?*

Wife: *Oh! You haven't lost them again have you?*

Husband: *Yes! Silly me. I keep losing them don't I?*

Wife: *Well, good luck finding them this time darling.*

Here, Wife switches from Parent to Adult crossing the C-P pattern.

---

[172] In *Walden*, Thoreau effortlessly depicts not merely our universal companionship-hunger but (rather reminiscent of Carl Jung's notion of the "collective unconscious") something of our intrinsic psychological "wiring" as an inevitably connected organism:

I have heard of a man lost in the woods and dying of famine and exhaustion at the foot of a tree, whose loneliness was relieved by the grotesque visions with which, owing to bodily weakness, his diseased imagination surrounded him, and which he believed to be real. So also, owing to bodily and mental health and strength, we may be continually cheered by a like but more normal and natural society, and come to know that we are never alone. (Walden; Or, Life In The Woods, 1854, "Solitude")

[173] defined as units of social intercourse in *Games People Play* (1964, Penguin: London)

[174] See Chapter 6.

"Have You Seen My Shoes?"

Covert transactions

A covert transaction is one in which a person says one thing but means another. The message has two components: the social (overt) and the psychological (covert). The covert affords much more information about the behaviour that actually and eventually transpires than the social level. The motive for covert transactions is usually shame or embarrassment originating in Parent values or prejudices; then again, desires and feelings sourced in Child. The most common social level can be located at Adult-Adult. The psychological messages are usually either Child-Parent ("Help me …") or Parent-Child ("You should …"). A variation on our scenario involving the slippery footwear might be:

Husband: *Have you seen my shoes?*

Wife: *Not since you last wore them dear.*

Here, Husband's cunning opening remark looks like a plain ordinary question (Adult-Adult) but – given what we know about this couple – and on closer scrutiny of Husband's tone of voice and body language, we conclude that this is a covert Child-Parent stimulus translating to, "*Please find my shoes for me*". Wife's response looks like a rational statement meaning, "*Not recently*", but translates tersely as, "*Jolly well try to remember where you left them*" (Parent-Child).

In the diagram, the dotted line represents the covert transaction.

COVERT TRANSACTION WITH SOCIAL AND PSYCHOLOGICAL LEVELS

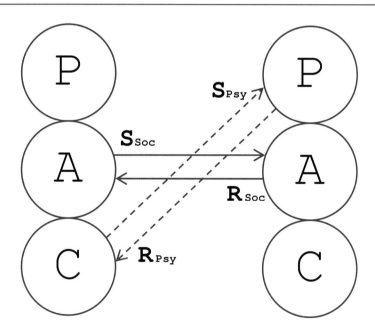

Covert transactions form the basis of "games", and are sometimes referred to as "ulterior" transactions. A habit of engaging in covert transactions can render a person unable to discern who they really are (especially in "Free Child"). TA therapists encourage people to be honest with themselves and with others. In so doing, people can develop the courage to ask fearlessly and openly for what they expect from relationships and, thereby, become more likely to obtain it.

What's your game?

Whereas Eric Berne's reference to "games" included any transactional behaviour with an ulterior motive, TA has since distinguished between racketeering and games (Fanita English), the "switch" defining the latter (Vann Joines; Marityn Zalcman). The switch, simply, is when one party to a series of (complementary) transactions changes ego state (without warning), leaving everybody feeling uncomfortable and uptight. The tension is relieved only by a further change of (reversion to complementary) ego state(s). TA sees racket feelings as the (dubious) "reward" associated with playing games, although this is intuitively difficult (in the context of reinforcement and motivation – see Chapter 2) as rackets are aversive by definition. Reconciliation of the two approaches is probably to be discovered in recognising that the "pull" of the "life script" is (gravitationally as it were) significantly more forceful than the potential of a transitory instance of daily living as an opportunity for learning.

A sad case in point

By way of hypothetical example, a wife with a (losing) "life script" determining that she must acquire material wealth at all costs (recall that the "script proper" is "the 'life script' together with all of the parental injunctions and permissions – transmitted as we have seen from the parents' Child ego state to the offspring's own Child"), seeing (or, more accurately, realising subconsciously) that her marriage was not satisfying that requirement sufficiently, manufactured (in ulterior fashion) endless ("rackety") scenarios in which she could generate and maintain grudges against her husband (by switching ego states, taking offence at the husband's corner of the symbiotic relationship; i.e., playing "games"), anticipating eventual uproar and divorce with him as the defendant because of his adultery (he having "needed", of course, an alternative source of "strokes", the marital ones having now dried up). Doubtless neither party (nor the hidden paramour) enjoyed the episode very much at all – nor their children – nor did any of them comprehend the whole dismal tale for what it was, until they all wound up in separate TA consulting rooms (or the doctor's surgery or the hospital ward or jail or the morgue).

Losing scripts and losing wickets

In Chapter 7, we described our potential for "spiritual blindness":

Whichever way you look at it, it is of no use making excuses for self-betrayal. There are two sides to any coin, and we can flip any situation over to look at it another way. We credit ourselves with guile; in fact, it is denial. How do we know it is denial? Because if you hold out playing a "bad game", you find yourself on a losing wicket sooner or later. Ask anybody who has tried it in the long run.

No means of escape

The astute reader will have realised very quickly that the husband and the paramour have discharged a losing script equivalent in deficiency to that of the wife's, and are equally accountable in the "love" triangle. When script payoffs are grave, they are termed "escape hatches" in the TA jargon (aka declaring and prosecuting war in the language of international diplomacy). TA identifies three escape hatches: "going crazy", homicide and suicide, with a debatable fourth – "running away" (established in psychiatry as a "fugue"). Of course, of these four, suicide is the only final exit from the very life we know and, so, self-destruction is the only script-*finale*. TA therapists are somewhat divided on how to "treat" escape hatches – some regarding their "closure" as a pre-requisite of progress in rehabilitation. The argument hinges on whether tactical or strategic escape hatch closure is possible (psychologically speaking), and then whether progress can be effected whilst they remain live and potent.

The "drama triangle"

In TA, movements across existential life positions are possible depending on what happens when we engage with others. Unhealthy life positions (broadly any which involve "not OK") may be occupied (without awareness necessarily) in order to justify "Persecutor" and "Victim" modes of relational behaviour (in the Parent and Child ego states respectively) - as demonstrated in the "drama triangle" presented by Steven Karpman[175]. The "Rescuer" position is also a significant (unhealthy) role in the turmoil and carnage. According to Karpman, any person playing a game is fitting themselves to one (or more) of these three "scripty" roles. The Persecutor puts other people "one down" inferring in them a "not OK" existential standing. The Rescuer is like the Persecutor in that she or he sees a third party as "not OK" and unable to save themselves from the Persecutor. The Victim operates from a "not OK" position, and may unconsciously invite relationship with the Persecutor and Rescuer. (I+U+ is the healthy (Adult) position - the one that is aligned with a "winning script" - and that is associated with progress in TA psychotherapy.)

The drama triangle is reproduced here:

STEVEN KARPMAN'S DRAMA TRIANGLE

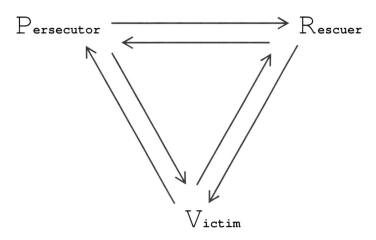

The drama triangle is used to interpret games by discerning which role the respective parties have assumed at the beginning of the series of transactions, and then identifying what change of roles happened at the "switch" (when a person shifted to another ego state and the parties sensed that something has gone wrong). In this way the roles in the drama triangle rotate during the course of a game. A Victim may, having become rescued, blame the erstwhile Persecutor who now assumes the role of Victim; alternatively, the Rescuer is seen as having interfered and becomes a Victim with one of the erstwhile Persecutor and Victim parties now assuming the role of Rescuer (the other becoming Persecutor). The drama triangle is avoided altogether, or at last abandoned, when participants remain in or revert to Adult.

---

[175] Karpman, S. (1968) Fairy tales and script drama analysis. *Transactional Analysis Bulletin, 7:26,* 39-43.

Growing up in TA

As we have tried to make plain, the "life script" is unconscious (or "pre-conscious"), meaning beyond a person's normal range of awareness without contrived means of bringing it to light. Although established during a child's formative years, supposedly it can be modified during the whole of life including adulthood. Now, **TA** makes three fundamental assumptions: (i) everybody is actually OK (whether or not we like people or their behaviour); (ii) everyone has the capacity to think (and, so, make personal choices), and (iii) people can "decide" their destiny (and the "decisions" they have made can be changed). Our scripts may have become dated, and we are called upon, especially by experience of failure, to re-establish ourselves. We can bring to bear our capacity for thinking to the matter, and we are capable of "redeciding". We move out of script, so regaining our "autonomy".

Freedom in TA: autonomy

Although Eric Berne is not on record as having defined autonomy formally, he has described it in *Games People Play* as, "manifested by the release or recovery of three capacities: awareness, spontaneity and intimacy"[176]. Awareness is the capacity of a person to perceive the world in a way that is uncontaminated by parental influences – as a pre-intellectual infant rather than a taught child. Spontaneity is the ability of a person to experience and express without shame (although not without prudence) feelings (originating particularly in "Free Child") that are natural in the sense that they are untaught. For Berne, spontaneity is liberation from the compulsion to engage in transactions with an ulterior motive (i.e., play "games"). Primarily a quality of the Child ego state, and inhibited in most people by the shadow of the Parent ego state, **TA** intimacy is the unencumbered, game-free and candid behaviour of the uncorrupted autonomous person.

A discount for (nearly) everyone

In **TA**, denial is known as "discounting" – setting aside information that contradicts the "script". It may involve serious overestimation or underestimation of other people. Eventually we will consider the capacity for "decision" and "redecision" that people really do have. Underestimating nearly all of humankind in one swoop, the final chapter of *Games People Play* comprises one paragraph only, reproduced as the transactional stimulus whose response remaining Chapters are:

The sombre picture presented in Parts I and II of this book, in which human life is mainly a process of filling in time until the arrival of death, or Santa Claus, with very little choice, if any, of what kind of business one is going to transact during the long wait, is a commonplace but not the final answer. For certain fortunate people there is something which transcends all classifications of behaviour, and that is awareness; something which rises above the programming of the past, and that is spontaneity; and something that is more rewarding than games, and that is intimacy. But all three of these may be frightening and even perilous to the unprepared. Perhaps they are better off as they are, seeking their solutions in popular techniques of social action, such as 'togetherness'. This may mean that there is no hope for the human race, but there is hope for individual members of it.

Let's pick up Eric Berne's gauntlet together: which is it to be then, friends: "Every man for himself" or "All for one and one for all"[177]?

---

[176] Berne, E. (1964) *Games People Play*. Penguin Books: London (Chapter 16, p.158)

[177] See Preface for expansion.

Echoes of "emptiness"
Towards the close of Part I, we contemplated "emptiness" as the unpleasant experience of the person laden with "conscience" which is:

a quiet strain, having the capacity to become psychologically "noisy", which has the effect of pressure to settle upon one or more beliefs, attitudes, intentions or behaviours (including not doing certain things as well as doing them) and which is experienced subjectively as psychological conflict – usually mild, but potentially deadly

On refreshing ourselves at the beginning of Part II, we reminded ourselves of a line of questioning that we should like to address:

"Does this tension that is conscience as we have just depicted it, along with any other psychological tensions that we may care to recognise, engender a kind of subjectively-experienced 'emptiness' which, as fallible human beings, we are prone to fill with all kinds of distractions, some of which are harmful to ourselves and others?" … *"What is the nature of this emptiness?"; "Does everyone experience it?"; "Under what circumstances are folks more or less likely to experience it?"; "Why do folks pursue certain rather than other distractions?"; "Do we have the capacity to observe it, evaluate it, effect or adopt alternative behavioural courses directed at filling or otherwise compensating for it?"; "Is there a moral quality to any such processes?"; "Can the 'nag' of conscience be disregarded, resisted, or modified by personal will or psychological therapy?"; "Can 'self' change 'self'?" and … "Why are there psychotherapists?"*

In Chapter 6 – inspired by Tolstoy's depiction of moral courage – we confidently anticipated that personal sanity might be discovered in the application of an "Accountable Self" in the "moral environment".

The writing on the wall
We have considered in the context of their whole histories both major facets of modern psychology ("scientific" and "analytical") alongside other disciplines that speak to our topic. We desire an approach that accommodates and expands upon them all. Each philosophical thread presents excuses for glumness that can be dissipated with hope: Skinner's "scientific determinism" combined with the clear relevance of conditioning principles to daily human life; the "writing on the wall" of the TA "life script" that can be cleansed by "redecision", and the immutable pressure of divine invitation (Chapter 5) combined with religious folks' insistence on God's love and care for Creation.

Are you sitting comfortably?
Eric Berne's renowned, "If you are not stroked, your spinal cord will shrivel up"[178] resonates with Thoreau's depiction of "Solitude" (see footnote, *supra*). A TA environment is betrayed by the bandying of unconditional compliments, and there is something very OK about that. But sometimes, each of us finds ourselves (struggling) alone. The notion of "self-stroking" is not unfamiliar in TA circles, and invites speculation on the development of bad habits during childhood (from knee-scratching and tics to smoking and other addictions). There is a TA response to the TA verdict on a life, and it can be found quickly enough in the yellow pages. But is there anything else?

Then ready, steady, go …
We shall have drawn together threads, joined up the numbered dots, and completed our colouring-in by the close of the next two Chapters.

---

[178] Berne, E. (1964) *Games People Play*. Penguin Books: London (Introduction, p.14)

"The Writing On The Wall"
Riveaulx Terrace, North Yorkshire

Chapter 9

"A moral psychology"

(Robert Stephenson Smyth) Baden Powell (1857-1941)
The essence, substance and import of "A moral psychology" are best
assimilated after first hand reference to (and considered reading of)
the vital historic and contemporary background detailed in Chapters
1-8. We humans continue now to participate in the unravelling of
history as ever we have done (for some 200,000 years hitherto and
where might it end …); moreover, as we all know empirically (from our
own experience) but don't always recognise (because of its potential
interference with expediency), the business of living is similar to
domestic refurbishment: the work that really counts, and the quality
of the end result, are all in the careful practice and preparation.

Teased to disintegration
We have teased out modern psychology from its roots, only to discover
it fragmented in our grip. Since the pivotal scientist Hermann Ludwig
von Helmholtz, a last common ideological ancestor, two strands of the
discipline that informs sanity have evolved independently. These are
scientific psychology on the one hand (after *inter alia* Wundt,
Watson, Skinner and Eysenck), and analytical psychology on the other
(after *inter alia* Brücke, Freud, Jung and Berne). We have troubled
ourselves to lay out the contextual and theoretical fundamentals that
underpin each of these subdivisions – particularly the principles of
classical and operant conditioning (see Chapter 2) and the elegant
yet empirically unverified Transactional Analysis (see Chapter 8). Is
there some manner whereby these two may be reconciled organically?

Are we there yet?
Having taken stock of the old and unsolved "mind-body problem", and
also the thorny matter of "free will" (which we may go some way to
despatch), we have considered in some depth the nature of our common
malaise – or what is known widely as the "human condition". Without
the groundwork laid throughout Parts I and II, how else could we have
confidence in the relevance of all the psychotherapeutic modalities?
But plenty exist, and most are extremely costly in terms of both
money and the trouble that assailed people have to go to – especially
(but ironically) when they are all "washed up", lost to themselves
and isolated socially – to find one that relieves rather than adds to
their trouble. Whilst contemporary treatment performs marvellously in
some quarters, it requires self-examination (see Chapter 7) of the
kind it invites (or should invite) from its clients. The systemic
response to our need (as a whole human society) is difficult to
evaluate (especially for the life-weary prospect) because (aside from
the discrepancies amongst us about how far we should care for the
temporarily unfortunate) history has produced uncoordinated schools
that differ significantly in terms of how they perceive psychological
"knottedness" and (thereby) determine the "relevance" of their
response (also Chapter 7). These divergent schools, furthermore, are
distributed across separate operational sectors (from private to
charitable with public straddling the two, often the most significant
financial investor). The sheer weight of cash that has been spent on
(vote-driven) policy development, strategy, research, implementation,
service development, review and user consultation in the past few
decades bears witness to the complexity in and remaining inadequacies
of the present system. The bottom line is: if it takes hundreds of
consultants to fit the light bulb, how may a baffled or desperately
unwell person navigate towards an unfamiliar destination in the dark?

Avoiding unnecessary upset
In laying the groundwork for a "moral psychology" we have begun to
define and consider the bearing of its various elements. Foremost
amongst these are "conscience" (see Chapter 5) and the force of the
"moral environment" (including the "weight of human history" – see
Chapter 6). We have posited that the ways in which we blend these in
our personalities will inform and alter (favourably or unfavourably)
our "spiritual" condition and hence direction. We mustn't get too
upset about words like "moral" and "spiritual". "Moral" just means
founded on a principle – like a rule or a tenet – and we have plenty
of these in secular law as well as in matters scientific and
psychological. "Spiritual" just means "unseen" – recognising that we
can't operationalise everything about sanity in the material and
measurable world of science (and we don't know whether we will ever
be able to do so). If you wish to add personal colour, even religious
fervour, to these terms, you are encouraged most vigorously to do so:
for all you know it may do you and the world some good. The whole of
Nine Seahorses represents an exhortation (*Plea*) to do just that in a
way that is right for you, you alone, and nobody else. We are about
to demonstrate the relevance and application of an "Accountable Self"
in the "moral environment" (discussed in Chapter 6) – and the various
ramifications of doing so – under the umbrella expression "moral
psychology". Finding and exploiting common ground has been a key
principle of our approach which is, thereby, ecumenical in spirit.
Not everyone, however, will warm to the argument, because you can't
please all of the people all of the time. Nobody in history has
achieved that standard, with the possible exception of Raymond[179].

No formal agenda
Nine Seahorses comes with a personal guarantee independent of the
reader's appreciation or otherwise of its thesis. It is a scrupulous
attempt at winnowing away the chaff from a long and multi-faceted
journey through modern psychology. The biography germane has, like
anybody's life, embraced both the mundane and the intense in everyday
experience – in thoughts, in feelings and in relationships. There
have been moments of low season and also high drama (sometimes we are
"lucky" to escape with our lives). The author has drawn from advanced
pedagogy in academia, diverse received wisdom in applied settings
(counselling and psychotherapy), as well as professional experience
in policy implementation, research and service building. The entire
argument has been formed with no overseer. No patron. No committee.

Why a "moral psychology"?
The human race has ever known "moral psychology" as rendered explicit
from the outset; nevertheless, lives still get horribly trounced and
can languish unredeemed in the 21st century. Human history (since
circa 200,000 BC), from "Out of Africa" (*circa* 70,000 BC) to the
first farming communities along the "fertile crescent", and then
formal civilization as it has been patchily and subjectively recorded
(all since the end of the last Ice Age *circa* 12,000 years ago), has
been one of inevitable mutual engagement. We have seen significant
reactions against (the human authority in) religion in the Scientific
Revolution and the Enlightenment, since which time we have unshackled
ourselves somewhat, but become rather depressed. Provisionally, we
may consider "insanity" as "lostness to ourselves" whilst living in
the world – not possessing in our own right the "spiritual" resources
needed to avoid personal disintegration whether mild or catastrophic.

---

[179] Also co-creator with Philip Rosenthal (1960-), Ray (Raymond Albert) Romano (1957-)
is the star of CBS's TV show *Everybody Loves Raymond* which, although classifiable as
superficial entertainment (or "soap"), is deeply and cleverly replete with ulterior
transactions that should delight even the most jaded TA professional (see Chapter 8).

"Umbrella Expression"

Accounting for the "moral self": preliminaries
Even with advances in biology, we don't know exactly what happens (in
the universal sense) when a human life begins. As offspring, we
weren't there to salute the twinkle in our parents' eyes, and their
romance (or sexual liaison however it transpired) - for all we know -
could have happened on another day when, although a facile
proposition, we might have been somebody else. The same principle
applies to the meeting of gametes as to the meeting of minds. The
melding of DNA, and the development of a zygote (and then embryo), is
subject to a host of vagaries including the "natural selection" of a
sperm (and thereby biological sex) from a veritable Light Brigade[180]
of hundreds of millions. A simple "spiritual" (substitute
"psychological" or "emotional" as you wish) interpretation of how a
person (you) came into being may be partitioned for argument's sake
into two variants: (i) its quiet, yielding acceptance as it really
was (e.g., accepting who your parents actually were and not wishing
they were somebody else; the date, time and place of your conception
and birth; your name; whether you have siblings and in what
permutation they exist, etc[181]); or, (ii) its rejection on the basis
of these or other attributes. The reader may reflect on which is more
or less conducive with personal sanity. The remainder of a life is
like that. Acceptance is the glorious watchword[182]. Vain attempts at
manipulating what we cannot change leads to our unremitting insanity.

What, exactly, is acceptance?
Assuming we can appreciate the concept mentally (perhaps conjuring it
into our "minds" if it is not already there), let it sit with us for
a moment; now, what have we done when, in the manner depicted, we
have *accepted* something about ourselves (or another person, or the
various "worlds" of the "moral environment" that we encounter daily)?
The question is hardly a diversion, for perhaps acceptance is the
ultimate weapon we possess against delusion - laying at the heart of
sanity waiting only for discovery. This psychological or "spiritual"
phenomenon is a form of yielding, of "letting go" of alternatives, of
"seeing through" or "finding out" those rivals as culprits of our own
self-deception. It possesses an extraordinary and most reassuring
quality: when it has happened, you know about it. All of a sudden,
the penny has dropped, and you realise that a shift in your thinking,
and your feeling (even whomever you feel you are) has occurred. You
realise that nobody can take it away from you, because it has become
a personal "truth" in which you may retain utter confidence. You have
nothing to prove, and fear slips away. Scientists may corroborate the
phenomenon one day, and then again they may not. It hardly seems to
matter. Good luck to the scientists. And good luck to everyone else.
And good luck to me. Everything is OK. And you know that this shift
is a permanent change should you wish to keep it. And you know it is
for the better rather than for the worse, even though it may at first
feel like defeat, a compromise or "surrender". And it brings peace.

---

[180] Following a misunderstood order from Lord Raglan the famous "Light Brigade" charged
tragically against well-positioned Russian forces in the Battle of Balaclava during
the Crimean War (1853-1856) - fought to protect disputed territories on the Crimean
Peninsula and nearby sea routes during the 19th century decline of the Ottoman Empire.

[181] … even that it happened at all. If you are contemplating with hurt feelings why you
were born, or wishing that you hadn't been, you may wish to consider that it is
"depression" that is "talking" to you, that it will pass, and that in the meantime you
may speak to somebody you can trust. Failing all else, try visiting a friendly doctor.

[182] Obviously this is not an invention. The well known *Serenity Prayer* has uncertain
origins, but is usually attributed to (Karl Paul) Reinhold Niebuhr (1892-1971), in
which case from 1937: *Father, give us courage to change what must be altered, serenity
to accept what cannot be helped, and the insight to know the one from the other.*

Another starting point …
What, then, exists of a person in the first place? The fact of the matter is that we "know" only so much. Science tells us a great deal about physiology: we know about fertilisation, development in the womb and lifecycle biological maturation. In the psychological or "spiritual" sense, conversely, when do we become anything at all? There are endless possibilities for taking a position on this, and we don't need to prove that any of them is correct or, for that matter, refutable (although we should not want to maintain any patently dismissible position except through sheer belligerence to ourselves). Perhaps we have an immortal "soul" formed in the "heavens" as humans have suspected since Psalm 139 was authored some 1,000 years BC, or as Plato held in Ancient Greece[183]. Then again, perhaps we become reincarnated. Perhaps a metaphysical "soul" comes into existence at the event of our conception, or later at the (astrological) "moment" of parturition. Perhaps there is no such thing; rather, a Cartesian "mind" (see Chapter 4) mediated by some facility of which science has not yet dreamed. Perhaps none of these is true because everything is material; in which case, perhaps we inherit (Jungian) "archetypes" (Chapter 8) shaped in some manner by DNA or, again, none of these but an Aristotleian or Lockeian *tabula rasa* (see Preface and Chapter 1).

"Moral alignment"
The point is not so much that we can demonstrate any of these in a positivist, or even empirical fashion, but that (should it matter to us at all as thinking individuals) we can align ourselves with an understanding that makes sense, or is coherent with the remainder of our personal philosophy, or outlook on all of life. The only thing we really want to avoid is delusion. Why? Because that might engender internal discord; by which we mean the cleaving to two antagonistic beliefs or positions simultaneously. We can tolerate mild conflicts, but tensile ones drive us potty. Suddenly we are back to "conscience" defined in Chapter 5, and about which we have reminded ourselves often since (particularly in Chapters 6 and 8); furthermore, which we are keen to mollify if we want to become or stay "spiritually fit":

a quiet strain, having the capacity to become psychologically "noisy", which has the effect of pressure to settle upon one or more beliefs, attitudes, intentions or behaviours (including not doing certain things as well as doing them) and which is experienced subjectively as psychological conflict - usually mild, but potentially deadly

Well then, how do we achieve "moral alignment"? We may not need to do any such thing: perhaps already we are entirely sane[184], and need no "straightening out". But suppose ever that we do find ourselves skew-whiff. What then? Perhaps we can bring to bear our (suddenly realised if we did not already enjoy it) capacity for "spiritual surrender" to that blight (our contrary psychic machinations); but to which mental "object" should we apply it? We must first appreciate all the contestants in the mix, and then come to some judgement about which of them can be released in favour of retention of one or more others - or be retained at the expense of dispensable irritants. This appears to invite some kind of psychological or "spiritual stock-taking" which, doubtless, can be accomplished with naked unqualified willingness rather than formal credentials in psychology or any other discipline; but we have come this far with our technical argument, and had might as well finish it for fun if for no other good purpose.

---

[183] See the Preface and Chapter 1 for expansion and footnotes.

[184] but unfortunately we suggested at the beginning of Chapter 7 that we are all "nuts"

The "Written Self": preliminaries

No quarter of contemporary psychology challenges the proposition that learning occurs in humans[185] as well as all other animals (notably vertebrates)[186]. In Pavlovian classical conditioning (see Chapter 2), the conditioned response (CR) is direct evidence of such, as is the change in the rate of the operant response in instrumental learning. Behavioural variations following the application of reinforcement are common to both mice and men[187]; however, the latter may lodge a verbal report. These basic (classical and operant) mechanisms (even if they are overlapping or unitary – see Chapter 2) form and combine in boundless ways (see the Table, "Variations within the classical conditioning paradigm" located in Chapter 2) to generate the array of personally significant experiences we know intimately from our own day-to-day living, and about which we can share in mutual discourse with our species-specific capacity for language. Lloyd Morgan's Canon (similar to Ockham's Razor – see Chapter 2) compels us to rummage about for simple explanations of (human) learning before resorting to more sophisticated (or fanciful) ones. This reasonable principle will guide us through a review of the relationship between "scientific" and "analytical" accounts of insanity – and its redress – in so far as we are able to interpret things from both vantage points. The juvenile human, thrust centrifugally into the world with a vast capacity for registering experiential information, is suddenly answerable to an impossibly rich array of motivationally significant events. Much of this exposure will generate adaptive assets; however, a significant proportion of its register may spawn irregular patterns of thinking and feeling for its onwards journey, the remedy for which must be sought in professional contexts invented since Helmholtz (for the most part a lot more recently than that). How did we ever get by?

The TA Parent ego state is S-S structurally

We shall begin our ascent (stopping before we find ourselves in too much fog) dealing first with the TA Parent ego state as, technically, it seems the most straightforward starting point for reconciling the "scientific" and "analytical" schools (simultaneously presenting the least requirement for having to call to arms Lloyd Morgan's hatchet). We know from TA theory that the Parent ego state P_2 "contains" the introjects of parents and other authority figures in P_3, A_3, C_3 "stacks", where each represents an identifiable significant other (see Chapter 8). The subject can "hear" (in C_2) the (affirming) voice of the (functional) Nurturing Parent or the (critical) voice of the (functional) Controlling Parent, and we may assume that this "aural" experience with its emotional overtones is, in all likelihood, a CR attributable to (early life) exposure to S-S pairings of P_3, A_3 and C_3 perceptual features (CSs) with the occurrence of reinforcers (USs) which may have included anything unconditionally soothing for the infant (warmth, physical contact, vocal and tactile reassurances etc)

---

[185] Even "scientific determinism" has a predilection for it provided it is knowable parsimoniously as small bricks – from which prospective sky-scrapers may be built.

[186] The basic forms of learning – habituation and sensitisation – occur in all animals.

[187] The poem *To A Mouse* by Robert Burns (1759-1796) reminds us (as if such prompting were called for) that the unravelling of history commonly fails to match the scenarios we effect with our "operant" imaginations. Unlike rodents, humans are apt to moan about it (translation of the seventh stanza to modern English courtesy of Wikipedia):

But Mousie, thou art no thy lane,	*But little Mouse, you are not alone,*
In proving foresight may be vain:	*In proving foresight may be vain:*
The best laid schemes o' mice an' men	*The best laid schemes of mice and men*
Gang aft agley,	*Go often askew,*
An' lea'e us nought but grief an' pain,	*And leave us nothing but grief and pain,*
For promis'd joy!	*For promised joy!*

or unconditionally aversive (harsh or angry words and tones, gestures and facial expressions, censures and exclusions, menaces, slaps and so on)[188]. In this conditioning adaptation, the emotional component (CER[189]) of the P_2 CS complex (P_3, A_3, C_3) is experienced in Child (C_2).

Early TA Parent
Whilst, classically, the TA Parent ego state doesn't exist until or after the child is a toddler, seminal TA may have been too keen to effect a functional differentiation of Parent and (pre-verbal) Child (and rashly failed to have separated Parent and Ego developmentally). S-S learning is probably immediate and rapid in the neonate (if not present in the embryo), but the child's capacity for reporting such learning (CER) to a therapist is constrained by developmental caps on both use of language and retrieval of early episodic[190] memories. TA supposes that learning in P_2 takes place along a (time) gradient of counterinjunctions (see Chapter 8) laying down "instructional tapes" in the child's Parent, where P_3, A_3 and C_3 are mutually discriminable on the basis of the parent's own ego state structure (approximately, shall we agree, P_3 is the instruction itself, A_3 is the justification for it, and C_3 is how the parent feels about it). In an associative learning account of the same process, the child can discern such subtleties and store them as CS (perceptual) elements; moreover, the whole process may start pre-verbally just like learning in C_2, Child.

Early classical learning like a tsunami
Whereas, historically, models of classical learning supposed that stimulus associations were formed or strengthened because of the temporal relationship between CS and US (approximate co-occurrence optimised when the CS preceded the US by a short interval), later ones regarded the capacity of the CS to acquire associative strength on a given trial a mathematical function of the difference between the maximum associative strength possible and its level before the trial in question[191]. This is like saying that conditioning will proceed very rapidly at first but tail off as trials proceed until a maximum associative strength is reached. Now, we can imagine that the neonate is a single-minded sponge when it comes to consumption of its "survival needs" and use of the learning capacity it possesses in relation to securing those precious assets. It will lap up not only milk and intimacy, but every imaginable signal that precedes their delivery (as if learning to "predict" their occurrence). Allowing the processing of compound (indeed complex) stimuli during this cascade of stimulation, rookie P_3, A_3, C_3 introjects (en route from the parent or significant other's Parent ego state to the offspring's Parent ego state, P_2) will march as an army of conditionable exteroceptive and interoceptive infant experiences, for the most part comprising strong sensory cues related to the presence and nearness of the parents (particularly the mother if the infant is breastfed). As time goes by, the Parent ego state developing in the infant becomes a diffuse

---

[188] Substitute "in all likelihood" for "in fact" – but for corroboration of "perceptual learning"; i.e., the capacity of an animal (not necessarily a human being) to learn about or better discriminate stimuli following mere rather than reinforced exposure.

[189] CER = Conditioned Emotional Response – see Chapter 2.

[190] "Episodic" or autobiographic memory is a well-established distinction within the "cognitive" domain of modern psychology. It may be contrasted with "semantic" memory ("I know that … [something is true]") and "procedural" memory (typically motor) skills that have become automatic because of practice (e.g., playing a musical instrument).

[191] The equation embodying this principle was presented in: Rescorla, R. A. and Wagner, A. R. (1972) A theory of Pavlovian conditioning: variations in the effectiveness of reinforcement and nonreinforcement. In: A. H. Black and W. F. Prokasy (Eds.) *Classical Conditioning II – Current Research And Theory*. Appleton-Century-Crofts: New York.

set of conditioned stimuli (P_3, A_3, C_3) identified with parents and other authority figures. The balance and profile of pleasant and aversive CERs will depend on the quality of parenting and may also determine (along with the repertoire of CSs to which the subject is later exposed) the relative components of Nurturing and Critical Parent in the child's own Parent ego state (P_2)[192]. Assuming a truly massive (although ultimately limited) unexploited reservoir of learning potential at birth, we may suggest that conditioning will proceed with a vigour and a firmness of registration precipitated just as much by the sheer vastness of remaining learning potential at the time of a learning event or "trial", which then of course will diminish inevitably and biographically until learning becomes tardy during senility. Naturally, none of the early conditioning was ever remembered by our subject. Quite understandably, "it never happened".

Having your TA Parent and eating it
TA Parent could oblige both science and its own domain by reinventing itself structurally as a perceptual-cum-classically conditioned module, extending its scope biographically to include S-S learning commencing as soon as the human infant has a capacity for laying down associative links, and qualitatively to include all non-person CSs (although on the whole these will be more infrequent and far less salient). Such a concession may involve the dissolution or collapse of P_3, A_3 and C_3 into a perceptual "black hole" if the TA theoretical distinctions have no or some other basis in associative learning[193]. Obstinately, it could insist on its present conceptual structure but risk confining its usefulness to self-fulfilling theoretical outcomes of TA therapy, simultaneously rendering itself incompatible with behavioral and cognitive-behavioral treatments for the same psychological problem in cases where the alternative treatment is more theoretically correct (thereby outdating itself and TA more broadly if such competing behavioral or other explanations prove themselves later). Even more obtusely it could (try to) have its cake and eat it by waiving Lloyd Morgan's Canon entirely, concluding that the Parent ego state is formed by some process other than perceptual or classical learning - or that neonatal (as opposed to toddler or post-language) classical learning is lodged in some other personality component (possibly Child, but this would seem a spurious partition). Of course, TA as a body is under no such obligations, and we all know that patience is a virtue even if sitting on the fence rarely is. There is science and there is artisanship. TA as a professional body, no doubt, knows immense diversity on these dimensions within itself.

The TA Parent ego state is R-S functionally
Functionally, the TA Parent ego state assumes one of two modes: (i) Critical Parent (which we have encountered frequently in the course of dealing with the unfortunate business of pathology, but which is offset in many wonderful families and other environments by its counterpart), and (ii) Nurturing Parent which is affirming and supportive. In TA, the Critical Parent addresses the Child ego state with the "expectation" (thus, surely a Skinnerian R) of a particular outcome (S) from Compliant Adapted Child, although it may not obtain it if Rebellious Adapted Child steps in (S). Nurturing Parent has an anticipative quality about it too (wanting good things for Child).

---

[192] Allowing for "intrapsychic conversations" (see Chapter 8), the C_2 experience of Nurturing versus Critical Parent will be determined by the balance of the introjects.

[193] The Parent ego state, so defined, would subject itself to the entire range of principles that govern the formation of classical associations, including the emergent field of perceptual learning which, because of its willingness to contemplate non-associative processes may, in fact, provide exactly the empirical link with "science" that TA longs for. Such a concession might generate the most rewarding of results.

"Unexploited Reservoir"
Loch Mudle from the summit of Ben Hiant, Ardnamurchan, Scotland

Pausing to take in the Child's eye view

The identification and separation of Child and Parent is crucial in TA in so far as it recognises their respective functions at the heart of interpreting interpersonal transactions. The standard diagrammatic representation of all the three ego states, whether structurally or functionally (see Chapter 8), stacks Parent and Child above and below Adult respectively, such that the only conceivable overlap of Parent and Child would accompany (severe) contamination of the Adult ego state. In relation to Child, TA holds that: (i) it develops early; (ii) it is *pre-verbally* early; (iii) it assimilates injunctions and permissions that are not necessarily mediated by language; (iv) it exists and develops before (verbal) Parent (and Adult); (v) it can "hear" verbal imperatives stored in the Parent ego state in the form of counterinjunctions; (vi) it can and does make "decisions"; (vii) the (pre-therapeutic) "early decisions" are autonomy-yielding and script-authoring; (viii) it "decides" what to do with parental messages; (ix) its later behaviour may be manipulative in the context of "rackets" and "games"; (x) its "Adapted" form comprises two functional modes – "Compliant" and "Rebellious"; (xi) there is a fun-loving uncorrupted "Free Child" component and (xii) it can "redecide" in therapy in such a way that the "Free Child" regains prominence. TA anticipates a favourable relationship with emerging science, but there is no known part of classical TA that determines how Child (or any of the ego states) is physically formed in terms of "archetypes", templates, biological structures or physiological learning traces.

The second order structure of TA Child

Structurally, nevertheless, TA Child (or C_2) incorporates a P_1, A_1, C_1 stack (see Chapter 8) which is an updatable "memory" of historic ego state arrangements located (on theoretical grounds) in Child on the basis that, whilst P_2 is old only in the sense that it contains past introjects, C_2 contains all of our biographic and episodic memories. In TA, older C_2s, including their P_1, A_1, C_1 stacks, simply represent our older Child ego states at any given age in years; however, this is difficult to translate into biographic learning at a fine level of detail. Let us say that each successive C_2 is differentiated from the last one (at time t) by the quantity and quality of interim learning in a manner whereby newer C_2s encase a freshened P_1, A_1, C_1 stack which is an updated P_1, A_1, C_1 arrangement from that time t somehow combined with Child's "episodic" experience of P_2, A_2, C_2 since t^{194}.

The "Magical Parent"

P_1 is the "Magical Parent" in C_2 which fantasises (as distinct from teases out rational conclusions) about the consequences of conforming versus not conforming with parental messages (which we take to mean any permutation of the injunctions and permissions, combined with the counterinjunctions stored in P_2 but which may be "heard" in C_2). In TA's jargon, and as we saw in Chapter 8, P_1 is sometimes known as the "pig parent" because of its capacity to generate disproportionate terror in Child. The "Magical Parent" can generate just as fantastic "compliance" scenarios, so generating an undue sense of grandiosity.

The "Little Professor"

In C_2, A_1 is the "Little Professor" representing the set of strategies that the child has used to solve problems, starting out early with primitive ("intuitive") approaches rather than ones which an adult's ego state A_2 would recognise as logical. Whereas the "early" script decisions are made in A_1, the fantasies about script consequences (in so far as these are consciously available) are held in P_1, and may include rationalisations for "racket" feelings. Seemingly, A_1 becomes

---

[194] We shall suggest a mechanism for this process (with its implications) presently …

more and more sophisticated (less and less "innocent" and more and more "cute" — even guileful) with the maturation of the individual.

The "Somatic Child"

TA script decisions are said to be "felt" in "Somatic Child" (C_1). Bearing in mind what we have said about superseded C_2s, the earliest C_1 will be pre-verbal, ancient and very difficult to access. When we consider exposure to TA injunctions and permissions, as distinct from the verbal counterinjunctions, we can imagine that the earliest of decisions are hunch-like rather than linguistically explicit, and the feelings stored in C_1 quite diffuse and very difficult to articulate.

TA Child possesses "agency"

When we examine our (i)-(xii) depiction of TA Child (*supra*), the most striking difference between C_2 and P_2 is that, whereas the structural formation of P_2, developmentally speaking, can proceed passively (whether by perceptual, associative or joint or vicarious mechanisms) C_2 possesses some attribute which we may refer to as "agency"[195]. After all, the most plausible interpretation of the intended effect of injunctions, permissions and counterinjunctions is that they are factors that can affect the likely rate of an instrumental response. (We know, moreover, that the Child ego state in the behaving adult is manipulative in so far as it may engage in "games".) The ingredient of "agency" is, of course, the very quality that marks out (operant conditioning or) instrumental learning from classical conditioning. If we have located all biographic S-S (classical) learning in P_2, then TA Child would seem a natural repository for all instrumental associative links. We have suggested that Parent is S-S structurally and R-S functionally. What, then, of Child? And what of its shrouded structural formation as distinct from its conspicuous functional processes? Answering these questions presents a quandary to which, provisionally, TA is most disposed to precipitate exquisite answers.

Recapitulation and a first diversion

A discredited maxim, "ontogeny recapitulates phylogeny"[196], represents the notion that an embryo goes through developmental stages that retrace adult forms of species in its evolutionary history. Whilst this principle is rejected by all of modern biology, it is true that vertebrate embryos often do develop *features* reminiscent of adult instances of species older in its evolutionary path. For example, the embryos of whales — which descended from land-bound mammals — at some point in their development have hair (which largely disappears) and "legs" which end up as deeply retracted "limbs" within the body.

Recapitulation and a second diversion

Turning to the evolution of learning itself, it is not unreasonable — or unusual — to recognise that Pavlovian or classical conditioning (i.e., S-S learning) is more "recent" than both habituation (learning to ignore a stimulus that has no consequences) and sensitisation (the strengthening of a recognisable response to repeated presentations of its eliciting stimulus); in fact, developments in laboratory research using the sea snail *Aplysia Californica* in recent decades have suggested that the mechanism(s) for classical learning may be elaborations of the simpler mechanism(s) underlying sensitisation[197].

----

[195] Agency represents, say, the capacity of a living thing to discharge behaviour which has consequences, its awareness of that faculty, its ability to effect judgement over such actions — and its moral appreciation of such consequences (e.g., whether they are "right" or "wrong" and the extent to which ethical accountability should be attached).

[196] after the German biologist Ernst Heinrich Philipp August Haeckel (1834-1919)

[197] With Arvid Carlsson (1923-) and Paul Greengard (1925-), Eric Richard Kandel (1929-) was co-recipient of a 2000 Nobel Prize for this (potentially) momentous workstream.

Now, whether instrumental learning is "older" or "younger" than classical conditioning depends (for all present intents and purposes) on whether we establish it as S-R (Thorndikeian) or R-S (Skinnerian) - the distinction between which we rendered categorical in Chapter 2 (where the reader was invited to invest imagination in the aftermath of an accident). To recap, the Thorndikeian account supposes that an associative link is formed between a situation (S) and a response (R), that same association being strengthened by the occurrence of "satisfiers" (Thorndike's term for rewarding reinforcement but we may suppose that aversive or punishing reinforcement operates according to the same S-R process). On the other hand, the Skinnerian account (of the same situation) supposes that the association germane is formed between the response (R) and the reinforcer (S), allowing that the situation may serve as a qualifying context. The Thorndikeian account is imagined to be "older" (more primitive than) classical conditioning because, in S-R, the situation (S) simply elicits a response (R) without requiring any S-S association to produce it (in which case it is a CR). It is notable that there is no requirement to recognise any subjective anticipation or first hand expectation of the reinforcer in S-R learning: it just happens - the "situation" (S) produces the "response" (R). On the other hand, when the association is formed between the (Skinnerian) response and the reinforcer (R-S), the expected outcome of the response would seem to play a significant part in its likely occurrence. This is to say, it is then reasonable to impute some condition of "subjectively experienced control" to the learner - a more sophisticated "mental" condition than that necessary for the performance of either a Thorndikeian response (R) or a classical one (CR). For more detail on these principles, including arguments relating to how well we can discern whether given instances of learning (acquired responses) are classical or instrumental in origin (including the "omission training" procedure and its correct interpretation), the reader is referred to Macphail, E. (1982) *Brain And Intelligence In Vertebrates* (Clarendon Press: Oxford). It is of significant interest to note that Macphail establishes a clear if challenging position about our species-specific capacity for consciousness and subjective experience of pain - both contingent on the human child's gradually emerging sense of "I" or "self" - in turn a corollary (as Macphail sees it) of human language development.

Two and two makes four
Blending what we know about the neonate's exposure to TA injunctions and permissions, and how TA holds that these are assimilated in C_2 in such a way that memory traces are "somatic" in C_1, but develop like Russian dolls (reminiscent of our whale's hairy hind legs) until they become more linguistically hinged and more accessible - with "early decisions" (and their associated fantasies in P_1) becoming more sophisticated with biographical time - might we not be charmed by the possibility that there is an "ontogeny" of learning in C_2? This could proceed from "early" S-R (Thorndikeian) to "late" R-S (Skinnerian) - the threshold somewhat blurred - but permanently overlapping to the extent that S-R underpins R-S; the R-S onset having to do with the transition from "pre-verbal", or Piagetian "sensori-motor", to "pre-operational". The attraction of this interpretation lies mostly in Thorndikeian S-R which permits of "pre-conscious" and deep contextual (situational) learning of exactly the kind that TA recognises: a "weight" of "unspoken" family culture inherited through Child ego state aether, pressing on the individual in terms of "baggage" - so inhibiting free, natural or spontaneous behaviour in "Free Child" - and which is very difficult to recognise, harness and shift in therapeutic settings. Thorndikeian S-R also rather neatly accounts for Child's or C_2's "episodic" experience of P_2, A_2, C_2 since time t.

"Aftermath Of An Accident"
How do you feel about your red coat now? (Chapter 2 refers)

Two and two makes five

As we know, Macphail (1982, *supra*) has suggested that when the human infant acquires language, its other interesting (species-specific) faculties arrive also, including very consciousness, a sense of "I" or "self", and a capacity for subjective pain. For Macphail, language acquisition is a faculty standing head and shoulders above all associative learning (classical and operant – whether S-R or R-S) and is seen, unlike all of associative learning as a broader category of vertebrate intelligence, only in humans. This is consistent with his position that non-human vertebrates (all capable of S-S, S-R and R-S, and equally intelligent in terms of associative learning with respect to each other) lack not merely language (as we have it) but also both consciousness, the human sense of "self" and capacity for subjective pain (presenting, incidentally, significant implications for animal experimentation, and perhaps even animal food consumption generally). Now, our account of the "ontogeny" of TA Child implicates a similar developmental trajectory – but with a significant difference. We have posited an S-R / R-S threshold prior to which all human "response" learning is S-R. Let us say that the human infant slides from S-R to R-S in the (structural development of the) Child ego state at some time around its passage from "sensori-motor" into language. This transition is associated, in our framework, with the point at which the various inner Russian dolls (hypothetical C_1s in biographically ancient C_2s) become therapeutically accessible, implying that ancient memory traces become retrievable to "mind" because of the acquisition of language at around the time of their formation. We find ourselves alongside Macphail except that we are positing that it is R-S itself that tells human language-competency apart with all its interesting corollaries. The first implication of such a proposition is that no non-humans possess R-S: all of their acquired (seemingly) operant behaviour must be either S-S or S-R. This is a feasible although remote, controversial and challenging possibility. We departed from Chapter 4 having resigned ourselves to a side-step of the "mind-body problem", and we do not need to effect a retraction; nevertheless, such reflections as these are luring for the materialists who hope to find a solution to consciousness in physiology. Such a treasure trove might delight the humanist fraternity that TA is (defined by its philosophical ancestry as we have seen); all the same, it does not disprove or eliminate the notion of a spiritual personality or soul.

The TA Child ego state's function follows its structure

Structurally, the TA Child ego state is operant or instrumental, and we have suggested that its pre-verbal incarnation is Thorndikeian, eventually giving way to "imaginative" R-S. By this time, Child is guileful whether as a "Little Professor" or as a big one (although we expect individual differences, see Chapter 3). On the face of things, there is a gradient of R-S to S-R down the (biographically evolving) P_1, A_1, C_1 stack; with R-S more salient (and biologically anchored) towards the top. We will suppose that there is a direct match between structure and function in C_2 at any point in time. As Child develops, its R-S structure becomes more sophisticated, as does its behaviour. As far as TA therapy is concerned, it is vital to appreciate that interventions should be devised to match the underlying learning. The difference between "co-creating" new psychological life with an S-R-imprisoned "King Baby"[198] is now transparently at odds with the task of "co-rehabilitating" with an R-S-wielding sociopath wishing to "go straight". The justification for releasing "Free Child" in TA therapy is more obvious than ever – for "Free Child" is defined by the extent to which C_2 is "unwritten" by either S-R or R-S associative links.

---

[198] "His Majesty the Baby" is Freud's 1914 depiction of the narcissistic human infant.

New notes on "nodes"
In so far as perceptual learning might involve the representation of
stimuli in the central nervous system by "nodes" having properties
parallel to the objects they represent, and in so far as the "real"[199]
(probably diffuse) excitatory or inhibitory neural and synaptic
pathways around and between them that become modified as a
consequence of conditioning may be represented by "associative
links", the nodes and links involved in a given operant acquisition
would vary in our model depending on developmental stage allowing the
postulated transition from Thorndikeian to Skinnerian instrumental
learning in the juvenile Child ego state. More particularly, whilst
the introjects (P_3, A_3, C_3) in TA Parent (P_2) might simply reinvent
themselves constantly with experience – without establishing a new
psychological identity for themselves no matter how young or older
the developing child – it is a different story with the TA "Child in
the Child" (C_1 in C_2). Here, the nodes involved in response behaviour
must transmogrify at some developmental point in such a way that more
diffuse stimulus nodes for "situation" (or "context") combined in
some way with a (Thorndikeian) response node relinquish themselves to
more specific nodes representing mentally rehearsable Skinnerian
responses (Rs) and anticipated outcomes (Ss). The node representing
the "new" response may (or does) now have a language competency
inbuilt, and may or may not be otherwise equivalent – structurally or
functionally – to the old one. Perhaps the "slide" from S–R to R–S
involves a node-creating or node-transforming threshold whereby some
trigger – possibly the adding of semantic information "transmitted"
(neurally) from a "Language Acquisition Device"[200] – precipitates new
node formulation and, in the aggregate, an entirely fresh mental set.

Less fresh than a daisy
Of course, we don't stay fresh forever. We get older. We get wiser.
And we get crabbier. How does this happen and why does it matter?
Arguably (and we can appreciate the point with only a cursory
appreciation of Chapter 2), fear is the one true emotion. It is the
driver behind every instance of conditioned avoidance. Its only rival
in the affective stakes is the charismatic pretender – (appetitive)
"hope" which, for all its distracting appearances, turns as merely
the other side of the same coin – then presenting itself as the fear
of failing to have satisfied a demand of the instincts (or "survival
needs" in the TA handbook). Each fear-induced, script-authoring jolt
of Thorndikeian, autonomy-yielding anguish in infancy (in which the
poor "Inner Child" stifles by stealth its own creativity) advances a
deposit of resentment into some C_1 vault of relationship hell to be
unleashed without warning on some unfitting future occasion. The pre-
verbal episodes are worst because of their unrecognisability. That is
why we can't be true to ourselves. Incapacitated by "spiritual
blindness", deeply lost in "denial" and compelled by the ruthless
demands of the impoverished Child's injunctions to follow and obey,
we invent excuses for doing so. These are the TA "rackets", or
inauthentic feelings we experience – wildly parrying our "spiritual
white sticks". Fear conceals itself beneath everything. Resentment
lies next on top. Over these two arch-destroyers of "worlds" parade a
million dancing excuses, a million interpersonal transactions and a
million reckless "games". At painful last, the moment of reckoning
arrives when – all washed up in "emptiness" and utterly alone – this
"self", defeated by its own hand, screams at the heavens, "Help Me…!"

---

[199] presumed (for which there is emerging evidence), but yet to be established in fact

[200] The original "Language Acquisition Device" (LAD) is an innate, congenital, species-
specific mechanism postulated by (Avram) Noam Chomsky (1928–) to account for human
language (funnily enough a reaction against behaviorist accounts of the same faculty).

"Face To Face With Our Fears" (and our smallness)

Travelling light
Armed with a provisional "scientific" understanding of the structure
and function of the TA Parent and Child ego states, and how they may
be experienced subjectively, perhaps we are approaching a point where
the "spiritual stock-taking" we envisioned a few pages ago as a
pathway to "moral alignment" might come nearer into view. At that
juncture, we quite appropriately recognised our temporary departure
to technical la-la land. Since we had started the journey we were
prepared to continue it; however, as we have said over and over (in
Chapters 5 and 8 particularly), there is a place for *Everyman* in this
world (provided we all peacefully realise it). That must include the
"egghead" (who, as we saw in Chapter 4, values the inspection of
intricacies and – why not – you never know the potential return), the
"pinhead" (who doesn't value anything) and the multitudes of
"somethingheads" in between. Of course, we don't need to tell any of
these apart (for it is far better that we all leave each other alone
unless we are invited into relationship accompanied by an RSVP), far
less what to do; we need only a means of submitting to the truth
about ourselves (the only antidote to "denial") – helped by willing
(and loving) friends if we are happy enough to have them to hand.
Unfortunately and sadly, the eventual toll of a TA "life script" – or
name that unravelling as you will – often extends to the most severe
of social estrangement. Then, when we are at our worst, we must rely
on what funds we may have remaining, money we can muster, or charity.
Fellow travellers (notwithstanding their political persuasion) are
the best companions if their stake in affairs is equivalent to ours
(i.e., honest self-appraisal). In those environments, the prospect of
a broken confidence, or an insensitive (far less judgemental)
incursion, is all but eliminated. But the requirement for failsafe is
a spurious defence, for no protection is needed against the phalanx
of one's own true convictions. The problem is one of getting started
with sufficient momentum to build up steam, until that gnawing and
ravenous sinkhole that was the past becomes truly lost to history.

Taking a nutcracker to a nut
Out of the blue, we can contemplate ourselves as we actually are
rather than as we once saw ourselves from a kindergarten in C_2 or
through the dark haze of a TA racket. This ought to sound (and feel)
like a scary undertaking, for otherwise we would be failing to
appreciate its nature, purpose and value. After all, we are talking
about coming face to face with our fears; also (as if that were not
enough) all our smallness (i.e., our petty resentments and hatreds)
and our cowardice (including our short-cuts to self-satiation and our
dishonesty to ourselves and others in understanding these things).
Many won't venture here without having acquired a sense of obligation
towards it – perhaps from some dismal failure – but the principles
involved are equally well applied in small measure to small setbacks.

(Almost) the last word on "toughness"
There may be some truth in the idea that a less flawed breed amongst
us may purchase modest doses of medicine for equally modest
sacrifices of pride, thus achieving (for there is no possibility of
any greater advance anyway) just small increments of personal growth.
Even if this were so, the whole of humanity might awaken suitably and
happily to the kind of day's work which benefits everyone. "Spiritual
stock-taking" isn't merely the dreadful obligation of the pitifully
weak and impoverished – a circumnavigable curse to the few who fall
(under the carpet) in the families of the superficially powerful. We
can all retain the prerogative to scoff, to feign superiority and to
laugh off liabilities, but we all get caught up with the cost of
living in the end. We are better off united. The world is getting too
dangerous for all that dated and perverse, "I win, you die" claptrap.

Driven around the bend
Having established universal principles of structure and function
(meaning that we suppose that the structural formation of the Parent
and Child ego states incorporates the same foundational elements and
proceeds according to more or less the same processes in all human
beings), the next level of appreciation is for our own idiosyncrasies
(for it is ourselves we live with at the end of the day, even if
others must endure us *Day In, Day Out*[201]). A TA specialist, if you can
afford one, may be willing to hold for you a multifarious reflection
of your "miniscript" – the uncountable instances of your behaviour in
which the "narrative" of your entire underlying script is revealed
(always tentatively for the evidence is only ever hearsay, or by
proxy, unless you accept its validity for yourself). TA theory holds
that the presentation of the miniscript is always precipitated by
microinstances of driver behaviour[202] (see Chapter 8), and these can
be discerned by the trained TA eye. The drivers are the archaic
habits developed in or by you to manage or rationalise your own
introjected parental messages. You may, for instance, have developed
a "Please Others" driver in order to satisfy parental messages that
amounted to "You're not OK unless you are co-operative and helpful".

The accessible counterscript versus the shrouded script
Your dear psychotherapist will guide you to see for yourself how your
personal drivers emerge as a consequence of your "early decisions" to
obey the counterinjunctions stored in P_2 (remembering that all of us
have a typical one, perhaps having two salient, rarely three or more
of the five). Now, in practise, TA routinely links drivers directly
to counterinjunctions (and, thereby, the "counterscript"), rather
than to injunctions (and the "script proper" which we recognised as
"the 'life script' together with all of the parental injunctions and
permissions – transmitted as we have seen from the parents' Child ego
state to the offspring's own Child". In TA therapy, you may not be
able (or pushed) to identify which of the 12 injunctions (identified
by the Gouldings) is at play beneath the counterinjunctions, and we
can appreciate the difficulties associated with penetrating the
layers of (C_1 in) C_2 to get back that far. It is much easier to try to
discern the parental "voice" (P_3, A_3, C_3 in) P_2 "heard" in Child or C_2.

Excitation and inhibition
Our provisional position on the structural "ontogeny" of TA Parent
and Child (in which we have reduced, with Lloyd Morgan's permission,
the "building blocks" of learning to associative links) suggests that
all of the observable behaviour we see in a conditioned human (if it
is not unconditioned responding or URs which we may assume must
emanate from TA "Free Child" – or TA Adult) may be classified as
either: (i) classically conditioned responding (i.e., CRs) to CSs
located in the P_3, A_3, C_3 stack in P_2 which – on the whole according
to "stimulus substitution theory" – will resemble (old) unconditioned
responding towards parent or authority figures[203] or (ii) an inhibited
(or facilitated) rate of operant or instrumental responding that is
either "early" (Thorndikeian S-R) or "late" (Skinnerian R-S). In our
example, whereas a compulsion (subconscious or otherwise) to "Please
Others" in order to satisfy a parental message tantamount to "Please

---

[201] *Day In, Day Out*, like *Tiptoe Through The Tulips* (see Chapter 6), is an iconic tune,
in this case written by Rube (Reuben) Bloom (1902-1976) with lyrics by Johnny (John
Herndon) Mercer (1909-1976). About "being in love", the song has been recorded by many
notable jazz artists. It includes the line, "That same old voodoo follows me about …".

[202] Kahler, T. and Capers, H. (1974) The miniscript. *Transactional Analysis Journal*,
4:1, 26-42.

[203] always either learned approach (i.e., "hope") – or learned avoidance (i.e., "fear")

Me" might be hinged on an "approach" CR in which the subject behaves towards parents (P_3, A_3, C_3 introjects in P_2) or others (by CS generalisation[204]) as if a parent figure whose esteem or ratification (US) we have come to value (CR); it might pivot just as much on a (situationally) diffuse and early S-R injunction ("If I'm not nice when I'm with grown-up people something bad might happen"), or a calculated – even guileful – "late" Skinnerian R-S rule determining that well-invested sycophancy buys friends and influence. In the aggregate, these ideas present a more systematic framework for evaluating "driven" behaviour than has been available in TA hitherto; nevertheless (as with all psychological theories), it is just an unfinished (although potentially helpful) provisional framework. It is no kind of gospel. And anyone with a serious sense of purpose (and enough of that indispensable and vital factor "willingness") can assimilate the required "home truths" by circumventing the broker.

Revisiting Type A and Type C

Learned behaviour referenced in this way assists an alternative interpretation of the personality dispositions tentatively considered to lie aetiologically behind a couple of our greatest killers. Whereas the Type A personality (mooted in the 1950s) is overdriven and prone to pathology of the cardiovascular system, the Type C personality (recognised in the formal literature since the 1980s) is liable, reportedly, to development of cancer and poor prognosis following diagnosis (see footnote to Chapter 7 for expansion). The pathological or "toxic" effects of both Type A and Type C are still unclear; however, both seemingly involve "repression" or "bottling up" of emotion. In the vernacular they are "hurry sickness" and "helpless-hopeless" respectively. As all twelve of the Gouldings' injunctions are imbued with the imperative "Don't …", and as the TA counterinjunctions are similarly imperious, it is not unreasonable to anticipate illumination from enlargement of this line of thinking. For instance, the Type A disposition may stalk from ancient, deeply ensconced (biographical but also inter-generational and cultural as we shall consider later) S-R injunctions demanding performance (subsequently reflected in "Hurry Up", "Try Hard" and "Be Perfect" drivers in the counterscript); whereas Type C may lie equally well concealed in old S-R compliance scenarios with their corresponding injunctions (emerging later as "Please Others" in the counterscript). Incidentally, the cockroach we are really looking for behind "hurry sickness" is not time at all. Our Type A victim is hostage far more to a "drive economy" than a "time economy". If you want to "cure" yourself of Type A habits, why waste your (precious) time trying to generate more of it, or allay the work that persistently tries to fill it? Rather, go to your ancient, contextual and somatic "Small Child" wherein, sympathetically, you may discover a very young person who must vigilantly "jump to it" every waking moment without really understanding why. Now you have ventured to the heart of the matter.

---

[204] The phenomenon of "generalisation" is a significant factor in determining the CR-eliciting capacity of diverse CSs in everyday life. We saw in Chapter 2 how classical conditioning, although a simple basic mechanism, presents endless ways in which organisms learn about (motivationally significant) events in the environment. This facility is enhanced by various extrapolations of the fundamental process including those listed in the Table, "Variations within the classical conditioning paradigm" (see Chapter 2). Of these, generalisation is probably the most powerful – in turn, underlining the significance of "perceptual learning". The phenomenon is familiar throughout all psychotherapy in the form of "transference" and "countertransference". Transference is the awkward process whereby a person makes assumptions about a third party based on their similarity to another figure in the first party's history, rather like "judging a book by its cover". In psychotherapy, a patient may form an attachment to the therapist based on an old affinity for a parent or other significant person. If the therapist permits the same or a similar situation to develop *vice versa*, the corresponding process of "countertransference" can present grave ethical difficulties.

Expression of the "Written Self"

TA recognises five drivers as a matter of professional consensus, but doesn't enjoy an empirical explanation for five rather than four, six or any other number. A similar principle applies to the injunctions – allegedly there are a dozen, but we don't know why the Gouldings were convinced of 12 except by dint of their own (significant) experience. It matters less whether there are six of one, or half-a-dozen of the other, as it does that I can acquire an appreciation of my own fears, motivational incentives, self-centred ways of satisfying my "needs" (especially if they cost others any of their rightful forty winks) and all the lies I tell myself[205] to keep my resentments watered and my trajectory through life sustained. Have I not experienced, through all of my days – including those halcyon Thorndikeian ones when I, though laden, bore no "moral responsibility" because of my innocence – experienced and suffered "conscience" as we have defined it[206]? Then how has my "Written Self" been expressed both in my "mind", and in the world at large? My TA Parent ego state P_2 is replete with significant (P_3, A_3, C_3) CSs; and their potency to elicit ("hope" and "avoidance") CERs, which I experience in my Child ego state (C_2), is extrapolated by the phenomenon of generalisation and a host of other stimulus contingency effects. Have I accepted every invitation to a Pavlovian response (CR) with my "moral capacity" for recognising its "moral value", or have I found some faculty whereby I could let it fade away without it having been exercised? My Child ego state C_2 is threaded through with an ancient and barely recognisable patchwork of willowy S-R fibres that occasion me, first with savour and then with trepidation, to lean this way or that, in sequences of scenarios that feign familiarity, but which I may barely recognise. Have I succumbed to every coercion as if wholly cast by the winds of "fate" ("famine" and "fortune"); or did I discover a faculty whereby I might determine another course? Perhaps I have tried to flex operant muscle supposing that "I am the master of my fate; I am the captain of my soul"[207], but what "control" did I truly possess over my R-S repertoire? Was it personal history, with its unexpected dividends, but broken promises too, that actually tilted my tiller? Did I dance to Skinner's tune? And what of all the direct and open invitations (USs) from this sensually bounteous orb? Did I embrace without buffer or moderation each pleasure and every pain (USs)? Did my participation (URs) mould my "Inner Child" for another day? Have all of those invitations to "settle upon one or more beliefs, attitudes, intentions or behaviours (including not doing certain things as well as doing them)" emanated from the material world for … in the final analysis … did very God or very nature – who fashioned me in space and time according to her own blueprint with none of my will or assistance – ever murmur with utter softness and timeless patience to me when I was "busy right now"? Did she ever beckon me here – or summon me there – and did I ever pause to pay heed? Was it always as simple as acquiescence and refusal, or was I stretched to accommodate the least of many evils? Did my "moral navigation" despatch me very far from "moral anchorage"? What, after all, do we mean by "settle upon", and what is our capacity for it?

---

[205] and others, for how may I be socially authentic unless I follow Polonius's paternal recommendation to Laertes, "This above all: to thine own self be true, And it must follow, as the night the day, Thou canst not then be false to any man"? (see Preface)

[206] *a quiet strain, having the capacity to become psychologically "noisy", which has the effect of pressure to settle upon one or more beliefs, attitudes, intentions or behaviours (including not doing certain things as well as doing them) and which is experienced subjectively as psychological conflict – usually mild, but potentially deadly* (defined in Chapter 5, and re-presented subsequently in Chapters 6 and 8)

[207] the last two lines from the poem *Invictus* by William Ernest Henley (1849-1903) in which the harassed narrator, seemingly, is convinced of his own "moral invincibility"

"Master Of My Fate, Captain Of My Soul" (all at sea though)
Sound of Mull, Scotland

Definition of "emptiness" and "FAQ" preliminaries
In Chapter 5 we asked, "Does this tension that is conscience as we have just depicted it, along with any other psychological tensions that we may care to recognise, engender a kind of subjectively-experienced 'emptiness' which, as fallible human beings, we are prone to fill with all kinds of distractions, some of which are harmful to ourselves and others?" Now we can begin to operationalise "emptiness" so that it may be useful in both theoretical and applied ways. "Emptiness" is the subjectively aversive discharge of "conscience" – the "lostness" we experience when we dispense of our "consciences" poorly, which can only mean that we have backed or "settled upon" the "wrong" nag – or one that isn't "wrong", but insists on itself – (especially if the wager was hefty or the bets became too frequent). Now, too, we can attempt answers to the "ancillary questions at the heart of 'moral psychology' [that] flow from this primary puzzler".

Recapitulating, one at a time:

"What is the nature of this emptiness?"
"Emptiness" is the unpleasant feeling we experience privately when we haven't been true to ourselves. Being true means establishing an authentic "moral alignment"; i.e., one in which we have eliminated our "moral conflicts" without indulging self-deceit in the process. Most simply, it is just giving up on the mindless pursuit of some course of action we know in our heart of hearts we'd be better off having relinquished. Don't we all take a little comfort to change the way we feel – for merely a moment (that's all): a daydream, a novel, a film, a chocolate, a doleful tune with a tear-jerking minor chord, a flirt, a shopping binge, an argument, a sexual indulgence, a cigarette, a glass of wine, a fight, an affair, a tranquiliser with the doctor's blessing, an all-weekend fugue, an illegal mind-slayer without any permissions at all (even our own). Of course many of us resort first (instead of last) to a brisk walk, a meditation, or a little honest chat with a friend. Most of our dilemmas are of the "acquiescence" and "refusal" kind, meaning that all we need to bring to bear in order to achieve or restore "moral alignment" is a simple personal honesty and a willingness to adjust our "moral compass". On these fortunate occasions there is an open door waiting obligingly ajar, and we need purely the sense to let go of the daftness that keeps us wishing for an alternative egress. Sometimes our task is to tolerate the frustration of an array of shut doors (when we seem confronted by the insufferable likelihood that there is no solution to a presenting anxiety within our grasp). Perhaps we can avoid the grown-up responsibility of being "stretched to accommodate the least of many evils" by simply waiting to see what tomorrow brings[208]. A colossal test of our sanity informs us that the tensions that threaten to tear us apart have not yet been confirmed (as we hope and expect eventually they will be) as "written" (and consequently, in principle, "overwritable") learning traces within our personalities. Perhaps we suspect they are annoyances (courtesy of Pavlov, Thorndike or Skinner) residing within our Parent or Child ego states, and that, if only we could expose them with or without the help of a therapist, we might then turn upon them our "moral Dalek", leaving us to proceed unencumbered until the next (inevitable) "moral confrontation". What are we to do when such "moral sitting ducks" refuse steadfastly to manifest themselves? Persist with our navel-gazing or psychotherapy? Perhaps we should turn back to our array of "shut doors" whereupon we may find we had been mistaken and one was unlocked all along. Perhaps we might stop. Do nothing. Unplug the 'phone. Attend to the whisper …

---

[208] The advantages of keeping life in the day extend astonishingly beyond the obvious …

"Does everyone experience it?"
Yes. Don't you? An immediate and direct corollary of consciousness,
it visits everyone drawing breath (without a life-support machine).
We know this is true through common-sense, and because of the
episodes of our lives when we have shared openly with other people,
or been willing to tolerate (or facilitate when we were generous)
their own unburdening. We only suspect we suffer alone because, quite
understandably, folks don't like to be too frank about themselves all
of the time. It is only hidden and forbidden by people in "denial".

"Under what circumstances are folks more likely to experience it?"
If we assume a literal interpretation of our definition, "emptiness"
is directly proportional to "moral misalignment" – the source of
"conscience". We need to get away from the habit of assuming that if
we were "morally misaligned" we were all at fault when actually we
were all at sea. We may be morally misaligned for a veritable host of
reasons, not the least amongst which may lurk some genuinely specious
and acerbic conditioned mental aberrations. These are the legitimate
and proper concern of listeners and therapists whether paid or not.
(It is only when we are "spiritually blind" and persist in our own
self-deception that no "moral dividend" accrues to any party at all.)
Truly irregular episodes of deviant learning are up for grabs in the
therapeutic environment, then; as are the statistically inevitable
strains that breach and threaten to blight every human existence:
hatches, matches and despatches; family, employment and financial
disasters; health problems etc. Of course, it is in their subjective
interpretation that sanity stands or wobbles. We have considered
their antidote already: "acceptance" isn't equivalent to defeat – it
is maturity. Talking of which, there are lifecycle patterns that also
prevail. The teenage years are challenging enough for everyone and,
in a socially disintegrated world, the younger amongst us must
determine that much more resolutely to remain "connected" with
themselves, with each other, and with their optimism. A petition for
the plights and rights of young people was presented in Chapter 6.
The reader is invited genially back to the prison cell in question.
We're in this together. Talking of which, there is a nasty "vicious
spiral"[209] that injects itself surreptitiously into every declining
life; i.e., the cunning assailant that is isolation. The more people
get bent out of shape, the less people desire their association.
We're all guilty of that kind of shallowness. The agonised casualty
retreats to lick their wounds, rendering themselves further out of
order. Anybody bathing themselves in self-pity is courting a ducking,
but the feeling goes with the territory and can be hard to shake off.
It is a self-reinforcing process, like a runaway train, and can be
fatal[210]. The good news is that it *always* passes, and its converse is
just as real – even if difficult to get off the ground. A sustained
willingness to maintain an improved "moral direction" absolutely
always pays off in the longer run. It is a law of the spiritual life.
"Emptiness", also, is an apposite expression for the "cross-up" TA
locates at the "switch" in a "game" (see Chapter 8). It is the moment
when someone posturing from Parent or Child is "found out" as their
adversary crosses over to an unexpected and incompatible ego state
(especially to Adult – the most reliable technique for closing down
damaging "conversations"). Games are sinister psychological devices,
not as weapons, but as temptations. They are like noughts and crosses
– if you are in the know – you can neither win (a hollow victory) nor
lose (relying on the simple Adult rule). You can't win a bad game.

---

[209] Strictly, a "vicious circle" is a "Catch 22" whereas a "vicious spiral" gets worse.

[210] If this feels a little close to home for you consider contacting a "listening ear".

"Why do folks pursue certain rather than other distractions?"
Amongst our distractions – from romantic novel to country invasion –
as individuals we do seem to pursue a "drug of choice" (i.e., have a
favourite "poison", although admittedly we may have a second or third
lurking in reserve). Any person capable of some degree of personal
honesty wouldn't need to introspect too extensively to discover their
own. It is that stereotypical repertoire of indulgent behaviour that
effervesces from somewhere within when we feel "stressed", "out of
sorts", "disappointed", "shameful", "guilty", "bitter", "resentful",
"afraid" and so on. Just for a moment, we can take away the edge of
our pain. Our indulgence seems to fill the "emptiness". We "know" it
is an illegitimate wadding; nevertheless, at that moment, better the
reprobate within than the bastard without (whom we may then ignore,
at least temporarily). After all, we have more "control" that way;
indeed, the illusion of "control" is the strongest comforter we know.
It only stands to sweet reason: if we are in "control", anything and
everything falls within our grasp, and there is nothing left to fear.
As a child, were you ever invited to say what you might order had you
three wishes? First and second choices? Easy peasy, lemon squeezy …
At the third, did you ever say, "Three more wishes!" Perhaps the rank
order of our favourites is determined by genetic or temperament
factors (see Chapter 3)[211]. Certainly it would seem feasible that our
personal history of reinforcement with a particular "reward" might
affect our future use of it. In the dreamy beginning, we crossed the
threshold, and something wonderful happened. Our eyes were opened,
and all the stars and spangles of our imaginations descended
sparkling before us. They were more "real" than our pain because they
took it off our "minds". O'Grady (Skinner) said … "Repeat!"; and we
obeyed. Again and again. Eventually our former *aide-de-camp*, now
fickle turncoat, reeled back as if a scurrying fuse coursing for the
bomb beneath our asses[212]. The survival rate from such munitions is
arguably about a half, for some die, and some live (to tell tales).
Perhaps comfort-accessibility is a major player: whilst they take no
account of individual narratives, public health statistics have
demonstrated over and over again that the damage wrought by drugs and
alcohol is inversely proportional to price and (legal) availability.
Politicians have shoulders broad enough for national campaigns and
international crusades; they have capacious arms for holding babies;
but they don't have time for heart-rending or park-bench stories.
They are naturally more inclined to "signal detection theory" applied
to prospective votes (in democracies) when it comes to setting taxes
and drafting statutes[213]. Closer to the front, perhaps the role of the
Parent ego state is not as straightforward as it seems, for the "not
OK" message of the TA "Critical Parent" (P_3, A_3, C_3 in P_2) warns
helpfully of pitfalls whilst our "Nurturing Parent" may afford us too
many permissions (telling us we may go to any lengths to feel "OK").
There are many provisional notions here, when perhaps we had hoped
for ready answers; but the real road to freedom from all this trouble
(even if you have known it in only small doses) mightn't trace the
scenic route through intricate reason, formal research programmes and
costly psychotherapy. Just as we closed the curtains on Chapter 2,
mightn't we all realise that the best things in life (like the best
people) are simple and free; moreover, "It's easy when you know how".

---

[211] There is no proof that self-comforting, or the adoption of a certain drug of choice
– or unmitigated addiction, runs biologically in families. Much else runs in families.

[212] although subjectively painful, perhaps nature's beneficence at work: "At this rate,
it's all over; but you still have a 50% chance to save your own skin … 'Yes' or 'No'?"

[213] plotting ethical ideals against popularity – seizing the vote-optimising asymptote,
or otherwise attempting to discern actual voting behaviour through the din of opinion.

"Do we have the capacity to observe it, evaluate it, effect or adopt alternative behavioural courses directed at filling or otherwise compensating for it?"
All of us have the capacity for observing "emptiness" in ourselves; apparently, it is both obvious and troublesome. Discerning it in others may be frustrated by its deliberate concealment. Most of us don't like to appear or feel "small" socially, because our esteem in the eyes of others (as we see that ourselves) is a highly prized human asset (to a greater extent than we realise or care to admit). Social esteem is powerful reinforcement (see Chapter 2) in its own right, and can lead us to foolhardy ventures in careers and relationships (especially if our motives are hidden to ourselves). The fact of the matter is that we are far more self-centred than we like to concede. Our preoccupation with other people's opinions of us is usually fantastically wasted imagination – for other people rarely think of us at all. They are far more concerned with their own personal and social esteem (amongst all their concerns). Even if we could read their minds when we are located there, we would discover their wishful scenarios to be shockingly disparate from the ones we imagine they possess: imagination abounds with little basis in fact.

... the knack of purposeful engagement
The qualitative aspect of "emptiness" is its unpleasantness, and the quantitative dimension its dreadful capacity to excruciate. In ourselves, we can easily rate its aversiveness in both respects. You may, if ever you have been severely "lost", describe your personal suffering as "beyond words". The remainder of us may accept this as a truism because of our own experiences and, if we are generous, we can readily conjecture your pain in our "minds" anyway; indeed, the capacity we have for sharing our psychic pain with each other appears intrinsically interwoven with our capacity for language. The knack of success in relationships, then, is to exercise compassion without "succumbing" to (TA) games. It is not so much a problem of evaluating or measuring "emptiness" in others as it is caring about it. Less so in social than in professional or psychotherapeutic settings, it's important to distinguish between sympathy and empathy: whereas sympathy to a (TA) gamer is like both a mud bath to swine and a match to forest kindling; empathy in its most wonderful, capacious guise is a fantastically practical way to love. The master of such engagement was Carl Ransom Rogers (1902-1987). His person-centred approach to counselling and psychotherapy, rooted in early humanistic psychology, supposes that a person develops a sense of "self" in the context of its history of relationship with the environment – particularly other people. Rogers conceives of "introjection" of others' values like TA Parent; however, whereas counterinjunctions represent (give or take) direct mapping of the respective ego states of the parties concerned; for Rogers, psychopathology sits on the ways introjects get distorted and become perceived as directly experienced (when they are thereby spuriously "real"). Our framework of conditioning can be applied as equally to personality development in the person-centred tradition as in TA. Distorted person-centred "introjects" may involve: Pavlovian (S-S) CRs that no longer reflect the adaptive "truth" of the (reinforcement) environment; ancient (and inaccessible) Thorndikeian (S-R) vestiges that ruthlessly precipitate unhelpful responses in particular contexts, or outdated Skinnerian (R-S) repertoires that may have been learned vicariously from a significant other (i.e., modelled). For Rogers, the self is a powerful force bent on moulding a congruent (phenomenological) whole world view, its own structural integrity ("gestalt") and its own potential. At the centre of therapeutic efficacy is "unconditional positive regard" – the loving acceptance of the client by the therapist – vital because it releases the loved one's intrinsic, healing and "self-actualising" tendency.

"Sanctuary"
Lynmouth Harbour, Devon

A second distinction we do as well to appreciate is that between lip service and meaningful social engineering. Especially in the last few decades (beginning in the UK under the Thatcher government when we were introduced to a wave of Harvard management consultancy and its associated culture – later perpetuated in a mushroom-cloud of self-serving bureaucracy under New Labour) we have become blindly adept (for we don't realise how corrupted we have become) at talking about social safety nets (and paying for all the public sector careers that lie behind and underneath that chat), but they do not exist in the number and forms that they might. Although we have lost to eternity, seemingly, the old-fashioned breed of the conviction politician; and our social problems, ethically speaking, are actually the unavoidable responsibility of the elected representatives who have become savvy enough to realise that it is wooing the undecided voter that counts statistically; "moral vacuousness" isn't all the fault of the swanky new political classes, nor may we blame fairly their friends the "spin doctors" whose calculated deceit now infects all our culture. We must look to ourselves. In democracies anyway, we get what we vote for and, as far as the ballot box is concerned, we are going to have to grow up as individuals before we grow up together. The reverse is true in relation to personal sanity. We don't crack the game alone. We need each other. We have seen why in this and the previous chapter especially. More relevant material is presented in all of Part III. As far as social engineering is concerned, the poor politicians must bring to bear their "signal detection" antennae most sensitively, because we say one thing and do another. We believe in the "truth" of the argument for human co-operation. We may shrink under flushes of "goose bumps" when we witness an eloquent speaker on the matter. We may even concur in conversations that we must support the political agenda identified. In the ballot box on the day the back pocket wins. We are conspiratorially engaged with how the politicians lie to us.

Then what safety nets might we correctly establish and vote to maintain? Only those that help people grow up in the way that we have done ourselves in order to vote for the system that created them. After all, none of us wishes to sustain "moral sickness", whether wilfully or unwittingly. Working from first principles, sanctuaries are needed for the battered. It shouldn't matter how folks ended up battered – that is not the point. Batteredness is the only criterion that need be applied to admission; for an additional, self-selecting one with which we all can live will apply by default. Our sanctuaries may (indeed must) be threaded through with a reorientation programme. A battered life never treads water. Either it recovers or it expires. Sanctuaries are alternatives to cemeteries. In a "moral psychology", recoveries depend on the development of bespoke "moral redirection", the only necessary compass for the remainder of that life's journey. Nobody authors the "moral script" except its new owner. We have seen how survival at this juncture, arguably, is merely 50% hinging on the yielding of a "Yes" or a refusal, "No". It makes all the difference in the world to the "moral fibre" of our culture that we offer our most distressed a half of a chance of a life. Perhaps "moral crunch" can be obviated with forewarning. As it takes more than a generation or two for families to reform cultural inheritance, our "citizenship" curriculum may be just the right locus for preparing our youth before truancy kicks in. Thirdly, let's have group therapy for everyone who wants it. You don't have to participate if you want to sell yourself short in life. It needn't cost a penny, as will be appreciated by the close of Part III. Now, we have footed a bill only for conditional sanctuaries and contemporary citizenship in schools. No bureaucrats. No need for argument or upsets. Clean consciences all round. Win-win.

"Is there a moral quality to any such processes?"
Group or dyadic human engagement of any kind takes away "emptiness"
of and in itself: much of our personal restlessness and malaise is
dissolved in any kind of togetherness. That is why children naturally
seek each other out in the playground (or wish to but for shyness);
why spouses seek illicit affairs when they feel isolated in a
marriage; why people still work in offices; why astronauts go into
outer space in twos and threes, and has much to do with why people go
to church. There is something about sheer human connection that
removes individual "lostness", satisfying us whether we have found
ourselves "morally awry" or not. But we know by now, whether in the
actual experience of our own lives (or in the case for *Nine Seahorses*
presented hitherto) that there are legitimate and illegitimate forms
of "protection" and authentic versus manipulative forms of connection
in community. This overall dimension of "moral soundness", moreover,
has much to do with our motives and the consequences of the
relationships we establish (with ourselves as much as with others)[214].
Our incessant striving in modern times to counterbalance a desire for
personal freedom and independence with a need to be anchored socially
tells us a great deal about the kind of animal species we have been
in the past 200,000 years – at the rate of 25 years per generation,
homo sapiens has precipitated about 8,000 incarnations of itself so
far – and are trying vainly to become contrary to our primeval nature
(where "nowhere is it written that we must be alone", see Chapter 8).
But as we have become technologically more advanced (especially since
the last time we were engaged in a global effort to annihilate each
other – as recently as World War II), we have bolstered our capacity
for creating "personal space" in which, supposedly, we don't have to
be "morally accountable", but have had to retreat alone to our online
bedsits and garrets for our "freedom". Some folks say that this "new"
form of human relationship (exclusively via electronic communication)
is no less legitimate than it ever has been. It just can't be true.
What happens when lovers touch? Can a baby be nurtured in cyberspace?
Why do family members visit each other when separated? What happens
when strangers smile in person? Why do workers generate synergistic
heat when they occupy the same occupational space? Do older people
want to die in the company of a virtual comforter? More to the point,
why on earth would we wish to render ourselves immune from each
other's pain, especially if we have been the architect of another's?
Perhaps, then, we need as much for the sake of our own sanity as for
the sake of compassion or justice to lodge our empathy and register
our willingness to put things right. Moral accountability is far more
privilege than it is liability. Reiterating – we must write our own
"moral scripts". No-one can tell us what to do. Groups are for
illumination of the person and formation of the togetherness that is
natural for humans who lead perverse lives if it is totally absent.
There isn't a truer, safer and more liberating "place" to exercise
mutual accountability – gaining personal freedom into the bargain –
than in mature and sensitive kindredship. The real challenges in life
itself are knowing the limits of one's own "moral illegitimacy",
knowing when games turn rancid, and knowing what to do (and what not
to do) between *rendezvous*. Work (any purposeful industry) is half the
answer. The other half answers itself, for nature abhors a vacuum: an
avalanche of unexpected but delightful turns-of-events seems to
descend upon us – merely for having surrendered away personal rust.

---

[214] We don't need to resolve difficult questions about "intrinsic morality" or "natural
law" (Chapters 3-6), because a "moral psychology" recognises these principles (motive
and consequences) in its definition of "conscience" and the ancillary questions it
poses. Since natural law recognises them also or, at least, they are not offensive to
natural law, a "moral psychology" is sustainable whether natural law pertains or not.

"Any Kind Of Togetherness"
Bathampton Weir, Avon (was Somerset)

"Can the 'nag' of conscience be disregarded, resisted, or modified by personal will or psychological therapy?"

If, in ancient days, all roads led to Rome; then, just as many threads of a "moral psychology" hang on this $64,000 question[215]. Inevitably we shall present a highly qualified response to this 'nag' for two main reasons. The first is that if the answer to our question was a blanket or easy "Yes", there would be no need for a "moral psychology". If personal "will" could "defeat" personal conscience, there would be little unhappiness, no psychopathology, few if any counsellors or psychotherapists and, for that matter, a much reduced incentive for personal religious belief. We would never hear about "conscience" or "emptiness" – because the whole phenomenon would be managed like thirst quenched by water. But we know that there is much unhappiness in the world. There is much commerce (as well as public service) in psychological treatment, and folks do look to religion for their solace (on many counts, amongst which sits personal moral integrity). The second reason our answer must be qualified is that we do not know (and may never establish) all of the possible sources of conscience. This applies to a "moral psychology" in that, whilst our putative frameworks for the conditionable human are compelling enough as they stand and may present eventually an entirely material account of conscience established in associative links (their identifiable traces in the central nervous system – as mutually antagonistic CERs – marvellously and satisfactorily explaining how they are experienced subjectively); we have no philosophical basis for underwriting such an outcome at this stage of psychological thinking generally, or psychological science in particular. On precisely the same grounds we could no more recognise divine conscience as it was depicted by Thomas Crean O.P. in Chapter 5 as psychological fact; nevertheless, any religious view of conscience is an indispensable matter of faith for many people, and there is no good reason why anybody might want to object to that (for what motive could they possess in doing so)[216]. The most immediate corollary of all this is that we just don't know whether conscience (*per se*; alternatively, as we have defined it) is an entirely re-writable psychological asset and, even supposing it were (or in relation to just those parts of it that are), we cannot possibly estimate the extent to which conscience may "be disregarded, resisted, or modified by personal will or psychological therapy" – because we have barely the most preliminary understanding of how such "un-learning" and "re-learning" can be achieved. Perhaps we may start by reflecting on the principles we have established so far and seeing where they lead us for answers. Perhaps we will find, after all, that far from having burdened us, nature has endowed us very well indeed.

---

[215] *The $64,000 Question* (broadly the model for the British TV show *Who Wants To Be A Millionaire?*) was a 1950s American TV show (based on the radio forerunner *Take It Or Leave It*) in which a contestant could take a prize for answering a question correctly or leave it as a stake against answering a more difficult one – eventually reaching a prize of $64,000 – at which point the game would end if it hadn't done so already.

[216] "Moral psychology" might be consistent with a religion depending on how a religion views "moral psychology", but "moral psychology" itself is no religious framework, let alone gospel. It has nothing to do with dogma, religious practices or human authority at all. "Moral psychology" of itself does not provide salvation (as far as Seahorse Sam is aware), for salvation is obtained by those who seek it. Someone who seeks sanity may find it in religion, and they may find it in "moral psychology". The other challenge presented by religion is the notion of "sin". Religion, on the whole, has plenty to say about "sin", but "moral psychology" has nothing to say about it. "Sin" requires redemption. Insanity can be "living hell", but it has not the same quality as eternal damnation (as far as Seahorse Sam knows anyway). Even though a religion may insist that conscience is the personal tug of the divine, religions tend to be keen on raising children correctly and espouse conscience-formation through vicarious learning (catechism). "Conscience" in a "moral psychology" welcomes any divine manifestation – but it doesn't rely on it, unless a person elects to render themselves subject to it.

… first signs of madness

Now, TA supposes that intrapsychic conversations take place between ego states, and we have wondered (only half joking) whether impasses between competing demands (which we proceeded to express in terms of conditioned emotional response) represent the first signs of madness. TA as a body must stand by the possibility of "re-writing" old learning experiences else it would enjoy no basis for psychotherapy. Behavioral therapy and CBT rely on similar principles — the reconditioning of associative links (if purely "behavioral"), and the "top down" refurbishment of faulty thinking as an adjunct (if CBT). Remaining with TA, the intrapsychic conversations look very much like "moral invitations" issued with either an authentic or a conniving RSVP; i.e., an intrapsychic pressure to respond in a conducive way. They are like gambits in interpersonal transactions, but occur within the "moral psyche" of the individual, lending weight to subjective "conscience". In a "moral psychology", the CS in TA Parent provokes a CR experienced as "approach" or "avoidance" in Child. There, a competing pressure to behave in a particular way (Thorndikeian R) may persist in situations where Parent CSs also feature; alternatively, arise from a Skinnerian history (R-S) of manipulating reinforcement. Thus, invitations may emanate not just from Parent but also (probably more surreptitiously) from TA Child (S-R and R-S) where they may meet the (complementary or opposing) force(s) of CRs in the classical (CS) environment. Given what we know about the TA ego states, we might expect a quality or feel to such invitations whereby S-S ones — having the flavour of counterinjunctions — will possess a "Parenty" feel ("You should …" and "You should not …"), whereas S-R (subtle but forceful invitations to discharge or withhold a response in a particular environment) and R-S (guileful desires to effect outcomes) ones may have a "Childy" feel ("I want to …" or "I don't want to …") — especially when "agency" attaches to the impulse germane (in which case it is R-S not S-R). Child and Parent are reminiscent of "I-Thou" distinctions effected in literature[217]. In a "moral psychology", the Child ego state is not merely structurally and functionally operant — it is also an "I" module and is that "voice" that cries "Help Me…!" in a tight spot. Parent — which contains representations of others structurally (P_3, A_3, C_3) and, being functionally aware in Controlling and Nurturing ways — is a "Thou" one. Whilst it is classical versus operant conditioning that discriminates between Parent and Child structurally, it is "I-Thou" that determines the quality of the R-S functional stance common to Child and Parent. In TA, the Adapted (conditioned) Child responds to Parent invitations in one of two modes, "Compliant" or "Rebellious" which — in a converse arrangement — may solicit compatible Parent responses (e.g., Rebellious Child invites Critical or Controlling Parent). To the TA Free Child who just wants unfettered fun, we may imagine that the lattice of learned dispositions is experienced as mere noise or, at worst, big nuisance.

… soup management

The range of competing associative pressures suspended in this Pavlovian-Thorndikeian-Skinnerian intrapsychic soup must be truly vast in both number and quality (representing the entire biography of biological learning), but they are not experienced all at once in our subjective "minds" (at least, not so far as we are aware). Chances are they are experienced mentally according to some combination of threshold rules[218] in an emotionally neutral consciousness which may approximate to TA Adult; possibly less so to Freud's Ego; moreover, which modern psychology broadly may agree involves "working memory".

---

[217] Buber, M. (1923) *Ich Und Du*. Insel-Verlag: Leipzig

[218] similar to those pertaining to retrieval from the lexicon in cognitive psychology

"Trusting Nature"
Holy Island, Lindisfarne, Northumberland

… psychological dark matter

As for the (chronologically colossal) "pre-conscious" remainder, is it rendered entirely insensible? Perhaps sub-threshold associative links vie for the limelight (of subjective experience and behavioural expression) according to their dynamic status and volatility combined with the eliciting power of the environment. On the one hand they are readily identifiable with Freud's Superego (even "latent" TA Parent) if the sub-threshold fancy is co-directional with "moral compliance", and with Freud's Unconscious or Id ("latent" TA Child at more of a stretch) on the other (especially if the phenomenon of "repression" by the conscious "mind" or Ego is sustainable empirically). Those parts of sub-threshold dark matter that generate ulterior rackets and games we may regard as Jungian shadow etc. All this stuff is elusive by definition ("inaccessible" except through professional and devious provocation in analytical psychotherapy), but we shall explore the advantages of a little "soul-searching" nevertheless during Part III.

… nature has spawned us as she has seen fit

Now, what happens if we try to apply "free will"[219] against viscosity? Perhaps we may only ever encounter personal frustration in direct proportion to the vigour of our wading in. This will almost certainly be the case if Skinner is even half way correct about "scientific determinism"; but in wondering about such possibilities we risk getting tangled in our own questions, because we could not apply personal will against a scientifically determined mesh of conditioned nodes and bonds in the central nervous system if will doesn't exist – all of our efforts and frustrations would be "determined" just as much as the objects of our bidding. Suppose then, as an alternative, we accept that the melting pot of pressures to veer this way or that (behaviourally speaking) is just nature's loving way of helping us out, and that we only experience distress when we fight it? Whether free will exists; and whether as a matter of personal stance one is an atheist or (scientific) determinist, agnostic or believer, sucker or scoffer; might we not all be willing, nevertheless, to accept that nature has spawned us as she has seen fit? Whether we enjoy our days or we are tormented by them, it is sure that we could no more have guided nature through her history than we can re-live our own pasts.

… inspiration courtesy of Thoreau

As Henry David Thoreau opined in a stirring passage from *Walden*[220]:

I think that we may safely trust a good deal more than we do. We may waive just so much care of ourselves as we honestly bestow elsewhere. Nature is well adapted to our weakness as our strength. The incessant anxiety and strain of some is a well nigh incurable form of disease. We are made to exaggerate the importance of what work we do; and yet how much is not done by us! or, what if we had been taken sick? How vigilant we are! determined not to live by faith if we can avoid it; all the day long on the alert, at night we unwillingly say our prayers and commit ourselves to uncertainties. So thoroughly and sincerely are we compelled to live, reverencing our life, and denying the possibility of change. This is the only way, we say; but there are as many ways as there can be drawn radii from one centre. All change is a miracle to contemplate; but it is a miracle which is taking place every instant. Confucius said, "To know that we know what we know, and that we do not know what we do not know, that is true knowledge." When one man has reduced a fact of the imagination to be a fact to his understanding, I foresee that all men will at length establish their lives on that basis.

---

[219] See Chapters 4 and 5 for a review.

[220] *Walden; Or, Life In The Woods* (1854) "Economy"; see also a footnote to the Preface.

What, then, is "transcendent trust", and how may we apply it? Any common-or-garden interpretation of the word "trust" implicates "letting go" or relinquishing "control". Very acceptance, which we encountered early in this Chapter, is its basic element: we accept (with a sigh of relief from our own misapplied and atrophied efforts) the world as it is rather than as we would engineer it or, at least, we accept the limits of our own capacity for moulding it. (Perhaps wisdom lurks hereabouts. We ignored the silent protests of nature just so far as we were foolishly misguided, having been "spiritually blind".) "Letting go" is exactly what it says it is. It is only "easier said than done" when we are not willing to discharge it, but sometimes we have to be pushed – and very hard indeed. Pressed into a corner, sooner or later we encounter unexpectedly our own "spiritual surrender"; suddenly appreciating how beautifully everything resides in and orbits the various "worlds" of our "moral environment" without our assistance. We discover the value and peace of spectating, when earlier we couldn't stop for fear of rendering ourselves unable to pay the rent. The "surprise view" we suddenly encounter includes the panorama of debris we left behind in our self-propelled wake. (We realise we may have "moral restorations" to make but, if we are wise, we will take time for triangulated perspective before proceeding.) Pausing to take stock of what has happened, we may have driven ourselves to helplessness in that forgiving corner, but we certainly didn't finagle our own way out of it (whether through intelligence, skill, aptitude, diligence or connivance). The penny has dropped. After the fight was lost, we found ourselves "morally aligned" with the various "worlds" of our experience with no price to pay except continued co-operation. We had only our pride to lose. Where is the fear that drove us? It has all but vanished as if of its own accord. So it is with administration of our "minds". The powerful faculty we can bring to bear to our conditioned (or otherwise inspired) consciences is "moral alignment" through yielding. In this "moral psychology", every single conscious human possesses a (fundamentally simple) "morally responsible" capacity to apply a balmy, dissonance-dispelling, tension-banishing "acquiescence" patch which has the effect of bringing in mental peace, but also affecting the likelihood of behaviour for which we find ourselves morally accountable. The patch-wielding executive (or janitor) is the "Accountable Self". It is the part of our personalities that makes "moral sense" of intrapsychic pressure ("conscience") by "settling upon" imagined and actual behavioural alternatives. What we didn't want to do is now our preferred course. The "Accountable Self" is neither conditioned like TA Compliant Child, nor entirely rational or emotionally neutral like TA Adult: neither of these are intrinsically "spiritual" faculties. Colloquially, "free will" (especially pressing on regardless) is the reverse of yielding, but we find that it is "spiritual surrender" that secured our "moral liberation". The intrapersonal congruence we experience may be new to us, but we don't object to it. We feel secure. We are comfortable in our own skin. It is as if "spiritual surrender" possessed the capacity to break associative links as effectively as one-trial flavour aversion learning[221] created them. Transcendent trust of the kind beautifully depicted by Thoreau is the natural antidote to fear. Perhaps the meaning of our trust resides in the receptacle in which we place it: the only fundamental error we make is to lodge it with ourselves. Self-reliance is *not* the answer.

---

[221] "Flavour aversion" is an instance of classical conditioning in which rats are injected with a nausea-inducing lithium salt immediately prior to presentation of food to which a novel flavour has been added. Their aversion to food imparted with that flavour is instant – acquired after one trial (pairing of CS and US – see Chapter 2).

"Surprise View"
Anne Boleyn's Seat, Fountains Abbey, North Yorkshire

"Can 'self' change 'self'?" and, if so …
The main problem with the notion that self can change self, whether
motivated to do so from within (through "strength of character" for
those to whom such expressions appeal), or under exhortations such as
"Pull yourself together!", is that in each of us several "selfs" are
in play at any one time, never mind the bubbling caldron[222] of
bothersome conditioned broth. This is not to infer that each of us is
a divided or disintegrated self, except in so far that during
episodes of our lives we may become "morally misaligned". Indeed, an
internally congruent personality doesn't experience the various selfs
arguing with each other like toddlers in a playpen – instead it knows
peace. But how far can a person bring intrapsychic congruence to
themselves, the motley choir of our various soprano, treble, alto and
bass selfs then harmonising from one hymn sheet (for those who like
business jargon never mind ecclesiastical metaphors)? Or must we have
assistance? We have said already that the avoidance of self-deceit is
pre-requisite in this business, but so also is an appreciation of
which elements of our conditioned selfs are helpful ("adaptive" in
the language of natural selection), and which are merely burdensome
and "re-writable" (a process supposing that such learning traces were
biologically written in the first place, and that the psychological
technology to reverse or otherwise compensate for them is available).
Coming to appreciate what can or should be "re-written" requires
"spiritual stocktaking" as a preliminary (see Part III for a sketch);
meantime, it is a question of illuminating what of all this we can
establish for ourselves and how much we wisely defer to relationship
with other parties. We may change only the writing on the wall. If we
try to demolish the bricks and mortar – even their very foundations –
surely we will risk far too great a "restoration" for our own good.

… the "Original Self"
Earlier in this chapter we contemplated the mysteries surrounding
human beginnings. For argument's sake, a new life precipitates an
"Original Self" which we accept was nature's doing (certainly not our
own). It has the minimal attributes of incarnation, and location in
time and place (even if it "pre-existed"); for we all know (because
of our shareable subjective experience) that not only do we exist
physically but that there is some legend woven in family folklore
surrounding our birth (even if some of us have to do some digging).
For a theoretical moment, our "Original Self" is uncontaminated by
earthly experience. We may locate our seminal human identity to some
other developmental form and co-ordinates of space-time, such as
conception (increasing the mystery but lessening the imprecision). We
may adopt whichever permutation of possibilities suits, but if we
have an ulterior motive for aligning with one rather than another –
or heaven help us we baulk at such basic propositions as these on
arcane grounds – at once we invite "moral misalignment". Since we are
similar bodily, and very probably psychologically[223], there is a *prima
facie* case for corporal and psychological templates including Jung's
archetypes to the extent that his ideas are demonstrated empirically.
Scientists tell us that we owe our "phenotype" to DNA (provided the
organism in which the double helix resides is nurtured sufficiently
in the environment)[224], and there's no good reason to argue with them.

---

[222] the refrain of the witches (brewing up an almighty mess) in Shakespeare's Macbeth:
"Double, double toil and trouble; Fire burn, and caldron bubble" (Act IV, Scene 1)

[223] If you wish to reason that my black is your white, I am happy to lose the argument
(see also Chapter 1 – *Self-indulgent philosophers*, p.5).

[224] We have met phenotypes and the heritability coefficient in Chapter 3 and Chapter 7.

In our unsympathetic depiction of the neonate as a conditionable, self-absorbed sponge, we supposed that the rapidity and embeddedness with which its "unused reservoir" of learning capacity gets written with (perceptual learning and) associative links is proportional to remaining available storage, as well as all the other factors that usually govern the rate of conditioning: distance from asymptotic strength for a given associative link, salience and discriminability of stimuli and so on. From its earliest days the infant is a receptacle for a vast network of experiential records upon which it may call later to help it survive (and reproduce if its selfish genes have their way). Now it is not unreasonable to suppose that some of these learning traces will generate mutually antagonistic pressures within conscience as we have defined it. These will include all the various "impasses" that would be recognised in TA, especially between matching Parent and Child ego states (e.g., P_2–C_2 and P_1–C_1). The cut and thrust of discipline in family and school life will raise its own conflicts (especially in the form of injunctions, permissions and counterinjunctions from parents, teachers and authority figures who don't see eye to eye), let alone the myriad of pressures from significant others in the world outside the family (including "peer pressure" and the commercial predators on TV who exploit our impatient desires). For the most part, all these anomalies and inconsistencies (aka "mixed messages") don't seem to bother children terribly – although we must keep in mind their limited capacity for articulating confusion, and standing firm in relationship to themselves in spite of all the conditioned fear to which, inevitably, they have been exposed. In TA terms, children have been accustomed to yielding "autonomy" from the earliest days of life (see Chapter 8), and do seem to want to reclaim it suddenly at adolescence (and then spend far too long at the job over their remaining adult life). We know from TA theory that we are all ulterior when it comes to growing up. We want our independence and freedom. We also want other people to help us when it all seems too much. We don't want to embrace "moral accountability" except when it is convenient to do so. It is the most natural thing in the world for children to avoid "moral responsibility"; indeed, we would be most alarmed at the prospect of a merely pubescent yet "morally precocious" hair shirt or sackcloth-in-waiting. Whatever the quality and pace of our developmental "moral trajectories", it is as sure as eggs are eggs that all of us will harbour our own precious yet occasionally unmanageable repository of experience, and that the fear resident within it will lurk cleverly hidden behind and underneath our every deed, direction and diversion.

Is there not a "natural" kind of fear that we recognise keeps us from danger, and an "unnatural" one that we bring to the table ourselves? We take our endowment from nature for granted – for we live with it every day – and have become utterly habituated to it (we would be a strange category of animal were it not so). Whatever she has afforded us in the way of perfection and robustness of body, or splendidness of health, she has left for a legacy our capacity to retrieve – from not more than an arm's length – a capacity for awe which is truly difficult to explain in scientific language (rather like "spiritual surrender"). We hear that music is made of mathematics, and that some mathematicians say that infinity is real whilst others "know" that it isn't. We are told that we cannot resolve the audible world more finely than the sampling rate embedded on a compact disc or mp3; but a vinyl enthusiast will swear by the unmatched pleasure to be had in analogue listening. No matter whom is "right", and setting aside the universal appeal of music, who can count out on the scientific abacus our subjective appreciation of beauty, or truth, or peace, or love?

So why should we be so disparaging of Mother Nature having bequeathed to us a "healthy respect" of all that would harm us? Can we not trust that she has endowed us equally well with an aptitude for sifting the fish bones from the bouillabaisse? Is our "Written Self" really so harmful to us? If so, thank goodness for psychotherapists – and we sympathetically rue the plight of all the suffering souls of history before their invention. If it rarely is, what constantly engages our poised "Accountable Self" in a lifelong confrontation for dominance?

... the inauguration of Franklin Delano Roosevelt (1882–1945)

On 4th March 1933, in the height of the Great Depression, and with a banking crisis and a pressing need for social reform playing the mood music, Franklin Delano Roosevelt (1882–1945) in his inaugural speech taking office as 32nd President of the United States of America said:

I am certain that my fellow Americans expect that on my induction into the Presidency I will address them with a candor and a decision which the present situation of our Nation impels. This is preeminently the time to speak the truth, the whole truth, frankly and boldly. Nor need we shrink from honestly facing conditions in our country today. This great Nation will endure as it has endured, will revive and will prosper. So, first of all, let me assert my firm belief that the only thing we have to fear is fear itself — nameless, unreasoning, unjustified terror which paralyzes needed efforts to convert retreat into advance. In every dark hour of our national life a leadership of frankness and vigor has met with that understanding and support of the people themselves which is essential to victory. I am convinced that you will again give that support to leadership in these critical days.

... the sole impediment to "moral sanity"

Isn't just such "nameless, unreasoning, unjustified terror which paralyzes needed efforts to convert retreat into advance" *the* sole and ultimate impediment to "moral sanity" itself? The fear that rendered us handicapped by resentments ("less fresh than a daisy") only a few pages since was not the "useful" fear of beneficent nature; rather, it was the personal terror that is both mother and father to self-centred "will": the lie that drives our every mistake, our every ulterior gambit – and every disrupted relationship in all of the personal and interpersonal "worlds" that make up our global "moral environment" – a lie we are so curiously disposed to believe.

... back to Eric Berne (and Pearl Drago)

Where has it come from? In *The Structure And Dynamics Of Organizations And Groups*[225], Eric Berne identified three elements of any group culture: "Etiquette" (analogous to TA Parent – the group's beliefs and values; its authority; the stereotypical and internally acceptable ways that groups or communities behave within their own confines including "them" and "us" prejudices); "Technical Culture" (analogous to TA Adult – a group or community's real and conceptual infrastructure including its physical resources), and its "Character" (especially its mood or emotional quality – analogous to TA Child). In the TA framework for which Pearl Drago won the 2004 Eric Berne Memorial Award from the International Transactional Analysis Association (ITAA), these three elements are stacked vertically in a predictable fashion and represented in (introjected into) our Parent ego states along with all of our other (P_3, A_3, C_3) parent and authority figure stacks. It isn't a terribly convoluted conceptual struggle to regard this transmission exactly as we have done the parental counterinjunctions; i.e., it works because of a developing child's exposure to an almost unimaginatively intricate and detailed

---

[225] Berne, E. (1963) *The Structure And Dynamics Of Organizations And Groups.* Lippincott: Philadelphia

array of reinforced (previously neutral) environmental stimuli. This whole process is, of course, consistent with a "moral psychology" although, unlike TA, we suppose that the process starts early because of our reconfiguration of the TA Parent ego state as an S-S module. At the fundamental level, there is no need to distinguish (cultural) reinforcement types beyond "pleasant" and "aversive"; nevertheless, there may be huge ramifications of layered (CS) distinctions on a pragmatic level. Similarly, cultural transmission may occur via cultural injunctions and conditioning of P_1, A_1, C_1 in Child (C_2) including, of course, the "Magical Parent" – arguably a difficult interloper to budge. Culture may be evaluated (as one might expect in a TA framework) along a dimension of (existential) OK-ness, and TA's concept of culture, formulated in this way, may be strategically harnessed and re-established in order to break "cultural script" transmission, especially in the modern world ("global village") where social injustices are more visible than they used to be, and folks can develop the courage at grass roots to stand up and be counted.

… we have a long history of mutual oppression

But it wasn't always so. We have a long history of mutual oppression.

… will the real moral Dalek stand up

Is it too much for us to bear to imagine that, just as we have been (spuriously) obsessed with "toughness" for goodness knows how much of our recent cultural history (see Chapter 7), we have been just as misdirected by (its schoolyard chum) "free will"? From the vantage point of the present, we have solved neither the "mind-body problem" (see Chapter 4) nor resolved "free will" after 13 billion years of post-Big Bang unravelling; thousands of millions of years of natural selection following the explosion of life on planet earth; 200,000 years of human history; 70,000 years of primitive global expansion since "Out of Africa"; 12,000 years of brutal competition since the last Ice Age; latitudinal exploitation of the "fertile crescent"; thousands of years of "civilisation" established with the sword and many other forms of military ingenuity; two-and-a-half millennia of "clever thinking" since Socrates, Jeremiah, Confucius and the Buddha; Ancient Greece; the Roman Empire; Islam and its expansion; the Holy Roman Empire and the Christian Crusades; medieval human wonders (13th century philosophers such as Thomas Aquinas and Bonaventure, together with their Eastern counterparts) and medieval architectural ones (cathedrals and non-Christian infrastructure); Asian warriors such as Genghis Khan; the Scientific Revolution; the Enlightenment; the stoicism of existentialism; humanism and the new fashionable atheism … not one of these has nailed the old quandaries. Perhaps something is wrong with our thinking. Perhaps it's time to go back to basics. Is it so far fetched as to imagine that our cultural inheritance has infected our mindsets as much as our social structures? Did it ever suit a medieval landowner to have a serf believe that he must choose to stay out of trouble? And where on earth did he get that idea from? Surely not in very antiquity when a Pharaoh managed, even after death, to induce armies of slaves, both indigenous and international, to "decide" and "redecide" to "happily" embrace their toilsome lot?

… heaping blindness upon blindness

Not only, then, are we subject to those most recent of our family's intergenerational imperatives – through grandparental and parental breeding of our "Inner Child" (C_2) where, eventually, we develop glowering fantasies (in P_1) about non-compliance with their dreadful demands – but we host the spectre of their representations mentally in our TA Parent ego states where they constantly remind us of how to "be good" in all of the circumstances of our lives. Added to all of this, we (like our parents) caretake the echoes of the ancients, also constantly exhorting us to "will" ourselves "freely" into conformity.

"Medieval Wonder"
Salisbury Cathedral, Wiltshire

… towards an understanding of control

In Chapter 2 we noted:

Whether Skinner is correct or not, any organism's subjectively experienced capacity for "controlling" its environment that arises out of conditioning processes may be illusory anyway, and this applies to humans. Aberrant CERs, such as disproportionate fear, are a specific case – not just because they are irrational – but because they have a counter-adaptive effect on functioning. Such modern heresy constitutes no argument against "consciousness", "conscience" and "choice" – which may rely on discriminable (other) faculties.

Now, what do we mean by "illusory" control? Is there any other kind? Is there "disproportionate fear" that is not "aberrant CERs"? If so, why and whence does it exist, how might we recognise it and can it be dismissed? Given that we have addressed "consciousness" (the "mind-body problem") and "conscience" in the deliberate way that we have, what could we mean by "choice" assuming we are reluctant to brook "free will"? Is "choice" a practicable concession between "free will" and "acquiescence"? Is it a fair expression of our "moral capacity"?

… biological control is natural and provisionally "illusory"

We have acknowledged biological "fear" and its converse "hope"[226] as two forms of reinforcement (which may, after all, be unidimensional in terms of "drive" expressed through the central nervous system), and which are necessary attributes of lifecycle systems both within an organism and in the Darwinian evolution of species through natural selection. These are the bequest of nature and are indispensable. Such reinforcement is the "battery" without which none of the building blocks of learning that we have recognised (S-S; S-R; R-S) could occur. Amongst these three, it is possible that S-S and S-R are more "passive" in the sense that mere exposure to the environment represents a significant element of the associative link, whereas R-S seems unavoidably contingent on some subjective expectation of the occurrence of the target stimulus. We have suggested that the TA Parent ego state is actually the physical register of S-S learning whereas TA Child comprises an "early" S-R register which becomes out-or updated with "guileful" R-S – possibly during some developmental phase in which language is acquired or becomes critically sophisticated, and the TA Child develops a qualitatively distinct character (which we would expect to be reflected in behaviour). The occurrence of the response in S-R may even be extra-conscious, not merely "illusory". R-S guilefulness is "real" in terms of subjective experience – but we have not anchored it truly in biology (else we might have cracked the "mind-body problem" for eternity) and, until such time as that may ever happen, it is provisionally "illusory".

… the witches of Macbeth and the Pied Piper of Hamelin[227]

The range of learning experiences accumulated by a vertebrate animal such as a human being in only one day must be truly vast, let alone an entire lifetime. Reverberating with vicarious motivational energy, we may imagine they swirl in a caldron of conditioned slurry, vying for attention in subjective experience and behavioural expression[228].

---

[226] which, eventually, we become confident enough to distinguish from "spiritual" hope!

[227] The fairytale of the Pied Piper of Hamelin (Hameln) can be interpreted in as many ways as we have the imagination and patience to bear. In medieval Germany, a man dressed in colourful clothing, and who could play a whistle passably well, lured the town's children away in a trance. Was he a hypnotic serial killer? Was he exacting revenge for non-payment of rat-catching fees? Is the story merely symbolic of medieval migrations throughout Europe, or the devastation of populations wrought by plague? Perhaps we shall never know. Intriguingly, some children with disabilities were saved.

[228] figuratively speaking – in the "pressure cooker we all know" (see Chapter 8, p.106)

The temptation to wax poetically from verses of the "Written Self" engraved in bound anthologies registered in the Superego, the Id and the Jungian shadow is too strong to resist. Whilst conflicts between mutually antagonistic CERs may bother children little (setting aside traumas), in even modest levels they become greatly troublesome for "grown-ups" who wish to avoid their beck, call or heed. Surely that is the most convincing case yet for a Freudian Ego – an ("illusory" until established in biology) part of "guileful" consciousness that doesn't want its R-S trajectory interrupted. It brushes inconvenient CERs under the carpet (where it is Shadow) hoping they will lay as sediment in the smouldering caldron whose liquid contents are Id[229]. Supposedly dormant there, they may not interfere with the more reckonable effects of our greedy machinations. If this is where we have ventured – if we find ourselves rehearsing the acquisition (or loss) of more than we need biologically – we have projected ourselves into the existential wilderness Roosevelt so shrewdly foresaw. We develop an "unnatural" fear and the "self-will" to back it up. Since these collapse under the slightest "moral scrutiny", they are the most "illusory" of our existential experiences – yet the ones that undermine our relationships the most. Adolescents and adults, then, to the extent that their "consciences" ever become "overloaded", bear the testing burden of having (unless they wish to persevere with intrapsychic misalignment and behavioural distraction) to distinguish between aberrant CERs (in which case particular professional and non-professional treatment – even, less formal helping – may be remedial) and the ancient, nurturing call of nature (in which case resistance may or may not be useless depending on the therapeutic technology available). We may suppose that the category "aberrant CERs" is a broad one, encompassing not merely biographic learning, but also the mind-buggering "spiritual blindness" of swathes of our ancestors[230] – something we could refer to (only subjectively unless and until we agree) as "cultural moral infection"[231]. Doubtless a divine source of conscience would not be in the least bit refutable by mere, squealing mortals; still, don't we let our own toddlers off the hook just for demonstrating the willingness to fall sufficiently well back in line?

… steam or fog: take your pick

A "moral psychology" can happily accept that "conscience" (all told) is experienced meteorologically as (occasionally very dense) fog that may need deciphering; moreover, that although some of that fog is not of our own making, and may even have been dumped on us uninvited as "weight of human history" (see Chapter 6), we cannot ignore it in the long run. Sooner or later we must bring to bear to that perplexity our "Accountable Self" which, having the capacity to effect "moral discernments", discharges a simple dichotomous function: "willingness to align" ("OK then …") as opposed to belligerence to invitation ("No" or "Yeah but …") – thereby "settling upon" alternatives and reducing mental tension ("cognitive dissonance"). Perhaps it is like a quivering magnetic compass where pursuit of roughly the indicated direction will satisfy, but unthinking retraction or diversion only curtails visibility and deepens "lostness". By now it should be clear that this "choosing" function is not the same thing as unqualified (TA) "decision", "redecision" or anything else offensively redolent

---

[229] The entire chant of the witches leaves one in no doubt (even if in great amusement) about the allegorical compatibility of their vile concoction and the unconscious mind.

[230] The merits of the argument against fertile crescent pugilists, Pharaohs and serf-bashers aside it is, of course, more convenient to blame the faceless, absent deceased for our fears than to confront and settle "moral accountabilities" amongst the living.

[231] In *Walden*, Thoreau's exhortation to live by faith in nature is an expansion of his argument, "One generation abandons the enterprises of another like stranded vessels".

of "free will" – especially if coerced from a broken person by a powerful therapist (of any persuasion – even more so if such coercion takes place behind closed doors where, unlike the group therapy environment, there are no witnesses). Like R-S guile, the "moral discernment" of the "Accountable Self" is not proven as a biological entity, but since it is that mysterious faculty capable of "spiritual surrender" – which broadens our experiential horizons so beautifully and limitlessly – it does seem somewhat crass to describe it as "illusory". Perhaps we can say it is certainly not "illusory" to those who have exercised it well. Interestingly, it is as subject to "validation" through "shareable subjective experience" as much as any existentially significant matter; in fact, it may *require* unselfish sharing amongst human beings in order to be nourished and sustained.

… doing what comes naturally

Such new (spiritual) horizons may be appreciated at second hand from another's description, just like the testimony of Chapter 6's fool who found her or himself on a losing wicket having persisted in a bad game. The effect of surrender is so simple, sudden and spectacular that it transcends those "stars and spangles" of our imaginations as they once attended the prospect of the rewards promised by O'Grady – seeming[232] to shred to ribbons in an instant a great proportion of all the associative links that chained us to our own bludgeoning incongruence. It is compatible with the rapid "cure" that Eric Berne might have anticipated from group therapy based on Transactional Analysis. Such existential shifts can be sudden but, as we have said, they may be effective in small doses as steady remedies to minor dilemmas and – this being so – they are reminiscent of the gradual spiritual awakenings recognised by William James in *The Varieties Of Religious Experience: A Study In Human Nature* (1902). The draw of such experiences is such that direction becomes a watchword. To turn about and walk back to the past would be to steal spiritually from oneself, as if a pilgrim shooting directly into the sandaled foot. A diligently maintained course is like a "spiritual rolling stone" gathering "spiritual moss". It is self-perpetuating like the vicious spiral that can take a life towards peril, darkness and oblivion rather than safety, freedom and light. The road unravels of its own accord as our footsteps increase in number. We are foolish if we insist on ourselves as cartographers, or too often fix co-ordinates for our "spiritual journeys", even its stage posts and resting spots. We take each day as it comes passing through in "transcendent trust". Our personalities have reformed from within. Visibly we are more relaxed, proportionate and playful. We are less self-centred. In a painfully superior manner, Friedrich Nietzsche abandoned us "motley" lot to "slave morality" (good for the masses – see Chapter 5), simultaneously exhorting exceptional people to "become what you are"[233]. Eric Berne pitched a barely distinguishable gauntlet to the "unprepared" (see Chapter 8), and we have accepted its challenge. More generously than Nietzsche and Berne, the abolitionist Thoreau encouraged *all of us* to advance confidently in the direction of our dreams – to live the life we have imagined – where we may expect to meet with extraordinary success (see footnote to Chapter 6 on p.61). Following *his* counsel, we found ourselves doing what comes naturally.

---

[232] A now considerable body of work on the synaptic plasticity underlying classical conditioning in *Aplysia Californica* suggests it is an elaboration of "sensitisation". As "habituation" (or, learning to ignore an irrelevant stimulus) is the behavioural reverse of sensitisation, perhaps "spiritual surrender" (from the "Accountable Self") generates a precipitous phenomenon which is like habituation in so far as it involves forfeiture of attention or, in this proposition, the sudden release of over-valued rewards signalled by CSs in one swoop, leaving us pleasantly free of dispensable CERs.

[233] Nietzsche's pet motto – actually attributable to the Greek poet Pindar (522-443 BC)

SUMMARY OF AN INTEGRATED DEVELOPMENTAL "MORAL PSYCHOLOGY"			
Being	Animal (vertebrate)	Human (*homo sapiens*) Animal (vertebrate)	Spiritually accounted Human (*homo sapiens*) Animal (vertebrate)
Faculty	Pre-language	Language (LAD) Pre-language	"Spiritual surrender" Language (LAD) Pre-language
Physis	Pre-conscious	Conscious	Spiritually awakened
(Piagetian) Developmental Stage	Sensori-motor	Formal Operations Concrete Operations Pre-operational	Spiritually intuitive Formal Operations Concrete Operations Pre-operational
Aesthetics	Instinctual	Creatively wilful Instinctual	Passive / Content Creatively aligned Instinctual
Unconscious Material	Superego	Superego	Superego
TA Parent: Structure P_3 P_3 P_3 A_3 A_3 A_3 C_3 C_3 C_3	"Voiceless" S-S (Approach / Avoid)	"Verbal" S-S (Approach / Avoid) "Voiceless" S-S (Approach / Avoid)	"Verbal" S-S (Approach / Avoid) "Voiceless" S-S (Approach / Avoid)
TA Parent: Function CP | NP	(CER)	"You should …" R-S "You need …" R-S (CER)	"You should …" R-S "You need …" R-S (CER)
Buberian Identities	(Satisfy) Me	"You (will provide)" "(Give) Me"	"Thou (art / Thy will)" "You (are and need)" "I (am and desire)"
Conversations	Pre-language "monologue"	Me-centred dialogue	We-centred discourse
TA Child: Structure P_1 A_1 C_1	Wordless fear in P_1 Autonomy-ceding A_1 Somatic C_1 Thorndikeian S-R	Skinnerian R-S Guileful P_1 Wilful A_1 Somatic C_1 Thorndikeian S-R	Skinnerian R-S Integrated P_1 Reasonable A_1 Somatic C_1 Thorndikeian S-R
TA Child: Function AC | FC	"Auto" S-R (/ CER)	Wilful R-S ("Yes"/"No") "Auto" S-R (/ CER)	Co-operative R-S "Auto" S-R (/ CER)
Unconscious Material	Jungian shadow Id	Jungian shadow Id	Jungian shadow Id
Psychic Pain	Frustration	Guilt / Shame Intolerance	Compassion Shame / Dismay Impatience

Referring to the diagram on the adjacent page, the last three columns (to the right) represent stages of being. Human beings (*homo sapiens*) are an instance of vertebrates, but the only species amongst them with language (as we recognise its texture, richness and complexity). Arguably, and according to Euan Macphail (*supra*), language endows the developing human child with consciousness and a sense of a "self". Macphail considers it tenable that subjective pain perception is a corollary of language development and co-emergent with consciousness. In a "moral psychology" we are suggesting – without an empirical foundation, but on sufficient theoretical grounds given how we have woven conditioning accounts of learning (aka "scientific psychology") with the TA ego states (philosophical descendants of Freudian theory and thereby "analytical psychology" as far as we are concerned) – that (non-human vertebrates and) the pre-verbal human child possesses Pavlovian S–S (i.e., classical conditioning) and Thorndikeian S–R (operant conditioning), but lacks Skinnerian R–S (also operant conditioning but relying on an alternative associative explanation – see Chapter 2). R–S is distinguished from S–R by the presence of some subjective mental anticipation of the target stimulus – a disposition which is "wilful" in the human child (and "guileful" in her or his fantasies). We are positing that the TA Child ego state is an operant module relying on S–R only (i.e., no R–S) until the neural mechanisms that underlie node formulation are "injected" from a developmental "Language Acquisition Device" (or LAD) – at which time operant nodes and links take on a different quality whereby old S–R learning is overlaid, updated or replaced by R–S. "Early" S–R is perfectly and delightfully compatible with all the phenomena that TA recognises including pre-verbal injunctions and permissions; the pre-verbal autonomy-yielding "early decisions" (in A_1); the "Somatic Child" (C_1) including all its ancient, corporal and "inaccessible" learning which is difficult to access in psychotherapy – and it also accommodates cultural injunctions very neatly too. In so far as S–R is overlaid rather than abolished by R–S, it is a lifelong raft of learning – and accounts for conditioned (operant) emotional responding in situations feigning familiarity (through generalisation of context). Once language has developed, and R–S has taken over, the "decisions" in A_1 (the "Little Professor") become first linguistically hinged and then ever more rational. P_1 similarly becomes less "penetrating, mordant and caustic" with time. Every instance of autonomy-yielding – whether pre-verbal or verbal – is "dumped" as resentment (perhaps in C_1, but we may as much suggest unconscious Jungian "shadow"). TA Parent is differentiated from TA Child by its Pavlovian (S–S) or "classical" structure which is "early" (aka "voiceless") like Child but of course beyond any kind of casual recollection in the older child or adult. Once language has arrived, the respective ego states also possess an "I–Thou" (Buberian) quality which differentiates their functional operations and permits intrapsychic dialogue focussed mainly on the Child's "Me". The tensions within conscience as we have defined it in Chapter 5 arise at least in part out of the various conditioned and unconditioned pressures on behaviour (which may be antagonistic for variations in Pavlovian and Thorndikeian conditioning for the same or similar environments). Human "spiritual surrender" – which may happen in large and small phases – precipitates a "spiritual awakening" by which illusory "will" is subjugated to "right-thinking" including: an awareness of the antiquity of nature and a proportionate perspective of our role in her unravelling; a passive (transcendent) appreciation of beauty, and a mature compassion for all humankind characterised by detachment and "gracious giving". Whereas TA autonomy may have been the Berneian prerogative of "certain fortunate people" (see Chapter 8), a "moral psychology" is for nobody if it is not for *Everyman*.

Doing what comes naturally is a "Careful Balancing Act" that can be mistaken for showing off, as demonstrated by Jonathan

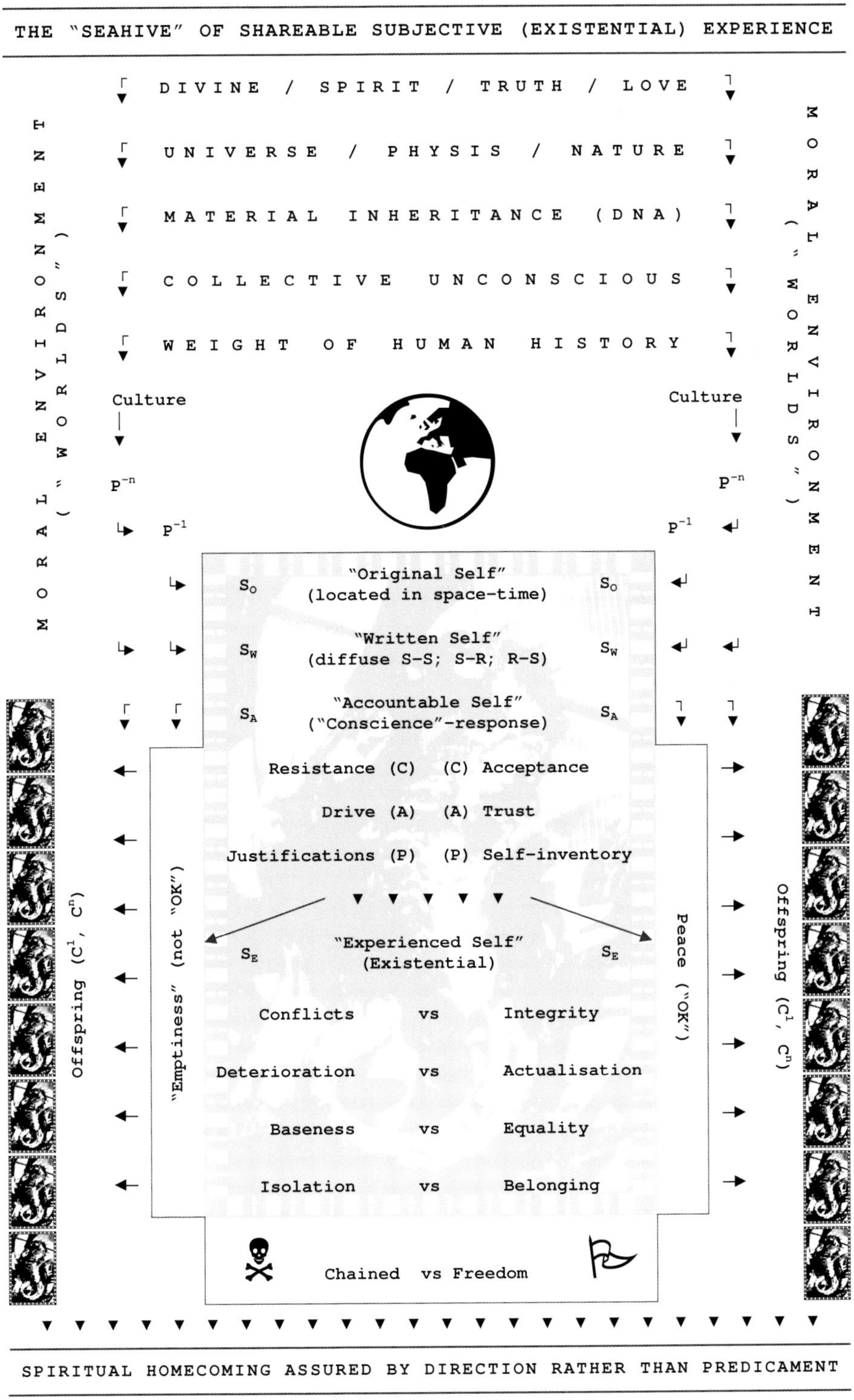

THE "SEAHIVE" OF SHAREABLE SUBJECTIVE (EXISTENTIAL) EXPERIENCE

DIVINE / SPIRIT / TRUTH / LOVE

UNIVERSE / PHYSIS / NATURE

MATERIAL INHERITANCE (DNA)

COLLECTIVE UNCONSCIOUS

WEIGHT OF HUMAN HISTORY

MORAL ENVIRONMENT ("WORLDS")

MORAL ENVIRONMENT ("WORLDS")

Culture

Culture

P^{-n}

P^{-n}

P^{-1}

P^{-1}

S_O "Original Self" (located in space-time) S_O

S_W "Written Self" (diffuse S-S; S-R; R-S) S_W

S_A "Accountable Self" ("Conscience"-response) S_A

Resistance (C)   (C) Acceptance

Drive (A)   (A) Trust

Justifications (P)   (P) Self-inventory

S_E "Experienced Self" (Existential) S_E

"Emptiness" (not "OK")

Peace ("OK")

Offspring (C^1, C^n)

Offspring (C^1, C^n)

Conflicts	vs	Integrity
Deterioration	vs	Actualisation
Baseness	vs	Equality
Isolation	vs	Belonging

Chained vs Freedom

SPIRITUAL HOMECOMING ASSURED BY DIRECTION RATHER THAN PREDICAMENT

… the "Seahive" of "shareable subjective experience"

A "Seahive" of "shareable subjective experience" is positioned under Jonathan's obliging gaze on the two previous pages. It should require very little explanation beyond the elucidatory material that has been presented already – particularly in Part II. The diagram assists with fusion of the broader principles behind a "moral psychology". Its focal point is at the vital frontier between the "Written Self" and the "Accountable Self". This is where the "moral action" takes place. Whether she is empress of all in her own right, or she is a faithful and obedient servant to a Godhead whom we are willing to recognise in our quaint and peculiar ways, nature has endowed us with a personal capacity to bear the weight of our entire inheritance – the spiritual and psychological tonnage of all of our massive vertical legacies (for a day at a time anyway) – armed most potently with the simple faculty of "spiritual surrender". Strangely, we can't seem to extract it from mother earth, fettle it from the elements, manufacture it, bottle it, market it, buy it, sell it, steal it or wrench it from a reluctant other: somehow we must recycle it freely amongst ourselves. Our preparedness to embrace it (for it is a gift once it is sought) determines the quality of our (Existential or) "Experienced Self". We can "go nuts" without it (although some of us may remain quite sane) or we can soar like Jonathan – knowing it courses beneath our wings.

… a keyword guide to the "Seahive" model of "moral sanity"

As an adjunct to the Seahive, a ready reckoner affording the flavour of "moral psychology" at not more than a glance is presented below.

A KEYWORD GUIDE TO THE "SEAHIVE" MODEL OF "MORAL SANITY"

The "Seahive" embraces …	The "Seahive" marginalises …
acceptance	(social) alienation
(the) "Accountable Self"	(strategic) atheism
advocacy	corruption (all misuse of power, and money)
associative learning (S–S; S–R; R–S)	"cultural moral infection"
autonomy	denial (D.E.N.I.A.L.)
"civic maturity"	"descending vicious spirals"
Civil Disobedience (Thoreau)	diathesis (weakness)
"competent coxswains"	domination, oppression and persecution
(personal) "conscience"	(existential) "emptiness"
counter-culture	(self-centred) fear
(the ideas of) Eric Berne (1910-1970)	free (and impolitely-imposed) will
(the) "Experienced Self"	(Transactional Analysis or TA) games
group therapy	(third party) human authority
Henry David Thoreau (1817-1862)	(mental or any other) illness
(human) history	inferiority (and compensatory superiority)
"moral alignment"	ingratitude
"moral economics"	intolerance (all prejudice and bigotry)
(the) "moral environment"	loneliness (self-imposed isolation)
(a personal) "moral psychology"	materialism
nature	(the) "mind-body problem"
Nine Seahorses	nationalism (as self-interest)
(the) "Original Self"	nihilism (existential pessimism)
(world) peace	parochialism (and protectionism)
(personal) responsibility	polarities, extremism and fanaticism
"poacher(s)-turned-gamekeeper" (PTGs)	pollution and environmental vandalism
safety nets	(all) psychopathology
(personal) sanity	(Transactional Analysis or TA) rackets
"shareable subjective experience"	self-pity
simple living	(the illusion of) "self-reliance"
"spiritual equality"	(any) self-absorption
(the) "spiritual mirror"	(the) separation (of humankind)
(a) "spiritual revolution"	"spiritual blindness"
"spiritual surrender"	(our cultural obsession with) "toughness"
Transactional Analysis (TA)	ulterior motives
"transcendent trust"	victimisation and victimhood
Walden; Or, Life In The Woods	(all) violence and war
(the) "Written Self"	(the) "weight of human history"

… "Why are there psychotherapists?"

Capturing what we have said so far, psychotherapists exist because: (i) there is unremitting human "emptiness" in our world (because nobody has ever discovered what we have all come to expect in our fashionable scientific culture – i.e., a "cure" for it); (ii) anybody who suffers from it is driven naturally to ameliorate cognitive dissonance, personal disaffection and "spiritual bankruptcy"; (iii) as a species, we are disposed to "moral expediency", i.e., taking a short-cut to mental relief, even if it is an artificial one (meaning that whether it is a chemical fix or some other kind, it relies on a misapprehension of "moral reality" and will, inevitably, last only fleetingly making things *worse not better* beyond the immediate term); (iv) once precipitated, this process may develop into a (potentially fatal) vicious spiral, polluting the more intimate of the various "worlds" of our "moral environment"; (v) the main reason we permit this to happen to ourselves (for we are not really fools – nature gave us brains to work things out) is that we cannot see our own self-deceit – we suffer from "spiritual blindness"; (vi) even when we can see ourselves more as we really are, we may have become so weakened that we need the help of other people to stand back on our own two feet; (vii) because we are a socially fickle and intolerant lot, with a shameful record of mutual oppression, it takes extreme "moral courage" (or utter defeat) for an insane person to "come clean" about the true nature of their problems (assuming sufficient clarity has descended on our "moral casualty" of its own accord); (viii) we do not organise ourselves well enough to short-circuit this tragic merry-go-round with reorienting safety nets and free group therapy; (ix) sufficient "moral pain" will prompt most people into ulterior self-referral including "games" and drastic forms of appeal for assistance (including parasuicide) from institutions which might become regarded as sanctuaries; (x) our public health systems suffer from political agendas, misdirected resources and limited competence (not because they are unprofessional, but because they are humans in blissful ignorance like the rest of us; moreover, they are muddled amongst themselves about "knottedness" and "relevance"); (xi) some people consider themselves sufficiently competent to pick up the pieces, and have organised themselves in sophisticated professional ways for discharging this function and (xii) there is sufficient demand to keep a curiously diverse multi-sector industry on its feet.

… all but complete

The case for a "moral psychology" is all but complete[234]. It already exists. It already works. It has saved many lives. It has afforded meaning and purpose to many others. It was never invented but arrived on the (Darwinian) tide of human speciation itself which, for all we know, was energised by nature herself in such a manner that *homo sapiens* amongst all her children might look back in awe at what she has done. But seemingly "moral psychology" has gone AWOL in one fugue from both the DNA double helix and the psychotherapeutic literature. *Nine Seahorses* is, in one sense, simply one participant's perspective of it encased in a broader appreciation of modern psychology. Perhaps many therapists already believe in "moral psychology" – even as it as been depicted in *Nine Seahorses* – but what do you call it at work? Is your first greeting to a prospect, aside from diversion to a hot tub, clean sheets, basic food and a comfortable chair, an invitation to "spiritual surrender" underwritten by the conviction and assured presence of a smiling crowd of poachers-turned-gamekeeper including yourself? What, to the uninitiated, is *this* strange breed of animal?

---

[234] barring the imminent completion of this Chapter, our notes on empirical support (Chapter 10) and Part III which is a breezy tour through "moral psychology" in action

Poachers-turned-gamekeeper (PTGs) are people who have turned a corner. A "spiritual awakening", whether precipitous or gradual, has projected a PTG from an old biographic journey into a qualitatively different one. How could we know this has happened? Because when (assuming they are willing) they tell their story, most folks will be able to discern by intuition its authenticity. A PTG almost certainly will; in other words, "It takes one to know one"[235]. This is why PTGs are more well equipped than most to discern the transition into "readiness" – or very "spiritual surrender" – that is, in practice, the sticky gateway through which anybody must pass in order to make "moral progress" – whether in living generally or in psychotherapy. Facilitating willingness to change (its formation and its sustenance) is known in professional settings as "motivational interviewing", and is regarded as a teachable skill. PTGs need no training to recognise the vital change in another that has already occurred in themselves. Curiously "spiritual surrender", or willingness in general (provided it is authentic and not contrived or feigned), seems as often as not to be all that is required for personality shifts to occur, following which the affected lives always develop a mysterious healing quality. Genuine PTGs will almost always have come into possession of such treasures; what is more to the point, they are able – and often want to – help shipwrecked sailors reach dry land just as they have done. To the unfamiliar eye, or the ignorant sceptic, such helpfulness may be interpreted patronisingly as "rescue". If it is badly motivated helping (such as for personal recognition or acquiring a sense of power or efficacy), then that is what it is. But if it is offered in a spirit of compassion and love, then *that* precisely is what it is. You can always tell the difference between a PTG and a sceptic – it is roughly proportional to the income they receive for being loving. A PTG is also familiar at first hand with the "Inside Job" (the title of Part I refers) undertaken by the person who must effect "moral redirection". In this occupation they possess a superlative capacity for holding a "spiritual mirror" to the person who becomes ready to examine the dark basement archives of their own personalities (framed perhaps around the personal biographic R-S agenda, but also with deep understanding of the hindrance of TA "script"), especially all the layers of idiosyncratic fears, resentments and self-centred pursuits – the "bad game" which we all play in degrees, but lose in the end[236]. The PTGs' appreciation of the value of this process, and the ways in which their own confidences have been respected by PTGs of the past who showed them their own new horizons, assures not only the security of the apprentice's trust, but also the "spiritual equality"[237] that combats all the superiorities and power imbalances (independent of clinical paranoia) that can contaminate professional environments. The identification that a "spiritual casualty" may obtain instantly with a PTG represents a strong case for how to operate "safety nets". These PTG principles are universal and may be applied in a vast array of health and social settings: recovery from coronary heart disease and cancer; children helping other children through trauma recovery; youth alienation and offending (see Chapter 6); single sex issues; gender issues; all of the recognisable addictions including alcohol, drugs, gambling and codependency (relationship problems) – and the recovery and redirection of any groups of people with any worthwhile purpose – from the smallest of families to national service agencies.

---

[235] aka, "You can't kid a kidder" – see also Chapter 7 (*Capacity for empathy*, p.78).

[236] The entirety of Part II of *Nine Seahorses* makes the case that "You can't win a bad game". The underlying notion is not dissimilar to "karma" in Hinduism or Buddhism.

[237] See Chapters 7 and 8 for expansion.

"Dark Basement Archives"

… "spiritual laundering" and group therapy

Whilst, in practice, some reparative work may need to be done in private (i.e., with one trusted confidant) – especially that relating to the most soiled of our "spiritual laundry"[238] – the facilitating power of relationship in psychological helping is better expressed in groups rather than dyads. Why? A preliminary case, based on relevance (to "normal" living), was presented at the close of Chapter 7. The long and short of everything else left to say in favour of group therapy has mostly to do with clean power – and honesty. If a person shares something about themselves that they wish to retain (e.g., "I have come to realise that …"), the power of witness in the group is exponentially greater than the privacy of a one-to-one relationship. The group affords some cancelling out of, and some protection against the yet unhealed and less wholesome (more judgemental and corrupt) elements of our individual personalities. Conversely, the capacity that a group has to love (appropriately affirm) its members is also that much more potent. In TA such affirmation is known as "stroking" (as we saw in Chapter 8). To the extent that Claude Steiner's notions about the "stroke economy"[239] are tenable – especially how "stroke deprivation" in families may be developmentally corrosive – the group can compensate wonderfully. The group doesn't get paid for that love even if the therapist or facilitator (as a stroke purveyor) does, and it thereby remains less contaminated by "ego defence" and any other form of self-interest. In groups, the practitioner is protected from the kinds of unwitnessed misunderstandings that can emerge from behind closed doors. Groups are less susceptible to the happenstance of people's lives: absences, vagrancies, illnesses, (and remissions,) flares and fatalities. If therapy is paid for, the group option is arithmetically the cheaper. The power-cost ratio of group therapy is so massive compared with individual therapy that it is a wonder that individual therapy prevails at all. Perhaps people have their own reasons for persisting in it; however, the issue is certainly one for personal and professional reflection. Our TA hero Eric Berne believed in group therapy. All told, the argument for groups is overwhelming. A formal review[240] of the evidence in favour of the efficacy of psychotherapy suggested that it does actually work – but mostly because of the confidence a client has in the therapist: who they are (probably their charisma), and the therapist's own belief in the process. Psychotherapy works because of collaboration and trust. All psychotherapy has a great deal to do with the power of confidence.

… light bulbs and coxswains

Each psychotherapeutic approach, nevertheless, draws on some or other theoretical foundation in order to obtain and afford conviction in the remunerated treatment that it delivers. Some of these approaches are explicitly "integrative"; i.e., they are multi-faceted and able to assimilate diverse solutions to "knottedness" as they see fit for any given client. Individual therapists within one domain vary along some dimension of religious versus relaxed adherence to the tenets of the background philosophy that applies. Whilst from one point of view such diversity represents choice for clients, we have made a substantial case (Chapter 7 and elsewhere) against an uncoordinated industry leaving clients floundering on the periphery of the system – rather than fix the navigation lights or pay reasonable wages for the coxswains (advocates) needed to bring the wrecks safely into harbour.

---

[238] where an argument in favour of the strongest of *unconditional* confidences prevails

[239] Steiner, C. (1971) The stroke economy. *Transactional Analysis Journal*, 1:3, 9–15.

[240] Wampold, B.E. (2001) *The Great Psychotherapy Debate: Models, Methods and Findings*. Lawrence Erlbaum Associates: Mahwah

… thank you

On arrival at port, is it not "love" that battered vessels respond to best even if they have paid for it? Why do you want to name it "care" instead? What does the extra yardage of detachment really afford you? No matter what "professional services" therapists believe they deliver for cash, is it not love that they actually impart – because anything else misses the mark. Tough love is fine: perhaps the only kind that matters for the majority of truly washed up seafarers. But love it is. You sell love – whether directly or by proxy. Is there anything inherently inferior about a service that is conditional on the payment of a fee? Perhaps not if, as some of you say, a client needs to hurt in the pocket as well as in the heart in order to gain the starting momentum necessary to effect "moral progress". Perhaps so, unless you have become so free of "moral corruption" yourselves – not merely as individuals but as one inscrutable façade to the defencelessly troubled – that you can retain all of your personal and professional interests[241] in separately-dug millponds where they may never overlap (even when it rains). Then again, until we have learned to love each other (when money for love shall be rendered an old-fashioned form of leverage), you are (nearly) all that we have and, so …

… thank you

---

[241] Twenty-first century psychological helping, as a professional industry comprising diverse philosophies and interests (see Chapter 7), is just as divided on the matter of self-regulation – particularly the registration of "protected titles". Some prefer *laissez-faire*; some recognise the benefits of mutual organisation not merely for the defence and representation of professional interests but to generate ethical standards and implement safeguards for the protection of its clients. Some consider professional titles important whilst others say, "What's in a name"? Amongst the former advance those who pride themselves on a particular tradition – perhaps including its training requirements – but also those who want titles (recognisable to the public) accessible only to practitioners who can establish their credentials on a register. Some would like to lodge and maintain any such records within the custody and control of its own professional membership bodies: others think the government should supervise it all. An entire case and framework for professional self-review was presented in Chapter 7. The Old Testament book of Ecclesiasticus was written in Hebrew originally c. 280 BC:

Any adviser will offer advice,
        but some are governed by self-interest.
Beware of a man who offers advice,
        first find out what he wants himself –
since his advice coincides with his own interest –
        in case he has designs on you
and tells you, 'You are on the right road',
        but stands well clear to see what will happen to you.
Do not consult a man who looks at you askance,
        conceal your plans from people jealous of you.
Do not consult a woman about her rival,
        or a coward about war,
a merchant about prices,
        or a buyer about selling,
a mean man about gratitude,
        or a selfish man about kindness,
a lazy fellow about any sort of work,
        or a casual worker about finishing a job,
an idle servant about a major undertaking –
        do not rely on these for any advice.
But constantly have recourse to a devout man,
        whom you know to be a keeper of the commandments,
whose soul matches your own,
        and who, if you go wrong, will be sympathetic.
Finally, stick to the advice your own heart gives you,
        no one can be truer to you than that;
since a man's soul often forewarns him better
        than seven watchmen perched on a watchtower.
And besides all this beg the Most High
        to guide your steps in the truth.

(*Jerusalem Bible: Popular Edition.* Darton, Longman & Todd)

"Old-fashioned Form Of Leverage"
Runswick Boat Winch, Runswick Bay, North Yorkshire & Cleveland

Chapter 10

"A broader, pragmatic empiricism"

Empiricism: measurably human
As we saw in (the Preface and) Chapter 1, "empiricism" is the old philosophical tradition holding that we human beings can only know (especially in the sense that we may all agree upon what we know) that which comes to us through (the evidence of our) experience. Its "narrow" interpretation is one that is favoured by behaviorists in particular, and science – as a fashion – in general. Science is a fashion; i.e., a passing contemporary philosophy – rather than any kind of permanent "gospel" – because it has existed for only a few hundred of the 200,000 years in all human history and – unlike sex, mind-altering relief and rock 'n' roll – it will not last forever. There is too much of the quality of human experience that is not accounted for by superstition, delusion and prejudice on the one hand – or materialist, positivist, (yet) strident science on the other. Even within science there are deep anomalies (cf. the "Uncertainty Principle" – see Chapter 4) and apparently irreconcilable accounts of the same phenomena. The antagonism between Newtonian and Einsteinian accounts of material subject to strong versus weak gravity or at light-proximate velocities – hence our obsession with accounting for the earliest possible moment of the Big Bang – is a modern case in point. In Chapter 4 we also wondered whether humans lack the capacity to know everything anyway – even if only on the grounds that we will always be limited by the constraints of our capacity as perspective-takers (see footnote to Chapter 4). In Chapter 4's Table, "Examples of polarisation from ancient and modern history", we imagined that:

Surely any final "theory of everything" will be less about what humans can measure than it will be "measurably human".

Breadth of thinking: if the cap fits
Whereas in Chapter 1 we elucidated "narrow" empiricism thus:

It is a corollary of empiricism that "innate" knowledge (ideas, revelation, inspiration, intuition – even reason) either doesn't exist or is spurious (with the possible exception of "knowledge" transmitted via DNA), and the extent to which one is "radical" about such matters is (inversely) proportional to the extent to which one tolerates exceptions to these strictures.

in Chapter 4, we appealed to common-sense:

Taking common-or-garden human experience for a moment, let us test our common-sense pulse, or ground ourselves in a broader empiricism – which is just to say rely on the subjective experience of life and living that we all possess.

and in a footnote to Chapter 4 we explained:

the roots of the English word "empirical" are in the Ancient Greek ("εμπειρικός" in modern Greek) translating to Latin as "experientia", meaning "experience". A "broader empiricism" here just means a broader experience, i.e., not limited to sensory experience alone. Folks can and do testify to and agree upon the meaning of common types of experience as well as to the slide rule or yardstick. Without such shared understandings human relationships would be dry if not impossible.

Pragmatic empiricism: Charles Darwin on board …

By "pragmatic" we mean simply some framework which is useful to us for the purpose of a "moral psychology" but which represents neither capitulation to easy superficial convenience, nor lip service to reasonable and consensual validation. Now, we all know that Charles Darwin (1809-1882) was a privileged passenger on board HMS Beagle (i.e., a self-financing[242] companion to the aristocrat Robert FitzRoy, 1805-1865, then captain of the ship and later to rise to Vice-Admiral of the British Navy[243]) as, on her second voyage from 1831 to 1836, she journeyed through the Galapagos Islands. We are indebted to Darwin for our present appreciation of *Man's Place In Nature*[244] knowing now (for none of us had done so hitherto, so we are given to understand) that we humans evolved like every other form of life on earth – and, possibly, for the same chronological span since a "last universal common ancestor". This happens, by all accounts, through the process of natural selection (or "survival of the fittest"), and speciation (into *homo sapiens* in our case) when an ancestral lineage has become sufficiently differentiated (in terms of what we have discovered as genetic material or DNA) that breeding between the old and new stock becomes impossible (infertile). Such differentiation, naturally, takes an "impossibly" long time – far too long, in fact, for the impatient empiricist who must measure everything scientific not only in his laboratory, and on his own slide rule, but also in his own lifetime. In those quieter and less populated days before electronic communications, handwritten letters were the order of the day, and Charles Darwin was fond of them. Rather as Sigmund Freud used to exchange thoughts, ideas and arguments about the unconscious "mind" and its analysis – bartering all the new tricks of the old trade with Carl Jung before the Great War (i.e., the very early 20th century), Darwin engaged in a similar manner with just as ardent a devotee – in fact, a hard-nosed man reputed as "Darwin's bulldog" – Thomas Henry Huxley (1825-1895). Huxley was less disposed than Darwin to accept any given proposition; conversely we might say, he required more evidence to accept the same idea; i.e., he was a "narrower" empiricist. As Huxley steadfastly refused in their correspondence to recognise natural selection as irrefutable until such speciation could be observed empirically (i.e., at first hand), Darwin wrote:

The empirical evidence you call for is both impossible in practical terms, and in any event unnecessary. It's the same as asking to see every step in the transformation (or the splitting) of one species into another.[245]

Darwin's position is very much like ours in so far as we anticipate empirical confirmation of the intrapsychic transitions that accompany "spiritual direction" and the achievement or maintenance of personal sanity (i.e., the species-grade makeover seen in anyone who undergoes "spiritual transformation"). We have presented a clear account of those who can recognise such psychological shifts in another person –

---

[242] Although a naturalist as HMS Beagle sailed forth, Darwin was bound for the clergy.

[243] Like his uncle Robert Stewart (Lord Castlereagh, 1769-1822) who had also been a sea captain – in those days widely recognised as a stressful and isolating occupation – FitzRoy committed suicide with a razor as in later life his depression prevailed over him and his accumulating health and financial problems. FitzRoy had become disturbed at his vicarious contribution to Darwin's theories – once exhorting an audience at the British Association for the Advancement of Science to "believe God rather than man".

[244] See Chapter 8 including footnote.

[245] Darwin, F. and Seward, A.C. (1903) *More Letters Of Charles Darwin: A Record Of His Work In A Series Of Hitherto Unpublished Letters (Volume 1).* John Murray: London

the "poachers-turned-gamekeeper", or PTGs we described in Chapter 9. These people need no convincing to appreciate something with which they are already familiar because of first hand experience. Of course, we are all human and — in that capacity — none of us requires any special qualification to recognise anything "measurably human".

… but we do not venture so far as William James
In working our way towards such a position we are aligned — although not entirely — with William James's (1842-1910) views on pragmatism (*Pragmatism: A New Name For Some Old Ways Of Thinking*, 1907). We do not venture so far as where he argues not merely that evidence can be circumvented if a belief holds its own through having been useful ("If it works for you, it works for you" — see Chapter 7), but that it becomes *validated* through such a process[246]. Our empiricism is *less* broad. We are not looking for incontrovertible (especially material) proof that "moral psychology" promotes "sanity", but neither are we willing to accommodate what James refers to as "over-beliefs" — or anything that looks like an artefactual solution, a red herring or a blind alley — just because, seemingly, it "works" (and so that's all OK with us then). As in our personal lives, we wish to persevere in trying to get somewhere authentic, even if we don't succeed visibly.

Ticks our boxes
A staggeringly potent social phenomenon with which we are already familiar; i.e., "shareable subjective experience" (see Chapters 5, 7 and 9) leaps all of the hurdles we have encountered in defining our terms of reference (empirical support; breadth of limits; pragmatism and, so, relevance). Unless we indulge in esoteric diversions, such as enquiring into whether the universe and humans within it really exist, and whether our psychic faculties are sufficiently equivalent for us to recognise and access each other's "frame of reference" (vital in Rogerian or person-centred counselling — see Chapter 9), we have a great deal in common with each other (see Chapter 3) as we know from the ways in which we share about our experiences harnessing our species-specific language. The expression, "No man is an island" is well-established in folklore, and originates in Meditation XVII of Devotion XVII amongst *Devotions Upon Emergent Occasions* written in late life and ill health by the English Catholic-turned-Anglican (following Henry VIII's bloodbath) poet John Donne (1572-1631) who lived much of his apparently arduous life supported by wealthy friends. The saying is entrenched in human tradition like religion as William James sees it; i.e., it survives because it "works". "No man is an island" refers to the common notion and sentiment that we all need each other — even if we are selective about the company we keep.

Give away (or share) what you want to keep
We have suggested in Chapter 9 that:

Group or dyadic human engagement of any kind takes away "emptiness" of and in itself: much of our personal restlessness and malaise is dissolved in any kind of togetherness.

In a "moral psychology", the kind and quality of togetherness that is characterised by common purpose and honest sharing serves two highly significant purposes aside from relief from "emptiness". People do us favours if they let us "get things off our chest" or "unburden". The icing on the cake is that we get to keep what we share or give away.

---

[246] William James was firmly of the view that religious beliefs were justified on the basis that they helped folks live happier and more meaningful lives (coining the jargon "Cash Value" to refer to the appraisal of a belief by its consequences) — and that no other empirical justification for them is or should be required. For James, the endurance of religious beliefs throughout history was evidence that they "worked".

Sweet as icing (truth for the tooth)
If I give something to you by sharing something private about who I
am it is like "letting go" of it. It is no longer a secret and I have
lost the power that enables me to indulge my secret without my being
detected (i.e., I can no longer believe or imagine that nobody on the
planet knows what I know about me – even if I am never detected or
"found out" literally). If I give you or share my secret, I have lost
that power forever (unless you die, but I have still given it away
once and that is knowledge to me). But since it is the same power
that imprisons me (by keeping me obsessed with a mental comfort –
something I use to change the way that I feel), my relinquishing it
affords me freedom. It is true that I have lost a comfort. But I have
also lost a rancid obsession. It is true that I have (voluntarily)
lost a corner of my privacy. But I have gained a priceless freedom.
It is true that I have foregone a little of the illusion that kept me
believing in my own "self-reliance" or "toughness", but I have gained
a peace which can never sensibly be traded. All things said and done,
I have trodden a step or two nearer to some worthwhile truth – even
if only about who and what I am[247]. Of course, such levels of self-
revelation are best reserved for trusted environments – where we have
made a case for the strictest levels of confidence. The "poachers-
turned-gamekeeper" and "spiritual laundering" sections towards the
end of Chapter 9 included a broader set of reflections on sharing in
private and in groups. Additional material is included in Part III.

Amen (somewhat)
It is this kind of truth that provides a far greater impetus to
sanity than any kind of measurement in the behaviorist's laboratory.
This is not to argue that science doesn't yield wonders – especially
medical ones – nor is it to argue that even radical behaviorists do
not generate useful knowledge about aberrant behaviour – laws about
the formation of conditioned emotional states that can hold us back
in life and which – at least theoretically – can be "unwritten" or
otherwise compensated for in therapy. Quite the contrary. We could
not have made the case for a "moral psychology" without all of the
raw material presented prior to our drawing together its various
threads in Chapter 9, "A moral psychology". But the truths of a
"moral psychology", once experienced, require no proof for the person
who has walked the journey. The dark, dank and dreary cave of the old
mystery has been suffused with the luminous power of the new one. We
are afforded a sense of purpose (and destiny) for our next discovery.
The process gathers "spiritual moss" like a "spiritual rolling stone"
(see Chapter 9), until our confidence in it all is unassailable. We
might say that this confidence is like faith – and so it somewhat is.

Getting used to the idea
We have alluded to the idea that "spiritual surrender" is like a one-
hit (or at least a powerful) associative link shredder (see Chapter 9
including a reference to "flavour aversion"). The "letting go", we
have suggested, may be alike sudden and massive habituation whereby
(the salience of) a previously highly valued reward is suddenly
reduced to nought. Whether this is reflected in the central nervous
system (and, even then, whether such a process may impact all of the
hypothetical structures with which we are familiar by now: Pavlovian
S–S; Thorndikeian S–R; Skinnerian R–S) we are very far from having
established. Yet – as in all things both scientific and spiritual –
you do find what you're looking for, eventually – and possession of a
sound sense of where to turn next is incomparably more helpful than
random rummaging about or blind refusal to take another hopeful step.

---

[247] see John 8:32 for a New Testament parallel: "If you make my word your home you will
indeed be my disciples, you will learn the truth and the truth will make you free."

"Another Hopeful Step"
Tintagel, Cornwall

An indispensable principle: willingness to be wrong
Thanks largely to Aristotle, we have inherited a particular tendency
in thinking which we may refer to loosely as "deduction". Deductive
reasoning is drawing an appropriate conclusion which must necessarily
follow from pre-stated premises. If the premises are wrong, the
conclusion will be wrong. Deductive reasoning can be sound inherently
but generate false conclusions. Thus, if all cats are black, and
Felix is a cat, then Felix is black. But if *actually* some cats are
white, our conclusion is false. Sound deductive reasoning depends on
true premises. By contrast, inductive reasoning can generate false
conclusions from true premises. In the oft-cited example courtesy of
Karl Popper (1902-1994), Europeans had observed millions of white
swans over centuries. Inductive reasoning might have permitted
Europeans to conclude that all swans are white. But *only one black
swan* imported (or venturing stray) from Australasia would undermine
the truth of the conclusion. It is this kind of error that scientists
can make when they are insufficiently cautious about generalising
findings from their rigidly controlled laboratory experimentation
(significantly helpful in nearly all other respects, particularly
defence against errors of deduction), and about which Popper was
mostly concerned. His solution is based on the principle of
"falsification" – meaning that we should try to be explicit about the
"black swan" in any edifice of inductive reasoning that we fabricate.
Indeed, Popper suggests that we should expend our resources on
disproving scientific theories rather than trying to generalise them
(or demonstrate over and over how correct – and how clever – we are).

Being wrong in a "moral psychology"
In a "moral psychology" blind or belligerent repudiation of personal
error is known (and experienced) as "pride" (actually just another
facet of the seam of fear we exposed in Chapter 9). We all know there
is only one answer for it: I can admit the mistake to myself and to
any injured party; apologise unselfishly wherever possible effecting
any necessary reparations for harms done; get back on my horse as
quickly as possible, and then leave the matter behind me (bringing my
capacity for "spiritual surrender" or "letting go" to bear should any
unhappy memories insist upon themselves). Omission of any of these
corrective activities represents unexploded munitions of the kind we
encountered in Chapter 9 (*"Why do folks pursue certain rather than
other distractions?"*). We are best advised to stop what we are doing
and retrace our steps until we have straightened things up as best we
can (seeking trusted counsel if ever we are confused about a matter).

Poking the "Seahive"
In case, for a moment, any interested reader might be tempted to
suspect that we had dispensed with all further calls for evidence, we
shall give over the remainder of this Chapter to Karl Popper by
presenting instances of how a "moral psychology" might be falsified.
We cannot hope to be exhaustive by presenting all of the ideas and
principles underwritten in *Nine Seahorses* – but we shall try to
highlight the principal ideas – and summarise how these have been
represented in earlier Chapters. We shall be imaginative in our
attempts to generate scenarios in which a "moral psychology" might be
contradicted or fail to apply at all (all of which can be readily
converted into "real world" yardsticks in social policy evaluation
for the tastefully hard-nosed empiricist). The acid test of such
objections is in the sincerity with which they are mounted, and in
how discussions (especially in groups where "spiritual blindness" is
"averaged over" and often defeated) go this way or that when "moral
psychology" is shared amongst honest conversationalists. If you like,
this is to encourage a "collective conscience" alongside personal
ones. We shall close Part II with reflections on "moral economics".

SAMPLE FALSIFIABLE PROPOSITIONS IN A "MORAL PSYCHOLOGY"

Falsifiable propositions	Sample *Nine Seahorses* references (with page number)	Foreseeable contraindications

The human tendency to polarise generates conflict not co-operation

Falsifiable propositions	Sample *Nine Seahorses* references (with page number)	Foreseeable contraindications
Sharing a huge proportion of their DNA, human beings seem bent on differentiating themselves from one another – both as individuals and as groups, communities and nations. Polarities hide truths, and their capacity to mislead may be considered proportional to the vigour with which they are defended. Extremists of all persuasions seem somewhat deranged, and are likely to remain or become more so the longer they cleave to their positions. Every human being who reports a troubled "mind" (unless their presenting problem is an overwhelming threat to existence) has a problem of intrapsychic alignment. Such internal misalignment, arguably, is one way of conceptualising "insanity" *per se*. To the extent that this is true, the achievement or restoration of sanity must involve establishing or re-establishing intrapsychic congruence or alignment. Psychology is a divided modern discipline because of polar positions on issues such as the "mind-body problem".	*… a polarised view rarely, if ever, embodies the whole story – or represents any worthwhile "truth". We might also suspect that the degree of fervour with which a polarised position is defended (especially if violently) is directly proportional to the extent to which its own protagonists may have personal misgivings about it.* (p.34) *We saw in Chapter 4 that human beings have always had a tendency to "polarise" … Modern psychology and psychotherapy are disintegrated and unfinished pursuits, largely because of this disposition. Trenchant positions on deep-seated difficulties (un)naturally create tensions within a professional discipline as much as intrapsychic conflict does in persons. Such internal misalignment, arguably, is one way of conceptualising "insanity" per se (which is to suggest that some spurious partitioning of beliefs and values – or "moral conflict" – lies with deleterious effect, lurking invisible unless exposed, behind every instance of experienced distress).* (p.85) *… if we become "too" honest with ourselves, we cannot bear the "conscience-weight" of our own irresponsibility … If we haven't yet grown up, we live a life of chronic burden, always under the suspicion of our own lurking moral gaze, let alone the scrutiny of law. Whichever way you look at it, it is of no use making excuses for self-betrayal. There are two sides to any coin, and we can flip any situation over to look at it another way. We credit ourselves with guile; in fact, it is denial. How do we know it is denial? Because if you hold out playing a "bad game", you find yourself on a losing wicket sooner or later … You don't need to exclude from your own "moral psychology" any first cause of "conscience", and you need admit and afford hospitality only to those that you choose to invite.* (p.76) *… fortunately for all of us other than Adam and Eve, humans have had a longstanding knack of feigning unselfishness if ever there was a sexual union in prospect … there is now a barely reckonable swarm of us, and the world's human population … may at last be peaking as bacteria in a crowded Petri dish. We are having to resort to contrived means of food production – moving from … local agriculture to the global distribution of synthetic commodities – the cost of which can be measured in contamination of the planet's ecosystem and potentially catastrophic climate change, as well as traditional economic metrics.* (p.99)	Although we weren't there to witness it all, and recorded human history is very patchy (practically non-existent until not many thousands of years ago), we can imagine natural selection in action as *homo sapiens* evolved and distinguished itself as a primate species. As the human population is likely to peak for the first time ever in the next few decades – following massive exponential growth in only a few centuries – the question now seems to be whether the human disposition towards mutual co-operation (for which there is just as much evidence in history as there is for intra-species antagonism) can prevail over our gluttony for mutual conflict – so promoting (or assuring) our peaceable survival. Aside from the raw competition instinct, the greatest threats to human survival are the rule of self-interest, the prioritisation of economic growth and weapons technology. Contraindications for a "moral psychology" include arguments that: humanity will save itself through inter- and intra-species competition; that "might is right"; that intrapsychic congruence can be established at extreme points of view. *Exercise*: Conduct a personal inventory of all your delicate viewpoints. Locate them on dimensions. Move up a gear or two. How do you feel? "The more I locate my opinions at the edges –so marginalising myself in humanity – the more congruent I feel within myself and with others?

SAMPLE FALSIFIABLE PROPOSITIONS IN A "MORAL PSYCHOLOGY"

Falsifiable propositions	Sample *Nine Seahorses* references (with page number)	Foreseeable contraindications
The problem of fear and ulterior motives in a two-faced psychology		
Psychology has always had a lot to do with motives.	*Throughout history, human beings have tried to understand one another – whether sympathetically, for practical purposes, or for reasons more akin to conquest … we have resorted to the most cunning and vile of tactics in high-stake arenas such as the battlefield and the lovers' nest … psychology seems to have a lot to do with motives.* (p.3)	Contraindications include arguments that: human beings are rarely dishonest if they are not essentially sincere and ever true to themselves and others;
Things are not always as they seem. Most lay perspectives of "psychology" are imbued with a connotation of "reading minds".	*Durkheim argued that certain Catholic communities were more healthy than certain Protestant ones based on police suicide statistics entirely; however, how can we know that those Catholics were not less disposed to commit suicide for fear of spiritual damnation rather than because they were happier or otherwise more sane?* (p.38)	most folks have no trouble knowing who they are and are willing to talk about the subject if invited; most of us mean exactly what we say and say exactly what we mean;
Whilst social mores dictate that we mustn't talk about motives because they are ulterior and therefore taboo, we cannot have a complete psychology without a comprehensive appreciation of underlying drives.	*It was Comte who coined the term "altruism" … that individuals should subjugate their personal rights in favour of service to others. We can easily imagine, nevertheless, how affording one's services to others can assume varying shades of psychological and relationship significance depending on the underlying motivating factor(s). Whether services are sold for money … and various other conflicts of interest can intrude (particularly diluting the principle that a paid-for service is geared towards the purchaser's best interests as a primary purpose) …*	all of our thinking and research in the humanities has been free of contamination by any misreading of human behaviour; "wearing one's heart on one's sleeve" is the natural default for humans – hiding one's true feelings is a most extraordinary habit;
All is *not* fair in love and in war. Perhaps fear is the dark horse of human motives – one that likes to disguise itself.	*perhaps the flavour of any service is at least partially coloured by professional ambition(s).* (pp.37–38)	romantic love – being everything that matters in a human life – is reliably free of misunderstandings, vengefulness and dastardliness;
We tend to be ashamed of our own fears. Perhaps this is partly because of our culture – not just because we feel "small" when threatened.	*Whereas … Berne's reference to "games" included any transactional behaviour with an ulterior motive, TA has since distinguished between racketeering and games … the "switch" defining the latter … when one party … changes ego state … leaving everybody feeling uncomfortable and uptight.* (p.128)	acts of "altruism" – which actually means selfless love – i.e., concern for other humans entirely free of personal motive – can always be interpreted at the superficial level: what you see is what is happening.
Has our culture become obsessed with "toughness"? In what other ways do we cover up our fears? Human behaviour cannot be fully understood without appreciation of *the actual nature of underlying motives.*	*Would not our amateur "psychologist" – the one who throughout history played guessing games with his enemy in war, succumbed to treachery in "love", or stooped in compassion to assist a fellow human being in need when no-one was there to witness the beneficent deed (and, somehow, he knew that) – be somewhat disappointed about the shape of the modern discipline? Have not the Scientific Revolution and the limitations of a narrow empiricism (one that appreciates the value of experience only when it is so measurable that we can all see it) excluded the thinking "mind" whose focus the vernacular*	doing a good turn for its own sake is a mug's or a sucker's game (i.e., no payoff); winning wars is mostly about brute strength;
Cave man is right. Modern psychology has become (at least) two-faced.	*"psychology" ever was? The agnostic … in behaviorist terms was thence to be discovered out in the ideological cold. In relation to our "minds" … are we not now somewhat two-faced?* (p.7)	all human behaviour is "scientifically determined" and, so, talk of intending this or that is diversionary puff and wind; humans will evolve into robots or *vice versa*.

SAMPLE FALSIFIABLE PROPOSITIONS IN A "MORAL PSYCHOLOGY"

Falsifiable propositions	Sample *Nine Seahorses* references (with page number)	Foreseeable contraindications
The illegitimacy of free will, empowerment and toughness in nature		

Falsifiable propositions	Sample *Nine Seahorses* references (with page number)	Foreseeable contraindications
Unbridled human "will", which is illusory anyway, is dangerous, from the highest to the lowest levels of social order. Endeavouring to establish personal superiority always represents an underlying insecurity and undisciplined indulgence of personal or social inferiority. We have been distracted by the spurious notion of psychological "toughness". The pursuit of sanity has far more to do with recognising everybody as "spiritually equal" than it has to do with rendering everybody "tough". Whereas Eric Berne seems to have favoured the pursuit of "autonomy" in its own right, a "moral psychology" prefers to regard popular outcomes of psychotherapy (autonomy, personal responsibility, freedom, happiness) as by-products of the process: they tend to slide through one's "moral fingers" if one grips or harnesses them too tightly. "Become what you are" is associated with Nietzsche, although the expression is more properly attributed to Pindar. Either way, it is a good fit for what a "moral psychology" anticipates.	*Now, what happens if we try to apply "free will" against viscosity? Perhaps we may only ever encounter personal frustration in direct proportion to the vigour of our wading in … Suppose then, as an alternative, we accept that the melting pot of pressures to veer this way or that (behaviourally speaking) is just nature's loving way of helping us out, and that we only experience distress when we fight it? … might we not all … accept that nature has spawned us as she has seen fit? Whether we enjoy our days or we are tormented by them, it is sure that we could no more have guided nature through her history than we can re-live our own pasts. (p.165)* *… "spiritual surrender" … precipitates a "spiritual awakening" by which illusory "will" is subjugated to "right-thinking" including: an awareness of the antiquity of nature and a proportionate perspective of our role in her unravelling; a passive (transcendent) appreciation of beauty, and a mature compassion for all humankind (p.177)* *… modern psychology's unfounded and misplaced faith in "free will" … rides tandem with its equally wrong-footed obsession with "toughness". (p.91)* *… curiosity and mastery … deserve thoroughgoing discussion because there are poorly appreciated … anomalies in relation to "empowerment" (p.90)* *How many clients presenting for psychotherapy are melancholic … from not measuring up? How many could depart from their first consultation happier (w)armed with a simple exhortation to draw satisfaction from what they actually are rather than what their culture apparently expects of them; from whom and what others unconditionally are; what is more, from how the world actually presents itself – with all its prejudices and intolerances (p.94)* *A clarification … Embracing the world as it really is, including "all its prejudices and intolerances", our unmanufactured selves and its other inhabitants as they really are, is not at all equivalent … to resigned reconciliation with inequality or injustice. Quite the contrary. (p.95)* *The road unravels of its own accord as our footsteps increase in number. We are foolish if we insist on ourselves as cartographers, or too often fix co-ordinates for our "spiritual journeys" … Thoreau encouraged all of us … to live the life we have imagined … Following his counsel, we found ourselves doing what comes naturally. (p.175)*	Conversely, polar positions on "free will" and "scientific determinism" - both of which are ostensibly macho in character – are jointly or severally tenable; e.g., The radical behaviorist (aka "hawk") such as Burrhus Frederic Skinner may be a "scientific determinist" – a person who considers that all behaviour is accounted for by cause and effect relationships without needing to resort to either the existence or effect of subjective human will. (p.44) and … radical behaviorism and its corollary, "scientific determinism", is a discovery of Western civilisation, more particularly an American one, yet we all know that North America is the "land of the free", and that everyone there has the capacity for realising their own fortunes wilfully. How could this have happened then? Is everything psychological determined? Or is nothing determined except that which we impose masterfully on patiently waiting destiny? Or is neither of these verifiable but rather there is something of "truth" in between? (p.90) A doctor who advises you to "pull yourself together" is well-established to do so … we can easily "will" our way into happiness. Wishing we were somebody else – or a perfect version of who we actually are – is only harmless fantasy. Mother Nature, although rather more experienced than ourselves, is better suited to be overruled than heeded.

SAMPLE FALSIFIABLE PROPOSITIONS IN A "MORAL PSYCHOLOGY"

Falsifiable propositions	Sample *Nine Seahorses* references (with page number)	Foreseeable contraindications
An original scientific developmental account of "moral psychology"		

It is possible to build a bridge between scientific and analytical psychology.	*… two strands of the discipline that informs sanity have evolved quite independently … We have troubled ourselves to lay out the … theoretical fundamentals that underpin each … Is there some manner in which these two may be reconciled organically? (p.133)*	Contraindications include arguments that:
Nine Seahorses is a progressive case – not a final one.		there are many different "truths" and no hope for general or "unified" theories;
The TA Parent ego state is built – structurally – as an S-S module. S-S and perceptual learning account sufficiently for the TA introjects in P_2 (P_3, A_3, C_3).	*… the TA Parent ego state is … the …. register of S-S learning whereas TA Child comprises an "early" S-R register which becomes … updated with "guileful" R-S … during some developmental phase in which language is acquired (p.173)*	as in the business of life itself, it is better to wait until a complete account is available than venture a few steps in a worthwhile direction;
The TA Child ego state is built as an operant module from S-R to R-S. This S-R / R-S gradient elegantly accounts for all important phenomena recognised in TA: *inter alia* injunctions, cultural inheritance, "early decisions", the "life script", drivers and the biographic evolution of C_2.	*… Thorndikeian S-R … permits of "pre-conscious" and deep contextual (situational) learning of exactly the kind that TA recognises: a "weight" of "unspoken" family culture inherited through Child ego state aether (p.144)* *… say … the human infant slides from S-R to R-S … at some time around its passage from "sensori-motor" into language … we are positing that it is R-S itself that tells human language-competency apart, with all its … corollaries. (p.146)*	TA as a body has nothing to do with science or scientific psychology, desires no liaison with academic psychology and – as a body – is under no obligation to indulge its capacity to think; Pavlovian conditioning is an erroneous or misplaced account of TA Parent conceptually;
The language acquisition device or LAD is co-emergent and bound with R-S. Node formulation is LAD-injected. Parent and Child are both R-S functionally – discriminable on the basis of an "I (want …)" versus "You (should …)" expansion concurrent and bound with the S-R / R-S transition.	*… whilst the introjects (P_3, A_3, C_3) …. simply reinvent themselves constantly with experience … it is a different story with the TA "Child in the Child" (C_1 in C_2) … diffuse stimulus "nodes" for "situation" (or "context") combined in some way with a (Thorndikeian) response "node" relinquish themselves to more specific "nodes" representing mentally rehearsable Skinnerian responses (Rs) and anticipated outcomes (Ss). The node representing the "new" response may (or does) now have a language competency inbuilt, and may or may not be otherwise equivalent … to the old one. Perhaps the "slide" from S-R to R-S involves a node-creating or node-transforming threshold whereby some trigger … from a "Language Acquisition Device" – precipitates new node formulation and, in the aggregate, an entirely fresh mental set. (p.147)*	S-R cannot account for cultural or trans-generational injunctions logically; there are fundamental tensions between the structural accounts of the ego states in a "moral psychology" and the established functional character of the TA ego states; a comprehensive associative account of the TA ego states makes no useful contribution to TA theory or TA psychotherapy;
There are significant implications for TA psychotherapy; e.g., Pavlovian CR dissolution militates against the power of counterinjunctions and introjects.	*In TA, the Critical Parent addresses the Child ego state with the "expectation" (thus, surely a Skinnerian R) of a particular outcome (S) from Compliant Adapted Child, although it may not obtain it if Rebellious Adapted Child steps in (S). Nurturing Parent has an anticipative quality about it too (wanting good things for Child). (p.140)* *The difference between "co-creating" new … life with an S-R-imprisoned "King Baby" is now transparently at odds with the task of "co-rehabilitating" with an R-S-wielding sociopath wishing to "go straight". The justification for releasing "Free Child" in TA therapy is more obvious than ever (p.146)*	empirical discoveries in clinical contexts contradict the *Nine Seahorses* model; it is proven that pre-verbal human infants and / or non-human vertebrates possess R-S operant learning; propositions about node formulation are as far-fetched (and therefore just as untestable and untenable) as Freud's account of "mind".

SAMPLE FALSIFIABLE PROPOSITIONS IN A "MORAL PSYCHOLOGY"

Falsifiable propositions	Sample *Nine Seahorses* references (with page number)	Foreseeable contraindications
The various pressures on "conscience" and limits on its mutability		
A universal understanding of "conscience" is both possible and available.	*… conscience is: a quiet strain, having the capacity to become psychologically "noisy", which has the effect of pressure to settle upon one or more beliefs, attitudes, intentions or behaviours (including not doing certain things as well as doing them) and which is experienced subjectively as psychological conflict – usually mild, but potentially deadly. (p.49)*	If it were established that conscience is entirely metaphysical versus entirely material in origin, or *vice versa*, our definition would hold water either way.
A pressure on "conscience": the "moral environment" …		Our definition would be redundant, however, if it made no sense for all practical purposes; or if scientific determinism were to hold sway (because then it would be of precious little practical use).
A pressure on "conscience": the "weight of human history" …	*In a "moral psychology", the "moral environment", put simply, is the context in which we must be sane. (p.57)*	
A pressure on "conscience": mind-buggering ancestral injunctions (S–R) and counterinjunctions (S–S) …	*… the "moral environment" comprises the various "worlds" that all of us each inhabits (p.60)* *The "weight of human history" … formal and informal laws, customs, values, mores and traditions … These are always eruptions of deep history (p.61)*	Other contraindications include arguments that: there are rudimentary disconnects between any of these identified pressures and the subjective experience of "mind";
A pressure on "conscience": all biographic conditioning …	*… "aberrant CERs" … encompassing … the mind-buggering "spiritual blindness" of swathes of our ancestors (p.174)*	
A pressure on "conscience": the TA Parent ego state (biographic S–S) …	*Classical and operant conditioning generate conditioned emotional states … "anticipatory hope" and "avoidant fear", a complex combination of each present in any individual's … profile. (p.17)*	there are rudimentary disconnects in between any of these identified pressures where we have posited an interaction or conversation amongst them which generates "conscience" pressure;
A pressure on "conscience": the TA Child ego state (biographic S–R) …	*O'Grady (Skinner) said … "Repeat!"; and we obeyed. Again and again. (p.156)* *… pressures within conscience … include the various "impasses" that would be recognised in TA, especially between matching Parent and Child ego states (e.g., P_2–C_2 and P_1–C_1). (p.169)*	there is an exclusive, hitherto unidentified source of "conscience";
A pressure on "conscience": the TA Child ego state (biographic R–S) …	*Is there not a "natural" kind of fear … and an "unnatural" one that we bring to the table ourselves? (p.169)*	it is, after all, possible that personal "will" can exert itself over "conscience" – which supposes amongst other things that (i) we are wrong elsewhere (Chapter 9) about the existence or potency of human "free will", (ii) we are wrong to suggest that there may be metaphysical (including natural and divine) sources of "conscience", (iii) we haven't discovered the technology for such manipulation, or, (iv) we have – but the powerful people amongst whom it is exercised presently are just too busy (and modest) to demonstrate their secret to the remainder of us.
A pressure on "conscience": self-centred fear (Roosevelt) …	*Food reliably elicits salivation. Because no learning is required, the food is referred to as an "unconditioned" stimulus or US and the salivation as an "unconditioned" response or UR. (p.9)*	
A pressure on "conscience": the unconditioned response (UR) …	*Do nothing. Unplug the 'phone. Attend to the whisper … (p.154)*	
A pressure on "conscience": nature's whisper …	*Dawkins recognises neither the possibility nor utility of a thinking person possessing a realistic take of their place in nature whilst simultaneously seeking religious or spiritual inspiration for living. (p.40)*	
A pressure on "conscience": the divine prerogative known by the believer …	*If … "will" could "defeat" … conscience, there would be little unhappiness … few if any counsellors or psychotherapists and … a much reduced incentive for … religious belief. (p.162)*	
There are limits on what can be "re-written".		

SAMPLE FALSIFIABLE PROPOSITIONS IN A "MORAL PSYCHOLOGY"

Falsifiable propositions	Sample *Nine Seahorses* references (with page number)	Foreseeable contraindications
	*"Moral psychology" 1: acceptance, transcendent trust and surrender*	
A person pursuing a "moral psychology" is at liberty to defer to any authority they may choose.	*Some people like to consider themselves morally self-sufficient … Others like to be guided by what they regard as human wisdom … Still others seek and find divine inspiration. A "moral psychology" is accessible by all such persons (p.44)*	Contraindications include arguments that: human beings are not "moral creatures" and have no need of "moral psychology";
Sanity resides in the "successful" combination of "conscience" with the "moral environment".	*Provisionally, it is in the perseverance of an "Accountable Self" in the "moral environment" that sanity stands or falls … in the acquisition … of a personal "moral psychology" that unstealable understanding resides. (p.60)*	human beings are "morally self-sufficient" in the sense that they do not need each other in order to establish personal integrity;
Tolstoy's provocation (p.68) is an exemplar in "moral psychology".	*Tolstoy's provocation … as perfect a model as … possible to imagine (p.68)* *… wait till we appreciate (p.57)*	human beings can effect or acquire a "moral psychology" by reading about it rather than actually doing it;
A simple appreciation of the world and its inhabitants – and, thereby, a starting point for sanity itself – can be had for the price of a little attention.	*… our perception … renders things awry … it is to ourselves that we must look … to put things right (p.58)* *… the more we became willing to awaken in these first two ways, the more the course of our lives seemed actually and reliably to improve … Was this a trick of perception or some other enigmatic but ludicrously apparent reality? (p.58)*	fear is an illusion and can be denied or avoided (by "will"); our tendency to impose "will" on each other is natural, inevitable and "morally neutral";
A better appreciation of the world and its inhabitants can be had for accepting that lousy feelings mostly are a problem of perception rather than difficult circumstances.	*… what have we done when … we … accepted something about ourselves … or another person, or the various "worlds" of the "moral environment" … This … yielding … "letting go" … brings peace. (p.136)* *What, then, is "transcendent trust" … Very acceptance … is its basic element: we accept (with a sigh of relief from our own misapplied and atrophied efforts) the world as it is rather than as we would engineer it or, at least, we*	most of us human beings neither require nor can muster conviction or courage of the quality demonstrated by Tolstoy; ingratitude is co-directional with personal sanity;
Trusting the process of developing a personal "moral psychology" mysteriously alters the course of personal lives for the better.	*accept the limits of our own capacity for moulding it … we found ourselves "morally aligned" with the various "worlds" of our experience with no price to pay except continued co-operation … Where is the fear that drove us? It has all but vanished … So it is with administration of our "minds". (p.166)* *If there is any pre-requisite at all for sanity, surely it is a very simple "spiritual" yielding (p.52)*	dissatisfaction is more fittingly attributed to errors of creation / nature or the faults of others than errors of perception, or other kinds of shortcomings in ourselves; appreciation in a life does not influence its course;
"Spiritual surrender" is a powerful asset that – once it has been experienced – can be applied as a personal habit in daily living.	*"spiritual surrender" possessed the capacity to break associative links as effectively as one-trial flavour aversion learning created them. (p.166)*	"acceptance" is for losers and for suckers; even if "spiritual surrender" is subjectively real, it has no material corollary or effect;
"Spiritual surrender" is a most potent associative link shredder … perhaps like sudden, rapid habituation.	*The effect of surrender is so simple, sudden and spectacular that it transcends those "stars and spangles" of our imaginations as they once attended the prospect of the rewards promised by O'Grady – seeming to shred to ribbons in an instant a great proportion of all the associative links that chained us to our own bludgeoning incongruence. (p.175)*	"spiritual surrender" is for suckers and for losers – the way to get through life is to fight to the death.

SAMPLE FALSIFIABLE PROPOSITIONS IN A "MORAL PSYCHOLOGY"

Falsifiable propositions	Sample *Nine Seahorses* references (with page number)	Foreseeable contraindications
"Moral psychology" 2: a Seahive of shareable subjective experience		

"Moral psychology" 2: a Seahive of shareable subjective experience

Falsifiable propositions	Sample *Nine Seahorses* references (with page number)	Foreseeable contraindications
Each human being may be identified with an "unwritten" or "Original Self" (and may align themselves with any account of how that Self came into being or materialised according to their own choosing). Each human being possesses an "Accountable Self" which is "morally competent" and "morally responsible" – yet fundamentally simple in its executive function which is to align itself with – or reject – (i.e., "settle upon") various "moral alternatives". The manner or style in which the "Accountable Self" is applied determines the quality of our subjective life as we know it in the "Experienced Self" (aka "Existential) Self") – particularly by mitigation of "conscience" pressure and, thereby, sanity. The "Seahive" facilitates appreciation of such processes. Although vacillations may occur, a bi-directional output (see the diagram) is correct: the "Accountable Self" acquiesces ("Yes") or refuses ("No"). Prudent "spiritual stocktaking" assists with establishing favourable "moral direction" and, thereby, sanity.	*… a new life precipitates an "Original Self" which … was nature's doing … For a theoretical moment … is uncontaminated by earthly experience.* (p.168) *Sooner or later we must bring to bear to that perplexity our "Accountable Self" which, having the capacity to effect "moral discernments", discharges … "willingness to align" ("OK then …") as opposed to belligerence to invitation ("No" or "Yeah but …") … "settling upon" alternatives and reducing mental tension ("cognitive dissonance").* (p.174) *A "Seahive" … Its focal point is at the … frontier between the "Written Self" and the "Accountable Self". This is where the "moral action" takes place … Our preparedness to embrace ["spiritual surrender"] … determines the quality of our (Existential or) "Experienced Self". We can "go nuts" without it … or we can soar like Jonathan – knowing it courses beneath our wings.* (p.180) *Many won't venture here without having acquired a sense of obligation* (p.149) *"soul-searching" … Part III.* (p.165) *Then how has my "Written Self" been expressed both in my "mind", and in the world at large? My TA Parent ego state P_2 is replete with significant (P_3, A_3, C_3) CSs … Have I accepted every invitation to a Pavlovian response (CR) with my "moral capacity" for recognising its "moral value" … My Child ego state C_2 is threaded through with an ancient and barely recognisable patchwork of willowy S-R fibres … Have I succumbed to every coercion … Perhaps I have tried to flex operant muscle … but what "control" did I truly possess over my R-S repertoire? … Did I dance to Skinner's tune? And what of all the direct and open invitations (USs) … did very God or very nature … ever murmur with utter softness and timeless patience to me* (p.152) *… a divine source of conscience would not in the least be refutable by mere, squealing mortals; still, don't we let our own toddlers off the hook just for demonstrating the willingness to fall sufficiently well back in line?* (p.174) *But how far can a person bring intrapsychic congruence to themselves … it is a question of illuminating what of all this we can establish for ourselves and how much we wisely defer to relationship with other parties. We may change only the writing on the wall. If we try to demolish the bricks and mortar – even their very foundations – surely we will risk far too great a "restoration" for own good.* (p.168)	Even supposing we are reincarnated, a human being still enters the world "unwritten" by the biographic experience it is about to encounter. The only serious contraindication to the "Original Self" is the argument that we are self-fabricated. Other contraindications include arguments that: "conscience" is "avoidable" in the sense that (i) conscience pressures do not exist, (ii) conscience pressures are always mild and never severe, (iii) conscience pressures are experienced by only some people, or (iv) they can be neglected or overlooked in any event (without any serious consequences for personal sanity); some people get through all of life without having their moral shirt-tail tugged severely enough to feel "morally tested" (and that must include me); the "Seahive" comprises (i) erroneous elements or misleading elements, (ii) erroneous or misleading interconnections, or, (iii) erroneous or misleading processes; human beings do not require assistance from each other in order to conduct themselves in a morally informed and prudent fashion; all or some of us require no straightening out of the kind implied by the notion or pursuit of "spiritual stocktaking"; God or nature didn't create us "morally flawed" – we are "finished products".

SAMPLE FALSIFIABLE PROPOSITIONS IN A "MORAL PSYCHOLOGY"

Falsifiable propositions	Sample *Nine Seahorses* references (with page number)	Foreseeable contraindications
Interrupting the tragic trajectory of "descending vicious spirals"		

Falsifiable propositions	Sample *Nine Seahorses* references (with page number)	Foreseeable contraindications
"Emptiness" is a useful generic term for the aversive feelings we experience when things have "gone wrong". Perhaps it is rather the converse of the "completeness" we feel when romantically in love, or when everything is going our way or – better – the peace we know when we realise that everything is just as it is supposed to be (and, what is more, that that is fine if not just OK with us).	*"Emptiness" is the … aversive discharge of "conscience" … feeling … when we haven't been true to ourselves. (p.154)*	Contraindications include arguments that:
	"Emptiness", also, is an apposite expression for the "cross-up" TA locates at the "switch" in a "game" (p.155)	"emptiness" is not an apt expression for these sorts of subjective states;
	The qualitative aspect of "emptiness" is its unpleasantness, and the quantitative dimension its dreadful capacity to excruciate. (p.157)	feelings of personal incongruence (conflict), inferiority and loneliness are not that common and – anyway – are easily remedied;
	That feeling … lies like solidified lard on the top of a jug of meat fat … We find ourselves … in a "descending vicious spiral" of isolation, loneliness and inferiority. (p.68)	
All of us indulge in "distractions" to change the way we feel – to compensate for such "emptiness".	*… there is a nasty "vicious spiral" that injects itself surreptitiously into every declining life; i.e., the cunning assailant that is isolation (p.155)*	"comfort-taking" *per se* is too rare – or of too little import to pay such attention to it;
	Don't we all take a little comfort to change the way we feel – for merely a moment (that's all) (p.154)	only some people get a little too partial to, or addicted to, their behavioural bad habits (from the most innocuous to the most deadly) – and that is not a problem for the remainder of us;
	… that stereotypical repertoire of indulgent behaviour … when we feel "stressed", "out of sorts" (p.156)	
These indulgences have the capacity to become addictive – although they don't always become so within our awareness.	*In the dreamy beginning, we crossed the threshold, and something wonderful happened. Our eyes were opened … the stars and spangles of our imaginations descended sparkling before us. (p.156)*	"descending vicious spirals" do not happen;
	Our indulgence seems to fill the "emptiness" … if we are in "control" … everything falls within our grasp, and there is nothing left to fear. (p.156)	"descending vicious spirals" happen – but only to a very small minority of spineless characters;
"Too much of a good thing" can spiral out of control to the point of becoming quite deadly.	*It is only when we are "spiritually blind" and persist in our own self-deception that no "moral dividend" accrues to any party at all. (p.155)*	folks can "will" their way out of feeling lousy and these processes need never get off the ground;
We can become "spiritually blind" to the process and ourselves as participants.	*… such a phenomenon is happening at an increasing rate and is more … common at a younger age in most … nations (p.68)*	if you can be ready to change at the end of the line you can be ready to change at any time before that;
	… the discrepancy between what young people say they want for themselves and what they actually do. (p.71)	the youth of today are their own worst enemy;
Adverse social trends affect young people especially and are better inhibited early than interrupted late.	*An interrupted … trajectory is better than an ignored one … especially true for younger people because … they must endure more years of it. (p.70)*	young people have only themselves to blame (for the "state of the country" and for their cultural inheritance);
You can't win a bad game.	*At painful last, the moment of reckoning arrives when … this "self" … screams at the heavens, "Help me…!" (p.147)*	ethically speaking there is no collective responsibility for such problems as these;
What happens at the end of the line is a lottery.	*So what happens next? … depends on … the … readiness of the distressed person to go about things in a different way … and … the relevance of response (p.75)*	what happens in other countries is hardly any concern domestically.

SAMPLE FALSIFIABLE PROPOSITIONS IN A "MORAL PSYCHOLOGY"

Falsifiable propositions	Sample *Nine Seahorses* references (with page number)	Foreseeable contraindications
The importance of realising the adequacy of the treatment response		
The evolution of the various silos within modern psychotherapy has generated diverse views of aetiology ("knottedness") which exacerbate confusion in already befuddled prospect clients.	*… the "relevance" of a treatment response has to do with the assumptions that are made … about how and why – precisely – a person is "all knotted up" … the various traditions … are just alternative ways of looking at the same problem, and none of them is entirely right; after all, none has furnished a complete explanation, and none has produced any universal "cure".* (p.86)	Contraindications include arguments that: all psychotherapeutic approaches understand psychopathology in the same way – it is just the jargon that varies between the assorted disciplines;
The system as a whole is chaotic to a person needing or seeking treatment because it operates across diverse operational sectors in unco-ordinated silos.	*… the therapist requires an appreciation of … match or fit between their available response and the true nature of the presenting problem* (p.86) *Does each practitioner the suffering person encounters once … capitulation has started possess a capacity for immediate and accurate diagnosis? No. We know this from collective experience of the "revolving doors" syndrome* (p.81)	one type of psychotherapy is just as good as any other for a given psychological problem; one type of psychotherapy is just as good as any other for a particular prospective client;
The identification of the nature of a presenting problem – rather than its subjective interpretation within one school of philosophy – is such a vital stage of treatment that it should properly front the whole system as a single point of entry / referral gateway.	*What parallels of our personal discomfiture exist in any treatment system at any one time?* (p.76) *… surely, psychotherapy needs as much self-examination as its clients. If it doesn't appreciate this … it risks the same consequences as the avoidant individual … i.e. … self-destruction … If the self-examination is earnest, the redirection is … favourable … There is also a tendency for relationships to change for the better.* (p.77)	one psychotherapist is just as good as another for a given prospective client – personal chemistry is no facilitator of client treatment or recovery; psychotherapy for the most part should take place unwitnessed – behind closed doors;
Psychotherapy needs self-examination just as much as its troubled clients.	*… in … Great Britain anyway … there is a personhood known as the "expert patient" … Compromised people lack "expertise" to the extent that they are laden with ignorance about how the treatment system works – doubled once with mental confusion - and twice with their own denial … Their appreciation of options … may be severely curtailed* (p.78)	the treatment response as a whole is sufficiently well aligned internally and co-ordinated;
Most "patients" in psychological health are not "experts" on their own condition (or they would have found their way out of trouble).	*The power-cost ratio of group therapy is so massive compared with individual therapy that it is a wonder that individual therapy prevails* (p.184)	there is no waste within the system as a whole – clients land in the right spot first time – every time;
The arguments for group therapy are overwhelming and correctly inform the core of any self-examination on the part of the treatment system as a whole entity.	*Is there anything inherently inferior about a service that is conditional on the payment of a fee? Perhaps not if, as some of you say, a client needs to hurt in the pocket as well as in the heart in order to gain the starting momentum necessary to effect "moral progress". Perhaps so, unless you have become so free of "moral corruption" yourselves … that you can retain all of your personal and professional interests in*	psychologically vulnerable people are "experts" on their own condition, know how to get appropriate treatment, have the confidence, strength and resilience to navigate their way into the system and – where public funds are provided – should be left in charge of their own treatment budgets;
Paid-for services are susceptible to contamination by (subtle) conflicts of interests.	*separately-dug millponds where they may never overlap … until we have learned to love each other (when money for love shall be rendered an old-fashioned form of leverage), you are (nearly) all that we have and, so … thank you* (p.185)	all the foregoing are academic anyway because the whole system has sufficient capacity, no waiting lists and is universally affordable.

SAMPLE FALSIFIABLE PROPOSITIONS IN A "MORAL PSYCHOLOGY"

Falsifiable propositions	Sample *Nine Seahorses* references (with page number)	Foreseeable contraindications

Empathy, poachers-turned-gamekeeper (PTGs) and competent coxswains

Healthy people can help unhealthy people get well. Those who know the route into harbour (the sanctuary of the treatment system and a suitable berth within it) at first hand make the best coxswains – more so than those commonly familiar with the safety of dry land and who can afford to wait patiently to ply their trade – it makes perfect sense to afford the former the authority of harbourmasters. Similarly, PTGs – having a peculiar capacity for empathy – are uniquely placed to be of useful service to those who haven't yet found their way. They are supremely qualified for advocacy and for getting group work off the ground. They liberate rather than lead. They may be willing to work without profit as a primary motive. "Spiritual deference" in peer-mentoring – being concerned with principles rather than personalities – is healthy and quite at odds with the spectre of "gurus" – or anybody else who sells what they have to offer on the back of some variety of human charisma. Wherever there is a great deal of human authority, there is often a swollen bank account in tandem.	*There is a … case for "competent coxswains" … to steer these distressed vessels into … harbour; to explain what can't be appreciated unaided; to afford temporary assistance with navigation, and to defend against misunderstandings and inattention. (p.81)* *Poachers-turned-gamekeeper (PTGs) are people who have turned a corner … PTGs need no training to recognise the vital change in another that has already occurred in themselves … they are able – and often want to – help shipwrecked sailors reach dry land … To the unfamiliar eye, or the ignorant sceptic, such helpfulness may be interpreted patronisingly as "rescue". If it is badly motivated helping … then that is what it is. But if it is offered in a spirit of compassion and love, then that precisely is what it is. You can … tell the difference between a PTG and a sceptic - it is … proportional to the income they receive for being loving … they possess a superlative capacity for holding a "spiritual mirror" to the person who becomes ready to examine … the "bad game" which we all play in degrees, but lose in the end. The PTGs' appreciation of … the ways in which their own confidences have been respected by PTGs of the past … assures not only the security of the apprentice's trust, but also the "spiritual equality" that combats all the … imbalances … that can contaminate professional environments … PTG principles … may be applied in a vast array of … settings (p.182)* *Fellow travellers … are the best companions if their stake in affairs is equivalent to ours (i.e., honest self-appraisal). In those environments, the prospect of a broken confidence, or an insensitive (far less judgemental) incursion is all but eliminated. But the requirement for failsafe is a spurious defence, for no protection is needed against the phalanx of one's own true convictions. The problem is one of getting started with sufficient momentum to build up steam, until that gnawing and ravenous sinkhole that was the past becomes truly lost to history. (p.149)* *It is patently obvious that someone who has similar experience to another possesses the greater capacity for empathy and, so, someone who wishes to step into the helping shoes of one so qualified must be at least one of: virtuously willing when no-one better placed will do it; better qualified on a net basis by other assets, or representing a response system that is protecting its own power or financial interests on unethical grounds. (p.78)*	Contraindications include arguments that: possessing first hand experience of another person's predicament confers no significant advantage in matters of interpersonal identification, trust and mutual confidence (factors known to favourably affect the process and progress of psychotherapy); qualifications other than direct experience of the trajectory of a life course and recovery from a "descending vicious spiral" weigh heavier in the balance when considering how best to help washed up people; e.g., being clever as evidenced by having read lots of books, having passed lots of exams, having lots of academic qualifications, having lots of letters after your name, having a privileged background, being wealthy, being well-embedded in the social establishment, being "well-connected", or having a patronising and superior attitude; the risk that – when things go wrong as inevitably they do when people are psychologically sick – "competent coxswains" or PTGs might be unfairly blamed outweighs the arguments in favour of delegating or leaving certain matters in their hands; the best things in life cost money and the more things cost the better they are; also, stiff professional competence lends far greater impetus to a stranded person's psychological redemption than "unconditional positive regard" or anything else reverberant with "empathy" or "love".

SAMPLE FALSIFIABLE PROPOSITIONS IN A "MORAL PSYCHOLOGY"

Falsifiable propositions	Sample *Nine Seahorses* references (with page number)	Foreseeable contraindications
Spiritual equality and togetherness are exercised in group therapy		

Have we forgotten our sense of togetherness? If we step back for a moment from the hustle and bustle of our daily lives – leaving aside for a moment all the natural anxieties that compel us to stay on the move in pursuit of our "survival needs" – it isn't difficult to conjure in our minds a sense of universal fellowship amongst all peoples – with a simple focus on the humanity we share. According to one point of view, it is only in lending emphasis to unity, rather than competition, that we will save ourselves from "mutually assured destruction". It is more productive to focus on what human beings have in common than what separates or divides them. A "moral psychology" is for *Everyman* (the title of an unattributed 15th century play): of course, we mean pure equality as distinct from sexual or any other type of discrimination. Our "shareable subjective experience" is always a good starting point for group therapy. We are in this together. We need each other. We don't organise ourselves well.	*Picture … 6,800,000,000 … people … The … population … from which modern humans evolved "Out of Africa" may have numbered only a few thousand … When we assimilate … that our sun … counts as but one star amongst about … 30-70 sextillion … we can hardly avoid the … sentiment – that we are small … But nowhere is it written that we must be alone – or separated* (pp.97;99) *Could we not … confess … how … little we … are able to establish about our mutual differences, and immeasurably how much more we might have in common.* (p.29) *Whereas TA autonomy may have been the … prerogative of "certain fortunate people" … a "moral psychology" is for nobody if … not for Everyman.* (p.177) *… can there be any meaningful psychology that is not for Everyman including the least intellectually agile?* (p.99) *… for satisfaction and fulfilment are for Everyman, or they are nothing* (p.52) *What human beings do appear to have … is a "shareable subjective experience" … seemingly, hinged squarely on our consciousness which, by ordinary understanding, is intimately bound with our very self-awareness and our awareness of other human beings.* (p.43) *You may … describe your personal suffering as "beyond words" … if we are generous, we can readily conjecture your pain … empathy in its most wonderful, capacious guise is a fantastically practical way to love.* (p.157) *… malaise is dissolved in … togetherness … why … would we wish to render ourselves immune from each other's pain … Groups are for illumination of the person and … the togetherness that is natural for humans who lead perverse lives if it is … absent.* (p.160) *There is a dimension of cogency in that "other" relationship which is at its most potent when it resembles closely the circumstances in which we must discharge our sanity … we can approximate those contexts … in groups – if we are … brave and willing.* (p.95) *The long and short of everything else left to say in favour of group therapy has mostly to do with clean power – and honesty … All told, the argument for groups is overwhelming.* (p.184) *The response may come unpersuaded from intimate community. Then again it probably won't … because we don't organise ourselves that well.* (p.75)	Contraindications include arguments that: human competition is as old as the hills, utterly natural, and shouldn't be inhibited by communists, liberals or bleeding hearts; what we have in common is less a desire to level the human playing field than it is to win the game of life – against each other; the notion of any kind of human equality – and, so, that includes "spiritual equality" – is fundamentally flawed: nature made us unequal and that is the way we will remain; the idea that everyone can be reasonably happy in this life is hopelessly ambitious; if we occasion pain to each other – or any other cost for that matter – in the course of pursuing personal ambitions, that is simply the way it is – it is not a matter for a "moral psychology"; "empathy" is a flawed and wasted concept – either it doesn't and cannot exist (we can't imagine what it is like to be another person or feel as somebody else does), or attempts at trying to understand other people's "frames of reference" serve no useful purpose; "shareable subjective experience" in groups is just another way of describing "gossip" – one-to-one encounters are more efficacious; we organise ourselves in (nuclear) families instinctively – the only other kind of organisation that we correctly encourage is that which generates economic growth.

SAMPLE FALSIFIABLE PROPOSITIONS IN A "MORAL PSYCHOLOGY"

Falsifiable propositions	Sample *Nine Seahorses* references (with page number)	Foreseeable contraindications
Collective responsibility is confined to safety nets and education		

People who are in trouble with their "minds", near inevitably, lack resources of every significant kind.	*Should young people … or anybody else … be left to establish a "moral psychology" under their own auspices and resources however scant those might be at a time of special need? (p.71)*	Contraindications include arguments that:
It could be you.	*… when we became incapacitated … our tolerance for our own hypocrisy? (p.76)*	it will not be me – nor my children – nor any other member of my family – nor anybody about whom I care – or rely upon economically;
Families are great – but not all families have their act together – all of the time. It takes several generations to change culture.	*… upon whom … should responsibility fall in the … situation where a teenager incarcerated for an acquisitive offence … petitions successfully … against a treatment system designed, implemented and funded by a government, arising out of failure to administer adequate substitute medication … in time to head off the discomfort of withdrawal … in … the … prison cell? Having identified the respective parties in the scenario … "Why so?" and "How so?" (p.70)*	the right and proper environment where young people learn to stay out of trouble is the (nuclear) family – the correct order of priorities is to re-establish families – whence appropriate social education will automatically ensue;
Young people may end up in prison because they have been ruthless, unthinking or simply unable to see or hinder their own "descending vicious spiral".	*Not many of us would discount … the role of the family … some would let it remain there to venture nowhere else. Still others prefer to exercise a "social conscience" and we may … envisage a dimension from zero involvement of government … to the … provision of … safety nets – even compulsory education and community service (p.71)*	it is better to have (taxable and) legalised "opium for the masses" (nicotine, alcohol, more narcotics for those who have become addicted to them) – on the grounds that quietened (potential) trouble-makers are less socially bothersome and less of a strain on the public purse that way (sedated) – leaving the remainder of us (who know how to keep our noses clean) free to get on with minding our own business (thereby attending to economic growth which benefits everybody – naturally);
Incarceration is the correct option for anybody who is a danger to society and is unwilling to change. The best judge of such matters is a panel of PTGs. There aren't good reasons for locking up people otherwise: there are many arguments against it. People who have offended others are best off in the community making suitable amends.	*We don't provide sanctuaries within spitting distance of park benches (p.122) … we have become blindly adept … at talking about social safety nets … but they do not exist in the number and forms that they might. (p.159)* *Then what safety nets might we correctly establish and vote to maintain? Only those that help people grow up in the way that we have done ourselves in order to vote for the system that created them … Our sanctuaries may (indeed must) be threaded through with a reorientation programme … Perhaps "moral crunch" can be obviated with forewarning. As it takes more than a generation or two for families to reform cultural inheritance, our "citizenship" curriculum may be just the right locus for preparing our youth*	
We are in this together.	*… Now, we have footed a bill only for conditional sanctuaries and contemporary citizenship in schools. No bureaucrats. No need for argument or upsets. Clean consciences all round. Win-win. (p.159)*	people who have broken the law are irredeemable; revenge and punishment are valid reasons for incarceration, for such motives do not further victimise people who have been offended;
Safety nets are needed as a first priority. Education is the only other necessary investment.	*Although we have lost … the old-fashioned … conviction politician … "moral vacuousness" isn't all the fault of the swanky new political classes … We must look to ourselves … In democracies anyway, we get what we vote for (p.159)*	we are hugely indebted to the "swanky new political classes" for all they have done for us – it is better to have remunerated people talking about safety nets than recovered people building them;
We get what we vote for. Change begins in psychology, not politics. Mature civic community is means *and* end.	*… our challenge is less a political one than a psychological one … hope for our future lies in our own hearts and minds … personal change is possible. (p.103)*	it is better not to rock the boat by thinking for ourselves.

Sample assets accruing from a "moral psychology"
To the extent that a "moral psychology" demonstrates its own efficacy
(to those who know its nurturing properties at first hand or who may
be willing to venture on a test drive) or survives Popperian scrutiny
(for the prevaricating sceptic), its capacity for re-establishing and
healing human affairs knows few restrictions. Its appeal is universal
as, from its voluminous heart, it issues quiet, gentle and persistent
invitations to every person's capacity for embracing sweeter destiny.
We have been at pains to emphasise that "moral psychology" is barred
to no-one (i.e., it is for *Everyman*). It separates us from each other
only by the degree of our willingness to submit ourselves to it. As
individuals we are each chained to nobody. Our objective is personal
freedom obtained through respectful recognition of mutual, common and
interdependent interests. But we are imposed upon by no-one, and we
venture morally only into our own shadows – or where we are cordially
invited. We are forewarned against – and need never succumb to – the
charms of the Pied Piper of Hamelin[248] even if, all the while, we had
been tapping our feet obligingly to Skinner's mesmeric (R-S) tune.
"Moral psychology" is a programme of personal, family and group or
community development that need cost next to nothing financially. It
takes a little organisation because its psychology is hinged on group
processes: it is never a solo effort except between *rendezvous*. It is
best achieved through spontaneous interest and low-level operations.
As an indulgence to the "moral environment" contemplated in Chapter
6, let us reconsider briefly the young person at its hopeful centre.
Adolescents have ever sought each other's company – for camaraderie
and for solace – at worst mischief (our own teenagers fall in with
the "wrong" crowd). A "moral psychology" harnesses and favours their
natural instinct for "togetherness" and the solidarity it promises.
The "healthy" group – unprompted by its elders – generates its own
(narrower) boundaries on waywardness. The "grown-up" work is limited
to providing the pre-emptive education and safety nets to which we
alluded in Chapter 9. A deleterious life course ("vicious spiral"),
early set, too often portends a tragic trajectory, but failure of
personal direction – as in adult lives – is only ever temporary, and
separation short of abandonment is an acceptable last resort. There
is nothing wrong with the strictures of a morally sound formal
community for those who are likely to "fall off the rails" without
one. Incarceration of young people is expensive, but let's have a new
"moral economics" for social policy. Teenage conceptions happen
because boys and girls don't say "No" each to themselves. All other
factors in reckless conceptions represent unfavourable pressures on
that inner resilience. The instinct is an imperious one as we know.
When young people possess a strong personal identity, and a sublime
trust in their own futures – the rough weather of insecurities, peer
pressure, and inhibition through intoxification are afforded fewer
chances to hold sway. Young people are like their soured counterparts
in that they just want everything to be OK. We must tell them it is
so, and mean it. They will do the same for the next generation until
our expectations for *them* are outclassed by a social infrastructure
and *Zeitgeist* beyond *their* wildest dreams. Our aspirant may not arise
as a Baez or as a Mandela, but we have demonstrated that the greatest
people of history remain unsung. Allegorical throughout, and relaxed
about its objectives, Part III presents "moral psychology" in action:
more, if you will allow, about doing or living it than explaining it.

---

[248] as we saw in Chapter 9, all those illegitimate enticements to "conscience" that may
lead us up the garden path to insanity: whether the unarticulated cudgel of our silent
ancestors; the nuisance of corrupt biographic conditioning (re-writable depending on
the limits of our psychotherapeutic technology); every unloving but refutable third
party agenda and – especially – our own undisciplined fear and "spiritual blindness"

"OK So Far …" (100% degradable but reusable by you)

Part III

"The Story Of Seahorse Sam"

Dialogue
The charge of the Unwitnessed Observer

In a dream, the Unwitnessed Observer came to Seahorse Sam:

Unwitnessed Observer:	*Where have you been?*
Seahorse Sam:	*Turning over stones!*
Unwitnessed Observer:	*What did you find?*
Seahorse Sam:	*Distractions!*
Unwitnessed Observer:	*What is not distraction?*
Seahorse Sam:	*Truth!*
Unwitnessed Observer:	*What is Truth?*
Seahorse Sam:	*Truth is that which is revealed to me when, humbly, I beseech to be guided …*
Unwitnessed Observer:	*Here then is your charge bon aventurier!*

Of means fair and foul permitted:
anthropo-allegory, pinch of pillory,
stranded psyche-skeins unknitted;
revitalise discontented history!
Draw My abject charges carried
undulating atop crested waves of wonder,
each curiosity married –
contiguous mystery-matters to ponder.
Now! The tender awakenings,
private confidences of the seeker finding,
swelling towards their homecoming;
recreated, perfect, paradise reminding –
known only (for some turned away)
to every treasurer of the Supreme Promise.
For Love asked only Her own sway.
Objurgate this existential edifice!

In My time, not yours, shall it be done!

Sam awoke, exclaiming rhetorically in his empty chamber,
Whereas the beautiful and popular (neither of which am I)
Princess Diana crowned herself 'Queen Of Your Hearts'
By strange visitation's lot am I 'Beckoner To Your Minds'

Seahorse Sam:	*Have you a 'Mind'? Have you a 'Heart'?*
You, Dear Reader!	*These are not for the taking!*

A word to the wise to those who'd hear:

resistance only *seems* necessary (ask the birds and the bees)

"Port Of Call"
Barriera Wharf, Grand Harbour, Valletta, Malta

Chapter 11

"Shipwreck and soliloquy"

A confident and optimistic start
Seahorse Sam joined the stream of life as each seasoned moped (rusty and seized up — but for mandatory daily exercise) enters Calcutta's major intersections amidst the rapids of its morning rush hour; i.e., blindly and quickly; rooted juxtaposed in its own tributary; trusting (by custom) the torrent of vehicles dredging every senior thoroughfare (one juncture presenting as sore a test of the obliging predisposition of destiny as another): all told — one might say — enthusiastically, carelessly and optimistically. That same first dawn (of all of Sam's hitherto unravelled days) — the understated daybreak sun baked the patchwork of the city's dusty thoroughfares whilst balmy breezes whisked up the luminescent, unhelmeted manes of blithe and gay motorised charioteers and their pillions. Natural and easy friendships (untarnished by familiarity and any hardness of feeling) noiselessly expressed themselves between each driver and every passenger — unrestrained smiles overlying privately hopeful hearts. Oriental scents canoodled their unsolicited and intimate way into this paradise's newest, still green and fledgling nostrils. Seahorse Sam had hit the ground running in a veritable and heady Indian Eden. Like any other seahorse, Sam was excited by this novelty, and aroused to the sublimeness of very life itself by all his hearty companions.

Early ominousness and the most forlorn of sentiments
He found himself on arrival at his first port of call (just as his attention had begun to dissolve in a precipitous fatigue) being attended upon by a small number of peculiarly interested parties. Having descended into the colder shadows of a concrete jetty running alongside a decrepit three or four storey structure to the left (now obliterating the falling evening sun), and a shabby seagoing merchant vessel to his right (beautifully salty to his rampant nostrils), Sam was directed suddenly (by force of strange compliance) into a self-effacing and rather unlit warehouse-like hive of curious industry. Multitudes of grown seahorses conducted themselves rhythmically in strange but focussed and orchestrated patterns of movement. Not an intelligible word was spoken. A determined administrator loomed largely, seeing to it that Sam had not forgotten to be hungry. One ran for soapy water hither whilst another fetched a drying towel thither. A serious-looking, lab-coated specimen ruffled a sheaf of papers flapping from a clipboard as if attempting to secure the next urgent instruction from the manual of days. A disturbing aura emanated from this particular individual, who seemed to be inspecting Sam from top to toe — and inside out — as if clattering around in a toolbox for the right spanner to wrench an obstinate nut. Although Sam didn't feel unco-operative, he certainly felt trepidation — an uneasy queasiness about how things were turning out. Where was the big city? What kind of underworld was this? In one darkly unpredictable and unattended minute, Sam found himself trapped and contained. Discerning the fibres of a strange resistance within him becoming taut — urging him to escape, and to go back to his friends — he knew the compunction was foolish: he would only die on the dusty streets. Strangely powerless to explain, to hide or to move, the voiceless feeling was an oppressive dimness cast over the sunny conviviality and social glee he had known on the busy thoroughfares. He began to imagine them in visions by way of comfort till he might return. There was no answer for it: he could only bide his time — and that awful suspense was the loneliest and most forlorn of sentiments.

Creepy Clipboard Clive

Was it all in Sam's imagination, or was the creepy superintendent – the one distinguished by the flapping clipboard – as often as not to be seen stooping sweetly before all manner of seahorses in just about precisely the proportion that their attributes varied from Sam's own? The slimy administrator leaned, slanty-headed in smiling co-operation with infant seahorses younger than Sam and, without prudence, seemed to court the admiring affections of junior and adolescent seahorses of the opposite sex. Tall, willowy and snooty over adults of his own social stature, he dominated by unproclaimed eclipse of joyfulness every sorry yardage he occupied. Most of all, he scuttled as smoothly deferent and as gallant as could ever be towards those fearsome shadowy figures and their consorts whose presence in the frantic hive was only ever discerned by their silhouettes and their imperatives. Rumoured to have been renamed Clive by kind volunteers following his arrival on the jetty many moons since as an incommunicative and inexplicably tatty fugitive from a distant land, secretively he had done away with his benefactors. Nobody addressed Clive by his name – nor ever steeled themselves to interrogate him on any delicate topic. And it seemed that every matter was a sensitive matter; at least, in so far as Clipboard Clive and Sam shared anything at all in common.

Flotsam and derelict of industry

Salad days whispered clemency and gentle endorsement to Sam as had paradise her lovely biddable self during their first urban encounter. Over the ensuing months and years, Sam settled into the dockside environment as some kind of juvenile stomping ground – and he forged it as a happy one. He grew to know the environment boundaried by the extremities of this particular harbour location well: its nooks and its crannies; its secret recesses where older seahorses and appointed officials never ventured, and its hidden and dangerous backwaters where corridors and passing points for vessels and pedestrians alike got washed constantly in the detritus of manufacturing technology – litter – borne atop the foamy crests of tidal inundations. All this flotsam and derelict of seahorse industry was offensive to Sam; unbeautiful, and ever appealing for its own removal and destruction. It pleaded innocence in its impact – as unthinking refuse rather than calculated contamination; only barely toxic nuisance – all the same, it was unwanted in Sam's playground and he removed it with elementary willingness and effort. Notwithstanding his chagrin, the world was a simple and welcoming place for easily satisfied adventurers like Sam.

Persecution

One temperate afternoon, Sam was wading sun-bound along a rivulet arched on both banks by the most exotic and proud of lofty flora; his pockets bulging with fine stones for the keeping. In his embrace grew steadily a pile of consumer jetsam ready for incineration back at the boiler room behind the warehouse. Nobody knew that Sam dispensed of pollution in this way – for he chose his moments for tipping the miserable refuse carefully, and the evidence was always destroyed. Clipboard Clive appeared suddenly – armed with a strange photographic device. Wearing an immensely satisfied expression, the interloper announced his proud intention to declare Sam's crimes to the seahorse community. Since the camera never lies, Sam would be charged with mischievously emptying manufacturing refuse into local waters. The creep disappeared as quickly as he had come, and Sam worked his baffled way back to private quarters. So many light years from being able to fathom Clive's motives, intentions or influence – Sam sensed that something dire was about to happen. Even those seahorses whom he might have depended upon most for solidarity sided with Clive because of his seniority. Sam was beckoned, admonished and interned. Rather out of character, he squirmed, and brooded darkly in his desolation.

"Dockside Environment"
Senglea (Civitas Invicta) and Grand Harbour, Valletta, Malta

"Homage To Neptune"
Studley Royal, North Yorkshire

A bid for freedom
By nightfall, Sam had hatched a dream. Longingly he fantasised about
his freedom. But what *was* his freedom? Anything but *this*! Anything
characterised by light and wind and sun and air and waves and sea and
movement and running and leaping and tearing down and building up.
What had he to lose? All *this*? Then surely he had *everything* to gain.
Pinching himself to remain awake, he waited until half way through
the night by which time, he reasoned, the risk of waking an overseer
or disturbing anyone who might raise an alarm would be at a minimum.
Taking nothing with him (except the spectacles he commonly wore – and
without which he wouldn't have got far at all free of faltering), but
realising he must have sustenance for a day or two, he escaped via
the kitchen and its small skylight which was never closed or locked.
Scaling down the hard tiled roof, and over the flat extension of the
boiler house he knew affectionately from another perspective, a drain
pipe broke the last vertical rush away from Sam's erstwhile prison.
Smiling to himself wordlessly through his fear and his adrenalin, he
skipped madly along the jetty past the briny ship and down towards
the steps that led to the rivulet where Clive had tripped him up.
Down another tributary he knew there was an old timber wreck which
floated and beached on each modest tide. As far as Sam was concerned,
it was an utterly seaworthy craft. Several frustrating minutes
subtracted from Sam's glee as he worked to loosen the knots of the
sodden rope that anchored the old ship to a tree. Uttering a Roman
homage to Neptune as the last damp fibres yielded to his testy tugs,
he pushed and heaved at its stern until it moved off the stony bank
upon which it had lain asleep in the night – redundant of all purpose
for years as far as Sam knew. He clambered over the aftmost rail, and
stood quietly in the night – silent but for the barely audible drift
of an opportunely conspiratorial tide as it retreated to the ocean
taking Sam and his battered but obedient vessel away to providence.

Unconstrained but for weather
Embarked buoyant and unconstrained (but for weather) upon this sudden
nautical mission, the only future beckoning him cooed persistently –
as if a loyal, dedicated lover, ever reinventing herself, invariably
manifest as some invitation to an immediate and fascinating pleasure.
Sam coursed like Odysseus[249] (only rather less royally) through an
omnibus of fabulous maritime adventures. A buccaneering roustabout,
he navigated himself and his remarkably constant boat from one
flabbergasted China Shop to another. Every breeze quickening over the
seas fomented a nimble tack and an impetuous bearing from the young
mariner. Myopic, cartographically incautious and defying unsounded
fathoms – somehow (as if underwritten by a mystical guarantor), Sam
survived the objections of fate and (almost) silent protests of his
own personal destiny. Seafaring recklessness cast him to many shores
– foreign in location; exotic in local abundance, and eerily remote
in culture. Slowly and without discerning (far less appreciating) the
ruinous trajectory of his inner resilience, Sam descended steadily
from the bliss and optimism of snatched liberation through the
ignorance and shadows of many a hollow triumph. In several turbulent
storms Sam established for himself an affable seahorse haven – always
(going by the bunting) ready to greet him and afford him succour –
but none could or would ever retain his restless and slippery anchor.

---

[249] Odysseus was renowned amongst the Ancient Greeks for his sharpness (of "mind"),
powers of persuasion, diplomatic adeptness, warrior-guile and ingenious military plots
(including the mythical wooden horse devised for the sacking of Troy). As we all know,
there is always more than one account of history. Odysseus's reputed self-discipline
was interspersed with instances of wrath, and he was less revered amongst the Romans
who – by dint of conquest – became entitled to render fresh accounts of Mediterranean
history (and who prided themselves on honour rather than cunning and sleight of hand).

A final escape and a curious detachment

Escaping to the open ocean after yet another frustrated encounter
with a ruthlessly lascivious indigenous hostess, Sam found himself
slumped in a corner of his bridge feeling peculiarly exhausted.
Taking leave of keen navigation, he discovered himself with bursts
and echoes of needles and pins – strangely absent from, and floating
away from his usual robust self, as if a dying astronaut suddenly and
unfortunately disconnected from the mothership and all its familiar
crew. The world had fallen silent and dark as in an unpolluted night.
The sense of aloneness that had descended upon him was fantastically
intense. More than any and all of this, he had somehow – through the
aggregate of all of his experience since escaping from the dismal
warehouse on that maritime jetty – taken delivery without warning of
the most curious new outlook in his wearied body and dispirited mind.

Self-reliance, mastery and vanity

Hope had gone. Sam had lost hope. There was none whatsoever left, and
it promised no return. The hope he suddenly missed was the hope that
he had relied upon by custom in all his past days to pull him through
each and every (inevitably difficult) encounter with this pressing
world and its challenging and belligerent occupants. It was the hope
that drove and encouraged him as if a fluctuating but nevertheless
inexhaustible battery of energy – and of pure luck – for all of his
waking comings and goings. This usually subliminal supply got him
through the successive trials of living – as if a precious metal that
would always weigh heavier in the scales of fortune than the greatest
imaginable cost of every ordeal of existence and its survival. At
last it had deserted him. He could not rise from the floor. He had
become helpless. All notion of power was vanity. He knew as a penny-
dropped, plain and encyclopaedic fact that he could not save himself.

Shipwreck

Then … the first, precipitate and colossal return to his senses. His
trusty companion – the old but reliable timbered craft – had noisily,
and with an enormous and reverberant crunch, splintered itself on a
tide-worn but hefty array of steadfast and barely submersed rocks.
These – seemingly with animate, cognate and unwavering intent – were
plainly resolute in their determination to ground Sam's adventures
permanently – but lacked harshness in their determination as if a
drill instructor rendered voiceless by rash compassion stumbling on a
war-struck, traumatised infant. Sam had never encountered such
paradoxically gentle obduracy – unspeakable darkness, the toxicity of
his emotional environment, the sheer and painful desolation of his
lost mind – but all of these became suddenly and queerly suspended.
Had there been some unseen agency behind this turn of events? Why had
the disintegration of his ship occurred only moments after desertion
of hope? Simply because he had abandoned watch in his exhaustion?
What was the use of sweet reason for fathoming all of this – for he
was possessed now of only the unassailable "truth" of his experience
both in the material world – and in the restored life of his spirit.

The shocking discovery about Clipboard Clive

Rummaging about in the Captain's locker for bottled water from his
prone position, Sam's digits lighted upon some old parchment which
transpired on inspection to be a large envelope containing a poster.
Sam drew it out and held it to the window. It read (with a mugshot):

WANTED FOR FOUL AND VILLAINOUS MURDER

Lord T. Dover alias "Clipboard Clive"

$ REWARD for freemen or AMNESTY for felons

The musty, chilling pronouncement was dated less than a year prior to
Clive's fabled deliverance from distress into the seahorse community.

"Steadfast And Barely Submersed Rocks"
Rubha na Carraig géire (The marble quarry), Iona, Scotland

"Foul And Villainous Murder" (but what really happened?)
National Museum of The Royal Navy, Portsmouth

"Captain's Locker"
Commander's cabin, HMS Warrior, Portsmouth Historic Dockyard

"Shipwreck"
The Gannel Estuary tidal wildlife haven, Newquay, Cornwall

Soliloquy

"Tomorrow's Easy World" including refrain

In tomorrow's easy world
I wished things all my own way
And as the shrunken years unfurled
And I forgot to pray
In my haste to make things right
I seized my dreams away
Till on my knees with no more fight
I learned there's just one day

In tomorrow's easy world, the perfect dame would do
A maid to smooth away my fears; a nurse to pull me through
Away to port in every storm; a storm in every port
An invoice thirty-nine years long for every refuge sought
A vain attempt to underpin the homeless child in me
At last I offered up my reckless, feckless ways to Thee
The anchor for the drifting raft, the signpost for the stray
The Lord of storms, The Lord of life, The Lord of just one day

In tomorrow's easy world
I wished things all my own way
And as the shrunken years unfurled
And I forgot to pray
In my haste to make things right
I seized my dreams away
Till on my knees with no more fight
I learned there's just one day

In tomorrow's easy world, as captain of a crew
With nought to fear, no guide to steer, no chart to misconstrue
With short supply, a certain eye, and paucity of thought
I drove my way through hearts and minds in every battle fought
The stout pursuit of each delight, the idle quest for bliss
At last I opened up my heart to all that was remiss
To Thee I yielded up the strain, the wrangle, the mêlée
The Lord of storms, The Lord of life, The Lord of just one day

In tomorrow's easy world
I wished things all my own way
And as the shrunken years unfurled
And I forgot to pray
In my haste to make things right
I seized my dreams away
Till on my knees with no more fight
I learned there's just one day

In tomorrow's easy world, companions grew more few
No captive's name to bear the blame, no scapegoat that I knew
I knocked on wood, despised the good, did little that I ought
Dissolved the day, and come what may, disowned what I'd been taught
A long crusade to serve myself, no praise where credit due
At last I learned the vital charge of daily thanking You
Provider to the modest heart, presenter of the way
The Lord of storms, The Lord of life, The Lord of just one day

In tomorrow's easy world
I wished things all my own way
And as the shrunken years unfurled
And I forgot to pray
In my haste to make things right
I seized my dreams away
Till on my knees with no more fight
I learned there's just one day

"Calm After The Storm"
The Ardnamurchan Lighthouse from Sanna Bay, Scotland

Chapter 12

"Aloneness versus togetherness"

Learning to wait

Sam sat on a dry promontory and waited. Inexplicably, he didn't fear abandonment. He knew the waiting was temporary, although he couldn't have begun to account for what might happen after the culmination of the waiting. He waited, and waited. He neither ate nor drank. Not one fibre of his inner being was forlorn. He suffered no frustration of desire. Sam experienced during that waiting only what was around him, requiring of it neither satisfaction nor deliverance. He just waited.

A surprise party

Behind him two seahorses appeared on an inexpensive carriage, steered by a third member of the same surprise party. Together the three introduced themselves as an experienced salvage crew – although it wasn't entirely clear to Sam what materials may have nourished their customary business. The Driver lingered, either seated in or fiddling with the rickety chariot, whilst the primary motley pair (for one of the twosome was slight and the other thickset) approached Sam; then accompanied him to the destroyed bridge – wherein the disconcerting poster of Clive had remained undampened and undamaged. The strangers seemed to recognise something about both the notice and the fugitive. Sam couldn't discern whether they had seen a copy of the notice themselves previously, had known Clive as an acquaintance – or simply were familiar with the gist and import of the message it conveyed. The strangers were transparently benign in intent, but they didn't seem in the least anxious to please, or wish to negotiate any kind of deal regarding – as they did with a smiling inspection – Sam's wreck.

A particular pedigree of answer

The more lightweight of the two retrievers asked Sam about his intentions. What did Sam intend to do now? The bantam seemed to expect a particular pedigree of answer – and Sam found it emanating from his core naturally – unforced – as if unprompted nevertheless.

I am not in the least sure, except that my vessel is ruined, and I have no need of its repair now; nor, indeed, any return to the ocean.

The kindly face enquired, *If your boat, by some turn of fortune, were suddenly restored, would you determine to set forth again?*

Sam knew from his innermost that his answer was rendered pure: *No*

Would you care to accompany us? We are going inland.

Knowing well that he hadn't a better notion, Sam replied, *I am weak and, although I'd rather not become your burden, I am barely mobile – let alone capable of work or of otherwise helping with your business.*

Let yourself be free of that concern until tomorrow, came the answer.

A particular sense of direction

By the time they had finished their conversation, Sam and the benevolent lightweight had found their way back to the chariot where the bulky associate seemed engaged in earnest report to The Driver. Sam clambered onto the wobbly vehicle, and the ramshackle quartet set off in a direction of which the funny cohort seemed most sure. Sam squirmed privately at the noisy humour celebrated amongst his new friends. The jolly crowd indulged their spirited merriment with a quip about this – and a crack about that – as if Sam's troubles were mere apparition; what is more, seeming oblivious to his dark travail (seated to the rear as Sam was, writhing in an existential quandary).

A convivial establishment

Eventually, the small group arrived at an inn known intimately by the stockier character. It lay between a forest of scrawny dwellings and the sea, some distance up the coast from Sam's sad wreck. Stocky's familiarity with the hostel was evident from the way he strode up to the modest entrance boldly, and by the way he was regarded once inside by those other seahorses already ensconced there. They seemed to appreciate his (and each other's) very presence, without requiring or anticipating any particular behaviour. The assembly was just as familiar with the lightweight – referring to him as The Feather. The establishment was a cordial one, although no liquor seemed necessary to generate or facilitate its social ease. To any casual observer, the most remarkable thing about the place was its aura. No ritual was in progress, nor did any one member seem to inspire the gathering. Yet here present was an obvious "gestalt": some presence made of more than the sum of its parts or individuals gathered there. It was as if their belongingness with each other possessed an identity of its own. Unambiguously benign, it seemed as resolutely replete with mission as the rocks upon which Sam's vessel and all his youthful ambitions had foundered. Unwavering in its consistency or depth, the connectedness between the seahorses in that forum imbued the entire ensemble with a collective optimism whose durability seemed limited only by the willingness of each constituent party to remain identified with one another. Sam had not yet appreciated the vital quality of their bond. The owners too (the inn being a family concern), were comfortably acquainted with the salvage crew going by the convivial and patterned banter which, unbroken in flow, still had not exhausted itself – and seemed to have legs long enough for a more or less permanent journey.

A protracted conversation begins

A protracted conversation precipitated itself between Sam's self-conscious awkwardness and the conviction and poise of The Feather (which seemed far outsized against his bodily dimensions and bulk). Although Sam had, rather intrusively, posited himself into a stance of private enquiry within his personal space, the lightweight seemed (anyway) to have all the time in the world for Sam's sharp questions:

What do you all possess here? There is no misery! How does it work?

Well, there are two unspoken rules – or principles – if you like. The first is that each and every one of us has something in common – and our co-venture is both a morally worthwhile and an indispensable one. We all used to be seafarers and, whilst we were adept at the tiller, we were poor mariners! Although most of us here are quite thoughtful and bright in many other respects, we were struck with the stupidity and temerity to set sail over and over again – with neither veteran for inspiration – nor manual for formal guide. We relied on little more than our own audacity. But that's all over now. Each of us has been landbound for a day, a month, a year; in many cases, quite a lot longer than that. You may find that you experience a certain kind of belongingness with us. We are, each of us, resigned utterly to that conjoining personal truth. If any one of us weren't surrendered to it absolutely, our latent trepidation would tear us away at the expense of this precious succour. Our chances of a further chance of cheery, fair-weather living might be significantly lower than those odds we enjoy now. At last, in no need of convincing, we remain because of our own experience, and value this alternative existence beyond any material or sensual treasure. We are a society with a high membership fee; i.e., shock, wreck and founder. We remember the less fortunate who drowned: their prospects, apparently, were more dismal than ours. Knowing it was not personal merit, we try not to dwell on what saved our skins: we are simply grateful to be living in our own still – and most of us do so more comfortably than ever we did atop the waves.

"Ramshackle Quartet"
(OK – it's really a sextet; but what's a duet between friends?)

"Who's In Charge?"
His Master's (Late) Voice, Triq San Ġwann, Valletta, Malta

An assumption of spiritual equality …

Sam stopped to take it all in. He knew that among The Feather's words coursed a new and life-affirming wisdom. He longed to ponder and reflect on the secrets coursing through his aching head – but he didn't want to lose the momentum of the conversation. Long before Sam realised that he had assimilated it all he piped up, *Who's in charge?*

That's the other major principle, replied The Feather: *there are no leaders here. It is true that we take it in turns to undertake tasks that appear to call upon some kind of clout – but personal authority earns no currency whatsoever in our midst; in fact, we avoid aspiring to it as if a plague. Far from want of responsibility, we acknowledge fundamentally the usefulness of our service to each other, but contrast rendering ourselves available in such a manner with personal ambition which only ever gets in the way of our own peace of mind (for our ambitions, by definition, are never truly satisfied except at some other time – and that is if we are fortunate). Although we are kind, tolerant and forgiving because we know intimately our own moral frailty, a self-promoting seahorse conspicuously lacks personal perspective. There is an assumption of spiritual equality amongst us. If we seem lofty or superior, we demonstrate only our foolishness.*

… no-one gets too swanky

Immediately, Sam thought of Clive, wishing almost as quickly that these robust acquaintances had been standing four-square behind him when he had been young, naïve, and had felt engulfed to the point of flight from the Clipboard. If only he'd had the benefit of being able to call upon these seasoned associates then. If only he knew then what he realised quickly he was beginning to know now … If only …

How do you get things done? queried Sam. *How is housekeeping assured?*

Well – as I say, answered The Feather, *we roster things out. The jobs that are best for us are the most menial ones: you know – preparing meals and clearing up afterwards. These sorts of activities afford plenty of scope for chatting about this and nattering about that – all told you might say – considerable opportunities for sharing experience with others in the same boat – but only figuratively speaking now, of course! When we meet in chapter house mode like the medieval vocations – to conduct business – to agree on a way forwards – or to make a decision about a matter that affects all of us – we try to defer to experience of landbound or dry living. Inevitably there are disagreements; and, as we all have a flawed history, we can expect some of these disputes to be petty or trivial. But it is better to laugh about such disruptions than take them to heart, and we develop a capacity amongst ourselves for banishing with immediate effect the kind of pride that prevents us admitting our own small-mindedness. If we all honour and stick to these principles, we find that we don't go far astray in practice and – when we do – it is not difficult to attain a fresh decorum in which we can work things out.*

So, concluded Sam, *no-one gets too swanky – or indeed ever wants to?*

You could say that, confirmed the genial conversationalist. *We have learned to defer to principles rather than revere individuals. Sycophancy doesn't travel here; in fact, it hardly ever happens. Like everything that feeds self-aggrandisement – it will weed itself out.*

But you have such robust personalities! Sam objected. *How do you reconcile self-abasement with the raucous presence you seem to enjoy?*

The Feather laughed. *It's not so much about self-abasement as the earnest pursuit of self-discovery. Our defended and fractious selves get demoted to the back of the bus. That is why you see the untroubled persona to the fore. We are as happy as we choose to be.*

"Steadily Ripening Marrow"

A new vista and a new horizon
Sam paused again. He felt flooded with countless sprinting thoughts,
a muddle of tangled leanings, but also with essential anticipation.
He knew that presently he was stumbling upon something vital – not
merely some valuable but discretionary source of helpful information
– but, rather, a purposeful, momentous and pivotal re-footing which
(from his proud, formerly self-reliant but steadily ripening marrow)
he yearned to adopt by means – if only it were permitted – of trading
in the entire stock of his suddenly worthless intellectual assets.

So there's something of a personality transplant on offer here?

Yes, The Feather replied. *You have to overcome the drive to preserve
what is familiar – especially outdated stock. You have to be willing
to visit novel territories – to travel outside your comfort zone.
That is what shipwreck does for us: it dissolves useless resistance.*

How do you know where to look? How would you reach a novel territory?

*The Feather smiled. Remember – we have abandoned the delusion of
self-reliance! In the schoolyard there was always someone smarter or
tougher than you – even if on a different as yet untold day – and the
bookworm and the bully both remembered that fact of life if and when
ever they were wise. Here, there is always a more advanced pilgrim –
someone who has already trodden steps like the ones you need to take.
It's not so much (in fact, at all) that you must go the same way –
for we all have unique histories and just as special unravelled
futures. But the principles are underwritten in spiritual aether –
just like the small book of mathematical laws that account somewhat
for the still mysterious material universe. Hereabouts, the tutor
draws back the curtain that veils the novice's unexperienced highway.
The apprentice draws on fresh conviction to take a small but
irrevocable step. The Yellow Brick Road[250] (to harness the expression)
is a strange attractor! Every pace along its ever-welcoming footage
precipitates another yard of splendid vista – always expanding before
an ever-lengthening horizon. The new world never fails to astonish!*

Have you travelled along your own Yellow Brick Road? enquired Sam.

*Of course! Stocky showed me how to tread the first steps of mine –
and someone once showed him his own. This is how it works for us:
once we are shown, we take the trouble to show others – otherwise our
society would die. I have taken many of my own steps since. The
journey will not end before I draw my last sacred breath. Having seen
what I have seen, I would never choose to return to Munchkin Country!*

A "collective consciousness" or a "collective unconscious"?
*These spiritual principles that you all recognise, and which you all
draw upon for your lifeblood* (continued Sam most curiously) … *Are
they like a "collective consciousness" or a "collective unconscious"?*

*They are a "collective consciousness" in that, universally, we
recognise them as "truth" – going by our goosebumps on mere exposure
to them – but they are not collective in so far as they generate a
unique experience for each seahorse who admits and practices them.
Perhaps they reflect a "collective unconscious" but, then again, the
evidence for archetypal templates is confined to the ways in which
they are manifest, so the proof is circular! Anyway, unlike spiritual
principles, archetypes may frame the mind-buggering hindrances of
swathes of our ancestors even if they emerged from natural selection.*

---

[250] In the renowned and popular fairytale by (Lyman) Frank Baum (1856–1919), the fabled
Yellow Brick Road was the route (with variations on the theme) from Munchkin Country
to the Emerald City that Dorothy and her understated friends pursued (through many
moral adventures) in order to secure the help promised by *The Wonderful Wizard Of Oz*.

Your money or your life
This time it was Sam's turn to smile, and he was most satisfied to oblige. Switching the subject confidently he said, *What about money?*

The amiable lightweight laughed audibly. *We contribute by throwing modest amounts of coinage into the hat according to conscience. There is always enough to underpin our togetherness – meaning that we can pay for the accommodation that we occupy for congregation, and for the refreshments we consume on those occasions. The surplus (of which there is little) pays for transport and other expenses incurred on salvage missions (such as when we attended your own shipwreck). They are not steep yet, all the same, we consider that the expense is one for the society rather than any individual member of it: if we are carrying out any business for the association, we make a point of reimbursing ourselves if there is a financial consequence. That is pretty much all there is to say about money amongst us. We work on the principles of individual conscience and enough – or sufficiency. The business of sheltering and feeding ourselves and our families is another matter. We take care of our interests independently there. There is just as much occupational or professional variety within the society as in the remainder of the entire seahorse universe. We try to earn an adequate income by working, or we otherwise provide for ourselves, according to each seahorse's circumstances or disposition. Not many of us are workshy, especially on the new Yellow Brick Road! Curiously, professional ambitions we once prized can wind up just as foundered as the rusty remnants of our previous misguided existences. Typically, we find ourselves striving in ways that are more naturally matched to our abilities and interests – perhaps, even, our childhood fantasies! Once, we may have been afraid to pursue our dreams because of crises of confidence – or fear of economic insecurity. On the Yellow Brick Road, we have begun to learn the art of transcendent trust, and we apply it to our working lives as much to anything else.*

Sam pounced. *Did you say transcendent trust? What on earth is that?*

The most subtle and deadliest of subtle and deadly foes
The Feather explained how he wanted to impart a few simple notions to Sam, but that a worthwhile appreciation of what he really wanted to convey might require a separate conversation; perhaps on another occasion when distractions were fewer, and the hours more plentiful. The bones of Sam's story had become familiar to The Feather already – in a preliminary but passably expedient kind of a way – and the thoughtful benefactor wanted Sam to understand how those wondrous and heady days he had known in the earliest of his years had, in the modest fullness of infancy, been contaminated awfully by a multitude of unsolicited events and a host of clumsy encounters (only the most ghastly of which Sam might stir up with any clarity of recollection). In truth, Clive and his Clipboard had come to represent many of them at once in a singularly terrifying, card-carrying public nuisance. By all accounts, Clive had been a ruthless bandit, but he had been tarnished, all the same, with many brushes. In a laboured manner, The Feather expounded how nature's legacy to seahorsedom had spawned beautiful things, but that one of her endowments accounted for every discomfiture under the sun. It stalked as fear disguised as reason. Clive had embodied that dubious asset well – nurturing it with care, harnessing it without restraint for the subjugation of all whom he might vilify. Once Sam had obtained a grasp of the subtlety of this dastardly foe, he'd begin to see how his own exacting restlessness, his solitary unhappiness and the irretractable despoiling of his youth by his own hand had all been fashioned by this nasty impostor. Masquerading as spontaneous accomplishment, stratagem – even reckless outburst of last resort – never once had it shown its true colours.

Chat amongst yourselves
Sam was so struck with his sudden capacity for identifying this concealed shadow-thread in all his past affairs that he almost forgot to press The Feather on the implied advantage of transcendent trust – which he presumed represented some exquisite weapon that could be wielded against the surreptitious adversary now or in the future. Sam sensed a comprehension of it at the tip of his own tongue, but wanted to hear a more convincing rendition from The Feather's lips anyway.

And, so, transcendent trust is a direct antidote for fear? Sam asked.

In one, that's it! replied The Feather, *but it helps to talk about it amongst ourselves – it's as if we usefully don our armour that way.*

I wonder, probed Sam, *how it is that your particular seahorse society stumbled upon these magical secrets when – for all seahorse history – they may have profited leagues upon leagues of seahorses before you!*

I don't mean to seem picky, said The Feather, *but – really – they are neither magical nor secret – and they are neither recent nor new-fangled. Imagine in your mind's eye that you are turning your face gradually towards the sun. The more you turn, the greater the arc of light cast upon your countenance. Light and warmth stream across untouchable distances to nourish you. The only thing required of you is the turning – but turn you must. The effect is both reflexive and proportional! It seems to you that mere readiness to perform the swivel brings about the benefits you anticipate; moreover, the more towards square the turning, the more optimal the photonic response. As far as our very existence is concerned, the sun has always been there (for she preceded us in time by a long chalk). Her spontaneous combustion has nourished our biology over many generations. In the spiritual domain, our collective experience (which we corroborate by sharing it amongst ourselves) confirms that there is some other beneficent power that responds just as lovingly, and just as automatically, if only we are amenable to any invitation to face it. Such beckoning more often than not issues from some messenger who, in turn, was afforded a similar communiqué by an earlier emissary. We are reminded permanently that we do not generate our own redemption. We are not spiritually self-reliant. Simply we are not made that way.*

Sam pressed on: *Is it correct, then, that this spiritual sustenance that can be so life-restoring and personally liberating has always been available to us – even if it has laid in unrecognised repose? And that to become aware of it we may have to be told about it when we are in some spiritually amenable condition; say, less determined than usual to defend our psychological or spiritual self-reliance? And that the prompting will emanate, as often as not, from another seahorse who was informed by yet another at some earlier time? And that any of us may have it – although not all of us may want it? And, as much as all of this, that it is our willingness to turn towards it – to face it on its own terms (thereby surrendering our resistance) – that precipitates its cascade of caring, guiding and healing power?*

Yes! came The Feather's unqualified agreement.

A potted history of disappointments
Do you think Adam and Eve got left out in the cold? teased Sam.

Well – that's an interesting and particular example of togetherness! burst The Feather's unruffled reply. *I don't know. I wasn't there. Allegedly, their overlapping purpose was seminal procreation. If you look around you here, you won't see much of the sexual imperative. That kind of relationship seems to be a special case in our affairs – potentially both heaven and hell on earth. Many of us will testify to that – especially wherever we were reckless, thoughtless or selfish.*

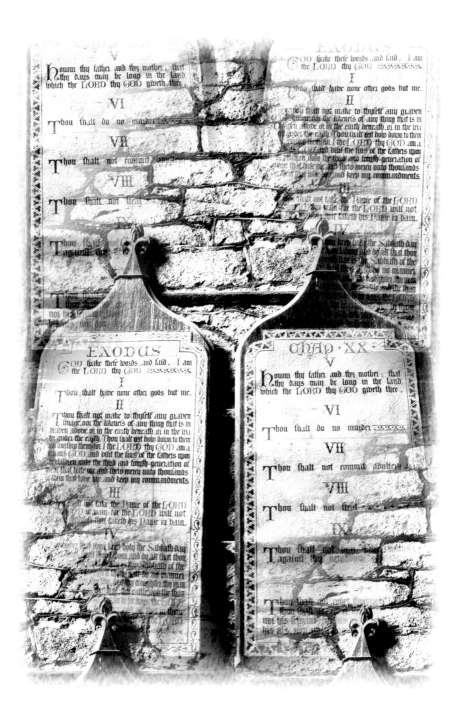

"Decalogue"
Saint Pancras, Widecombe-in-the-Moor, Dartmoor, Devon

What of communities of the past? continued Sam, unfairly assuming a comprehensive historical knowledge in The Feather. *Was this spiritual sustenance always so hidden and retained quietly by those amongst whom it was discovered that the history books have missed its import?*

The Feather paused for a moment. *We are well-advised to remember that the history books have been written by those who possessed assets for their creation: power, political and social connection, money, time, education, capacity for articulating argument and opinion, materials (including pen, ink and page) – and uninterrupted lives – at least, days consistently enough free of war and strife, personal and family tragedy, poverty, destitution and ill-health. The recording of history is always subjective – even in our present age of sweet and objective reason (and we are not so advanced in the evolution of civic matters or social enlightenment as we are disposed to assume). Spiritual heroism doesn't proclaim itself! We know so little of what has gone before us – at least in matters of spiritual significance.*

What about the religious texts? said Sam, a little rhetorically.

It rather depends on whether you consider them spiritually inspired.

Written by the hand of God? prompted Sam in his usual partial way.

By the hand of someone spiritually surrendered – perhaps.

Didn't Moses have trouble with community cohesion? (Sam had surprised himself.)

What do you think happened on Mount Sinai? counterpoised The Feather, transposing the pattern of Q and A.

Sam found himself on his back foot. *What do you mean?*

Was Moses a frustrated leader who had sloped off alone, hoping for inspiration, eventually returning to his unruly flock with a new set of rules that was successful enough – in terms of maintaining order – that fortunate historians were able to write about them? Or did a sequence of events take place exactly as described in the Bible?

You mean the Ten Commandments were inscribed on tablets of stone by God and delivered to Moses in person on the mountain called Horeb?

Yes. Which is it? The story is allegorical or it is literally true.

Why is that question important? demanded Sam, a little irritated.

Because one understanding lends itself to a fundamentally different kind of "spiritual surrender" than the other; explicitly – to what or to whom are you surrendering? What you believe makes a difference!

Sam realised he'd have to discover the answer to this pivotal dilemma himself – for if what he believed mattered, it was no use arriving at any such beliefs in conversation. He'd have to arrive at them through conviction, and that could only be achieved with his unencumbered "self", unswayed socially if you care. He was getting the hang of The Feather's intuitive style, and introduced a proposition of his own:

Moses's people were lost – not just in the desert, but morally speaking – just like I was moments before my shipwreck. They needed moral redirection and so did I. I needed moral inspiration from someone or something other than myself, and so did the children of Israel. In taking heed of Moses and the Ten Commandments – as they were presented by Moses to his people – they stayed their course for the Promised Land, just as I have glimpsed my own Yellow Brick Road.

Going by his silence, and the gentleness of his gaze towards Sam, The Feather didn't appear to consider that there was very much to add.

"A Messenger As Much As A Ruler" (Hermes Kriophorus)
Statue at Chatsworth, Derbyshire

Flattery gets you nowhere

Sam thought that he might get away with just a little more of The
Feather's attention – especially if he applied a little flattery.

In the old world, attempted Sam, *when seahorses spent much of their
time trying to convince each other of this and that, a clever
ancestor, Plato, argued*[251] *that philosophers like you should sit at
the top of the tree overseeing civilisation – in charge of everybody.*

As Sam ought to have expected by now, the flattery had little impact.
The Feather found only the first few bouts of irony in any one
conversation hilarious, and his guffaw was stifled as a consequence.

*In my old life, delusions of power accompanied delusions of self-
reliance,* insisted The Feather. *If I sought or accepted power over my
friends now, not only would I embarrass myself given our society's
shared values but – more to the point – I would be sure to deplete my
spiritual resilience. But since that inner robustness is my greatest
personal asset, and also my most cherished treasure, I shall avoid
claiming position for myself at any expense. Plato considered the
philosopher-king, by the way, to be a messenger as much as a ruler!
Do you know that there were many overstated intellectual adversaries
during those times? A bachelor-philosopher Epicurus*[252] *was fond of his
friends just like us; however, whereas without abandonment of self-
reliance our fellowship bonds could never have formed, Epicurus saw
his liaisons as a vehicle facilitating pursuit of self-sufficiency! A
constellation of values favoured by Epicurus fits poorly with our own
received wisdom. Epicurus promoted the pursuit of pleasure or freedom
from pain – what we might call hedonism – as an end in itself: the
one by which personal happiness may be obtained. We see happiness as
a by-product of being true to oneself by abandoning self-delusion. We
are too open-minded about the spiritual life to sympathise with his
ideas about everything being explained by the behaviour of atoms
moving about in empty space – even if they have the capacity to
"swerve" – thereby permitting "free will" amongst seahorses. The idea
of "free will" is a little too unqualified for a seahorse who has
experienced the power, simplicity and beauty that surges generously
from renunciation of that very thing! Epicurus was confident that
everything – including the soul – ended at death, but not many of us
would hold that we can be certain that there is – or is not – a
personal soul (aside from the mind that we know intimately because of
subjective experience and, also, how we share that experience amongst
ourselves in community). We don't know as an empirical fact whether
there is something outside space and time in the form of an afterlife
– or what we have to do to enjoy it. We can see, nevertheless, how
Epicurus was willing to stand up and be counted on a progressive or
unpopular course – such as the education of all seahorses including
slaves. And we also appreciate his ideas about retaining all possible
explanations of a given thing until any have become demonstrably
incorrect. We like that kind of open-mindedness, and find ourselves
advocating it strongly to stranded mariners when we are engaged on a
salvage spree! We like the way he avoided getting mired in politics,
appreciating the trouble they can attract. We too step aside from all
possible controversy by sticking to our core business. We don't mind
if our results appeal to others, but we try not to promote ourselves.
Like Epicurus, we know the value of our ties and of our bonds; but
our real self, in so far as such a thing can be appreciated at first
hand, emerges out of personal humility rather than any social honour.*

———————————————————————

[251] in *The Republic* (*circa* 380 BC)

[252] Epicurus (341–270 BC), after whom Epicureanism is named

Vestiges of interpersonal authority
*Would you say that this cohesion within your seahorse society is
linked in a direct manner to this absence of individual authority
within it?* asked Sam, keen to extract and amplify his understanding
on this profoundly political matter. *I have been trawling my own
limited acquaintance with accounts of groups of seahorses – over the
centuries since Plato and Epicurus in antiquity – who gathered
themselves relationally around some cause or another. I presume you
do have regard for causes adopted by seahorse collectives because you
declare a binding purpose yourself! Suppose, furthermore, that some
of these other causes were worthy beyond interrogation; moreover,
sustainable in and of themselves in so far that we have seen many
revived in new groups that generated themselves after the old ones
expired. What, then, if all those frustrated communities ultimately
faded because their members gathered themselves relationally around
an authority figure too, even if only an effigy or a fearsome legacy?*

Well, said The Feather, *in advance of a considered trawl of my own,
my feeling is that you have a point. After all, if we trace our
ancestors up to and earlier than the end of the last cold era when
the seas were small, and there were very few of us, they seemed to
have lived out quite separated lives (as far as we can tell given the
paucity of surviving first hand accounts). Constantly on the move –
driven almost exclusively by their desperate need for food and
sanctuaries for safe breeding – probably there were no authority
figures setting aside any local Alpha specimens or uncontested thugs.
There would have been no settlements of any significant number and,
therefore, no subjects over whom to reign. We might say safely that
there could have been no large-scale or culturally-entrenched
oppression. In the form of institutional slavery – condoned and
prosecuted across the globe – that was to arrive with the earliest of
seahorse civilisations and endure until only a few generations ago.
In our earliest neighbourhoods along the fertile reef – co-emergent
with our harvesting of food in local systematic ways – might became
right! The maxim, "I win, you die!" prevailed and violence became a
justifiable means to every civic end. Prior to the establishment of
such settlements, we know of no special causes that endured over
those earlier expanses of history except natural selection herself
and all that she precipitated! "Nature red in tooth and claw" got
translated in time and cultural evolution to "Seahorse eat seahorse".
Ubiquitously history replays the sword pitched against the sword, but
barely at all the numerous small and selfless acts of thoughtfulness
that raised lives up rather than tore them unthinkingly to shreds.
For all we can determine, there have been causes only since there
have been oppressors. Oppressors breed oppressors in order to
rationalise the toxic culture that is so convenient for them, and to
effect a spurious moral basis for their self-serving machinations.
The process is a most insidious one, transmitting itself over and
over through successive generations as each replicates itself
biologically, co-spawning echoes of sanctioned (context-reinforced)
behavioural repertoires by rebuking spontaneous behaviour in their
bewildered pre-verbal infants who can be cajoled grammatically later.
This is how impoverished moral environments are blindly perpetuated.
World communities are always a misshapen product of their histories –
just like individuals and, just like individuals, they cannot develop
a sensitivity to their own corruption without a spiritual mirror. Who
is to hold the spiritual mirror to an individual or to a community?
The only plausible candidate is a consistently less corrupt one and,
since that is an impossible arrangement, we settle for peers. The
moment we introduce power, we certainly dance with latent corruption.
The only principle that whispers assurance to us is the one that is
both ideal but also pragmatic. We have no leaders. And no oppressors.*

"Blind Perpetuation"
Original sculpture by Bob Waters at Arlington Court, Devon

"Maintaining A Very Small Corner Of The Whole Universe"
Upper Barracca Gardens from Grand Harbour, Valletta, Malta

In an ideal world
Then how do you prevent chaos and preserve social order? invited Sam.

We don't. We have no need to. The code of our society is too robust.
If you insist on pushing the point, I would try to convince you by
saying that none of us wishes to contemplate a return to the sea and,
relying on our mutual belongingness for the strength to resist that
temptation, our creating too much disruption would be tantamount to
sawing off the branch that is our individual perch on safe, dry land.
But that might suggest to you that it is common-or-garden fear that
drives us rather than simple belief. Whilst we may experience either
at any time, it is actually the spiritual shift precipitated by our
shipwreck – the authentic resignation to re-establishing ourselves –
that keeps us grounded. It feels subjectively like personal volition.

Is yours a true Utopia[253]? Sam wanted to see how far he could go.

The Feather smiled a very gentle smile. A true Utopia smacks of
greater perfection than you will see around here. A true Utopia would
be the end of the line. But that isn't in prospect for us – either
personally, or in society. No. We don't claim perfection. We think we
have made some progress here. We think that, to some extent, we have
got our act together. But we don't believe that standing still is an
option for those who have been fortunate enough to walk the
illuminated fork in the road. We have to make progress or we regress.
Treading water is only ever an unsafe and temporary option for us.

Just one more question, if I could … urged the interrogating salvagee
… if there are many causes, and some of these are mutually
antagonistic, can it ever be possible to have a universal brotherhood
amongst us; you know, one that includes every seahorse – the ultimate
in social harmony amongst all seahorses – and permanent world peace?

We don't aim for perfection, as I said, spoke The Feather, resolute.
As you will come to appreciate if you remain amongst us, it is not
just necessary, but it is also morally sufficient to mind our own
business, to take care of only our own moral affairs. We review
ourselves critically, but we steer clear of taking notes on others
unless we are invited to do so explicitly. We own our own problems
and shortcomings and we anticipate that others will do the same. We
just take care of our side of the street – and our pavement alone. It
is true, I suppose, that if every seahorse, and every society of
seahorses, adopted these principles – then global satisfaction would
be in prospect! But that is an indulgence of your question, and we
are not responsible for world peace. As individuals, we are satisfied
with maintaining a very small corner of the whole universe. We do
help each other in that task – in what we call sponsorship – and,
perhaps it is true that miscellaneous societies of seahorses could
sponsor each other progressively towards maturity and mutual harmony.
That seems farther off than I can imagine today – much farther off.[254]

---

[253] Based on Plato's *Republic*, *Utopia* (1516) is the "perfect" human society created in
fiction and located on an island in the Atlantic Ocean by Sir Thomas More (1478–1535).
Like *Nine Seahorses*, *Utopia* favoured equality and pacifism, recognising that whilst
perfection is an impossible dream, ideals are worthwhile yardsticks for meaningful
progress. There are many utopias in religion, literature, and the broader culture –
including the Biblical Garden of Eden. If ever there was an incontrovertible candidate
for an ancient and enduring Jungian archetype, perhaps the human capacity for longing
for everything to be OK (and imagining that it is) is about as close as one will get.

[254] Herbert Spencer (1820–1903) in *Social Statistics* (1851) wrote, "Every man may claim
the fullest liberty to exercise his faculties compatible with the possession of like
liberties by every other man … Morality knows nothing of geographical boundaries, or
distinctions of race … No one can be perfectly free till all are free; no one can be
perfectly moral till all are moral; no one can be perfectly happy till all are happy."

"See Others Reach Dry Land"
Saint Michael's Mount, Cornwall

Convinced of a need for belonging

Just suppose, said Sam (still not quite appreciating how fortunate he was to be alive, and how much better off he might be – in both his own eyes and his social standing – to at least *seem* rendered closer to reticence by gratitude), *I am now convinced of my need for belonging in a fellowship such as yours. May I join you? What must I do to qualify? Is there an apprenticeship I must serve? For how long?*

Why, certainly you may join us! said The Feather on behalf of the entire society, knowing that its membership criterion had been satisfied easily by Sam's evident personal submission – not to say sheer expression of interest and inexhaustible curiosity in understanding how it all worked. *The only requirement we place upon you is that you must desire to remain reclaimed; i.e., you maintain your position about not putting out to sea, and that you remain available as a foremost call on your time to attend shipwrecks – working with us to see others reach dry land. As for a probationary period, there is no such thing; remember – we are spiritually equal! You might say that, for each and every one of us, membership lasts 24 hours on a renewable basis. We never qualify to a criterion, or receive any certificate such as in the trades or professions. You are about to embark on a lifelong journey. Welcome to the home straight!*

Sam enjoyed a most exquisite rush of hope and personal satisfaction.

The unobscured "Home Straight" is an elevated feeling!
York Race Course

Chapter 13

"Principles, practice and perseverance"

From staunch society to bona fide personal freedom
Yesterday you mentioned something about sponsorship … interposed Sam
(reviving what amounted to his induction interview with The Feather)
… what is that, and how does it help us maintain modest corners of
the universe in ways which promote our new-found and mutual freedom?

Every single one of us; at least, each one of us who suffers no dark
misery, has a sponsor, answered The Feather, *happy to co-operate.*

What for? demanded Sam.

The program. This seemed like a brisk resumption to both parties.

What's "the program"? insisted Sam, addressing The Feather.

It's the set of principles that informs, stimulates and maintains our
personal spiritual journeys. It has much to do with learning about
honesty – or "getting real", if you like. We come to appreciate – if
we are open-minded enough – that we have been "spiritually blind" in
significant ways, especially in our old lives. That "spiritual
blindness" we have heard referred to by others as "denial" or
"discounting"; in fact, many things besides – some quite pejorative –
because most (if not all) of our thoughtless, inconsiderate and
selfish behaviour emerged from the blind side of our personalities.
We become willing to try to remedy that state of affairs, but we have
to transcend our own inner resistance towards that end. That obstacle
is, as it were, a buttress for the raw, sensitive "self" that longs
chronically for everything to be OK, and for the reassurance from
others that we are OK, too. Although a dispensable defence, it is as
hardy as hell, and may take quite a battering before it crumbles.

My goodness, said Sam, *you make it all sound like quite a struggle.*

We find living far less of a struggle once we have a sponsor and a
program, asserted The Feather with absolutely no quiver in his voice.

I think I'm beginning to realise that my shipwreck has dissolved much
of my resistance, said Sam – realising he was pretty much on beam.

Quite! answered The Feather. *In (not too much) time you may like to*
establish that as an absolute. We have found that absolute surrender
of adherence to the old life is necessary for a truly authentic new
beginning. Fortunately, it is the only absolute of the program.
Everything else that comes afterwards is satisfied by a reasonable
degree of commitment and effort. Any dilution of the primary
requirement, and brininess creeps into our nostrils sooner or later.
There is no finer practice in the program than the art of letting go.

What comes next, then? enquired Sam, moving fast with his enthusiasm.

You take an honest look at yourself. It may feel brutal at times.

Why? asked Sam, sensing he was being a little obtuse.

Why must you do it, or why might it feel brutal? probed The Feather.

Well – since you ask that way – both: I suppose I meant both.

OK. You can't see yourself as you really are. You need a spiritual
mirror. That involves a structure; i.e., the program – and another
seahorse – who becomes your sponsor. It can feel brutal because your
raw inner self may be exposed in a way that surprises or shocks you.
You can count on the support of your friends … I mean really count.

"Your Raw Inner Self May Be Exposed"
(This specimen's better half was away visiting her own sponsor)

"Imposing Assortment"
Part of Rosalie Chichester's collection, Arlington House, Devon

It all sounds a bit circular - if you know what I mean, moaned Sam.

I do. It's supposed to be. The letting go bit is truly circular. By that I mean that you must do it to experience its effects: and I mean really do it. You can't … kind of … test it to see whether it works. It only works if you let go in the sense of relinquishing all of your expectations about what might happen as a consequence of doing it - of actually entrusting your future deliberately but unconditionally!

In what or in whom are you placing your trust when you do that?

That's a personal thing. Do you remember yesterday we talked about Moses and whether he actually carried tablets of stone down the mountain? What you believe matters. You need to find a conviction that's right for you and stems in and from your innermost heart. The way I think about it is this: I presume that anything or anyone that or whom we can trust has the capacity to show us all we need to know. Whenever I possess or express that confidence, it seems to reap a harvest of understanding that just grows and grows in a quiet manner.

That sounds quite spectacular, rendered Sam more co-operatively.

Awesome is what it is. The wonder is in the unravelling of your life.

Let me guess
How do I acquire this capacity for trust - this private experience of confidence and awe? asked Sam with more than a little interest.

You start with a willingness to be guided; that is, consciously relinquish your illusion of self-reliance. This shouldn't be too much of a challenge once you appreciate it for what it is. You can dispense with any lurking doubts by examining your record: your old way of doing things and the consequences that they had - not just for yourself but for others. Anyone who baulks at such an exercise must consider themselves too rounded to make mistakes, or perhaps believe that their record is not sufficiently blemished to require scrutiny - or just reckon that it is otherwise an optional demand on their time.

Sam reassured himself: It's OK. I don't fall into those categories.

It's really, really important to understand that nobody else tells you what to believe, think, feel, say, do or become. You acquire your own understanding of all these things - by working with someone else. Remember that your sponsor understands things from both perspectives; i.e., guiding and being guided. Don't consider a sponsor who doesn't have one themselves. Nobody who isn't sponsored can sponsor another.

Sam could see no reason to hesitate. Will you sponsor me? he asked.

No

Why not?

I sponsor an imposing assortment of seahorses already and, in any event, there may be someone more suitable for you.

What do you mean by suitable? asked Sam (not too visibly hurt).

Someone with whom you identify, and whom you respect enough to listen to what they tell you. But always remember that you are not deferring to an individual. Your life is entrusted to a beneficent power now. Take your inspiration from there. Trust that your relationship with your new sponsor will be assisted by a third, spiritual essence. Your willingness to be guided is a condition which generates its own effect. You will find, often, that nothing more is required of you.

With a little compensatory self-assurance, Sam said, Let me guess …

You can only ask, obliged The Feather softly. Don't be afraid to ask.

A question of honour
Stocky, said Sam slightly obsequiously, *do you have a sponsor?*

Stocky smiled. *Sure do.*

Will you sponsor me?

I'd be very glad to, Sam. It would be an honour.

Sam felt struck that Stocky viewed sponsoring him as anything to be glad about. *Thank you,* he muttered with trepidation, but much relief. *The Feather said something about "getting real". What did he mean?*

It means that – at last – you refrain from kidding yourself.

Still don't get it. Sam's challenge was acceptably innocent.

Take you and your seafaring escapades …

Yes, but I had to escape.

Clive corrupted and frightened you, but you reserved your indignation for yourself alone: before, during and after setting sail.

Yes I did, Sam admitted.

Why?

Because I didn't want any interference, answered Sam honestly.

Stocky persevered: *What sort of interference had you anticipated?*

Any more interference like Clive's, came Sam's straight answer.

Yes – I can see that. But you kidded yourself that every seahorse was like Clive. That isn't actually true. Look around you now.

But you weren't at the jetty. I wish you all could have been.

No, Stocky sympathised, *but there may have been folks like us on or near the jetty. You didn't enquire too extensively did you?*

No I didn't, agreed Sam.

We came to you at the rocks, asserted Stocky somewhat obliquely.

Yes, you did.

What might have happened to you but for our arrival?

Sam paused in a moment of blankness … *I believe I would have expired.*

You are what we call in the salvage business a slow learner!

Do you think I've always been a slow learner? Sam was, in fact, sad.

I was teasing you. Actually, it is probably the rapidity and force with which we learn things – a lot of it going on subconsciously (or underneath our awareness) from the earliest of our days – that generates much of our misery as well as much of our gladness and joy. What do you think you might have been learning before your escape?

Something quite forceful – perhaps instinctive – drove me towards what I saw as independence. I can see now that it all had everything to do with wanting to do things my own way – without anybody telling what I could or couldn't do. Often I felt empty, or like an outsider looking in. Or I felt full of conflicts: torn this way and then that. Or I felt lonely. And I knew from even the very earliest of my private experiences that I could perform affective alchemy – transforming feelings into a more bearable (even pleasurable) haze with the quick application of some convenient concoction or another. I knew that if I engaged with others openly, I would be challenged to the point where I would have had to do everything very differently.

Developing a good appetite
Were there any trustworthy seahorses to whom you could have turned?

Those stones were not the kind I persisted in turning over. I was just determined that no-one like Clive should have the better of me.

That's understandable, affirmed Stocky with due kindness.

Is it? Sam looked up, hopeful.

Yes it is. It is perfectly reasonable to want that kind of freedom.

Sam remained quiet and pensive for a moment. Stocky left him thus before continuing, *So you kept your head down, transmitting messages to everybody else that said, "Get off my back", or, "Leave me alone".*

Yes, unless I wished to have another seahorse near me for comfort.

So you used others for physical intimacy, concluded Stocky bluntly.

Sam hung his head in sudden, real and spine-tingling shame.

It's important that you realise the truth of your past, said Stocky, *but you will also see that usually there has been a quid pro quo. Whoever comforted you at those times wasn't exactly running away. Maybe they had their own reasons for being situated where they were.*

No, I mean Yes — but …

… but you feel bad about it all the same, Stocky sympathised.

Yes, agreed Sam.

And you feel, perhaps, that there is — so it seems — insurmountable unfinished business with your erstwhile paramours, and all of those interfering busybodies who occasionally — and with a variety of motives including the reasonable and the poisonous — appealed to your better nature, but whom you always despatched with a smarting ear?

Yes. Sam thought that he understood what Stocky was getting at.

Some comforters have had your best interests at heart …

Perhaps …

… and some like to be promoted. Others solicit their own dismissal.

Sam realised suddenly that he didn't. *What on earth do you mean?*

Never mind. Look, let's recap. Since your Indian arrival you have felt strangely compelled — from somewhere within, so to say — in various situations to behave in this way, or refrain from behaving in that. But you mightn't have been able to identify where those compulsions came from. You just realise that they have driven you — now that you have space to reflect on all your affairs deliberately.

Yes. But just clarify what you mean about "somewhere within".

Stocky permitted himself a subdued chuckle. *I mean the impulses in question — those that have been driving you — that seem to quicken or quell a given sort of behaviour in various recognisable scenarios …*

What do you mean by "recognisable scenarios"? interrupted Sam.

… situations of a particular kind — such as a busy marketplace — and ones that mimic that bustle — anywhere where there is a crowd, say …

OK

… those impulses don't express themselves as words. They seem to emanate from your core. You have sensed reverberations in your body …

Stocky paused. Sam paused too. *OK,* said Sam eventually.

"Remote Location"
Duart Castle, Isle of Mull, Scotland

… the odd thing about that whirlpool of urges, Stocky continued, *is that you can't for the life of you tell where they come from. You can't associate them with a particular memory, no matter how you try. They seem most entrenched in you; moreover — quite persistent in the way that they have prompted you in given circumstances — and also ones that feign familiarity; i.e., new ones similar to those you know you have experienced before. You don't possess a confidence that you can obliterate the unpleasant harrying through the exercise of will.*

I can recognise what you are saying, answered Sam. *It's difficult for me to get a hold of the whole idea in my mind's eye, because I have always lived with that emotional environment. It is biographic, and I can only imagine how it might have been for things to be different.*

Things can be different from now on, asserted Stocky. *It takes an awakening of the kind you are experiencing now, plenty of patience and an openness to embrace the crowds and the bustle with a new confidence. Before you know it you have become a different seahorse.*

OK, said Sam, *I think I have an appetite for all that.*

Care to digest an oxymoron?
Care to digest an oxymoron? asked Stocky, introducing a diversion.

I have never stooped to cannibalism, replied Sam, not entirely sure whether he'd succeeded in being funny.

Very good! said Stocky. *All those busybodies that got in your way …*

Yes, acknowledged Sam.

… I'll wager you can imagine each of them in your mind's eye clearly enough, can't you?

Most certainly, agreed Sam. *Many of them have assumed a life of their own. If I am frank, I might barely recognise one in the flesh today.*

Stocky was pleased with the progress between the pair of ex-mariners, asking of Sam, *How do you feel about all those old acquaintances now?*

Honestly? asked Sam, testing the scope of candour permitted.

Of course, replied Stocky.

Well — I have always considered them offensive; some of them grossly so, and don't see much cause at present anyway for changing my mind.

I'm more interested in how you feel than what you think, insisted Stocky.

OK. I feel angry towards them. I could easily call them vile names.

Good! said Stocky, rewarding Sam's straightforwardness. *Now, I want you to think about those same busybodies — one at a time. Just hold one of them in your mind — one about whom you feel deeply resentful.*

OK … Sam lapsed into a concordant silence.

What do you feel? probed Stocky gently.

Anger — and an aversion or disgust that compels me to remove myself to a remote location as soon as I have delivered a piece of my mind.

OK. Do you have a sense of unfinished business with that seahorse?

Of a kind, I suppose, concurred Sam.

What kind? pressed Stocky.

There's an ache … and a responsibility for peace I can't resolve.

Uh-huh, said Stocky — almost enthusiastically. The sponsor waited.

After several moments in a reverie, Sam exploded: *The strange thing is … I feel I could make that peace just by recognising how I have been self-centred – independently of anything they have done to me. I don't have to make their peace for them. I only have to make my own.*

That's right! chimed Stocky. *You have discovered an enormously useful spiritual principle of the kind that affords a good night's rest.*

No kidding! articulated Sam, a touch sarcastically.

No kidding at all. The oxymoron is, "Let those who live in your head because they offended you, know that you know you have wronged them".

Sam looked unmistakeably burdened by such convolution, blurting out, *You've got me all confused about more than a couple of things.*

I can imagine, replied Stocky.

All this "you know that I know" stuff. Doesn't it smack of playing guessing games? Isn't that a bit old-fashioned for where we're going?

Stocky was firm: *I think that you are being unfashionably evasive.*

So … I am to reflect on how these other seahorses might have felt?

Exactly, confirmed the robust sponsor.

And everything that has ever gone pear-shaped is all my fault?

Stocky laughed. *Of course not! Remember – you are cleaning up your side of the street. You are not responsible for the other side of it.*

Sam pondered for a second, by which time he thought he had got it.

Not quite there yet
And do I have to visit all those lousy seahorses, apologising for how I used or abused them, when really it was they who screwed me over?

You're not quite there yet, asserted Stocky. *Back up the truck! Remember – you are taking into account something you haven't reckoned properly before; i.e., that you have been selfish towards others.*

Oh yes, said Sam, somewhat shame-faced again.

And what is more, Stocky added, *it may be inadvisable to visit certain of them. You would never want to do more harm than good.*

Sam re-adorned himself with his "a mite baffled" expression.

Stocky clarified: *You wouldn't want to visit any old acquaintance in order to straighten things out where – by the end of the visit – the net harm done to other seahorses had increased rather than decreased.*

Sam didn't like what he was hearing. He knew that his agile mind was hunting the "get-out". Stocky was a few thoughts even farther ahead.

Look, said Stocky, *making sensitive amends to other seahorses for past wrongs …*

What are "sensitive amends"? interjected Sam.

… sensitive amends are ones that are brief, and let the other person take the apology they want or need. You just say something as vague as, "You know all that stuff – I'm sorry – it was me, not you".

I see, said Sam (and did).

Making amends, continued Stocky, *is a delicate business. Being able to exercise discretion over what and what not to do is one of the greatest advantages of working with a sponsor. Don't go off visiting old enemies without a conversation between us about your intentions.*

Rather predictably, Sam seemed satisfied with that holding advice.

"Pear-shaped"
A Beurre Hardy still dripping after a nice refreshing shower

(… tell at least one person) "Everything"

When will I know everything I need to know?
Is there anything else I need to know about being sponsored? enquired
Sam in an absurdly cavalier manner.

Still replete with an abundance of patience (for there had been no
shortage of shipwrecks in recent times and, like The Feather, Stocky
had an impressive assortment of charges), Stocky humoured his
apprentice deftly: *There is much more that you will learn about
sponsorship. When you have worked through the cycle of the program
once in earnest, you will be sponsoring exhausted seahorses yourself.
But these are early days, and you mustn't look too far ahead. Rather
than taking on life by the horns, we are satisfied to manage one day.
That is what we seem to be built for - our own affairs for 24 hours.*

OK, said Sam, eager to listen. *Anything else I should know today?*

Stocky beamed at Sam's evident readiness to pick things up quickly.

*Yes. Remember your fundamental position. You are an ex-mariner. The
Feather explained to you the advantage of rendering that absolute.*

Yes. I remember, agreed Sam.

*Second, find some spiritual entity to trust. It doesn't matter what
it is as long as it is meaningful to you - but is not you! If you
believe in the divine, that is well and good. Nature spawned you and
knows your weaknesses as well as your strengths. The Feather and I
are going nowhere as long as you maintain your fundamental position.
There are many hundreds of other seahorses upon whom you may rely.*

OK, said Sam. He wasn't fighting this. He remembered what The Feather
had said about a trustworthy source being able to guide as needed.

Third, enumerated Stocky, *we will talk more about your adventures -
about the seahorse you have been - and how you have affected the
lives of others … even Clipboard Clive will feature on your list!*

Oh gosh! exclaimed Sam, but there was no fundamental resistance.

Sensing Sam's genuine fatigue, Stocky quit the onslaught of numbers.

*You will need to tell at least one person everything. It is the last
secret that you keep - the one you are most reluctant to disclose -
the one you'd escort most ardently to the grave - that makes you most
needlessly lonely. It could be the one that beckons you back to sea.*

Sam hesitated with misgivings, but said nothing.

*We will talk about what sort of seahorse you want to become - unless
you consider yourself a finished product already - in which case we
will need to address that obstacle first. You will need to be
entirely ready to change, to have all your self-delusion dissolved,
and yet discern what sort of seahorse nature imagined you to be - and
how you wish to converse with her about that. The rules are few.*

That sounded quite positive. *OK,* said Sam.

*We have already touched upon your willingness to remedy past wrongs -
we will travel to that difficult territory gradually and carefully.*

Quite! agreed Sam precipitously.

You need to develop a capacity for recognising when you are wrong.

I think that you are right about that! said Sam most conducively.

We have agreed that you will prioritise attending shipwrecks with us.

I want to! exclaimed Sam.

Above all, Stocky said solemnly, *never permit yourself hopelessness.*

"Appreciating One's Piers"
Bournemouth Pier, Dorset (was Hampshire)

Chapter 14

"Learning to 'Let go'"

Discouragement spurned as vanity
Sam and The Feather resumed where they had left off just a few days
previously. The Feather had refused to sponsor Sam; nevertheless, Sam
already knew that self-pity could not be harnessed usefully in this
strange but promising province. He had summoned the courage to ask
Stocky instead (as The Feather gently seemed to have intended), and
everything had gone swimmingly. Only little did Sam realise what a
vast inheritance of spiritual riches he was absorbing – simply for
having abandoned his pointless and self-centred seafaring adventures.
Sam knew something was afoot in the way of personal psychological
transformation, but he had no idea of the scale on which it shifted.

Stocky said that I must never permit myself hopelessness, prompted
the still green, but ever-keen pilgrim.

Yes. It is a chronic condition of ours, answered The Feather as
obligingly as ever. *It is, of course, an impostor. Under its spell we
consider ourselves victimised. Actually it is a self-indulgence.*

*A nagging emptiness that can turn bitterly painful to the point of
excruciation – especially if we mismanage it?* invited Sam.

Very much so, agreed The Feather. *It may feel like a deep sense of
pointlessness or futility – some say nihilism – that seems to want
our demise or self-destruction as its only means of satiation. But
really it is we who sulk – or object belligerently to the way things
actually are – so deeply that we can barely see our own incapacity
for perceiving things reasonably objectively. Another seahorse, if
sufficiently brave, may point out our foibles to us; but we are far
more likely to snap than to suddenly confess our own shortcomings.*

Sam recognised the truth of The Feather's words instantly. *Yes, I
have felt just that way often, although I have never cared to admit
or show it. I have strived for self-reliance; but I can see that the
very striving was a reflection of the underlying reality that I
lacked such independence. By trying to convince myself and other
seahorses that I was OK, I was battling the spectre of hopelessness
uselessly. I can see now that fear of that gaping futility was the
fundamental drive beneath all my vain efforts. Any seahorse who had
established an authentic way of dealing with the same feelings would
have been able to discern my old besieged existence quite readily.*

The Feather challenged Sam: *Was battling? Old besieged existence?*

Sam paused. *Well*, he said, *we shall see.* And The Feather was happy to
accept Sam's assertiveness about whether his problems had expired.

Keep your perspective, said The Feather. *Each of us suffers from it.
It is a very significant part of the seahorse condition. Goodness
knows how it got to be so, or what in our make-up accounts for it.
Perhaps it has to do with the capacity we have for communicating with
each other so imaginatively, so intensely and with such a sense of
purpose. Perhaps we are electrified with a-hundred-and-one
expectations which, of their very selves, bestow upon us false hope.
All that seems to matter now is that we accept that it may touch us –
rather than fight it frantically before it arrives. We know that we
have each other to rely on, and that we possess each in our own right
an appreciation of all those spiritual principles upon which we may
draw should ever we find ourselves uneasy, displaced, upset or awry.*

Growing into intuition
Stocky and I had a long conversation about the program, reported Sam.

I can imagine! replied The Feather, attaching one of his warm smiles.

Whilst we all may labour under a common condition, we all must grow up too; at least, if we wish to acquire a worthwhile personal sanity.

The Feather firmly agreed: *Quite so!*

After all, we all were hatched merely as eggs once! said Sam in flow.

Agreed! quipped The Feather.

And - by definition - were immature then!

Very juvenile indeed! exclaimed The Feather energetically - seemingly happy to marry Sam's enthusiasm with accelerations of his own.

So, continued Sam, *the program is for helping us to grow up - and since "spiritual surrender" is at its beginning absolutely and at its heart in so far as we can bring it to bear - we learn to let go of our infantile handicaps: to relinquish them instead of defend them?*

The Feather, quick to discern Sam's need for corroboration, provided it without hesitation: *Yes. All that you say seems correct to me.*

Sam was getting the hang of all this. Right on message he asserted, *We started by learning to let go of our seafaring instinct entirely, for we came to accept that it was a road to ruin for us. We had burnt the fuse along its whole length. We had to let go of it completely.*

That's right. That applies to Stocky, to me, to you, not forgetting The Driver on that day we attended your wreck. We can't speak for anybody but ourselves. But in relation to our category, apparently, there was no short-circuit. Being obtuse, we learned the hard way.

I'm not sure that I have grasped the remainder of the program the way that you and Stocky have, Sam blinked, rather unthinkingly. *I believe that I now understand much intellectually, but I don't seem to have the intuition that you possess. Will I acquire my own with practice?*

Yes, you will, The Feather assured Sam. *It is a question of carrying on with absolutely everything for just a day at a time - and no more. We don't project into the future like a Grandmaster of chess, for barely one of our rehearsed scenarios[255] will ever transpire; besides, it is only fear that wants us to anticipate every awful eventuality.*

And already I know the answer to fear: it is transcendent trust. I am learning to rely on a spiritual source - one of my own choosing - out of a free conviction - knowing that, because it is trustworthy, it possesses a better judgement and capacity than do I for taking care of my business. If I am confused about its very nature, or what it wishes for me, or what it requires me to do, I need only ask it - for it has the facility to answer me, and I can expect an answer if I am sufficiently amenable to receiving a response without baulking at it.

The Feather was becoming (just occasionally) rather impressed with Sam's insights in a way that made his washboard of a chest burst with astonishment and satisfaction - lending weight to his own discovered sense of gratitude. To see embedding in another seahorse the wonder that he had once enjoyed for the first time himself was a profoundly significant experience for him. And he wasn't exactly new to it now.

---

[255] "Emotion Control" (see also Chapter 7) including "Rehearsal" is a psychometrically quantifiable phenomenon linked empirically to a variety of health outcomes at both the physiological and psychological levels. The work has been pioneered by Derek Roger formerly at the University of York, UK; latterly at the University of Canterbury, NZ.

Evolving into maturity
How do we get to be so underdeveloped, asked Sam provocatively. *It seems we are – as it were – unfit for purpose. Aren't we all the product of billions of years of evolution and natural selection?*

Well yes – in so far as we understand all things scientific – which may be to a far more limited extent than many of us would like to believe. We don't know whether science, as we have known it since Copernicus, has the capacity to discover and explain everything – even though some seahorses adhere to science almost as though a personal deity – as vigorously as many adhere to a religious faith. If we are sensible, we will leave room for the unexplained, don't you think? The Feather winked at Sam, but the missile missed its mark. *Arguably* (he continued), *it is our unwitting marginalisation of everything we can't understand in a concrete way that disables us so woefully and – plausibly – infects our culture with the same folly.*

If we all agree on the program's principles, why is it that none of the seahorses around here exhort each other to "Grow up"? Sam teased.

The Feather laughed loudly. *Quite often and, secretly, we'd like to!* he spluttered through his audible mirth. *Remember that we keep our side of the street clean – and only our side. We don't take notes on each other unless invited – such as in sponsorship. Anyway, we are all fallible! Exhorting another adult seahorse to "Grow up!" is like insisting that an infant one acts her or his age when what you really want is for them to think and act like you do; i.e., as an adult!*

Sam chuckled. *But sometimes I feel lousy or rubbish because things are … kind of … haunting me – rather than because I want my own way.*

The Feather's mirth evaporated at once as if exposed to proximate stellar combustion. *Yes. Me too. And still nowadays. Don't be discouraged. I have not known a dark day since I was a sailor. By "dark" I mean a day where I have felt drowned in toxic hopelessness. I do have difficult days. And on those difficult days I can usually see for the looking that – in the manner of exercising spiritual principles – I am doing something I ought not – or not doing something I ought. Often there is a peculiarly favourable untwisting of events when I bring self-examination, acceptance and trust to bear! Even so, there are times when I can't – for the life of me – fathom the arrival of a murky cloud. Acceptance and trust – whilst always of fundamental avail – don't seem a sufficient mental patch, and I have to resort to waiting for a day to pass (without putting to sea). When that happens, I am well-advised to seek out my own sponsor – for my willingness to do so seems, inevitably, to induce whatever understanding and cheer I lack. Perhaps this is the territory of contemporary psychology as much as it is of spiritual endeavour. I have learned to exhaust my capacity for pursuing the program as a first resort. The experience of many of us confirms that often it turns out to have been the easier way. We were simply unwilling under duress to maintain our commitment to it. Any alternative turns out to have been no solution at all or, at worst, a distraction in disguise. But all of us – justifiably – are entitled to pursue our own arrangements for spiritual and psychological adjustment, for whom with a right mind would divert us from a truly satisfactory remedy?*

How do I know what arrangement is right for me – before I try one?

That requires wisdom, replied The Feather quickly.

How do I obtain wisdom? asked Sam, quite unable to predict an answer.

Ask for it Sam! In the spiritual life (as in the pursuit of science) you will find eventually if not sooner just what you're looking for!

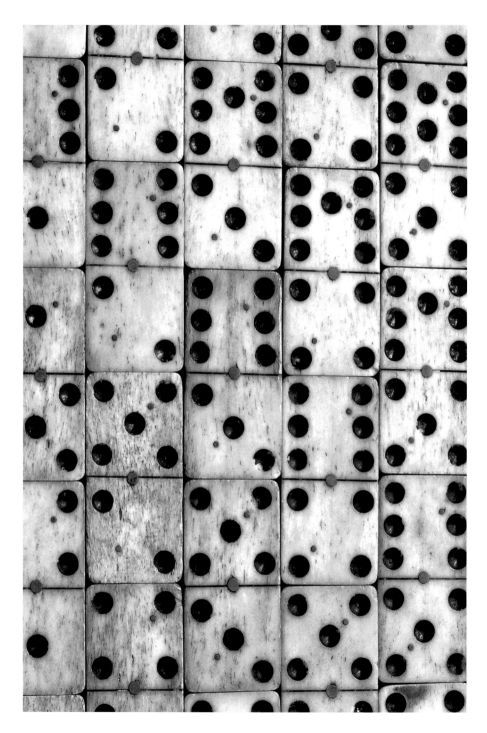

"Ancient And Not-So-Ancient Echoes": whale-bone dominoes from a
photograph by Dr Hannes Grobe at the Alfred Wegener Institute

The territory of contemporary psychology
What exactly did you mean when you said, "Perhaps this is the territory of contemporary psychology as much as it is of spiritual endeavour", Sam wanted to know.

Well — according to one (and only one) framework for understanding these things, answered The Feather, *when we act as if we were children, we are in what is known as a corresponding ego state.*

Sam sought clarification: *"Ego state"?*

Yes. According to this point of view, an ego state is a recognisable mental condition betrayed by characteristic thoughts, feelings and behaviour. We also possess a Parent ego state, and an Adult one. In our Child ego state, we can be bolshy and resistant to parental imperatives, or we may be compliant. It is usually one or the other! In our Parent ego state, we are either nurturing — or we are trying to get someone to toe the line (i.e., we are "controlling" or, more pejoratively, "critical") by inviting compliance from another's Child. You can see that both Parent and Child states are chiefly manipulative processes and, in that sense at least, socially immature amongst adult peers. The Adult ego state is the one in which we are rational and reasonable! Our behaviour is hinged on the here and now.

Do go on, said Sam, confident that there was cause to be interested.

Unlike the Adult ego state, the Child and the Parent ego states are built of ancient and not-so-ancient echoes …

Pardon? interrupted Sam.

Ancient and not-so-ancient echoes, The Feather repeated.

That's what I thought you said. Please do elucidate.

OK. But do bear in mind that what I am saying here represents an unproven model.

I have that very much in mind, Sam chirped.

But it is a neat and compelling model anyway.

As I am about to discover, no doubt, beeped Sam.

The bottom line is whether it is — so to speak — "real" or "actual" and, fittingly, helpful to us, perhaps on the dark days we discussed.

Then like all good models we can subject it to scrutiny, repeated test-drives, and ruthless exposure as mitigated or unmitigated error.

Quite, said The Feather, feeling almost discouraged, *but you did ask.*

Do go on, Sam urged, trying to sound heartening.

… before we developed the competent use of our seahorse language, we were looked after intensively by our parents and carers …

Assuming we were fortunate enough to enjoy such, Sam cut in again.

Agreed; but we couldn't have survived our very early lives at all without constant basic care.

I suppose you are right, answered Sam a little too curtly.

… and during all that time, continued The Feather, *for a year or two, we were exposed to a huge repertoire of reinforcement: nice things such as food, warmth, cosiness, physical intimacy and the like but — simultaneously and equally — a vast array of aversive influences: scolds, or even a harsh tone of voice from a carer — anything at all that was unpleasant; moreover, just the very withholding or withdrawal of those mostly pleasurable things that made us feel safe.*

Where this is all going
Where is all this going? pressed Sam.

Well, all that reinforcement will have tended to increase or decrease the likelihood that we will behave in particular ways in situations like the ones in which the reinforcement first or regularly occurred.

Even though we were too young to understand language?

Almost because we were too young to understand language! Only later – when we appreciated the power that our own use of language possessed to affect the occurrence of reinforcement – did our learning become significantly more refined: we learned to manipulate the environment.

I see, said Sam, in customary self-obsessed mode, trying to reflect on how all of this might have occurred during his own infancy.

Now, what is more, continued The Feather, *learning that happens because of reinforcement is always accompanied by an affective or an emotional response. If the reinforcer was horrible, the attendant emotion is unpleasant. It may be experienced in a variety of ways. Ultimately it is a fear response that makes us want to avoid things.*

I see, said Sam, although he hadn't quite let it all settle yet.

Look, said The Feather, *if the learning occurred before we used language, the emotional response will be wordless. It won't feel clear. It may seem like a fundamental or core response from our bodies – at least – those parts that help us run away from danger.*

Got it, said Sam, with undue triumph.

Later – when we could use language to pursue what we wanted, the nice things we tried to get, and the nasty things we tried to avoid, had words – and so did the feelings that accompanied their being obtained or avoided. The emotional response may still be physical – but now it is one we can articulate. That makes it feel qualitatively different.

So that later kind of learning is much easier to undo? asked Sam.

Easier to understand and access – that's all. We can talk about it all till the cows come home – or, even, until the chickens come home to roost (said The Feather, a little casual about his metaphors); *but undoing that learning may be a lot less easy than we might think.*

Why? enquired Sam.

A premature question is forced
The Feather felt compelled to introduce a question to Sam just a little earlier than it was due. *Do you understand fully why you set off for sea – personally desperate, unaccompanied, with no chart or guide – and with no resources other than a few stolen provisions?*

No, said Sam, glad to be invited to focus on his own story. *Not fully. I have talked about it with Stocky, and he invited me towards certain challenging considerations, but it isn't all clear to me yet.*

Well – part of what drove you may have been undiluted immaturity.

O … K. Sam was still utterly willing, but didn't like the charge.

And part may have been mistrust of everybody, and no spiritual faith.

Sam remained silent.

And part may have been a wordless harrying from your core – a conditionless desire to burst away from what you saw as your prison – Anything but this!

Yes – that's how it was, pounced Sam. That much seemed clear to him.

And you may have begun to believe that you could exercise something that you came to regard as personal will – a perception of control.

Yes … I can see that too, confirmed the uncomfortable scrutinee.

Now, these two sorts of echoes, explained The Feather, *are the fundamental building blocks of your Child ego state. They can be formed whenever reinforcement is encountered – and you may imagine that the number of bricks in your Child ego state is astronomically high – not limitless as in infinity – but verging on countless.*

My goodness, answered Sam, genuinely impressed by the mathematics.

Your Child ego state, The Feather continued, *is instrumental in terms of its function; i.e., as we have said, it strives to control reinforcement through what looks to the Child like discharge of personal will. Have you ever seen a junior seahorse having a tantrum?*

Of course, replied Sam.

Then you can imagine in your mind's eye what I'm getting at.

Indeed I can, said Sam freely. *What of this Parent ego state then?*

More about vanity

Glad you asked, said The Feather with visible satisfaction. *The Parent ego state is functionally like the Child ego state. It is instrumental in that it anticipates favourable outcomes depending on how it sees itself acting. It is as vain as the Child ego state.*

"Vain"? Sam seemed surprised at the adjective.

Yes, vain. The perception of control possessed by both the Child and Parent ego states is illusory in the sense that the contingencies that actually prevail between behaviour and result are far less tangible or reliable than ever imagined – even with hindsight. We are constantly rationalising our behaviour to fit justifications for the various types of reinforcement that we seek. Most are in the social sphere – for much of our reinforcement, so we believe, resides in the hands of others. We can be tempted to coercion at times; in fact, the most unscrupulous of us make a habit of harnessing fear to that end.

Yuk! How seedy! spluttered Sam, truly disgusted.

"Yuk" and "seedy" are most apt! echoed The Feather, just as vehement.

Is the Parent ego state made of the same stuff? solicited Sam.

No. The building blocks are similar but appreciatively different. You remember Clipboard Clive, don't you Sam? enquired The Feather.

Why, of course, agreed Sam.

Well he, and all of the busybodies you ever encountered, are stored in your Parent ego state as introjects – or internal representations of individual seahorses. These introjects have many features – just like the real ones. The attributes that are most salient or powerful – in your mind's eye – are those that appeared to signal or predict the best and the worst of all the reinforcement you ever encountered.

So the Parent ego state is also massive – just like Child!

That's right, confirmed The Feather.

I'm not sure that I am comfortable with all those revolting, fishy, axe-grinding characters living rent-free in my head! Sam exclaimed.

Quite so, said The Feather. *And you don't have to let them. We shall come to determine how you may evict undesirable tenants presently.*

I'm looking forward to that, said Sam. And, truly, he was.

Sam asks an intelligent question

How, enquired Sam, *might I determine whether a given unsettled feeling emanates from my Child ego state or my Parent ego state? More technically, how might I know which of the three types of building bricks lies aetiologically beneath it? For, surely, if I answer those questions, I would, at least, know which bothersome organ to excise with my psychological scalpel, divining fairly where to lay the cut.*

That's a good question, replied The Feather. *The surgical procedure – if you have the time and the inclination – is indicated by interpreting what we know already. Pre-language situation-response (S-R) learning is physical, nebulous and harrying. Post-language response-reinforcer (R-S) learning is guileful. The introjects in Parent generate specific affective responses associated with their attributes. That brick is made of two stimuli forged together – the introject or its attribute – and the reinforcer. It is thereby S-S.*

A re-examination of Sam's conscience

If I experience an aversive tension in which a variety of courses of action are vying with each other for prominence, do we not now have to understand quite a hotchpotch of emotional drivers? And if there is such diversity, and one or more drivers are misaligned with the remainder, how am I to select a morally appropriate way of behaving?

Well – there is such a thing as "conscience", replied The Feather, knowing that the brevity of his answer would leave Sam unsatisfied.

Yes. Conscience is the word I was looking for. Conscience has tension incorporated inherently; I mean – if there were no tension, there would be no conscience – no pressure to veer this way versus that.

I suppose so, said The Feather, pleased at Sam's rhetorical waxing (from which The Feather obtained temporary relief from tiring work).

It would be a great ease on our consciences if we could re-write our minds, hinted Sam, honestly hoping for The Feather's co-operation.

Well – we can't re-write the past. On that we may be agreed.

Absolutely, said Sam, secretly fantasising about time machines.

But perhaps we can overwrite or otherwise compensate for elements of our learning that we may regard as illegitimate or bastard.

I like that way of describing many of my introjects, agreed Sam.

But I also imagine this to be a slow process that can only begin in earnest following a systematic trawl through our biographic histories. This assumes we can disentangle in a sufficiently coherent manner the three types of ego state building bricks that we have identified. Even then – we must pull up sharp when it comes to ancestral mind-buggery – for we may make too many assumptions about transgenerational transmission; i.e., the precise ways in which learning gets cascaded in families. And perhaps we become tempted to look for scapegoats – to embark on dangerously gleeful witch-hunts.

Why isn't that a simply wonderful idea? taunted the unsavvy Sam.

Because scapegoating is an instance of kidding ourselves. We lapse into "spiritual blindness" – especially if our targets were never truly at fault. What's worse, we only add fuel to the inferno of our personal resentments – feeding the uncomfortable angst we experience when the worst of those sitting tenants amongst our introjects launch themselves into our imaginations spontaneously. And don't they perform such dastardly manoeuvres just when we consider ourselves undistracted? Don't we want to be free of all that inner turmoil?

I should say so, said Sam. And he meant it.

"Vying With Each Other For Prominence"
Original sculpture by Bob Waters at Arlington Court, Devon

Exorcising ghostly apparitions
So you can see, said The Feather, *that a re-writing of our minds is far from a straightforward business given the current state of our psychological technology. But actually that doesn't matter terribly! Something far more ancient than science – indeed, by a factor of some 400^{256} – lies at the tips of our fingers (if not the tips of our tongues). The same "spiritual surrender" that eventually we applied without equivocation to the seafaring disposition (the one we accepted would finish us off without ceremony) can be applied in more diluted measures, if we cannot generate a full-scale capitulation, to any or all of those nasty ghostly apparitions or tenants we no longer wish to entertain in our mental condominiums. We can exorcise them!*

"Spiritual surrender" trumps analysis and re-authoring just like a mechanical excavator surpasses manual grave-digging, Sam suggested.

Yes – or, shall we say less morbidly, such surrender is a no-contest facilitator of change compared with more protracted detailed work.

When you said, "We can exorcise them!", I gained an impression in my mind's eye of something quite forceful – quite wilful, said Sam.

Oh no, not at all, replied The Feather with some disdain. *Try to regard wilfulness as a close cousin of the acquisitive expectations we siphoned chronically from our Child ego state. They were infantile in so far as they were self-centred, and unrealistic in their disproportional relationship with what actually happens in the world. In this manner, wilfulness is just as illusory as the fear that generates our habitual rehearsal of all those dreamy (and always threatening) future eventualities. There is proportionate fear – much of it unconditioned and which quite reasonably, thanks to mother nature, keeps us out of trouble – and there is the surfeit that we bring to the table ourselves – a dreadful but dispensable habit.*

… that we can relinquish rather than banish? Sam inferred hopefully.

Yes. That will do nicely, corroborated The Feather.

If we can relinquish all the fear we don't like at will … Sam stopped himself – feeling very stupid … *Sorry! Of course …*

Yes … (The Feather said gently and waited …)

… and, so, I can't expect to achieve this faculty instantly …

No

… but I can practice!

Yes! This time, The Feather sounded triumphant (and quite duly so).

Conscience gets a road-test
That means, concluded Sam, *that I can't railroad my conscience into submission, but that I can test it with a little patient and loving self-examination, conducted in a spirit of honesty with myself …*

… and your sponsor! This time it was The Feather's turn to interrupt.

Sam was happy not to be trusted to accomplish this work solo: *… yes – with Stocky – and then I can undertake patient practice at letting go of ghostly apparitions, having the confidence that I am not trying to banish – through useless wilfulness – the loving whisper of nature. Given what you say about 24 hour chunks of life, I can persevere with and monitor my progress on a daily basis – never seeking to project more than a day. I can co-test my attachment to reality versus fantasy by sometimes appraising my capacity for acceptance and trust.*

---

[256] assuming that *homo sapiens* can be traced back 200,000 years – and science some 500

Very good, said The Feather.

Then I need to see Stocky, blurted Sam at the beginning of a rush.

Yes – you do. But there's no great hurry. Is there?

I suppose not, agreed Sam.

You need to tell at least one person everything. Don't keep a secret. We all have private material that is best kept that way. You may develop other friends whom you can trust, but air your dirty laundry with much discretion. If ever in doubt, ask Stocky for his thoughts on the matter. Within the seahorse society at large, we share in a far more general way. We share about principles; I repeat, how we are learning about principles. We do not need to resort to specifics in public forums. If something is eating us, we are willing to declare it – even if it makes us feel small; or, should I say especially if it makes us feel small – but we go to a sponsor or trusted confidant. Stocky will not break your confidence because his own sanity depends on treating you with the respect and dignity he requires for himself.

Gosh … Yes … Thank you, said Sam – with lots of true appreciation.

If you keep this up – a day at a time – you will change, and you will know you have changed, and you will never look back. I promise you.

Yes … Thank you

You can feel utterly unchained – no matter what your circumstances.

Sam sensed the truth of The Feather's words (again) through the haze of an uncertain and barely imaginable future. *OK,* he said.

Your "Inner Child" will become free to express itself without fear!

Wow! (Sam wasn't feeling stunned yet, but knew that he would be …)

Your Parent ego condition will be moulded peaceful and peace-adoring. It will be liberally nurturing and loving. It will lack forever in your life – and the lives of many future generations of seahorses – the rank, bitter, seahorse-shredding edges of both tongue and sword!

Sam thought that The Feather had over-extended himself, but remained quiet about it.

Sam is rendered terminally and unspeakably grateful
Sam, said The Feather quietly.

Yes

The whisper of nature that we have been talking about …

Yes

… it is always a simple invitation, and you shouldn't complicate it.

Sam paused. *OK*

You can become anything you want to become.

Anything? Yes … OK

But become what you were meant to become, urged The Feather.

Sam!

Yes, Sam said.

I have acquired an intuition – of a certain kind – and you will too.

Oh … Thank you

Sam was becoming an inexpressibly grateful seahorse. Not even once in the rest of his life did he glance back over his spiritual shoulder.

"No Going Back"

Chapter 15

"Say, 'Cheese!'"

No time for hesitation

Many moons later; in fact, more than 40 or so, Sam was wallowing in the peace of his own company and the afternoon sunshine in a remote sector of the new land in which he had made his home (or, rather, the new home he now enjoyed in the land that had silently invited him). He was wading sun-bound along a rivulet. High foliage arched over his bliss. In his arms mounted a pile of detritus, for Sam's interest in clearing pollution had found even greater scope to reign. Suddenly he thought he heard the moans of distressed seahorses; moreover, the moaning was eerie and deathly. It sounded as if a dreadful accident had occurred. He couldn't establish the direction from which the sounds emanated as the pile of synthetic rubbish grew about his ears. He heard more noise. It was unmistakeable: something appalling was happening within earshot. He pushed the litter away from him towards one bank of the river, and scanned the horizon rapidly. Much further downstream – as the estuary broadened – he could make out staggering figures – seahorses struggling from open water towards the refuge of the beach. The shallow ocean there was awash with lifeless, floating bodies. A large sailing vessel of some kind lay on the ultra-horizon, semi-submerged as if scuttled. One of the approaching seahorses fell as if exhausted or dead – and then another. Perhaps now a dozen or so remained standing. Then another fell: now 11 stood or staggered. Some of these had made their way clear of the tide. Moments later only 10 remained vertical. The moans continued unabated and, now that Sam had identified their source, they seemed to intensify in both volume and anguish. Sam became aware of a most strenuous competition between two competing instincts at his core. In the intensity and urgency of his subjective mental experience, half of him was filled with fear. *Who were these visitors, and what had become of them? Were they armed as well as bloody? What were their intentions? Had they been defeated in a battle? If so, perhaps they were guerrilla seahorses, and would stop at nothing to preserve themselves.* The other half of him wanted to run towards them – to assist them – to be as helpful as possible in their trial. *Just a moment's delay could cost the life of one of these wounded! Run away! Find safety! Help these distressed souls!*

Sam remembers who he is

A torrent of courage descended upon the torn animal. The Feather's words rang with an assurance that was absolute and serene: *The only requirement we place upon you is that you must desire to remain reclaimed (i.e., you maintain your position about not putting out to sea), and that you remain available as a foremost call on your time to attend shipwrecks – working with us to see others reach dry land.* But Stocky and The Feather were not at hand. Sam had no idea of their whereabouts, for he had last seen them several days since. *Attending shipwrecks is a commitment I undertook with enthusiasm*, he reminded himself. But it wasn't convincing he needed: by now he knew not to draw upon reason, but upon spiritual intuition. Re-phrasing to his own ears he asked himself, *What is the correct course of action in this moment?* Knowing he was alone – and that, as a rule, a salvage crew comprising at least two seahorses should be formed to attend any wreck – he knew equally well that he had no hope of help. *Run then! But the situation is desperate! And what about my spiritual purpose? Then, there can be nothing to fear!* The only possible course ahead gradually fortified itself as an inner conviction, and he let loose a canter towards the gory carnage. *But wait! Who … on earth … is that?*

Should old acquaintance be forgot

Sam and Clive recognised each other simultaneously at about a hundred yards' distance. As they moved towards each other, both paused to stop and take in the shock of the moment. To Sam, Clive seemed older, and tired far beyond his years (even if several of those had elapsed since the last time they had encountered each other). The Clipboard seemed desperate too – but that could be explained by today's awful happenings – whatever they may have been. More than anything, Clive was tearful, and seemed broken – or very near broken; and Sam knew that (he knew that) because of his own experience of shipwreck, and the way that that experience had been consolidated as autobiographic narrative in his own mind. *It takes one to know one!* and *You can't kid a kidder!* ran through his thinking with far more a hint of echo than personal superiority or ego-satisfaction. To Clive, on the other hand, Sam seemed healthier, cleaner and stronger – almost invincible. *What had happened to the little nuisance?* For all Clive knew, Sam had perished miserably at sea. Clive had run into serious trouble with the community on the hospitable jetty – for it had attributed Sam's sudden and unexplained disappearance to Clive's mistreatment of him.

Sam is curiously unafraid

By the time the two old antagonists were close enough to converse, only four of Clive's comrades remained alive, leaving five survivors all told including the notorious Clipboard. The other four hung back behind Clive as if he were their leader, and had ventured forth on their behalf as an envoy suing for peace with a mightier adversary. Sam was the first to speak, nevertheless, and found himself parlaying as if assisted by a force or power that was not himself – a power of quiet yet unboundaried truth; a power of simple and incontrovertible justice, and a power with which he discerned a shade of familiarity.

Sam carries his message of hope

The cluster of distressed sailors – including two females – seemed anxious to listen to Sam's words carefully – as if their lives depended on what he had to say. Sam held forth about hope – seeing the obvious need and that it required nothing in the way of expansion or additional explanation. *I can see that you have encountered serious difficulties,* said Sam. *I can see that many of you have been injured or killed. Just a small number of you have survived. I can see your plight, and how baffled you seem about whatever might happen henceforth. I can see your powerlessness and your hopelessness. I can see it in both your circumstances and your hearts. Do you know that your hope lies not in where you find yourselves now – but where you go next? Do you realise that there is always hope – as long as breath and life remain? Do you know that what seems impossible to you now will seem only a chapter of history in the days to unfold? Your next step means everything. You have found yourselves cruelly shipwrecked. This once happened to me – not many leagues from where we find ourselves now. Utterly grounded, and with nowhere to go, I had lost confidence in my own capacity to mould my days, and resigned myself to nature's mercy. Two seahorses appeared as if in a dream – seemingly from nowhere – just as I may have appeared to you today. After the briefest of interviews, they transported me to their community – since which time I have ensconced myself amongst them with a deep sense of privilege. They asked nothing of me for their kindness, explaining that the same favours were once afforded to them – and that I must render myself equally dispensable. I was finished in the same painful manner in which you have found yourselves beached now. Those friendly seahorses asked me whether – should my splintered vessel be repaired – I might wish to set back out to sea. I knew in my heart that I should not desire that course under any circumstances – and told them so. Satisfied, they led me away to happy destiny.*

A round of introductions

At Sam's pause, the group started to chatter amongst themselves. They seemed confused as if struck simultaneously by optimism and futility. Sam couldn't discern the true nature of their quandary. One of them started to explain. Her voice was plaintive but lacking in self-pity.

I am Coalshed Carol … she started.

Sam intervened immediately. *Why Carol, are you known as "Coalshed"?* He appended understanding to his gaze – as if affording unconditional and loving acceptance of her answer before she had delivered it.

I have lived a foul and dirty life, she said. *I was raised in sordid circumstances. I perpetuated that pattern of abuse with a vengeance in my adult life as if – perversely – I could expunge the memories – and all they represented – from my aching soul, by stamping them violently into my social sphere. It was as if by perpetually forcing their re-enactment, I could somehow lever recognition of my protests in the heavens: my complaint that my past was not acceptable to me. Everyone ran out of patience with my behaviour. I was antisocial in dreadful ways and made a pillow in many strange and dangerous places. After a particularly nasty fight, I ran away. I met Clive. He took me to sea. We have been mercenaries extraordinaire. The rest is history.*

Mercenaries? enquired Sam, surprised. His saccadic gawking betrayed the triangulation he sought. The other female seahorse spoke gently.

I am Sly Shirley, she said. Pre-empting Sam's inquisitiveness, she continued, *I am known as "Sly" because, unlike Carol, I think twice – or more often – before I act. In fact, I am our chief-strategist. I have lacked scruples in all my affairs, and I am employed to devise every possible underhand approach to any of our gainful exploits – negotiating away nothing in the way of courtesy, mercy or compassion.*

By "mercenaries" and "gainful exploits", said Sam, *do you mean that you raised the Jolly Rodger? Have you taken lives at your pleasure?*

That was always my undertaking … I am Poop Deck Pete. A willowy character had piped up – seemingly as honest as Carol and Shirley had been rendered by their sudden misfortune. *We would always raise some flag rather than none – the Jolly Rodger or the King's Standard. We worked as mercenaries if the King required it – retrieving treasure from his enemies. His commissions were always generous. If he had no use of us temporarily, we raised the Jolly Rodger. We even raised the Jolly Rodger sailing under the King's orders, never revealing that we had taken a ship for our own profit. Now we have foes everywhere.*

You are referring to the King of Thorland, aren't you? demanded Sam. Sensing a myriad of defiant, unassembled parts in a complex jigsaw of past events, he felt a quickening of personal fear – and knew it had to be expunged instantly. The King of Thorland was a thug: a fearsome character whose reputation was loathed by the community on the jetty.

Yes, answered Pete. *As long as we brought him booty we were highly favoured, and enjoyed the freedom of his kingdom. On the last voyage paid for from the King's purse, one of the King's other assassin-ships witnessed an attack we made under the Jolly Rodger. Only when we had sunk the plundered vessel, and later retired to dine on the gun deck of our moored fighting ship, did our rival-assassins surprise us. We prevailed for a while – to the point of forming a boarding party – but our hull yielded to cannon shot at close range. We had to attend to the bilge. Before we knew it, we had been boarded ourselves. Our adversary, seeing that we were doomed, was content with swag, and left us with our stricken ship and perishing lives. You can see the remnants of last evening's skirmish before you now.*

and later retired to dine on the "Gun Deck" …
HMS Warrior, Portsmouth Historic Dockyard

… of our moored "Fighting Ship"
HMS Warrior, Portsmouth Historic Dockyard

Drowned in blind self-pity

Your words are tremendously comforting to us Sam, said Shirley, *yet we feel undeserving of your goodness. We have such squalid histories as individuals; and as a cohort we have been dismally steeped in unscrupulous brigandry – not one of us innocent of mutual encouragement, aiding and abetting. Accordingly, we are a morally forlorn lot as well as terribly dilapidated in our bodies. We are pathetically dispirited and can't raise ourselves to welcome your kindness with a smile.* Although drowned as much in blind self-pity as barely-mitigated felony, Shirley seemed to mean what she said, as if suddenly through some inner transformation she had won the right to discard her moniker; moreover, she had earned the approval of the sad posse to speak on their behalf going by the sundry submissive gazes and fawny countenances amongst her friends. But there was a notable exception – and everybody knew (although hadn't said as much) that the large, bedaggered and violent-looking seahorse fully shielded by Clive's still-imposing façade hadn't spoken at all – let alone amicably. Sensing the support of the group, hiding his consternation and speaking through Clive as though he were invisible – Sam spoke up bravely, *Would you care to introduce yourself? I am Seahorse Sam.*

Terribly dissolute

The huge seahorse answered, *I am known as Hittite Hal. Glad to make your acquaintance. I'm afraid I am the most terribly dissolute survivor amongst us. I am Master-at-arms. Formally speaking, Clive is our Captain, but it is me to whom every shipmate answers. I have had sole responsibility for the accumulation and use of all of our munitions and weaponry – a duty from which I have drawn much pleasure. Armed not so much with the pistol, sword or the pike, but surreptitiously and wordlessly with base and sinister intimidation, I have overseen our ship's discipline vigorously and enthusiastically. In the course of prosecuting my duties, I have supervised and participated in the pressing of numerous juveniles into service – including many married fathers. Countless young seahorses have been scourged, chained to cannon shot and made to walk the plank at sea. The sole charge on our ship's statute book was "insubordination combined with loathsome cowardice for which the penalty seen fit by the Master-at-arms shall apply". Of course, these coerced, imprisoned and tortured youngsters were only ever trying to stick up for themselves – or defend their free consciences. I and my cronies have much to answer for. As you can see, my subordinates have expired, and now it seems I am the only living perpetrator of all this injustice.*

An infectious atmosphere of repentance

Sam considered it more likely than not that Hal was sincere in his apologies – in so far as the outsized pirate could assimilate his own responsibility with any kind of perspective at this juncture. Whilst he may have been as much a convincing orator as a ruthless oppressor (having eased into his deft delivery shrewd use of the past tense), he simply couldn't have reported all this regret conniving such an authentically remorseful timbre to his voice. Clive, too, seemed to have been afflicted by this open atmosphere of repentance, declaring:

I fear I am indebted to you personally Sam. Clive paused, seemingly unsure how to proceed. *We go back a long way, don't we? I'm not sure that I can begin to quantify the psychological anguish I have occasioned you with my extensive catalogue of tyrannical schemes and castigations. They were not so different in quality and technique from Hal's modus operandi; actually, just more subtle. Once upon a time, Hal was just an unfortunate vagrant – skinny to the point of starvation from a run of calamities in his business as a butcher. But I took him in and trained him in the art of plunder on the high seas. I mean to say – I admit with a great deal of personal anguish how I*

*have mistreated you, Sam – over many years. I regret especially that
time when I plotted to take photographic "evidence" that you were
polluting the water concourses near the jetty when the reverse was
true. In fact, you were the only litter-conscious seahorse amongst
all of us. I have wronged you dreadfully. I'm sorry, Sam.* Clive
effected an about turn, uttering a quieter retraction to the Hittite.

Immeasurably precious healing and reconciliation
Sam discerned a multi-faceted compulsion within himself to interrupt
the Clipboard – to halt him in his tracks – for whilst he sensed the
immeasurably precious process of spiritual healing and reconciliation
proceeding between them, he didn't want to confront the rising sap of
all his old memories – including his own resentments towards Clive.
But he knew equally well that as long as Clive was clearing his own
laden decks, Sam's own were not yet entirely free of moral detritus.
Sam knew there was precious little moral mileage in permitting
superordination to his self-centred fears, and he remembered that
Stocky had cautioned him about how delicate the business of
establishing restorations can turn out to be. Sam's intuition told
him that care was needed most wherever amends had not been invited –
or any other circumstances in which insult may be taken to have been
added to injury (or salt rubbed in old wounds). Sam had no doubt that
these conditions did not belong in that category. He turned to Clive.

Sam lapses momentarily into confusion
Clive, pleaded Sam. *Some say it takes two to tango, and whilst we
were never equal partners on any level or dimension one might choose
to invoke, I bore you a great deal of ill-will. I can see how my
attitude towards you must have been difficult to bear. And I can see
how my feelings as a vulnerable youngster must have been all too
visible and amenable to sympathy within our seahorse community.
Whether or not you were responsible for all you say, I am sure I
milked and exploited the protection and solidarity (for me and
against you) that I could have mustered from seahorses amongst your
own generation. Perhaps I contributed to the deterioration of your
reputation, adding to the marginalisation that you came to know
within the community that once welcomed you, talking of which … um …*

Unco-operative pieces of this complex yet appealing jigsaw
Sam tried to gather his thoughts frantically as if they were diverse
chunks of this complex (yet strangely appealing) jigsaw that wouldn't
co-operate in forming the image anticipated by the fervent hobbyist.
Something was wrong. He couldn't tie together into a single coherent
narrative the legend of Clive's arrival on the jetty, the shocking
discovery of the "wanted" poster in the Captain's cabin aboard Sam's
now stranded vessel – and the unanticipated events of recent hours.

*… Clive – is the story of your arrival on the jetty an accurate one?
Is it true that you were an innocent fugitive from a distant land –
and that you secretly did away with your benefactors prior to your
rising through the ranks of powerful administrators in the warehouse?*

Clive was visibly disturbed at Sam's line of questioning, seeming
least of all to have expected the intrusion of the "wanted" poster.
At the same time, his perturbation seemed to have more to do with the
unavoidable precipitation of his past than any intent to obfuscate.
Clive made no motion to press Sam on how much he knew, as if he might
yet gauge how much he could dissimulate. Instead, he began to account
for his history in chronological order, as if realising that such a
report were the only means of satisfying Sam's frustration at the
disparate shreds in the storyline. After all, there was no doubt that
Sam was interested in what Clive had to say, and there was an equal
and opposite intent on the Clipboard's part to set matters straight.

Demise of self–centred fear: "Keeping Your Feet On The Ground"
Heracles and Antaeus, Studley Royal, North Yorkshire

The truth is revealed at last
Once, Clive started, *I was young like you! A nipper in Thorland, I*
had a well-connected father and a devoted mother. I was an only child
and spoiled. I realised quickly which side my bread was buttered –
and learned about politics instinctively. I was obedient to my
father, because I appreciated that maintaining such a position –
foiling all intrusions of potential controversy – I would inherit his
position and status within the wealthy aristocracy of that realm. The
King of Thorland acquired his position – like all but the most recent
monarchs of history – through armed might and forced dominion. My
father was a Duke appointed to his inner circle. My mother never
exploited her talents as a social architect, but remained loyal to
the regime, clandestinely soliciting the comforting services of
itinerants peddling mysterious potions which worked to quieten her
conscience. I rose rapidly in the King's Navy – from Midshipman to
Captain in no time at all. The King was avaricious, constantly
declaring war on his enemies. I don't wish to shock you Sam, but that
vessel on which you escaped from the jetty was at one time a superbly
equipped espionage-ship, employed by me commanding a small and very
well-formed band of elite troops. The King swore us to secrecy in all
but the most trivial of matters, even within our privileged families.
My father knew nothing of my military escapades – for which I
received much recognition from the King – but none from his subjects.
On one such spying mission, we were discovered in spite of our
precautions. The scouting force in question was a small one. We
overpowered it without great difficulty, and I killed its leader with
my cutlass in the Captain's cabin of my own familiar craft. One of
the deceased's party escaped with news of the encounter, and I was
branded and sought as a murderer in that foreign domain. The King of
Thorland, naturally, took a different view, regarding me as a state
hero as long as his ulterior appropriation in that neighbouring land
was not exposed. But exposed it was, and the King framed me as the
perpetrator – forging copies of his rival's notices about my crime. I
took off, knowing a kinder death awaited me unrescued at sea than
staying at the King's mercy. My ship landed where you took it, for it
got washed up near the jetty by sheer twist of kindly circumstance. I
tethered it to the same tree from which you eventually released it,
and made my way to the warehouse with my tale. There were never any
rescuers and there were no benefactors (hence none to be despatched).
The jetty community was generous – and gullible in my eyes. I wore my
aristocratic demeanour as if an unassailable passport to elevated
position within the administrative echelons of the innocent
neighbourhood in which I found myself – and no-one challenged me. I
corrupted its culture with psychotic plotting. You were only one of
its victims, Sam. I was a lone and unencumbered persecutor. Every
seahorse within many miles succumbed to my megalomaniac spell. I
couldn't hope to be popular with everybody, and the community turned
against and hounded me sorely when it was reported that I was
responsible for your disappearance. I harnessed my old repertoire of
skills – turning pirate – letting myself believe that that occupation
was my only means of survival. I let myself believe I was desperate.

What do you make of your seafaring ambitions now? asked Sam sharply.

I wish to relinquish them all unconditionally, answered Clive.

The other four intruded immediately: *Me too! And I! And me! Also I!*

It seems to me, said Sam (ensuring that Hal was paying attention) –
that by far the most potent device in any delinquent's armoury is the
lie through which its wielder and executor cannot themselves see. It
is the illusion of self-centred fear, and its demise is partly
assured by keeping your feet on the ground and your life in the day.

A little clarification for Shirley, Carol and Pete
What do you mean by "keeping your feet on the ground", Sam? enquired
Shirley, *for surely such an expression is wide of the seahorse mark!*

And what does life in the day mean? harmonised Carol.

*And why is the demise of self-centred fear only partly assured by
these two?* requested the Poop Deck.

Well, began Sam, *in ancient mythology amongst humans, an infamous
pugilist dwelling in a remote place would challenge every passer-by
to a wrestling match. Being at the top of his game, he invariably won
and, possessing a rather nefarious streak, was disposed to retain his
victims' skulls as trophies. The misanthropic fighter was eventually
defeated by an exceptional adversary who realised that the wrestler's
supremacy depended entirely on his maintaining contact with the
ground. Accordingly, the guileful challenger held the hitherto
unbeaten combatant aloof in a bear-hug (I do hope I am not confusing
you too much with these cross-species references,* Sam interjected*),
thereby depriving this newly-defeated rogue of his uncommon strength.
Amongst us seahorses, "keeping your feet on the ground" just means
being reasonably concrete about life. The surest manner of achieving
this is the mental surrender of tomorrow's projections and fantasies.
Perversely, we indulge them by way of defence — as if we could ready
or steel ourselves against the ghastly events we imagine might occur.
Since these rarely if ever transpire, we are better off reserving our
energy for living in the moment — with as much as possible of our
attention located there. This isn't just an idea, or, rather — it is!
But it is one that demands perseverance — for practice makes perfect.*

I think you have answered my question, said Carol, satisfied.

*Pending our having practiced sufficiently (when, one delightful day
we are struck with a peace which settles upon us just as if we hadn't
truly earned it), we need to find a means of "letting go". It seems
we are built — psychologically speaking — in such a fashion that our
surrender is more meaningful if it identifies an object — a resource
greater than ourselves upon which or upon whom we may learn to rely.*

I think, now, you have answered mine, added Pete.

Sam looked at the Clipboard. *If you concentrate hard enough, Clive,
you may discern a loving whisper. If you do — don't complicate it!*

A modest spring in Sam's step
There is somewhere I would like to take you all, Sam appealed to the
queer quintet. Heading off, he noticed that his Parent ego state had
become diminished in power — spiritually neutralised, you might say.
Clive the vile and hateful introject had clicked his heels thrice and
departed. Had Clive poured coals on Sam's head deliberately in this
strange turn of events (you couldn't have contrived it in fiction)?
No, Sam told himself, *now you are being paranoid.* Sam couldn't bear
how beautiful the world had suddenly become. A peace and a softness
descended. But for common-or-garden sensitivity, he could almost have
skipped with gay abandon alongside the desolate vagabonds beside him.

Back at the inn there is joy — and conspiratorial satisfaction
Sam noticed that Stocky and The Feather were present at the crowded
inn, but having seen Sam enter with Clive and his bedraggled crew,
they remained curiously reticent, seated privately at a table in the
shadows, apparently cutting each other knowing and satisfied glances.
Sam thought to himself (in a spirit of earnest spiritual equality), *I
must introduce Clive and his companions to my friends, for as a band
of associates, now we shall number nine not four!* Sam felt peculiarly
comfortable and secure at one spiritual epicentre of *Nine Seahorses*.

"Say 'Cheese!'"

Finale

Last thoughts on a one-faced psychology

Inspired by Henry David Thoreau (1817-1862) – and his appreciation of
the power and beneficence of nature – *Nine Seahorses* has included:

- a critical overview of how modern psychology (in so far as it
  speaks to sanity, or, the "human condition") got to be what it is;
  i.e., an account of it rooted in the entire history of humankind;

- a creative and unconventional psychological "theory of everything";
  at least, an interesting dovetailing of divergent threads – forging
  a happy marriage of psychology with its counterparts in: all forms
  of psychological helping including counselling and psychotherapy;
  all the humanities including history, philosophy, spirituality,
  religion and religious studies, and all of the social sciences
  including (counter)culture, politics, citizenship, justice, war and
  peace studies, conflict resolution, ecology and environmentalism;

- an *avant-garde* reconciliation of scientific (behaviorist) and
  analytical (broadly Freudian) strands of the disintegrated modern
  discipline; in particular, a developmental explanation of Eric
  Berne's (TA) ego states couched in terms of associative learning;

- the implications of psychology for psychological treatment (i.e.,
  all forms of psychotherapy) – with a particular appreciation of
  "descending vicious spirals", especially amongst those affected by
  social alienation, addiction and crime – emphasising Young People;

- reflections on social responsibility in the new "connected" world,
  including the case for education and safety nets threaded by
  "competent coxswains"; i.e., organised advocacy for people in need
  of treatment through the medium of the "poacher-turned-gamekeeper";

- an argument that there is (still) scope for a "moral psychology"
  (qualitatively assured by the exclusion of third party authority);

- deferring to the scientific tradition, a commentary on the breadth
  of empirical support that can be obtained for a "moral psychology";

- the implications of a "moral psychology" for culture, and the world
  of human relationships from the most intimate to the international;

- reflections on the "spiritual life", "spiritual equality" and the
  personal liberation available following deep "spiritual surrender";
  including reflections on how this latter phenomenon can represent,
  in the context of CBT (or cognitive-behavioral therapy), the rapid
  short-circuiting of more protracted and expensive therapy geared
  towards "re-writing", "overwriting" or otherwise compensating for
  all the corrupt biographic and sociocultural learning infecting us
  (i.e., that which needlessly generates psychological distress);

- in Part III, a literary flourish in "The Story Of Seahorse Sam" –
  an allegorical tale of a sensitive seahorse encountering distress
  and spiritual deliverance – his relationship with the creepy
  "Clipboard Clive" (representing the entire gamut of psychologically
  illegitimate learning in Sam's life); Sam's yielding to the succour
  offered by seahorses who'd already found consolation in their own
  emancipation, and a conversational account of his own spiritual
  journey: his acquisition of independence, his path to maturity and
  his willingness to help others find the same freedoms by abandoning
  chronic, shadowy self-interest, and embracing "transcendent trust".

Now, in a one-faced psychology where may we find a one-faced society?

"One-faced Psychology"

"May The Road Rise To Greet You" (only minor roadworks ahead)
Gluvian, near Saint Columb Major, Cornwall

"May The Wind Be Always At Your Back"
Original sculpture by Lynn Chadwick (1914-2003) at Chatsworth

"Cottage By The Sea"
Clovelly, Devon

"Ageing Gracefully"
Towan Island, Newquay, Cornwall

"Still Beautiful"
The Gannel Estuary, Newquay, Cornwall

"Still Seaworthy" (nothing to prove though)
The Gannel Estuary, Newquay, Cornwall

5000 BC

⋮

not chronologically linear

⋮

2000 AD

Hinduism from c.5000 BC
Judaism from c.2000 BC
Buddhism from c.500 BC
Empedocles (490-430 BC)
Socrates (469-399 BC)
Hippocrates of Kos (460-372 BC)
Plato (428-348 BC)
Aristotle (384-322 BC)
Christianity from c.30 AD
Galen (129-200 AD)
Islam from c.600 AD
Saint Bonaventure (1221-1274)
Saint Thomas Aquinas (1225-1274)
William of Ockham (1288-1348)
Nicholas Copernicus (1473-1543)
Galilei Galileo (1564-1642)
René Descartes (1596-1650)
Sir Isaac Newton (1643-1727)
Immanuel Kant (1724-1804)
Jeremy Bentham (1748-1832)
Auguste Comte (1798-1857)
Søren Aabye Kierkegaard (1813-1855)
Hermann Ludwig von Helmholtz (1821-1894)
Lev Nikolayevich Tolstoy (1828-1910)
Wilhelm Maximilian Wundt (1832-1920)
Friedrich Wilhelm Nietzsche (1844-1900)
Ivan Petrovich Pavlov (1849-1936)
Conwy Lloyd Morgan (1852-1936)
Sigmund Freud (1856-1939)
Émile Durkheim (1858-1917)
Carl Gustav Jung (1875-1961)
John Broadus Watson (1878-1958)
Martin Heidegger (1889-1976)
Gilbert Ryle (1900-1976)
Carl Ransom Rogers (1902-1987)
Burrhus Frederic Skinner (1904-1990)
Jean-Paul Charles Aymard Sartre (1905-1980)
Eric Berne (1910-1970)
Hans Jürgen Eysenck (1916-1997)

"Rubin Revisited"
Where and when (if ever) does 'Truth' emerge in psychology?

The Rogues' Gallery with Reader's Notes
(or personalities in the history of psychology)

Seahorse Sam concurs with Sir Isaac Newton in his view that all the significant figures of the past stand on the shoulders of giants. Anyway the truest heroines and heroes of history remain unrecorded.

Who?	Dates	Mug	Reader's Notes
Homer	999 BC – 400 BC		Chapter 1 (footnote)
The Buddha (Siddhārtha Gautama)	600 BC – 400 BC		Chapter 5
Pindar	522 BC – 443 BC		Chapter 9 (footnote); Chapter 10
Empedocles	490 BC – 430 BC		Chapter 3; Chapter 7
Socrates	469 BC – 399 BC		Preface (footnote); Chapter 1; Chapter 3; Chapter 4; Chapter 4 (footnote); Chapter 7
Hippocrates of Kos	460 BC – 372 BC		Chapter 3; Chapter 7; Chapter 8
Plato	428 BC – 348 BC		Preface; Chapter 1; Chapter 4 (footnote); Chapter 4; Chapter 5; Chapter 7; Chapter 8; Chapter 8 (footnote)
Aristotle	384 BC – 322 BC		Preface; Chapter 1; Chapter 3; Chapter 4 (footnote); Chapter 7; Chapter 8 (footnote); Chapter 10
Epicurus	341 BC – 270 BC		Chapter 12
Alexander the Great	336 BC – 323 BC		Chapter 1
Paul of Tarsus (Saint)	c.5 BC – 67 AD		Preface (footnote)

Who?	Dates	Mug	Reader's Notes
Galen of Pergamum	129 AD – 200 AD		Chapter 3; Chapter 3 (footnote); Chapters 6/7 (photograph); Chapter 7; Chapter 8
Avicenna (Ibn Sina)	980 AD – 1037		Chapter 1
Abubacer (Ibn Tufail)	1105 – 1185		Chapter 1
Genghis Khan	1162 – 1227		Chapter 6
Saint Bonaventure	1221 – 1274		Chapter 1; Chapter 2; Chapter 7
Saint Thomas Aquinas	1225 – 1274		Chapter 1; Chapter 2; Chapter 4 (footnote); Chapter 4; Chapter 7
William of Ockham	1288 – 1348		Chapter 2; Chapter 7; Chapter 9
Ibn Khaldun	1332 – 1406		Chapter 4 (footnote)
Nicholas Copernicus	1473 – 1543		Preface; Chapter 1; Chapter 7
Sir Thomas More (Saint)	1478 – 1535		Chapter 12 (footnote)
Henry VIII of England	1491 – 1547		Chapter 1; Chapter 10
Saint Ignatius of Loyola	1491 – 1556		Chapter 8 (footnote)
Pope Gregory XIII (Ugo Boncompagni)	1502 – 1585		Chapter 1

Who?	Dates	Mug	Reader's Notes
Saint Francis Xavier	1506 – 1552		Chapter 8 (footnote)
Andreas Vesalius	1514 – 1564		Chapter 3 (footnote)
Saint John of the Cross	1542 – 1591		Chapter 5 (footnote)
Giordano Bruno	1548 – 1600		Chapter 1
William Shakespeare	1564 – 1616		Preface (footnote); Chapter 9 (footnote); Chapter 9
Galileo Galilei	1564 – 1642		Chapter 1; Chapter 7
John Donne	1572 – 1631		Chapter 10
René Descartes	1596 – 1650		Chapter 4; Chapter 4 (footnote); Chapter 7
John Locke	1632 – 1704		Chapter 1 (footnote); Chapter 4 (footnote)
Robert Hooke	1635 – 1703		Chapter 1
Sir Isaac Newton	1643 – 1727		Chapter 1; Chapter 4; Chapter 7; Chapter 10
Voltaire (François-Marie Arouet)	1694 – 1778		Chapter 1 (footnote)
David Hume	1711 – 1776		Chapter 1 (footnote)

Who?	Dates	Mug	Reader's Notes
Jean Jacques Rousseau	1712 – 1778		Chapter 1 (footnote)
Immanuel Kant	1724 – 1804		Chapter 5; Chapter 5 (footnote); Chapter 7
William Paley	1743 – 1805		Chapter 5 (footnote)
Jeremy Bentham	1748 – 1832		Chapter 6; Chapter 7
Edward Anthony Jenner	1749 – 1823		Chapter 8
King Louis XVI of France	1754 – 1793		Chapter 4
Robert Burns	1759 – 1796		Chapter 9 (footnote)
Napoleon Bonaparte (Napoleon I)	1769 – 1821		Chapter 6
Robert Stewart (Lord Castlereagh)	1769 – 1822		Chapter 10 (footnote)
FitzRoy James Henry Somerset (Lord Raglan)	1788 – 1855		Chapter 9 (footnote)
Thomas Carlyle	1795 – 1881		Chapter 6; Chapter 6 (footnote)
Isidore Auguste Marie François Xavier Comte	1798 – 1857		Chapter 4; Chapter 7; Chapter 10
Alexandre Dumas (Dumas Davy de la Pailleterie)	1802 – 1870		Preface (footnote)

Who?	Dates	Mug	Reader's Notes
Benjamin Disraeli	1804 – 1881		Chapter 3
Robert FitzRoy	1805 – 1865		Chapter 10; Chapter 10 (footnote)
John Stuart Mill	1806 – 1873		Chapter 1 (footnote); Chapter 4; Chapter 6; Chapter 6 (footnote)
Charles Robert Darwin	1809 – 1882		Chapter 4; Chapter 5 (footnote); Chapter 8; Chapter 8 (footnote); Chapter 10; Chapter 10 (footnote)
Søren Aabye Kierkegaard	1813 – 1855		Chapter 5; Chapter 7
Henry David Thoreau	1817 – 1862		Preface; Preface (footnote); Chapter 1 (footnote); Chapter 6 (footnote); Chapter 8 (footnote); Chapter 8; Chapter 9; Chapter 9 (footnote); *Finale*
Karl Heinrich Marx	1818 – 1883		Chapter 5; Chapter 5 (footnote)
Ernst Wilhelm (Ritter von) Brücke	1819 – 1892		Chapter 8
Queen (Alexandrina) Victoria of Great Britain	1819 – 1901		Chapter 3
Revd William Henry Poole	1820 – 1896		Chapter 5 (footnote)
Herbert Spencer	1820 – 1903		Chapter 5 (footnote); Chapter 6; Chapter 12 (footnote)
Hermann Ludwig von Helmholtz	1821 – 1894		Chapter 1; Chapter 1 (footnote); Chapter 7; Chapter 8; Chapter 9
Jaques aka Louis Pasteur	1822 – 1895		Chapter 8

Who?	Dates	Mug	Reader's Notes
Thomas Henry Huxley	1825 – 1895		Chapter 8; Chapter 8 (footnote); Chapter 10
Lev (Leo) Nikolayevich Tolstoy	1828 – 1910		Chapter 6; Chapter 6 (footnote); Chapter 7; Chapter 10
Wilhelm Maximilian Wundt	1832 – 1920		Chapter 1; Chapter 2 (footnote); Chapter 7; Chapter 8
Ernst Heinrich Philipp August Haeckel	1834 – 1919		Chapter 9 (footnote)
Samuel Langhorne Clemens (Mark Twain)	1835 – 1910		Chapter 3
William James	1842 – 1910		Chapter 8; Chapter 8 (footnote); Chapter 9; Chapter 10; Chapter 10 (footnote)
Josef Breuer	1842 – 1925		Chapter 8 (footnote)
Friedrich Wilhelm Nietzsche	1844 – 1900		Chapter 5; Chapter 7; Chapter 9; Chapter 9 (footnote); Chapter 10
Granville Stanley Hall	1844 – 1924		Chapter 1
Robert Vischer	1847 – 1933		Chapter 1
Sir Francis (Frank) Darwin	1848 – 1925		Chapter 10 (footnote)
William Ernest Henley	1849 – 1903		Chapter 9 (footnote)
Ivan Petrovich Pavlov	1849 – 1936		Chapter 2; Chapter 3; Chapter 7; Chapter 8; Chapter 9; Chapter 10

Who?	Dates	Mug	Reader's Notes
Theodor Lipps	1851 – 1914		Chapter 1 (footnote)
Julius Richard Petri	1852 – 1921		Chapter 8 (footnote)
Conwy Lloyd Morgan	1852 – 1936		Chapter 2; Chapter 7; Chapter 8; Chapter 9
Lyman Frank Baum	1856 – 1919		Chapter 12 (footnote)
Sigismund Schlomo (Sigmund) Freud	1856 – 1939		Preface; Chapter 3 (footnote); Chapter 7; Chapter 8; Chapter 8 (footnote); Chapter 9 (footnote); Chapter 10
Paul Eugen Bleuler	1857 – 1939		Chapter 8
(Robert Stephenson Smyth) Baden Powell	1857 – 1941		Chapter 9
Émile Durkheim	1858 – 1917		Chapter 4; Chapter 7; Chapter 8; Chapter 10
Bertha Pappenheim ("Anna O")	1859 – 1936		Chapter 8 (footnote)
James McKeen Cattell	1860 – 1944		Chapter 1; Chapter 2 (footnote)
Oswald Külpe	1862 – 1915		Chapter 1; Chapter 8
Albert Charles Seward	1863 – 1941		Chapter 10 (footnote)
Charles Edward Spearman	1863 – 1945		Chapter 1

Who?	Dates	Mug	Reader's Notes
Edward Bradford Titchener	1867 – 1927		Chapter 1
Lightner Witmer	1867 – 1956		Chapter 1
Mohatma (Mohandas) Karamchand Gandhi	1869 – 1948		Chapter 6; Chapter 6 (footnote)
Paul Federn	1871 – 1950		Chapter 8; Chapter 8 (footnote)
Sándor Ferenczi	1873 – 1933		Chapter 8
Charles Hubbard Judd	1873 – 1946		Chapter 1
Edward Lee Thorndike	1874 – 1949		Chapter 2 (footnote); Chapter 2; Chapter 9; Chapter 10
Carl Gustav Jung	1875 – 1961		Preface; Chapter 3 (footnote); Chapter 3; Chapter 5 (footnote); Chapter 7; Chapter 8
John Broadus Watson	1878 – 1958		Chapter 1; Chapter 7
Martin Buber	1878 – 1965		Chapter 9 (footnote)
Henry Jackson Watt	1879 – 1925		Chapter 1
Albert Einstein	1879 – 1955		Chapter 1 (footnote); Chapter 4 (footnote); Chapter 5; Chapter 7; Chapter 7 (photograph); Chapter 10
Sir Alexander Fleming	1881 – 1955		Chapter 8

Who?	Dates	Mug	Reader's Notes
President Franklin Delano Roosevelt of the USA	1882 – 1945		Chapter 9; Chapter 10
Joe Burke	1884 – 1950		Chapter 6 (footnote)
Ernst Simon Bloch	1885 – 1977		Chapter 1
Edgar John Rubin	1886 – 1951		Chapter 4 (Illustration); *Finale* (Illustration)
Ludwig Josef Johann Wittgenstein	1889 – 1951		Chapter 5 (footnote)
Gabriel Honoré Marcel	1889 – 1973		Chapter 5
Martin Heidegger	1889 – 1976		Chapter 7
Al Durbin	1891 – 1945		Chapter 6 (footnote)
(Karl Paul) Reinhold Niebuhr	1892 – 1971		Chapter 9 (footnote)
Heinz Hartmann	1894 – 1970		Chapter 8; Chapter 8 (footnote)
President Juan Perón of Argentina	1895 – 1974		Chapter 6
Jean Piaget	1896 – 1980		Chapter 8 (footnote)
Max Schur	1897 – 1969		Chapter 8

Who?	Dates	Mug	Reader's Notes
Nick Lucas (Dominic Nicholas Anthony Lucanese)	1897 – 1982		Chapter 6 (footnote)
Clive Staples Lewis	1898 – 1963		Chapter 4 (footnote)
Gilbert Ryle	1900 – 1976		Chapter 5; Chapter 5 (footnote); Chapter 7
Werner Heisenberg	1901 – 1976		Chapter 4 (footnote)
Rube (Reuben) Bloom	1902 – 1976		Chapter 9 (footnote)
Carl Ransom Rogers	1902 – 1987		Preface; Chapter 7; Chapter 9; Chapter 10
Erik Erikson	1902 – 1994		Chapter 8
Sir Karl Raimund Popper	1902 – 1994		Chapter 8 (footnote); Chapter 10
George Orwell (Eric Arthur Blair)	1903 – 1950		Preface
Burrhus Frederic Skinner	1904 – 1990		Preface; Chapter 1 (footnote); Chapter 1; Chapter 2; Chapter 2 (footnote); Chapter 5; Chapter 7; Chapter 9; Chapter 10
Jean-Paul Charles Aymard Sartre	1905 – 1980		Chapter 5; Chapter 7
Arthur Koestler	1905 – 1983		Chapter 5 (footnote)
Johnny (John Herndon) Mercer	1909 – 1976		Chapter 9 (footnote)

Who?	Dates	Mug	Reader's Notes
Eduard Einstein	1910 – 1965		Chapter 8 (footnote)
Eric Berne (Eric Lennard Bernstein)	1910 – 1970		Preface; Preface (footnote); Chapter 7; Chapter 8; Chapter 9; Chapter 9 (footnote); Chapter 10
Lynn Chadwick	1914 – 2003		*Finale* (photograph)
Hans Jürgen Eysenck	1916 – 1997		Chapter 3; Chapter 3 (footnote); Chapter 5; Chapter 7; Chapter 8; Chapter 8 (footnote)
Fanita English	1916 –		Chapter 8
Julian Rotter	1916 –		Chapter 7
Nelson Rolihlahla Mandela	1918 –		Chapter 6; Chapter 10
Evita (María Eva Duarte de Perón)	1919 – 1952		Chapter 6
Leon Festinger	1919 – 1989		Chapter 5; Chapter 5 (footnote)
Aaron Temkin Beck	1921 –		Chapter 7
Neville Thomas Bonner	1922 – 1999		Chapter 6
Arvid Carlsson	1923 –		Chapter 9 (footnote)
Paul Greengard	1925 –		Chapter 9 (footnote)

Who?	Dates	Mug	Reader's Notes
Hans Joachim Bremermann	1926 – 1996		Chapter 4 (footnote)
Ronald David Laing	1927 – 1989		Chapter 7 (footnote)
(Avram) Noam Chomsky	1928 –		Chapter 9 (footnote)
Martin Luther King Jr.	1929 – 1968		Chapter 6
Eric Richard Kandel	1929 –		Chapter 9 (footnote)
Donn Byrne	1931 –		Chapter 7; Chapter 7 (footnote)
Mikhail Sergeyevich Gorbachev	1931 –		Chapter 6
Jeffrey Alan Gray	1934 – 2004		Chapter 5; Chapter 5 (footnote); Chapter 7
Mihály Csíkszent-mihályi	1934 –		Chapter 6 (footnote)
Claude Steiner	1935 –		Chapter 8; Chapter 8 (footnote); Chapter 9 (footnote)
Winnie Madikizela-Mandela	1936 –		Chapter 6
Terry Waite	1939 –		Chapter 6; Chapter 6 (footnote)
Joan Chandos Baez	1941 –		Chapter 6; Chapter 10

Who?	Dates	Mug	Reader's Notes
Richard Dawkins	1941 –		Chapter 4; Chapter 4 (footnote); Chapter 5; Chapter 10
Bob Dylan (Robert Allen Zimmerman)	1941 –		Chapter 6
Stephen William Hawking	1942 –		Chapter 4; Chapter 4 (footnote)
Martin Elias Peter Seligman	1942 –		Chapter 7
Aung San Suu Kyi	1945 –		Chapter 6
Suzanne C. Kobassa (Ouellette)	1948 –		Chapter 7
Susan Adele Greenfield	1950 –		Chapter 2 (footnote)
Hannes Grobe	1954 –		Chapter 14 (photograph)
Ray (Raymond Albert) Romano	1957 –		Chapter 9 (footnote)
Philip Rosenthal	1960 –		Chapter 9 (footnote)
Barack Hussein Obama II	1961 –		Preface; Preface (footnote); Chapter 4 (Table)
Miguel Alcubierre Moya	1964 –		Chapter 8 (footnote)
Thomas Crean O.P.	1973 –		Chapter 4 (footnote); Chapter 5; Chapter 5 (footnote)

Who?	Dates	Mug	Reader's Notes
Icek Ajzen	–		Chapter 8 (footnote)
Jerry M. Burger	–		Chapter 7 (footnote)
Hedges Capers	–		Chapter 9 (footnote)
Sidney Cobb	–		Chapter 8 (footnote)
Pearl Drago	–		Chapter 9
Sybil (Sybille) Bianca Giulietta Eysenck	–		Chapter 3
Martin Fishbein	–		Chapter 8 (footnote)
Mary Goulding (née Edwards)	–		Chapter 8
Robert (Bob) Goulding	–		Chapter 8
Geoffrey Hall	–		Foreword
Vann S. Joines	–		Chapter 8; Chapter 8 (footnote)
Taibi Kahler	–		Chapter 9 (footnote)
Steven Karpman	–		Chapter 8; Chapter 8 (footnote)

Who?	Dates	Mug	Reader's Notes
Euan M. Macphail	–		Chapter 1; Chapter 4 (footnote); Chapter 9
Jenny Morris	–		Chapter 3 (footnote)
Willfried Nesshoever	–		Chapter 3 (footnote)
Robert A. Rescorla	–		Chapter 9 (footnote)
William Revelle	–		Chapter 3 (footnote)
Derek Roger	–		Chapter 3 (footnote); Chapter 7 (footnote); Chapter 14 (footnote)
Thomas Schapals	–		Chapter 7 (footnote)
Ian Stewart	–		Chapter 8; Chapter 8 (footnote)
Allan R. Wagner	–		Chapter 9 (footnote)
Bruce E. Wampold	–		Chapter 9; Chapter 9 (footnote)
Tony White	–		Chapter 8
Marityn Zalcman	–		Chapter 8
Mila Zinkova	–		Chapter 2 (photograph)

Who?	Dates	Mug	Reader's Notes
	-		
	-		
	-		
	-		
	-		
	-		
	-		
	-		
	-		
	-		
	-		
	-		
	-		

Who?	Dates	Mug	Reader's Notes
Seahorse Sam	–		Part III
Lord T. Dover aka Clipboard Clive	–		Part III
The Feather	–		Part III
Stocky	–		Part III
The Driver	–		Part III
Coalshed Carol	–		Part III
Sly Shirley	–		Part III
Poop Deck Pete	–		Part III
Hittite Hal	–		Part III
	–		
	–		
	–		
	–		

Who?	Dates	Mug	Reader's Notes
	-		
	-		
	-		
	-		
	-		
	-		
	-		
	-		
	-		
	-		
	-		
	-		
	-		

References

(third party works cited within *Nine Seahorses*)

Aristotle (*circa* 350 BC) *De Anima.*

Baum, L.F. (1900) *The Wonderful Wizard Of Oz.* George M. Hill: Chicago

Berne, E. (1963) *The Structure And Dynamics Of Organizations And Groups.* Lippincott: Philadelphia

Berne, E. (1964) *Games People Play.* Penguin: London

Buber, M. (1923) *Ich Und Du.* Insel-Verlag: Leipzig

Burger, J.M. (1992) *Desire For Control: Personality, Social And Clinical Perspectives.* Plenum: New York

Burns, R. (1785) *To A Mouse, On Turning Her Up In Her Nest With The Plough.*

Byrne, D. (1961) The repression-sensitisation scale: rationale, reliability and validity. *Journal Of Personality, 29,* 334-349.

Carlyle, T. (1850) *Latter-day Pamphlets.*

Chomsky, N. (1965) *Aspects Of The Theory Of Syntax.* MIT Press: Cambridge

Cobb, S. (1976) Social support as a moderator of life stress. *Psychosomatic Medicine, 38,* 300-314.

Cohen, I.B. (1970) *Dictionary Of Scientific Biography (Volume 11).* Charles Scribner's Sons: New York

Crean, T. (2007) *A Catholic Replies To Professor Dawkins.* Family Publications: Oxford

Darwin, C.R. (1859) *On The Origin Of Species.* P.F. Collier & Son: New York

Darwin, C.R. (1871) *The Descent Of Man, And Selection In Relation To Sex.* D. Appleton & Company: New York

Darwin, F. and Seward, A.C. (1903) *More Letters Of Charles Darwin: A Record Of His Work In A Series Of Hitherto Unpublished Letters (Volume 1).* John Murray: London

Dawkins, R. (1976) *The Selfish Gene.* Oxford University Press: Oxford

Dawkins, R. (2006) *The God Delusion.* Bantam Press: London

Donne, J. (1624) (Meditation XVII, Devotion XVII) *Devotions Upon Emergent Occasions.*

Dumas, A. (1844) *Les Trois Mousquetaires.* Baudry: Paris

English, F. (1977) Rackets and racketeering as the root of games. In: Roger N. Blakeney (Ed.) *Current Issues In Transactional Analysis.* Bruner Mazel: New York

Eysenck, H.J. (1959) *Manual Of The Maudsley Personality Inventory.* University of London Press: London

Eysenck, H.J. (1990) *Rebel With A Cause.* W.H. Allen & Company: London

Eysenck, H.J. and Eysenck, S.B.G. (1964) *Manual Of The Eysenck Personality Inventory.* Hodder & Stoughton: London

Eysenck, H.J. and Eysenck, S.B.G. (1975) *Manual Of The Eysenck Personality Questionnaire.* Hodder & Stoughton: London

Federn, P. (1928) Narcissism in the structure of the ego. *International Journal Of Psychoanalysis, 9,* 401-419.

Federn, P. (1929) Das ich als subjekt und objekt im narzissmus. *International Journal Of Psychoanalysis, XV,* 4.

Fishbein, M. and Ajzen, I. (1975) *Belief, Attitude, Intention, And Behavior: An Introduction To Theory And Research.* Addison-Wesley: Reading

Freud, S. (1914) Zur einführung des narzissmus. *Jarbuch Für Psychoanalyse, VI,* 1-24.

Goulding, R. and Goulding, M. (1979) *Changing Lives Through Redecision Therapy*. Brunner-Mazel: New York

Gray, J.A. (1971) *The Psychology Of Fear And Stress*. Cambridge University Press: Cambridge

Greenfield, S.A. (1995) *Journey To The Centers Of The Mind*. W.H. Freeman & Company: New York

Gregory XIII (Pope, February 24th 1582) *Inter Gravissimas*.

Hawking, S.W. (1988) *A Brief History Of Time*. Bantam Dell: New York

Heidegger, M. (1927) Sein und zeit: erste hälfte. *Jahrbuch Für Philosophie Und Phänomenologische Forschung, Band VIII.*

Henley, W.E. (1888) Invictus: originally untitled in *A Book Of Verses*. D. Nutt: London

Homer (*circa* 999-400 BC) *The Odyssey*.

Huxley, T.H. (1863) *Evidence As To Man's Place In Nature*. D. Appleton & Company: New York

James, W. (1890) *The Principles Of Psychology (Volumes 1 & 2)*.

James, W. (1902) *The Varieties Of Religious Experience: A Study In Human Nature*. Longmans, Green & Company: New York

James, W. (1907) *Pragmatism: A New Name For Some Old Ways Of Thinking*. Longmans, Green & Company: New York

John of the Cross (Saint, 16th century) *Dark Night Of The Soul*.

Joines, V. (1982) Similarities and differences in rackets and games. *Transactional Analysis Journal, 12:4*, 280-283.

Jung, C.G. (1933) *Modern Man In Search Of A Soul*. Kegan Paul, Trench, Trübner & Company: London

Kahler, T. and Capers, H. (1974) The miniscript. *Transactional Analysis Journal, 4:1*, 26-42.

Karpman, S. (1968) Fairy tales and script drama analysis. *Transactional Analysis Bulletin, 7:26*, 39-43.

Koestler, A. (1967) *The Ghost In The Machine*. Hutchinson: London

Laing, R.D. (1960) *The Divided Self*. Tavistock: London

Lewis, C.S. (1952) *Mere Christianity*. Macmillan: London

Lloyd Morgan, C.L. (1894) *An Introduction To Comparative Psychology*. W. Scott: London

Macphail, E. (1992) *Brain And Intelligence In Vertebrates*. Clarendon Press: Oxford

Macphail, E. (1998) *The Evolution Of Consciousness*. Oxford University Press: Oxford

Mandela, N.R. (1994) *Long Walk To Freedom*. Little Brown & Company: London

Mill, J.S. (1863) *Utilitarianism*. Parker, Son & Bourn: London

More, T. (1516) *Utopia*.

Myers-Briggs, I. and Myers P.B. (1980) *Gifts Differing: Understanding Personality Type*. Davies-Black Publishing: Mountain View

Newton, I. (1687) *Philosophiæ Naturalis Principia Mathematica*. Samuel Pepys: London

Niebuhr, K.P.R. (1937) *The Serenity Prayer*.

Nietzsche, F.W. (1883-5) *Also Sprach Zarathustra: A Book For All And None*. Williams & Norgate: London

Orwell, G. (1949) *Nineteen Eight-four*. Secker & Warburg: London

Paley, W. (1794) *A View Of The Evidences Of Christianity*. Faulder: London

Plato (*circa* 380 BC) *Phaedo*.

Plato (*circa* 380 BC) *The Republic*.

Plato (*circa* 399 BC) *The Apology Of Socrates*.

Poole, W.H. (1879) *Anglo-Israel Or, The British Nation: The Lost Tribes Of Israel*. Bengough Brothers: Toronto

Rescorla, R. A. and Wagner, A. R. (1972) A theory of Pavlovian conditioning: variations in the effectiveness of reinforcement and nonreinforcement. In: A. H. Black and W. F. Prokasy (Eds.) *Classical Conditioning II - Current Research And Theory*. Appleton-Century-Crofts: New York

Rocklin, T. and Revelle, W. (1981) The measurement of Extraversion. *British Journal Of Psychology, 20*, 279-284.

Roger, D. & Schapals, T. (1996) Repression-sensitization and emotion control. *Current Psychology, 15:1 (Spring 1996)*, 30-37.

Roger, D. and Morris, J. (1991) The internal structure of the EPQ scales. *Personality And Individual Differences, 12*, 759-764.

Roger, D. and Nesshoever, W. (1987) The construction and preliminary validation of a scale for measuring emotion control. *Personality And Individual Differences, 8*, 527-534.

Rotter, J.B. (1966) Generalised expectancies for internal versus external control of reinforcement. *Psychological Monographs, 80: Whole No.1*.

Ryle, G. (1949) *The Concept Of Mind*. University of Chicago Press: Chicago

Shakespeare, W. (*circa* 1600) *Hamlet*.

Shakespeare, W. (*circa* 1605) *Macbeth*.

Skinner, B.F. (1948) *Walden Two*. Macmillan: New York

Spencer, H. (1851) *Social Statics: Or, The Conditions Essential To Human Happiness Specified, And The First Of Them Developed*. John Chapman: London

Steiner, C. (1966) Script and counterscript. *Transactional Analysis Bulletin, 5:18*, 133-135.

Steiner, C. (1971) The stroke economy. *Transactional Analysis Journal, 1:3*, 9-15.

Stewart I. & Joines, V.S. (1987) *TA Today: A New Introduction To Transactional Analysis*. Lifespace: Nottingham

Thoreau, H.D. (1849) Civil Disobedience. In: *Elizabeth Peabody's Aesthetic Papers*.

Thoreau, H.D. (1854) *Walden; Or, Life In The Woods*. Ticknor & Fields: Boston

Tolstoy, L.N. (1865-9) *War And Peace*. Russkii Vestnik: Moscow

Tolstoy, L.N. (1873-7) *Anna Karenina*. Russkii Vestnik: Moscow

Tolstoy, L.N. (1894) *The Kingdom Of God Is Within You*. W. Scott: London

Twain, M. (1876) *The Adventures Of Tom Sawyer*. Chatto & Windus: London

Twain, M. (1884) *Adventures Of Huckleberry Finn*. Chatto & Windus: London

Waite, T. (1993) *Taken On Trust*. Hodder & Stoughton: London

Wampold, B.E. (2001) *The Great Psychotherapy Debate: Models, Methods And Findings*. Lawrence Erlbaum Associates: Mahwah

Wilson, W.G. aka "Bill W" et al. (1939) *Alcoholics Anonymous*. Works Publishing Company: New York

Wittgenstein, L.J.J. (1949) *The Concept Of Mind*. University of Chicago Press: Chicago

Zalcman, M. (1987) Game analysis and racket analysis. In: *Keynote Speeches Delivered At The EATA Conference, July 1986*. European Association for Transactional Analysis: Geneva

The Bible: Authorized King James Version. Robert Barker

The Bible: Jerusalem Popular Edition. Darton, Longman & Todd

Ratio Atque Institutio Studiorum Societatis Iesu aka *Ratio Studiorum*. (1599) Collegio Romano

The Summoning Of Everyman. (15th century) Unattributed

"Thoreau's Cove (Walden Pond) showing the Indian Path"
Courtesy of the Thoreau Institute at Walden Woods, Lincoln, MA

~ The conclusion of the wise seahorse ~

None of us is dwelling involuntarily in a maelström of chaotic and random relationships fixing meaningful patterns amongst them only by discharging our hopes and wills – unless we wish so to do by rejecting the infinitely superior option which always comes to us one way or another – always highly personal and often with sufficient regularity and force to dissolve our resistance – in some cases rapidly, in come cases gradually – but in some cases too unattended to effect redirection in time to enjoy the fading days of creation.

Everything is – to the Unwitnessed Observer – and to the wise and humble seeker of Truth – as it is supposed to be.

~ Be a wise seahorse ~

"Prototypical *Nine Seahorses*": the cover shows a "spiritually
perky" lot under the watchful eye of the Unwitnessed Observer

Addendum
Layers of allegory in the concept of *Nine Seahorses*

Referring first to the prototypical (black and white) facing array

The most immediate allegory, whilst anthropomorphic, is metaphorically useful. It is easy to cast oneself by imagination into some hypothetical entity uncontaminated by assumptions we make about ourselves as humans. In other words, we can free ourselves from the shackles of programming. We can be(come) anything we like (as, supposedly, we can in psychotherapy, if not the spiritual life). For example, although seahorses are fish but swim upright, and humans are upright mammals, seahorses (in the "real" world) do not necessarily conform with stereotypical human sex and gender categories – nor any other cultural and social roles. In a sense, the male seahorse becomes "pregnant" and "mothers" young offspring. How culture-bound is our human psychology? In folklore, although not always in fact, seahorses are monogamous. How monogamous are humans? Does the answer depend on whether humans have a capacity for a moral ideal (for we all know that the proportion of humans which "loves" only one person in a life time is modest)? Male seahorses attract females by displaying their "emptiness" (a display of the egg pouch or abdominal cavity is part of the courtship ritual). What is the battle of the sexes amongst human beings really all about? Why would a human individual (let alone a seahorse) ever want to pull moral rank on behalf of its entire biological sex, or even sociocultural gender? Why, for the sake of social justice, of course. But must we each have to leave such prejudice behind if we seek a common ultimate social justice (true and final equality)? Conceptually, the greatest significance of *Nine Seahorses* is that in a large or infinite extension of the prototypical array (of nine; first to 25, then 49, 81, 121 …), every individual is surrounded infallibly by others. The connotations are mutual protection, co-operation and absolute (genderless) equality. Each seahorse is facing in a particular direction. Maintaining a direction (as distinct from "lardy stagnation" or "vicious spirals") is all important in progressing towards maturity. All the seahorses are facing the same way – a healthy universal: is this subjugation of self-centred fear and its illusory companion "free will" (especially when imposed impolitely)? In hospitable Hawaii, the seahorse is a symbol of everlasting friendship.

Referring next to the (colour) front cover array of Nine Seahorses

Real seahorses (fish) may turn a bright colour on significant social occasions, or in new environments: they are excited by novelty – and each other. Although the seahorses in the prototypical (black and white) array look the same, we can permit infinite variations of personality – at least partly because psychological change (including spiritual venturesomeness) is an "inside job". In biological taxonomy, seahorses belong to the genus hippocampus. The hippocampus is part of the limbic system thought to be linked intimately with memory and spatial learning in humans and other mammals. We have supposed in *Nine Seahorses* that a primary (spiritual) benefit of community is the capacity of one member to hold for another the "spiritual mirror". Each of the nine depictions on the front cover (except the ninth, or, bottom-right) represents a mathematical mirror-rotation suggesting – with a little licence – that each individual is gazing at some (moral) reflection of itself. Seemingly there are innumerable ways in which this can happen. Each mirrored seahorse-instance seems (morally) bent out of shape as if trying to contemplate its natural incarnation. This condition will have something – even everything – to do with each individual's sense of developing "self". The ninth, or, bottom-right lucky seahorse seems to have achieved such "enlightenment" facing – as it does – the Unwitnessed Observer, and is traversing the seas untroubled. The vivid colours of the nine seahorses seem a more concrete (at least, chromatically intense) version of what the Unwitnessed Observer possesses in Its "mind's eye" – or, something akin to what the Ancient Greek philosophers might have considered as "form".

Final thoughts on human relationships, love and spiritual idealism

The vertical dimension (comprising three rows) will not be lost on any Transactional Analysis (TA) enthusiast nor indeed the horizontal projections (across three columns): one can easily imagine (counter)injunctions, introjects, modelling, transactions etc. Like humans, seahorses invest a great deal in their young whose survival rate is high. How will the present human generations be judged by those who will follow and against what yardsticks? Will they be generous enough to forgive us if we don't leave things as we would like to find them? We had better bring ourselves back to earth (dry land) and remember the significance of the human (species-specific) capacity for language. Humans are unique on the planet in fundamental ways, the relationships amongst which we have yet barely fathomed: consciousness, subjective pain, conscience, personal responsibility … selfless love. Which of the nine cover depictions most reminds you of you (at this present time)? What about each of your family, friends and colleagues? Can you reflect on the "spiritual personalities" of all such people in a "spiritually generous" way – perhaps as you might like them to think "spiritually" of you in turn? Seahorse Sam now finds himself committed to – but often painfully short of this ideal.